Praise for

Autism and the
Transition to Adulthood

"The most practical book I have read on developing measurable transition goals and real-life community based experiences for students and young adults with autism . . . An excellent handbook for teachers, preservice providers, parents, related services—all those involved in assisting with planning a successful life for a young person with autism."

—Sherrilyn K. Fisher, Ph.D.
President, Division on Career Development and Transition

"Finally, a comprehensive resource focusing on the specific and often idiosyncratic transition needs of individuals on the autism spectrum. Writing in a very accessible style, Drs. Wehman, Smith, and Schall have merged the relevant research with their clinical insight and extensive hands-on experience to produce a volume that should be considered essential reading for both parents and professionals alike. Highly recommended!"

—Peter F. Gerhardt, Ed.D.
President and Chair, Scientific Council
Organization for Autism Research

"A practical book that explores the realities of transition to life after public school for individuals with autism. This is a great resource for families, teachers, adult service providers, and individuals with autism looking ahead to the worlds of work and community living. For all students, adulthood comes quickly; now everyone can be prepared for productive citizenship."

—Cary Griffin
Senior Partner, Griffin-Hammis Associates
co-author, *Making Self-Employment Work for People with Disabilities* and *The Job Developer's Handbook*

"An invaluable tool for parents of middle and high school students with an ASD in planning for supports to maximize their child's potential and to ensure a positive future."

—Bradford Hulcher
mother of an 18-year-old with an ASD
Information and Referral Specialist
Autism Society of America, Central VA Chapter

D1196102

Autism and the
Transition to Adulthood

Autism and the Transition to Adulthood

Success Beyond the Classroom

by

Paul Wehman, Ph.D.
Virginia Commonwealth University
Richmond

Marcia Datlow Smith, Ph.D.
CSAAC
Montgomery Village, Maryland

and

Carol Schall, Ph.D.
Virginia Autism Resource Center
Virginia Commonwealth University
Richmond

with invited contributors

·P·A·U·L·H·
BROOKES
PUBLISHING CO ®

Baltimore • London • Sydney

Paul H. Brookes Publishing Co.
Post Office Box 10624
Baltimore, Maryland 21285-0624
USA

www.brookespublishing.com

Typeset by Integrated Publishing Solutions, Grand Rapids, Michigan.
Manufactured in the United States of America by
Sheridan Books, Inc., Chelsea, Michigan.

The individuals described in this book are composites based on the authors' experiences. In all instances, names and identifying details have been changed to protect confidentiality.

Library of Congress Cataloging-in-Publication Data
Wehman, Paul.
    Autism and the transition to adulthood : success beyond the classroom / by Paul Wehman, Marcia Datlow Smith, and Carol Schall.
        p.   cm.
    Includes bibliographical references and index.
    ISBN-13: 978-1-55766-958-2 (pbk.)
    ISBN-10: 1-55766-958-9 (pbk.)
    1. Autistic youth—Education—United States. 2. Autistic youth—United States—Life skills guides. I. Smith, Marcia Datlow, 1951- II. Schall, Carol. III. Title.
    LC4718.W44 2009
    371.94—dc22   2008036060

British Library Cataloguing in Publication data are available from the British Library.

2018   2017   2016   2015   2014

10   9   8   7   6   5   4   3

#24444038O

Contents

About the Authors

Paul Wehman, Ph.D., Director, Virginia Commonwealth University Rehabilitation Research and Training Center on Workplace Supports and Job Retention, 1314 Main Street, Richmond, Virginia 23284

Dr. Wehman is Professor of Physical Medicine and Rehabilitation with a joint appointment in the Department of Special Education at Virginia Commonwealth University. He received his doctoral degree from the University of Wisconsin and helped to develop supported employment at Virginia Commonwealth University in the early 1980s. Dr. Wehman has published more than 200 articles and authored or edited 37 books. He was recipient of the Joseph P. Kennedy, Jr. Foundation International Award in Mental Retardation in 1990 and received the Distinguished Service Award from the President's Committee on Employment for Persons with Disabilities in October 1992. Dr. Wehman was recognized as one of the 50 most influential special educators of the millennium by *Remedial and Special Education* in December 2000. He is also Editor-in-Chief of the *Journal of Vocational Rehabilitation*.

Marcia Datlow Smith, Ph.D., Psychologist, CSAAC, 8615 East Village Avenue, Montgomery Village, Maryland 20886

Dr. Smith is Assistant Executive Director for Programs and Psychologist at CSAAC, an agency that has supported children and adults with autism since 1979. She has designed a broad range of positive behavior supports that have allowed adolescents and adults with autism and challenging behavior to achieve community living and supported employment. In addition, she has directed federal research grants and worked on federal model program and replication grants for the treatment of autism awarded to CSAAC. Dr. Smith was awarded a Mary Switzer Senior Research Fellowship by the National Institute of Handicapped Research, and, in 1989, her work with autism was recognized with the Governor of Maryland's Health Care Professional of the Year award. She has made presentations both nationally and internationally and has written book chapters and peer-reviewed journal articles. Dr. Smith has authored several books, including *Autism and Life in the Community: Successful Interventions for Behavioral Challenges* (Paul H. Brookes Publishing Co., 1990) and *A Guide to Successful Employment for Individuals with Autism* (with Ronald G. Belcher & Patricia D. Juhrs, Paul H. Brookes Publishing Co., 1995).

Carol Schall, Ph.D., Director, Virginia Autism Resource Center, Virginia Commonwealth University, Post Office Box 842020, Richmond, Virginia 23284

Dr. Schall is Assistant Professor of Special Education and Disability Policy at Virginia Commonwealth University. She has been learning from and supporting individuals with autism for more than 25 years. Dr. Schall is involved in supporting individuals across Virginia through her work as the director of the Virginia Autism Resource Center. She is well versed in completing functional behavior assessments and using positive behavior supports to develop comprehensive plans for individuals from a person-centered approach. Dr. Schall is a nationally known speaker. In addition to her speaking engagements, she provides consultations to schools, families, and community services providers who support individuals with autism or related disorders. Dr. Schall's research interests include the use of psychotropic medication by individuals with autism spectrum disorders and training for parents and professionals who work with individuals with developmental disabilities. Dr. Schall is listed in the 2005 and 2006 editions of *Who's Who in America* and was honored by TASH with their Positive Approaches Award.

About the Contributors

Lori W. Briel, M.Ed., Coordinator of Post Secondary Education Initiatives, Virginia Commonwealth University Rehabilitation Research and Training Center on Workplace Supports and Job Retention, 1314 West Main Street, Richmond, Virginia 23284. Ms. Briel has extensive experience providing employment services, resource coordination, employment supports, and career development services for individuals with significant disabilities. She has coordinated numerous demonstration projects related to the transition from high school, to college, to employment for individuals with disabilities. Currently, she coordinates a mentoring program for college students with disabilities, collaborates in the development of self-determination modules for high school students with disabilities, and provides instruction in the teacher education program. Her specific research and career interests include transition from higher education to employment, internship supports, and career development for people with disabilities. She has presented nationally and has coauthored several journal articles and book chapters in these areas.

Elizabeth Evans Getzel, M.A., Director of Postsecondary Education Initiatives, Virginia Commonwealth University Rehabilitation Research and Training Center on Workplace Supports and Job Retention, 1314 West Main Street, Richmond, Virginia 23284. Ms. Getzel has extensive experience conducting research, evaluation, and training in the areas of transition planning for secondary students with disabilities, postsecondary education for students with disabilities, and career planning/employment for individuals with disabilities. She currently directs grant-funded projects focusing on supported education in postsecondary education, career development for college students with disabilities, faculty professional development focusing on universal design principles, and secondary education transition services. Ms. Getzel has authored or coauthored journal articles and book chapters on transition, career development, postsecondary education, and employment and is the co-editor of the book *Going to College: Expanding Opportunities for People with Disabilities* (with Paul Wehman, Paul H. Brookes Publishing Co., 2005).

Dawn R. Hendricks, Ph.D., Behavioral and Educational Consultant for Individuals with Autism Spectrum Disorders (ASD), Adjunct Professor, Virginia Commonwealth University, 1314 West Main Street, Richmond, Virginia 23284. Dr. Hendricks provides educational and behavioral consultative services to individuals with ASD and their families. She has more than 15 years of experience supervising programming and providing information on best practices through technical assistance and training. Dr. Hendricks was instrumental in creating coursework and a post-baccalaureate certificate program in ASD at Virginia Commonwealth University. She currently teaches at Virginia Common-

wealth University and works with the Virginia Autism Council, a state-supported council of autism professionals, to improve educational and training measures for personnel
who serve individuals on the spectrum.

Jennifer McFarland-Whisman, Ph.D., Behavioral and Educational Consultant, Adjunct
Associate Graduate Professor, Marshall University, 1 John Marshall Drive, Huntington,
West Virginia 25755. Dr. McFarland-Whisman is a behavioral and educational consultant and an adjunct associate graduate professor at Marshall University, where she co-
teaches courses on autism. She has 20 years of experience working with individuals with
autism spectrum disorders, 16 of which were as the associate director of the West Vir-
ginia Autism Training Center at Marshall University. She is on the West Virginia Positive
Behavior Support Network Leadership Team and the West Virginia Team Autism. Dr.
McFarland-Whisman coauthored the book *Autism: A Primer for Educators* (with Barbara
Becker-Cottrill, John Deaver Drinko Academy, 2007) and won the TASH Positive Approaches Award, as well as the Professional of the Year award from the West Virginia
Autism Society. She is interested in all aspects of positive behavior support and autism,
especially the areas of systems change, family and school support, and team planning.

Lucy Axton Miller, B.S., Training Associate, Virginia Commonwealth University Rehabilitation Research and Training Center on Workplace Supports and Job Retention
(VCU-RRTC), 1314 West Main Street, Richmond, Virginia 23284. As a training associate
with VCU-RRTC, Ms. Miller provides training and technical assistance on a wide variety of topics with emphasis on how paid employment affects Social Security disability
benefits and using work incentives to promote employment outcomes for Social Security Administration disability beneficiaries. In addition, Ms. Miller has more than 20 years
of experience in all aspects of supported employment implementation for adults with significant disabilities in both urban and rural settings. Before joining VCU, she served as
a vice president for Career Resources, Inc., a nationally recognized leader in One-Stop
and Welfare-to-Work services in the greater Louisville, Kentucky, metropolitan area. Ms.
Miller worked for more than 10 years at Seven Counties Services, a regional planning
authority for mental health, mental retardation, and chemical dependency services.

Grant Revell, M.S., M.Ed., Research Associate, Virginia Commonwealth University Research and Training Center on Workplace Supports and Job Retention (VCU-RRTC),
1314 West Main Street, Richmond, Virginia 23284. Mr. Revell has extensive experience
related to the use of performance-based funding of employment services and in the
areas of policy analysis and funding related to state-level and national implementation
of supported employment. He served as project director for the National Supported
Employment Consortium, a 4-year national study funded by the Rehabilitation Services
Administration of the U.S. Department of Education to research best practices in
supported employment services to individuals with significant disabilities and to dis-
seminate information on these best practices through technical assistance and training.
Mr. Revell currently serves as a state training liaison for the Region III CRP-RCEP. Prior
to coming to VCU-RRTC, he worked as a program specialist in supported employment
and as a vocational rehabilitation counselor at the Virginia Department of Rehabilitation
Services.

Pamela Sherron Targett, M.Ed., Director of Employment Services, Virginia Common-wealth University Research and Training Center on Workplace Supports and Job Reten-tion (VCU-RRTC), 1314 West Main Street, Richmond, Virginia 23289. Ms. Targett has served as the director of the employment services at VCU-RRTC since 1989. In this ca-pacity, she oversees a supported employment program that serves approximately 60 in-dividuals with significant disabilities each year. She also provides training and techni-cal assistance to other supported employment programs and has authored a number of works on disability and employment-related topics.

Preface

There has been an explosion of new information about autism in American society since the 1990s, perhaps accelerating even more over the past several years as the national media begins to provide dramatically increased coverage on the issues and challenges facing children with autism and their families. This type of national attention on a specific category of disability has not happened for a very long time, arguably since John F. Kennedy addressed the needs of individuals with intellectual disabilities in the early 1960s or James Brady, former press secretary to President Reagan, called attention to the challenges of those with traumatic brain injury.

The need for services and even a cure for autism, however, seems even more pervasive than the examples listed above, partly because we now live in an information age with the Internet, YouTube, and high-definition television, where the stories fly much faster and with much greater drama than ever before. Children and youth with autism have caught the eye of America, and there is huge interest in this topic—partly out of altruistic perspectives but also out of fascination with the myriad and complex characteristics of people with autism.

Clearly, the greatest attention in the research and book literature has been on early intervention and childhood programming, with appropriately heavy emphasis on applied behavior analysis as the desired mode of intervention. As we show in this book, however, toddlers and young children with autism do grow up. They become middle schoolers. They become adolescents in high school. They want to go to college. They want to work, and they want to live in the community. The strengths and weaknesses of autism will follow them into these community environments, but these young adults still have to deal with all of the issues of adolescence and adulthood.

In fact, this brings us to a major point that we ask readers to remember as they read this book. Young adults with autism are young adults FIRST and individuals with autism second. They will have as much sensitivity to criticism or compliments as other people do. They will enjoy the benefits of earning money and job promotion as anyone else. They will value friendships and romantic relationships as anybody else. They want to be independent and free to move around as all Americans are.

Therefore, this book focuses on how this can happen. We believe that competence leads to self-confidence and self-esteem. We also believe that competence leads to empowerment. We know that competence will not be achieved without the structured interventions that we describe in this book. We also know that competence in work settings, home, college, and the community can best be developed in those settings, not in an isolated classroom with students engaging in pretend activities.

This is a book about the potential of individuals with autism. Rather than offering random hope, this book explains what we can do to empower people to take full advantage of their potential. Although we acknowledge the importance of hope and faith in all ventures, we believe that young people with autism will prosper in highly organized and planned programs that facilitate their progressively greater independence and interdependence.

The 10 chapters in this book provide a number of case studies, programs, and ideas for use by practitioners and families, with emphasis on what we know that works. We identify three young people—Jeff, Craig, and Maria—and follow them throughout each of the chapters so the reader can see their different potential and success.

In conclusion, this book is an important step in the direction of bringing together the limited knowledge that is accruing on transition for youth with disabilities. We know in 10 years there will be much more, but those in the field cannot wait any longer. This book is a must right now.

Acknowledgments

The development of this book was enriched greatly by the participation of a number of people who kindly gave of their time and were very professional as well as sensitive to the needs of young people with autism. We are very grateful to our contributors, who are in most cases close colleagues. We would like to acknowledge and express our deepest appreciation to Pam Targett, who not only helped coauthor a number of the chapters but also graciously gave of her time in editing, brainstorming, and locating selected references that strengthen the book. We very much want to thank her for her efforts.

We also thank Dawn Hendricks, Grant Revell, Lucy Miller, Lori Briel, Jennifer McFarland-Whisman, and Elizabeth Getzel for their willingness to help write key chapters within this book. Their direct clinical expertise was definitely reflected in the chapters they developed.

Thanks is also due to Ian Paregol for his generous support throughout and to Jake Eidelman and Leslie Martone for their assistance during the writing of this book.

In addition, we wish to acknowledge our profound thanks to Jeanne Dalton for the incredible amount of time she spent on organizing the chapters, reformatting according to guidelines, tracking down references, and keeping the entire project on target. We most appreciate her ability to communicate so well with our colleagues in terms of hitting deadlines, getting permissions completed, and so forth.

There is no doubt that the work of Tara Gebhardt, our developmental editor at Brookes Publishing Co., was a huge time saver in terms of making our body of work much more readable and "user-friendly." We thank her for going beyond the call of duty to make this an outstanding book, one which is much easier to read.

Finally, we thank, with our deepest gratitude, Rebecca Lazo, our acquisitions editor at Brookes Publishing Co., who helped to "birth" this project and carry it through the planning and writing process, truly from beginning to end. It is obvious to all who know Rebecca how much passion she has for helping children and youth with autism. She was always providing us with the best guidance in terms of how to best communicate to readers so that our meaning would be understood and used.

To my children, Brody, Cara, Blake, Ragan, and Peyton,
and my loving wife, Lele, for all of their love and support
—PW

To my family: my husband, Tom Biery, my sons and
daughters, Christian and Danielle Schaefer and Jared and
Victoria Smith, and my parents, Gerald and Lita Datlow,
who introduced me to both psychology and autism
—MDS

To Mary and Emily for tolerating me while writing
this book. Also, to Jennifer, Michael, David, Clark,
Anne, John, Robert, and all of the other many individuals
who taught me so much about living with ASD as an
adolescent or adult. May your paths lead you to true
success beyond the classroom!
—CS

Understanding the Transition from School to Adulthood for Students with Autism

Carol Schall and Paul Wehman

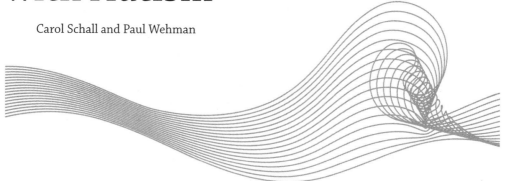

JEFF

Jeff is a 15-year-old young man who was diagnosed with Asperger's syndrome at the age of 12. He displayed a confusing set of characteristics for most of his life and had a variety of diagnoses, none of which seemed to fully describe the patterns of behavior he displayed. As a preschooler, Jeff appeared to be very bright. He knew a lot about maps and roads, liked to watch documentaries on television, and read early. Although Jeff's parents were pleased by his precocious reading and academic skills, their son also displayed many challenges, particularly around other children. For example, Jeff did not like playing at the park and would frequently run away when other children approached his space. He insisted that his parents do everyday tasks in the same way. For example, they always had to put his fork on the table after Jeff was in his seat and before they placed a spoon on the table. As a kindergartener, he was found eligible for special education services as a child with attention-deficit/hyperactivity disorder.

By the fourth grade, Jeff's behavior had become more challenging in school. He was upset when there was a change in his daily schedule or when he was interrupted during a preferred task. He rarely asked teachers or peers questions about themselves or asked for help when he misunderstood something. Instead, when frustrated with a task, he would scream, tear up his paper, and crawl under his desk. He would also blurt out answers in class.

Jeff's parents and his school team continued to address Jeff's needs. Now, at the age of 15, he excels in math and science and is making adequate progress in language arts and history. Jeff, however, continues to lag behind his peers in socialization and maturation. When he talks to others, he sounds as if he is giving a lecture. He does not seem to notice how loudly he talks or that he frequently makes socially embarrassing comments to others. Furthermore, he often makes unpleasant physical contact with others, such as stepping on another student's foot, tripping someone as he or she walks by, and even occasionally randomly punching someone in the arm. This behavior not only repels other students, but it also puts Jeff at risk for suspension from school. He has also developed a disturbing behavior of staring at women's feet and commenting on their shoes. He acts especially pleased if they are wearing sandals. The teachers and his female classmates find this unsettling.

In addition to his social problems, Jeff has limited work skills. He gets upset with directions given by the teacher and displays immature behavior. He does not like changes in his routine and does not like to be interrupted midtask.

Jeff has a lot of potential. He is bright, has energy, and would likely excel at a job one day. What would be functional objectives for Jeff's individualized education program (IEP)? How will these be achieved given his behavioral issues, social problems, and poor communication skills? How can the team capitalize on Jeff's strengths? Could Jeff perhaps start his own business someday? Could he live independently?

CRAIG

Craig is a 17-year-old young man with autism[1]. From the time he was born, Craig's parents knew that something was different. They frequently told the pediatrician that Craig seemed to be in a world of his own. He was not talking by the age of 2. At times he was content to sit and watch the door hinges on his bedroom door open and close for hours on end. He found the most pleasure in spinning in circles while flapping his hands. If he was not spinning himself, he sought objects to spin. He could spin anything, even a tissue box balanced on one corner. When he was alone, Craig seemed happy. Whenever other children or adults tried to play with him, however, he would scream and run away.

When Craig started walking, he would wander away and not respond to his name. This presented safety concerns. At 4 years of age, when Craig entered the preschool program for children with developmental delays at the local public school, he received a diagnosis of autism.

Craig received all of his services in a self-contained special education program. The teachers and therapists used different techniques to improve Craig's

---

[1]Since autism spectrum disorders represent several specific conditions and a range of functioning, and to make it easier on the reader, we have decided to use the word *autism* in this text when referring to any label related to *autism spectrum disorders*. Except when otherwise specified, the information, strategies, and recommendations apply to students with any condition that falls under the umbrella of autism spectrum disorders, regardless of specific diagnosis or level of functioning.

speech; however, at the age of 17 he uses only a few words and phrases, such as *no, eat,* and *go bathroom.* He frequently makes vocal sounds, and sometimes his teachers can judge his mood from the types of sounds he makes. Craig's behavior always worsens when there are significant changes in his environment. He displays some problem behaviors, including hitting his own head and biting his wrist. He needs close supervision in the bathroom to prevent him from stuffing papers, towels, and even his clothing into the toilet and flushing it repeatedly. Craig will require transition goals that target these behaviors.

Craig loves Special Olympics and is a very good athlete. He likes to swim and be involved in water sports. He really enjoys putting things together. For example, he once took apart his desk and put it back together. Although this made his teacher nervous, the desk was fine and worked quite well after he finished. Craig has very good visual alertness, visual memory, and visual-motor coordination. He can put difficult puzzles together quickly. He can find a cup of coffee instantly in a room full of cluttered desks. He remembers exactly where in the grocery store his favorite foods are stocked.

Craig has not yet had an opportunity to work in an actual job. As he nears the end of his high school years, he is receiving all of his education in a special education setting. Now that he is 17 and in a new school, his team is wondering how to plan his transition to adulthood, and they are scrambling to do so because transition was never approached with Craig at his previous school.

The questions regarding Craig's future are similar to those for Jeff's: What are the strengths he has to build upon? What types of positive behavior plan(s) are necessary? What areas are a priority? What might be done differently? Would inclusive schooling help? Would community-based training help, or supported employment and life skills training? Where should Craig live as an adult?

MARIA

Maria is 16 years old. She seemed to develop typically until about 18 months of age. She walked on time and even began to use some words. At the age of about 18 months, her social and communication development seemed to deteriorate. She would line up the objects in her house and would scream whenever her mother rearranged the furniture. Maria never played with the other children in their neighborhood or at her child care center. She seemed content to simply carry toys from one place to the next, lining them up wherever she stopped.

Maria developed language, but her use of language was not typical. Although she learned to use words quite well, she would ask for most things she needed by referring to herself in the third person and using the form of a statement. For example, when she had to go to the bathroom, she would loudly announce, "Maria go to the bathroom now." She also used language to engage in rituals. For example, she would recite long sections of dialogue from movies she had seen.

When Maria was in the fifth grade, she could recite the movie *Finding Nemo* from beginning to end. If she was interrupted while doing so, she would go back to the beginning and start again. Years later, she still recites portions of this movie whenever she is feeling anxious or stressed.

Despite these challenges, Maria learned to read and manipulate numbers to about the third-grade level. She received special education services in a resource room for reading and math but participated in science, social studies, music, art, physical education, computer, and library in the general education environment during elementary school. When she made the transition to middle school, she had a very similar schedule, except that she began to receive her social studies instruction in the special education room.

Now that she is 16, Maria is somewhat independent in her self-care but needs her mother to remind her to take showers, brush her teeth, and use deodorant. She does not cook or prepare any of her own food; she continues to rely on her mother to do this. In school, she now receives all of her core subject education in a special education classroom but attends elective art, chorus, and physical education in the general education setting. Maria has not had the opportunity to work, although her desire to purchase DVDs may be a good incentive for her to earn money. She has some challenging behaviors that need to be addressed in transition planning. For instance, when she is upset she scratches her arms or rips her clothing. She often does this in private, and her mother later finds the results of it—scratches on her arms and torn clothing. Very rarely she will become so upset that she throws objects. For example, when a family trip to the beach was canceled due to a hurricane warning, Maria retreated to her bedroom and threw her clock radio across the room.

Here are some questions for Maria's transition planning. Would a person-centered plan help the team chart her future and maximize her strengths? What type of behavior management plan is essential to help her to succeed? How does the current curriculum fit with her goals as an adult? Is a 2-year college experience a possibility? What kind of work would interest her and how can the team discover this? Where might she live? How independently can she make and keep friends? Where will she go to engage in leisure activities?

THE CHALLENGE OF TRANSITION

Entering adolescence and young adulthood presents many new challenges for all young people, especially those with autism. As Jeff's, Craig's, and Maria's stories illustrate, as individuals with autism prepare for transition from school to the adult world, they must prepare for life without the daily structure of school. In short, these young people, their families, and educators must wonder, plan, and prepare for the time when the schoolbus no longer takes them to school. While others without disabilities face the same eventuality, for individuals with autism, the issue is complicated by the uneven provision of adult services to assist such individuals.

Like other transition-age youth with disabilities, under the Individuals with Disabilities Education Improvement Act of 2004 (IDEA 2004; PL 108-446), students diagnosed with autism who have turned 22 or graduated from high school with a regular diploma no longer have a legal right to appropriate transition services, such as life skills training, transportation, vocational training, and individual and family counseling (although some state laws may provide for services beyond this age). Yet these are exactly the services young adults with autism need. Large numbers of youth with autism rated low on self-care tasks, functional cognitive skills, social skills, and communication when compared with the entire population of youth with disabilities served under IDEA 2004 (Wagner, Newman, Cameto, Garza, & Levine, 2005). Many families find that the services provided to individuals diagnosed with autism are not tailored to the needs of the children and young adults in this population. Families have also reported that locating, obtaining, and financing needed services for these young adults requires navigating complicated public and private medical, social, and vocational rehabilitation service systems (Autism Society of America, 2001).

More than ever before, people with autism spectrum disorders are participating in the mainstream of school (Kluth, 2003; Kluth & Chandler-Olcott, 2008; National Center for Special Education Research, 2007a), work (Griffin, Hammis, & Geary, 2007; Wehman, Targett, & Young, 2007), and the community (Wehman, Inge, Revell, & Brooke, 2007). Careful transition planning, however, is critical for young people like Jeff, Craig, and Maria to be successful in the community (Wehman & Wittig, in press). Growing up is hard enough for most teenagers; for those with autism, there are enormous additional barriers. Throughout this book you will follow these three students, whose stories will illustrate some of the concepts related to positive transition planning for youth with autism. You will explore how to design behavior support plans, how to determine and implement college and/or employment possibilities, and how to write and implement meaningful educational programs.

In this book, we open up a discussion about the sometimes exciting, sometimes frightening world of autism—specifically, growing up with autism through adolescence and into adulthood. We look hard at the road that must be followed by youth with autism to be productive and engaged members of society. We discuss the issues, challenges, and strategies that are involved in helping young people with autism participate in society. Our focus in this book is about what young people with autism *can do* and how to design supports to expand their opportunities and potential.

WHAT CHARACTERIZES AUTISM?

Autism is a pervasive developmental disorder characterized by severe deficits in social interaction and communication, by an extremely limited range of activities and interests, and often by the presence of repetitive, stereotyped behaviors. Autism is defined by a certain set of behaviors that can range from very mild to severe. There are five disorders under the umbrella of *autism spectrum disorder* (ASD): autism, Asperger's syndrome, pervasive developmental disorder-not otherwise specified (PDD-NOS), Rett syndrome, and childhood disintegrative disorder (CDD) (American Psychiatric Association [APA], 2000). The incidence of ASDs is currently best reported as 1 person in 150 (Centers for Disease Control and Prevention, 2007). Individuals across this spectrum have deficits in communication and social skills. ASD is also marked by "restricted, repetitive, and stereotyped patterns of behavior, interests, and activities" (APA, 2000, p. 71). The social skill deficits associated with ASD fall into four categories; to qualify for an ASD diagnosis, an individual must demonstrate behavioral difficulties in two of these four categories. The categories are briefly described in Table 1.1.

Autism is a lifelong developmental disability that affects an individual's ability to form relationships and to communicate. It also affects the person's ability to develop varied interests and to respond to life's changes and stresses (Attwood, 2006; Kluth, 2003). ASDs used to be considered rare, and many individuals with autism were misdiagnosed with intellectual disabilities or mental illnesses, such as schizophrenia. In some cases, children with autism received no diagnosis, struggled through their schooling, and remained a mystery to their parents, teachers,

Table 1.1. Social skill categories for individuals with autism

Difficulty establishing relationships with peers

Difficulty with social or emotional reciprocity. *Reciprocity* is social sharing—acknowledging another person's presence and interacting with him or her. It also implies *empathy*, or being able to perceive another's feelings and show sensitivity (putting oneself in the other person's shoes).

Difficulty sharing interests or being attentive to others

Lack of using and interpreting eye gaze, body positioning, gestures, and other nonverbal ways of interacting with others

Source: American Psychiatric Association (2000).

and peers. Since 1995, however, there has been a dramatic increase in the identification and diagnosis of ASDs in younger children (Grinker, 2007). Although there has been improvement in identifying young children with autism, some adolescents and young adults who have autism have not been identified due to the complexity and range of functioning associated with this disorder. Consequently, there may be students in middle and high schools who are on the autism spectrum but who are not diagnosed with the disorder (Schall, Doval, Targett, & Wehman, 2006).

Social Relationships

The social behaviors of individuals with autism make it difficult for others to understand and relate to them. Consequently, these behaviors not only isolate the student with autism but can mark the student for failure in vocational efforts. For instance, Jeff, who occasionally hits others, must learn to keep his hands to himself. If he were to hit someone in the workplace, it could be considered violence, and Jeff could lose his job.

Social skill limitations are a major reason so many individuals with ASDs have difficulty securing and holding a job (Hillier, Campbell, et al., 2007; Müller, Schuler, Burton, & Yates, 2003; Wagner, Newman, Cameto, Levine, & Garza, 2006). Much of the current focus of vocational rehabilitation is on learning job skills; little emphasis is placed on developing socially sensitive behavior. As a result, people with autism frequently learn how to complete job tasks well but struggle with learning how to interact successfully with co-workers. This also presents a challenge for vocational rehabilitation specialists, who seek to support individuals with disabilities in work settings. It is critical, therefore, that transition programs for students with autism focus on social skills, problem solving, and coping.

Communication Deficits

Youth with autism commonly experience difficulty in communicating or have unusual methods of doing so (see Table 1.2). It is important for students with autism to overcome these difficulties because communication—whether through words, gestures, sign language, pictures, or any other form—is a skill that is required not only for work or advanced schooling but also for general interaction with peers, acquaintances, and others encountered on a daily basis. Throughout school, members of a student's IEP or transition team, including the teacher, guidance counselor or school psychologist, behavior specialist, occupational therapist, physical therapist, speech-language pathologist, family members, and administrator, see it

Table 1.2.   Communication deficits among individuals with autism

According to the *Diagnostic and Statistical Manual of Mental Disorders, Fourth Edition, Text Revision* (American Psychiatric Association, 2000), individuals with autism must display at least one of the following difficulties in communication:

1. Repeating phrases or words previously heard (echolalia) or using words in unusual ways
2. When using speech to communicate, frequently unable to initiate or sustain a conversation with others
3. Not using words to communicate at all and not compensating by using gestures, facial expressions, or body language

Source: American Psychiatric Association (2000).

as part of their job and mission to educate the student and compensate for his or her communication impairments and challenges. This has become more necessary and prudent than ever with the move toward inclusion into general education classrooms. Teachers, to some extent, may work around students' language difficulties. It is essential, however, that transition planning for students with autism include reliable, acceptable, universally understood means of communicating. Once a student enters the workplace, he or she must be able to interact and communicate with employers, co-workers, and possibly customers, so it is important that he or she understands others and can be understood.

Behavioral Issues and Concerns

According to the *Diagnostic and Statistical Manual of Mental Disorders, Fourth Edition, Text Revision* (*DSM-IV-TR*; APA, 2000), individuals diagnosed with ASD must display at least one of the following characteristics:

1.   Demands for routines to be followed regardless of their importance to the activity

2.   Repetitive motor movements that are not functional

3.   Interest in parts of objects instead of the whole object

4.   Intense and focused preoccupation with subjects

These behaviors can be unusual, troubling, and even dangerous at times. Research shows, however, that it is possible to minimize some of these behaviors through good intervention or training programs; depending on the type of environment the person is in, it may even be possible for the person to capitalize on these behaviors (Carr et al., 1999). For instance, although Jeff's insistence that his daily routine remain the same sometimes leads to problem behavior, this quality is also likely to make him a very dependable employee who shows up to work on time every day. Craig's attention to parts of objects, as seen in his interest in taking apart and rebuilding things, may result in his being a highly detailed worker who completes tasks very accurately. In other words, with good educational and transition services and supports, adolescents with autism have strengths related to their disability that could be advantageous in the workplace. Among them are dependability, high attention to detail, intensive focus on particular topics, excellent rote memory, and exact repetition of motor movements (Quill, 2000).

Secondary Characteristics

There are also secondary characteristics related to autism, although not every person with autism develops these characteristics. Secondary characteristics fall into two basic categories:

- *Challenging behaviors*—Challenging behaviors are grouped into general categories and include but are not limited to aggression toward others, self-injurious behavior, darting or wandering away, excessive preoccupation with information or activities to the exclusion of all other activities or learning, and a high degree of overactivity.

- *Additional mental health diagnoses*—Individuals with autism may be more vulnerable to anxiety disorders and depression, particularly during adolescence (Attwood, 2006; Volkmar, Paul, Klin, & Cohen, 2006).

Challenging behaviors and mental health issues are troubling at any age, but children become stronger and harder to manage as they get older. Consequently, these types of behavioral issues are considerably less tolerated in schools, communities, and work. In short, during the early transition ages into adulthood there are social guidelines that must be followed or the individual will be quickly labeled and segregated. Individuals who display challenging behavior into adolescence or develop mental health problems are frequently the most difficult to serve in transition programs and to successfully place in post–high school employment. Fortunately, there are many supports and interventions that can be used to deal with these challenges, but the members of a student's IEP or transition team must be well trained. For these students, it is critical that the transition team consider these problems and plan sufficient supports that will provide for a seamless move into the community.

UNDERSTANDING EACH PERSON AS AN INDIVIDUAL

Although we have just described many of the unique behaviors and characteristics that an individual with autism may have, we have also provided examples of people who appear to respond to the world in vastly different ways from one another: Jeff, Craig, and Maria. People with autism, like people without disabilities, are individuals first. Not only does every individual with autism present a different set of disability-related characteristics, but each also has his or her own strengths, interests, and wishes. This is to say that autism is not one profile or set of behaviors that is common across all people with the disability. Rather, it is a collection of behaviors, and different people's behaviors may vary. Some people with autism do not use words to communicate, like Craig, and others seem to talk more than the average adolescent. Some individuals like to have their schedule precisely the same every day, like Jeff; others may spend all of their free time reading about a special interest. Some individuals like to be near peers and seek peer attention; others prefer to be left alone.

Because the characteristics of people with autism vary, professionals, paraprofessionals, and caregivers cannot assume that they understand a person with autism just on the basis of the diagnosis. All people providing care and services to a person with autism must discover the unique behaviors that define that person. Figure 1.1 shows a questionnaire that can be completed by the student and his or

Personal profile on: _____

Person completing form: _____

Relationship to the student: _____

What does he or she like?

_____

What does he or she dislike?

_____

How does the student tell you that he or she likes something?

_____

How does the student tell you that he or she dislikes something?

_____

How does the student tell you that he or she wants to stop doing something?

_____

How does the student tell you that he or she wants to be left alone?

_____

How does the student tell you that he or she wants something or wants to do an activity?

_____

What does he or she like to do during free time?

_____

What does he or she do when upset or frustrated?

_____

What kinds of situations seem to upset or frustrate the student?

_____

Who are his or her friends?

_____

With whom does the student like to interact or spend time?

_____

Are there people who are problematic for this student, people he or she does not like to be around?

_____

What other information about this student is important to share? (Think about personal, communication, social, medical, or behavioral issues that others should know about.)

_____

Figure 1.1.   Student personal profile questionnaire.

Autism and the Transition to Adulthood: Success Beyond the Classroom by Paul Wehman,
Marcia Datlow Smith, & Carol Schall © 2009 by Paul H. Brookes Publishing Co., Inc. All rights reserved.

her parents or caregiver to help the IEP or transition team create an accurate profile of the student. Collecting and sharing this information across service providers and caregivers will help team members communicate effectively about the needs that the person with autism may have.

COLLABORATING WITH TEAM MEMBERS

Considering the differences in individual strengths and needs and the multiple challenges associated with autism, it is critical to have many professional and caregiver perspectives supporting the adolescent with autism during the transition years. In short, it takes a team of people with different knowledge and skills to develop and coordinate an IEP and a transition plan for a student with autism. Table 1.3 lists some of the professionals who may be on such a team and the skills they might offer. Notice that the table lists the student and family members as important contributors to different skill areas.

Table 1.3 does not list just one team member for each skill area. This is because professionals may have expertise across several skill areas. To use the information in the table when supporting a student with autism, look at the left column, which lists the skills needed for supporting the student during transition. Consider whether the current team has a person or people with those skills. If not, look at the list of professionals in the column on the right and decide which, if any, of those professionals in your setting possess the needed skills and are available to serve on that team.

Table 1.3. Skills and potential team members for supporting adolescents with autism

Skill	Team members who may have this skill
Teaching social skills and developing a social skills plan	Teacher, psychologist, behavior analyst, speech therapist, occupational therapist, vocational rehabilitation specialist
Teaching communication and developing a communication plan	Speech therapist, teacher, behavior analyst
Analyzing challenging behavior and developing a behavior intervention plan	Behavior analyst, teacher, vocational rehabilitation specialist, psychologist
Assessing, planning, implementing, and evaluating core academic, functional, daily living, and recreational skill needs	Teacher, psychologist, behavior analyst, family members
Developing a transition plan and coordinating communication across team members	Teacher, vocational rehabilitation specialist, school or community-based case manager
Addressing environmental and sensory challenges	Occupational therapist, teacher, behavior analyst, vocational rehabilitation specialist, psychologist
Addressing psychiatric, behavioral, or mental health concerns	Psychiatrist, psychologist, licensed clinical social worker, behavior analyst
Identifying potential jobs, finding employers, designing successful work stations and environments, and teaching job skills	Vocational rehabilitation professional, job coach, vocational teacher, transition teacher
Providing the team with history of the student's past experiences; assisting the team with discovering the student's vision and dreams	The person with autism, family members, teacher, any other team member who has a long-term perspective of the student
Implementing all plans, collecting data on the plans, and providing feedback to the team about the success of the plans	Paraprofessional staff (instructional assistant), job coach, teacher, residential and community-based direct services staff

Because of the need for so many different skills and areas of professional knowledge, it is important that teams collaborate. Prelock (2006) defined *collaborative teaming* as "an interactive process that enables individuals with different backgrounds and expertise to organize and work together to define and creatively solve problems as a team, recognizing that no single person could have produced such solutions" (p. 90). This means that individual team members must share their professional information so that they can learn how best to support the student throughout the transition process. To do this, team members must be open to different perspectives and new ways of thinking about the student and the student's strengths and needs. They must also be open to using creative problem-solving strategies when they encounter problems in the transition process. Team members must feel free to share their thoughts about their own areas of expertise as well as listen to others' opinions. This requires that members meet regularly, develop trusting relationships by being accountable to one another, and work on maintaining open communication (Sharp & Hawes, 2003).

Although it is critical to have a team of support, it is not necessary to have a team member from every profession listed in Table 1.3. It is possible that some team members may serve multiple roles. For instance, a speech therapist may have additional training in sensory processing and may be able to help the team develop sensory supports. A parent may have discovered behavioral strategies that work with his or her child and can share this information with the team to address the child's challenges outside of home. In other words, although it is important to have a team to address the multiple needs of an adolescent with autism, it is not critical that every team have the same members.

CHARACTERISTICS OF
RECOMMENDED TRANSITION PRACTICES

Adolescents with autism require specialized support and planning throughout their transition from school to adult life. Thoughtful transition planning is needed whether the student is continuing on to college or is seeking employment with supports through a community provider or vocational rehabilitation agency. Consider the importance of having a framework or guidelines to follow in transition planning for each student. Each student is different, yet there must be consistency to approaching the design of a transition plan. It will be important for the transition team to use recommended practices when supporting the student with autism through this transition. The five guidelines or practices we see in transition planning for students with autism are

1. Implementing positive behavior supports to address behavior challenges

2. Matching the IEP to a vision for the future

3. Capitalizing on inclusive experiences

4. Providing a variety of community-based job and life experiences

5. Coordinating a smooth transition to new resources and service providers in the community

Each of these important practices and their relevance to individuals with autism are described briefly here and in more depth in other chapters.

Implementing Positive Behavior Supports to Address Behavior Challenges

It is clear that many individuals with autism display challenging behaviors. In addition, the characteristics of autism lead to a need for increased communication and social skills and decreased problematic or repetitive behaviors. Thus, it is important for parents, teachers, and other direct service providers to understand the purpose of students' behavior and develop positive behavior support plans for students. Chapter 2 provides an overview of the skills teachers need in order to analyze the purposes of students' challenging behavior and implement a plan to decrease those behaviors while increasing adaptive behavior.

Matching the Individualized Education Program to a Vision for the Future

Middle and high school mark important changes in the school curriculum for all students. Perhaps one of the most significant is the increased choice that young people have when they enter middle school. Instead of being provided with the same curriculum as everyone else in their class and year, middle school students are offered choices of classes and electives. This provision of choice in the curriculum demonstrates the acknowledgment that youth are beginning to explore their own interests and abilities and will eventually choose a course of study that leads them to their own personal career path. Some youth will go on to college and study science, human services, art, or music. Some youth will go to work in mechanics, in construction, or in administration. Curriculum choice reflects the importance of looking forward, not back. By the end of elementary school, all students leave behind the basics and, ready or not, move on to a course of study that matches their interests.

It is important that this same change occur for middle and high school students with autism. Rather than focus on the missing developmental skills a person with autism may have, his or her curriculum should look forward to the potential career path the individual will follow. This critical shift should be reflected in the IEP process. Adolescence is the time to identify skills that will result in meeting the vision that the person and his or her family have for adulthood. Even for individuals who will go on to college, it is critical to begin to shape the curriculum based on plans for the individual's adult life.

In short, the task of education from middle school forward is one of getting a life. When considering education from that point of view, it becomes clear that skill selection is a key process. The issue of getting a life also raises the question of what kind of life a person with autism should seek. The answer to that question is the life of the individual's vision and dreams. Chapter 3 will provide a roadmap for teachers seeking to understand this process and encourage the development of IEPs that match the student's strengths, interests, and vision for the future. In Chapter 3, you will read about the importance of assessment, career development, person-centered planning, and IEP development. All of these processes require that adolescents with autism be involved and, as much as possible, speak for themselves. When an individual cannot communicate his or her feelings or wishes about these matters, the team must consider how the student has expressed preferences through the varied experiences he or she has had in school. The result is an IEP that is focused on the student and has included the student in its development.

Capitalizing on Inclusive Experiences

The best place to teach many students with disabilities, including autism, is with their peers who do not have disabilities. Rather than a philosophy or movement, inclusion should be viewed as a tool that can address both academic and social skill development while meeting students' individual needs. Specifically, inclusive experiences present students with autism the opportunity to observe, learn, and practice social skills with peers who do not have disabilities.

When well supported and implemented, inclusion also affords individuals with autism the opportunity to gain access to the general education curriculum under the guidance of both special and general educators who are highly qualified. Thus, inclusion serves a very important role in helping adolescents with autism meet state standards while practicing social skills in natural environments. Chapter 4 describes how to properly plan and implement supports for successful inclusion to address the needs of students with autism in meeting state standards and accomplishing social skill practice in natural environments.

Providing a Variety of Community-Based Job and Life Experiences

One key to success in employment is having previous work experience. Working is a unique experience in that the types of relationships, the way tasks are completed, and the way co-workers interact are all governed by stated and unstated rules. Rules for customer care and reporting to a boss are unique to and only observed in work environments. Thus, they are best learned at work. Likewise, there are stated and unstated rules that govern other public environments, such as restaurants and grocery stores. The best place to learn the rules of these environments is in each environment itself. Because of the difficulty that many individuals with autism experience when attempting to generalize skills from one setting to another, it is important to teach them in the environment in which they will use the skills—in real settings outside the classroom, such as internships, work-study situations, part- or full-time paid work, or even volunteering. Chapter 5 presents strategies that will enable teachers to teach these skills, while Chapters 7, 8, 9, and 10 present strategies on developing and providing instruction in work-, community-, and home-based settings.

Coordinating a Smooth Transition to New Resources and Service Providers in the Community

An important aspect of transition planning is to connect the person with autism and his or her support system to all of the resources and service providers available to adults with disabilities. With a thorough understanding of families' needs and pertinent adult services, IEP and transition team members will be better suited to address students' and families' needs. This is the major way family support occurs for transition-age youth with autism. By connecting youth and their families with resources and service providers while students are still in high school, the teacher can continue to support students' transition in the classroom by implementing changes based on the recommendations of service providers and obtaining new services through the transition referral process. As the person with autism makes the transition from high school to the community, workplace, or college, more and more adult service providers should participate in the development and implementation of the plan. The teacher's role during this aspect of transition is to provide all of the necessary introductions across the team and to facilitate the development of a plan that allows the person with autism and the entire team to interact together successfully. Chapter 6 and the Resource Guide at the end of the book address teachers' and parents' need for information about those important services.

PULLING IT ALL TOGETHER

As noted previously, adolescence is a difficult time full of challenges. Students without disabilities struggle to find their way to their future. Students with autism face additional challenges due to their disabilities. The critical factor in the success of transition for adolescents with autism is determined by the people who comprise their team. In order to achieve success beyond the classroom, the team must listen well to the student and his or her parents regarding their vision for the future and plan carefully to assist the student in achieving that vision.

Positive Behavior Support

Marcia Datlow Smith

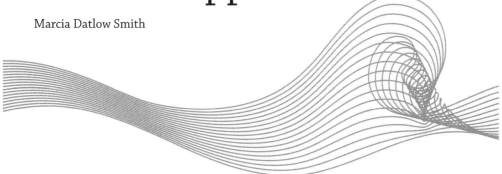

As noted in Chapter 1, people with autism and Asperger's syndrome frequently exhibit behavioral challenges. For example, the case studies of Jeff, Craig, and Maria demonstrate that problem behavior is a major issue for all of these students. Jeff steps on other students' feet, is argumentative, and on occasion has hit others. Craig injures himself by hitting his head and biting his wrists. Maria scratches her arms, repeats movie dialogue at inappropriate times, and has thrown objects when she has been really upset. All three of these young people would benefit from positive behavior support plans to decrease these challenging behaviors. This is frequently the case for individuals with autism (Matson & Nebel-Schwalm, 2007). Before we discuss transition planning in the next chapter, it is important to consider how best to assess behavior and develop positive behavior support plans so that young people with autism and Asperger's syndrome can become successful adults. This chapter explores the process for developing a behavior support plan that achieves the following: 1) helps students with autism reduce problem behaviors, 2) encourages more acceptable behaviors, and 3) helps students succeed in school and work despite the presence of challenging behavior.

The process for behavior change is systematic. It includes selecting goals, determining the purpose or function of behavior, and planning strategies that help the student learn new ways of behaving. Strategies might be implemented by the teacher, family, job coach, or even by students themselves. Occasionally other specialists are included, such as a psychologist, a speech or occupational therapist, or a psychiatrist (Hieneman, Childs, & Sergay, 2006; Kincaid, Chapman, Shannon,

Schall, & Harrower, 2002). The process of developing a behavior support plan and available resources for doing so are further discussed later in this chapter.

Students like Jeff, Craig, and Maria have many social needs, and they need to understand and navigate social contexts and learn which behaviors are acceptable. It is possible to select goals for change and help students learn more appropriate ways of behaving. It is also possible to help them learn more rewarding ways of interacting with others; however, selecting goals may seem overwhelming because there may be many needs to address. Once a student begins the transition planning process, priorities for behavior change become clearer. Targeted goals for a behavior plan can be developed based on the following criteria:

1. *Does the student's behavior hinder success on the job?* For example, Jeff's unwanted physical contact with others might result in his losing a job. If Jeff is to succeed at work and be able to keep a job, his behavior plan needs a goal that supports a reduction in aggression or unwanted physical contact.

2. *Does the student's behavior hinder social relationships?* Maria's constant reciting of *Finding Nemo* would certainly hinder social relationships. A goal that supports learning new topics of conversation would help Maria attract and retain friends.

3. *Does the student's behavior limit independence?* If a student cannot control his rage, his independence will be severely limited because he will need supervision to ensure that he does not injure himself. A goal that reduces violent self-inflicted outbursts and encourages more acceptable ways of dealing with stressful situations would help the student gain independence. Because the student often has these tantrums when being told no, teaching him to accept no as a response would be an important goal for him.

4. *Does the student's behavior present a danger?* The student's self-inflicted rage does present a danger. If he hits his head very hard, he could harm himself. If he were to do this in a public place, he could be arrested or removed by emergency services providers. Again, helping the student stop this behavior could be critical to his safety and the safety of others.

Goals must be observable; that is, they should be visible and measurable. Anger cannot be targeted as a goal because it cannot be seen or measured; however, "hitting others" could be a goal because hitting can be seen and measured. Frustration cannot be targeted as a goal for the same reason anger cannot. Instead, the goal might be "asking for help."

Goals can be developed that seek to reduce problem behaviors. In Jeff's case, goals would include reducing physical aggression. Maria's goals would include working quietly, respecting property (i.e., not throwing objects or ripping her clothes), and decreasing the frequency of scratching herself. A goal for Craig would be decreasing self-injury. Goals can also be developed that seek to teach more appropriate behavior, such as asking for help, greeting others, taking turns in conversation, and learning new topics for conversation.

Table 2.1 provides a list of common types of challenging behaviors along with suggested alternative responses that can be worked into goals for positive behavior change.

Table 2.1.   Acceptable alternatives to challenging behavior

Challenging behavior	Alternative behavior
Demands food or drink through verbal abuse or destructive behavior	Asks politely Gestures or signs Waits for scheduled opportunities
Escapes or avoids tasks or instructions through refusal, verbal abuse, negotiating, darting, or destructive behavior	Follows instructions Initiates and completes scheduled tasks
Demands favorite activities during scheduled tasks or assignments	Waits for scheduled opportunities
Misuses property by banging, slamming, breaking, or throwing	Uses property for its intended use Closes, handles, or puts away property gently
Engages in challenging conversations of personal questions, irrelevant topics, or repetitive, lengthy monologues	Respects privacy by asking appropriate questions Takes turns in conversation Takes into account interests of listener
Escapes or avoids instructions, corrections, reprimands	Accepts correction Accepts instructions Accepts suggestions
Demands sameness through refusal of changes in schedule or routine	Accepts changes in schedule or routine Asks for help with changes

FUNCTIONAL BEHAVIOR ASSESSMENT: FINDING PURPOSE IN BEHAVIOR

It is always important to find the purpose of a problem behavior. Without knowing the motivation behind it, attempts to correct the problem behavior are guesses, at best, resulting in failure to properly correct it. Before students can be helped to change and to achieve their goals, it is important to find out why they behave the way they do. The process of finding the purpose or cause of a behavior is called a *functional behavior assessment* (Carr et al., 2002; Carr et al., 1999; Machalicek, O'Reilly, Beretvas, Sigafoos, & Lancioni, 2007).

Behavior serves basic functions for people regardless of whether they have autism. Young people with and without disabilities exhibit many behaviors, both positive and negative, that serve certain purposes. Craig, for instance, has learned how to operate the microwave because he can use it to heat up pizza, his favorite snack. His problem behaviors also serve a function for him. His mother reports that she frequently gives him a soda to help him calm down when he hits himself. She also will give him something he asked for, even after she said no, just to keep him from hitting himself or to stop him once he has started. Craig has learned that if he hits himself (behavior), he will get something he wants (soda). He has also learned that if he is having difficulty and he bites his wrist, his teacher comes running to find out what the problem is and to help him out. His teacher might also take him out for a walk. His wrist biting thus has two purposes—it gets him extra breaks and allows him to go for a walk, which he likes. Other students who do not speak may at times act out by screaming, throwing things, banging, hitting themselves, and hitting others. These behaviors can serve such functions as obtaining desired items (e.g., food or drink) or being allowed to engage in certain preferred activities.

Problem behaviors can also serve more social functions, such as gaining attention, avoiding demands, escaping from tasks, obtaining assistance, and escaping from reprimands and criticism (Matson & Nebel-Schwalm, 2007). Jeff has learned that if he is having difficulty with a task and he yells and pounds his fists, his teacher hurries over to offer assistance. Jeff's tantrums serve the purpose of getting him help. If the teacher gives him a math assignment and he stomps his foot, the teacher backs off and gives him some time to read his magazine. Jeff learns that foot stomping helps him avoid demands and allows him time to do his favorite activities.

Maria has learned that if she sits quietly, her teacher and peers do not say much to her. If she starts to throw objects, however, the teacher will rush over, ask Maria what is wrong, and rub her shoulder. Maria enjoys this attention. Throwing objects has come to serve the purpose of obtaining her teacher's attention. It is likely that autism prevents Maria from seeing the throwing of objects as wrong behavior. Instead, she sees it as useful behavior—it brings her attention from her teacher.

Although the causes of problem behavior vary from student to student, there are common themes. Table 2.2 presents some common causes and examples of problematic behavior. To discover the function of a behavior, it is important to first find the patterns in the behavior. Finding patterns involves looking at what events trigger the behavior and what the payoffs are for the student.

Triggers

Triggers, sometimes referred to as *antecedents* are the events or tasks that set a problem behavior into motion. There are several categories of common triggers.

Social Triggers

Social triggers are events that occur in the form of social contact initiated by others, such as teachers, job coaches, family members, or peers. Social triggers for problem behaviors include being spoken to in a harsh or critical tone, insistently being asked questions, being teased, being talked to too much or in too loud of a tone, or having someone get too close physically. Being pressured or rushed can trigger problem behavior, as can absence of social attention. Maria's recitation of *Finding Nemo* might be an example of this. The behavior serves the function of bringing conversation her way.

Change

Individuals with autism can be sensitive to change, and changes can be triggers for problematic behavior. These may be unexpected changes in routine, schedule, and/or upcoming events. A substitute teacher, a substitute job coach, or changes in the family constellation can all serve as triggers for problem behavior.

Instructions and Demands

Certain kinds of instructions or demands made on a student with autism can trigger behavior problems. These triggers include assignments that are too difficult, instructional methods that are not suited to the student's learning style, repeated demands on the student, and nonacceptance of the student's refusal to do something.

Table 2.2.   Common causes and examples of behavior problems

Cause	Example
Desires food or drink, especially unscheduled, additional, or favorite food or drink	A student screams for iced tea when she sees her teacher drinking iced tea.
Desires attention	A student is left alone at his desk while the instructional aide assists someone else. The student begins to bang his forearm on the desk.
Desires favorite activity	A student darts out the back door of the classroom without permission to take a long walk.
Avoids task	A student is presented with a math task. He screams and bites his wrist.
Wants to escape from task	A student is stocking shelves at her part-time job. After 2 hours, she says, "Go home," and kicks the boxes.
Wants to escape from correction	A student is reprimanded for an error in his work. He responds by cursing his teacher and banging his fist on his desk.
Needs help	A student is making copies in the school office. The copy machine jams. The student starts to cry.
Wants to escape from social situation	A student works in a hardware store. A customer follows him around to ask him a question. The student hits the customer.
Has difficulty with change	A student gets a new job coach. She is so upset she refuses to go to work.
Experiences unexpected disappointments	A student has been counting on his usual Friday night bowling trip, but bowling is canceled due to snow. The student punches a hole in the wall.
Has disrupted routine	A student missed homeroom because her bus was late. She refuses to go to her first period class and keeps returning to homeroom.
Has interrupted ritual	A teacher tried to interrupt a student's dialogue to present a task. The student throws the work materials on the floor.

Denial of Requests, Interrupted Activities, and Waiting

Denying or interrupting a student's access to enjoyable activities or outcomes—such as telling the student no, interrupting a favorite activity (especially if the interruption is followed by a demand, such as "Stop playing video games and do your math"), and making the student wait unexpectedly for a long time (especially if the wait is for a pleasant activity)—can serve as a trigger for problem behaviors. Sometimes students with autism have certain rituals. Denying them time to do their ritual or interrupting a ritual can trigger a problem behavior.

Identifying triggers can help teachers understand the function of a student's behavior. If a problem behavior occurs in response to demands, the teacher might hypothesize that the student is engaging in the problem behavior to escape those demands. If a problem behavior seems to be triggered by denial of a preferred activity, the team can hypothesize that the function of that behavior is to acquire specific activities. If there are several triggers for a problem behavior, the team might want to explore the role that *payoffs* play in the problem behavior.

Payoffs

Problem behavior often brings some reward, or *payoff*, for students with autism. When Jeff screams, for instance, his teacher offers assistance. When Craig bites his wrist, his mother offers him a snack to calm down. These payoffs help ensure that Jeff and Craig will engage in the behavior the next time they need help or want a snack. Payoffs are also referred to as *reinforcers* (Hieneman et al., 2006), and the process of using reinforcers to strengthen behavior is known as *reinforcement*.

When looking for the function of the behavior, the answer is often found in the payoff. Looking at what the student gets as a result of the behavior can help pinpoint the function of the behavior. Problem behavior might result in several kinds of payoffs.

Social Payoffs

Attention—in the form of reassurances, help, and additional explanations—can serve as a payoff for problem behavior. Additional assistance or counseling from favorite staff or family members is another example of a social payoff.

Favorite Activities

Some students learn that when they act out, they are allowed to engage in favorite activities. Frequently, teachers and parents allow this because they think they are helping the student calm down, but in fact they may be helping to strengthen the very behavior they want to discourage.

Escape

Sometimes the payoff is that the student can escape or avoid a situation or task that has become unpleasant. For example, a student who screams when presented with a math assignment learns that the outcome is that the teacher withdraws the assignment. Avoiding math is the payoff for screaming.

Food, Drink, and Favorite Items

Sometimes well-meaning teachers and family members provide a student food, drink, and favorite items in their attempts to calm the student down. Again, this benevolent act may actually result in more problem behavior in the future.

By identifying the triggers and payoffs for a behavior, teams can develop sound hypotheses about the function of the behavior. In the next section, we share how teams for Jeff, Craig, and Maria did this.

Jeff's Behavioral Goals, Triggers, and Payoffs

Jeff's transition teacher arranged for a consultation with the school psychologist, who was skilled in helping to solve the social problems of students with autism and Asperger's syndrome. The school psychologist worked with the transition teacher and the instructional aide to develop a behavior support plan. The goals developed by the team for Jeff were

- Speaking politely to others (defined as no verbal abuse and no screaming)

- Respecting others (defined as no incidents of unwanted physical contact, such as stepping on toes, tripping others, and punching others)

- Respecting women's privacy (defined as not staring at their feet and not commenting on their shoes)

After targeting these goals, the team reviewed information on Jeff's behaviors to determine their function. The team interviewed his teachers and his instructional aide and reviewed classroom data on Jeff's behavior. These data consisted of write-ups of incidents, including noted triggers and information on how others responded to him afterward.

A pattern began to emerge. Incidents of yelling and name calling generally occurred when Jeff's teacher gave him instructions on new tasks, corrected his work, or interrupted him midtask. Yelling at his teacher often resulted in being given a few minutes to calm down, more assistance from the teacher or instructional aide, or having them ask him what was wrong. After he gave the reason for his yelling, they would seek to solve his problem for him. The team concluded that one function of Jeff's verbal outbursts was to obtain help when he experienced difficulty. The second function appeared to be to escape from criticism. He had discovered that if he screamed, his teacher would stop her criticism and give him a break. The third function was to be allowed to complete the interrupted task. If he yelled when interrupted midtask, the teacher would back off and let him finish.

The team determined that the function of Jeff's unwanted physical contact with others was actually to gain attention from his peers. If he stepped on someone's toes, the person would respond by saying something such as, "Hey, watch it." Jeff would then smile or laugh. He seemed to enjoy the social interaction his actions brought. Staring at women's feet seemed to serve a sexual function, as evidenced by other gestures that accompanied the staring.

Completing a Functional Behavior Assessment for Craig

As noted in Chapter 1, Craig's verbal abilities are limited to single words or short phrases in which he makes requests. The area that presented the most challenges for Craig's transition team was that of behavior. Craig sometimes banged his head, both with his fists and against walls and floors, and he required close supervision in the bathroom to keep him from purposely overflowing the toilet. Craig's transition team targeted several goals as part of his transition plan:

- Respecting himself, thus decreasing the frequency of self-injury (defined as Craig's hitting himself or banging his head)

- Correctly using the bathroom

Triggers and payoffs were examined to determine the function of Craig's self-injurious behavior. Data were kept for several weeks, during which time his teacher and also his parents kept track of incidents of self-injury. They wrote down the triggers to the behavior and what happened afterward. Triggers for Craig's behaviors included being told no when he made a demand for food or drink, being spoken to sharply, and having favorite items taken away, such as certain objects and tools.

A close examination of Craig's outbursts revealed that during and after an episode of self-injury, his family or teacher would attempt to find out what was wrong and provide him with what he was demanding. If an outburst was a result of having a favorite object taken away, the teacher would return the object. Although giving Craig what he was demanding quickly stopped the self-injury, it appeared that giving him favorite foods, drinks, and objects and meeting his demands were in fact payoffs for his self-inflicted outbursts. Craig had learned that hitting himself served his purposes of getting favorite snacks and extra time with his favorite objects.

Maria's Functional Behavior Assessment

Maria's transition team was planning work experiences for her but found her loud, insistent recitations of movie dialogue and her occasional behavioral outbursts daunting. Furthermore, her teacher was concerned about her occasional scratching of herself and was fearful of putting her in stressful situations. The team targeted several behavioral goals as part of Maria's transition plan:

• Helping Maria limit her movie dialogues to scheduled times

• Decreasing the frequency of property destruction, notably throwing objects and ripping clothing

• Decreasing the frequency of self-injury (scratching herself)

The transition team invited a consulting psychologist to help develop a behavior support plan for Maria to work toward the behavioral goals. The psychologist reviewed information on Maria's problem behaviors through interviews with her teachers and her mother. A diary was also kept in which details of problem incidents were jotted down, including observable triggers and payoffs. Triggers for scratching herself and tearing her clothing included being interrupted when she was reciting a movie dialogue, schedule changes, and being spoken to harshly. The psychologist also discovered that student teasing was a trigger for Maria's scratching herself, especially if the students were boys. Interestingly, the team also found triggers for reciting of movie dialogues. When new tasks were presented, especially a physically demanding task, or if Maria was asked to change the way she did a task or assignment, she would often start to recite a movie dialogue. She would also recite dialogue if she was corrected. Triggers for throwing objects included unexpected disappointments, such as the family beach trip being canceled (as mentioned in Chapter 1) or a field trip being canceled.

Review of the diary also revealed several possible payoffs. If Maria threw an object, the teacher or instructional aide would take her for a walk and attempt to calm her down by offering her a drink. Once she was calm, the teacher would counsel her and explain to her how she should have handled the situation. She would then have Maria apologize and restore the object to its original place. Similarly, incidents of torn clothing or scratching herself resulted in sympathetic reassurances from the teacher or aide. In addition, Maria would get lotion or ointment rubbed on her scratches. The extra attention and soothing lotion were payoffs for her behavior.

One payoff for reciting movie dialogues was receiving attention from staff and other students, as they would make comments, laugh, and goad Maria on. It became obvious that Maria was also using the dialogues to delay or avoid work assignments and to stop her teacher from teaching or correcting her; her teacher's efforts were silenced by Maria's rambling recitations.

In sum, it appeared that the function of throwing objects was to escape what for Maria had become a difficult situation. She was able to leave the classroom, get a drink, and gain the sympathetic attention of the teacher. Scratching herself and tearing her clothing also served the function of gaining sympathetic attention and assistance. The functions of reciting movie dialogue were three-fold. First, it probably was an activity that she found self-entertaining. Second, and likely more important, it allowed her to avoid tasks, correction, and instructions. Finally, it appeared to allow her to interact socially with other students, as she was unable to communicate effectively with her peers without reciting movie lines.

Summary Hypotheses from the Functional Behavior Assessment

By tracking the types of triggers for problem behavior and the payoffs a student receives in response to such behavior, transition teams can develop more accurate hypotheses for the function of the behavior. Below are some sample hypotheses for Jeff, Craig, and Maria that demonstrate how understanding the triggers, describing the behavior, and understanding the function can help teams plan effective behavior change strategies.

Behavioral hypotheses for Jeff are

1. When given instruction on a new task, Jeff will yell in order to get more assistance from his teacher or aide.

2. When corrected by his teacher or aide, Jeff will yell in order to get a break from the task and to be left alone.

3. When interrupted in the middle of a task, Jeff will yell in order to get his teacher to ask him, "What's wrong?" He then asks for more time on the current task.

4. When near others, particularly women, Jeff will step on or stare at their feet in order to gain peer attention and increased interaction.

Behavioral hypotheses for Craig are

1. When he is told no, or something he wants is taken away from him, Craig will hit himself in order to get the thing he wants.

2. When he is spoken to harshly, Craig will hit himself and bite his wrist in order to solicit sympathy and kindness (e.g., "What's wrong, Craig?").

Behavioral hypotheses for Maria are

1. When there is a change in routine, Maria is interrupted during one of her movie dialogues, she is spoken to harshly, she is teased by other students, or she is

very disappointed, Maria will scratch herself in order to solicit sympathy from her mother and teacher, get a drink during times of stress, or go for a walk.

2. When asked to complete a new task or change the way she completes a task, or if she is corrected, Maria will recite movie dialogue in order to get attention from her teachers and peers and to avoid completing work.

3. When she experiences great disappointment, such as the cancellation of an event she was looking forward to attending, Maria will throw items in order to get sympathy and attention from her caregivers.

These hypothesis statements demonstrate the three aspects of problem behavior discussed so far: the trigger (the phrase of each statement following the word "When"), the behavior (the statement after the words "[student] will"), and the function (the statements after the words "in order to"). Although these are hypotheses, they are based on the functional behavior assessment, which includes careful observation and documentation of the student's behaviors. Consequently, teams can usually rely on the results of functional behavior assessment to represent the current functions of behavior. Statements such as these allow teams to develop effective strategies to change behavior.

STRATEGIC PLAN FOR BEHAVIOR CHANGE

Once the function of a behavior is discovered, it is possible to select strategies for behavior change (Hieneman et al., 2006; Machalicek et al., 2007; Snell, Vorhees, & Chen, 2005). There are a wide variety of strategies to choose from (see Table 2.3); however, strategies cannot be chosen haphazardly. They should be chosen to address the function of a particular behavior. The strategies need to follow from an organized intervention plan for change that relies on what is known about triggers, payoffs, and functions of students' behaviors. The intervention plan will help team members and students work on the behaviors in one or more ways, which are discussed next.

Change the Environment to Encourage Success

Sometimes problem behavior occurs because individuals with autism are faced with confusing or even aversive environmental events. There are six ways a team might change the environment to increase success: 1) ensuring adequate supervision, 2) providing an individualized schedule for the student, 3) matching the instructional strategy to the student's task and learning style to ensure success, 4) providing more opportunities for the student to make choices, 5) eliminating any triggers, and 6) cushioning the impact of triggers.

Provide Adequate Supervision

Many students with autism require more supervision than their peers without disabilities. They may need smaller classrooms, a job coach at work, or even a one-to-one instructional assistant. Extra supervision might be occasional as a need arises, or it might be intense and full time. Sometimes the behavior support plan may call for a change in supervision to help the student succeed.

Table 2.3.   Strategies for behavior change

Type of strategy	Procedures	Examples
Trigger related	Remove the trigger.	Avoid harsh tones when providing correction.
	Cushion the impact of the trigger.	Provide an alternative activity if the main activity is canceled.
	Help the student cope.	Provide training on how to handle disappointments.
Access to favorite items	Allow free access to items the student wants.	Let the student have a snack anytime.
	Schedule access to items the student wants.	Schedule time for snacks.
Incentive plans	Rate the student for good behavior.	Rate the student on his or her work behavior and provide daily and weekly rewards for good performance.
	Reward the student for high productivity.	Reward the student for achieving production goals.
	Reward the student for longer periods of good behavior.	For each week of good attendance, slightly increase the student's salary.
	Give surprise rewards.	Several times per week, give the student an unexpected reward for cooperative behavior.
New ways of achieving function	Teach the student more acceptable ways to achieve his or her purpose.	If the student steals food from peers' lunches, teach him or her to ask for seconds.
Social skills training	Teach the student more acceptable ways to handle difficult situations.	If the student curses at work when having difficulty with a task, use social skills training to teach him or her to ask for help.
Safety precautions	Take precautions if explosive outbursts occur.	Train staff to prevent the student from hurting him- or herself if the student starts to bang his or her head.

Provide Individualized Schedules

Scheduling problems can lead to behavior problems. Individuals with autism and Asperger's syndrome can be very sensitive to schedules that change, are too demanding, provide too much down time, or are unclear (Conroy, Asmus, Sellers, & Ladwig, 2005; Snell et al., 2005). Individuals who have difficulty cooperating with the routine often benefit from a schedule that is made very clear for them. It is helpful for them to know exactly what activities and tasks they will be doing as well as start and end times for each task. The use of breaks in a schedule can be an important strategy for students whose problem behavior serves the function of avoiding tasks or work. With a schedule that defines exactly when breaks occur, students with autism frequently become more adept at tolerating work.

Written schedules can be used if the student can read. If changes are made in the day's school or work schedule, the written schedule can be changed accordingly. For students who do not read or speak, a picture schedule can be used. The individual is shown pictures of the day's planned activities, ideally featuring him or her participating.

Ensure that Instructional Strategy Allows for Success

Careful use of instructional strategies can help students learn. For students with autism, the use of sound, individualized instructional strategies are important for successful positive behavior support. If the teacher moves too fast for a student's learning abilities when the student is learning a new skill, or the teacher does not provide adequate demonstration of the skill, the student is likely to be frustrated and display that frustration through problem behavior. Likewise, moving too slowly might result in student boredom, which presents another opportunity for problem behavior to occur. Consequently, it is critical to use instructional strategies that match the task and the student's needs. Chapter 5 provides an excellent review of numerous effective strategies.

Offer More Choices

Individuals who are given choices in their schedules may be more likely to cooperate (Hieneman et al., 2006; Kincaid et al., 2002; Machalicek et al., 2007; Snell et al., 2005). Students who use verbal language can be asked to make choices; individuals who are nonverbal can be given choices by being shown pictures or actual items. Some individuals with autism who use problem behaviors to avoid certain activities will often be able to stay with those activities longer if given choices. For example, one student typically displayed oppositional behavior, such as sitting down and refusing to get up, when attending parties. His family would then have to escort him from the party and take him home. His family found that by giving him the choice to leave every 10 minutes he was more willing to stay cooperatively than when not given those choices.

A caution about choices, however: Sometimes individuals with autism are reluctant to try new things. Resistance to change is often a major issue. If allowed too much choice, or if asked to make a choice at a critical time, the student may shrink from important opportunities. Sometimes providing explanation and encouragement to try new things will help students expand their horizons.

Eliminate Triggers of Problem Behavior

Sometimes it is possible to simply eliminate the triggers that prompt the problem behavior. The behavior support plan can include removal of social triggers, task triggers, or event triggers (Lerman & Rapp, 2006). If a student is likely to engage in a problem behavior in response to harsh criticism, one strategy to address that behavior would be to train team members not to use a harsh tone of voice when correcting the student. If certain events, such as an unexpected schedule change, trigger problem behavior, the support plan might include procedures to eliminate unexpected schedule changes. So, for example, if unexpectedly changing Jeff's work schedule results in an angry response of banging on the table, team members should take care to keep his routine consistent.

Cushion the Impact of Triggers

Sometimes it is not possible to eliminate triggers. For example, if a student with autism frequently displays problem behavior in response to schedule changes, there may be nothing that a teacher or job coach can do to prevent some schedule changes. When triggers cannot be eliminated, it is often possible to cushion their impact by using strategies that help the student deal with the triggers. For instance, students can be given extra instruction and time to adapt to changes in their schedules (Conroy et al., 2005; Miltenberger, 2006; Snell et al., 2005).

Provide More Frequent Access to What the Person Desires

Craig's problem behavior frequently occurs when he is told no in response to requests for drinks, food, or particular activities. By providing regular access to the things he wants, his team may eliminate the need for Craig to request these things and then hit himself when staff tell him no (Miltenberger, 2006).

Teach a Better Way to Achieve the Function of the Problem Behavior

Students can be taught new ways to achieve the function of their behavior (Hieneman et al., 2006; Mancil, Conroy, Nakao, & Alter, 2006). For example, Jeff can learn to ask for help when he needs it rather than yelling at others. Craig can also learn to ask for a soda in place of hitting himself in order to get it. This is one of the most important elements of a behavior change plan. If students do not learn new ways to meet their needs, they will always resort to the problem behavior. It is absolutely essential that teams include a strategy to teach students a better way to achieve the function of their behaviors.

Respond Differently to the New Behaviors and Problem Behaviors

It is important that the behavior support plan include strategies for providing different responses to positive behaviors and negative behaviors. There are three ways to achieve this aspect of the positive behavior support plan: 1) provide motivation in the form of incentives, 2) remove payoffs for the problem behavior, and 3) spell out how the problem behavior will be handled to prevent injury or unwittingly encourage the behavior. Each of these is described further.

Provide Motivation for the New Behavior

Sometimes the function of acting out is to avoid work or to escape from tasks or situations. It may be necessary to provide incentives for the student to work well (Hieneman et al., 2006; Mancil et al., 2006). It might also be necessary to provide motivation for the student to make behavioral and social choices that will allow a successful transition into adulthood. Motivation is most often provided in the form of incentives. It is always best to take a look at the payoffs for the problem behavior and make sure that your incentive plan includes those payoffs. For example, if Jeff yells to get help on a new task, and he is now learning to ask for help instead of yelling, the most logical incentive for the new behavior is for his teacher or job coach to give him help when he asks.

Is it often necessary to provide incentives to the student for cooperative behavior because students with autism may have difficulty conforming to social and work demands that are necessary for transition. Even if a student has a paying job, the money itself might not be a strong enough incentive for displaying good work behavior. The student might not understand the power of money, or the paychecks may be too infrequent. An incentive program may encourage the student to work toward behavioral and social goals (Carr et al., 1999; Hieneman et al., 2006; Kincaid et al., 2002; Machalicek et al., 2007; Snell et al., 2005).

Rewards used as incentives might include favorite foods or drinks or other pleasant experiences, such as rubbing in lotions, smelling colognes, and participating in favorite activities. For Craig, who has difficulty with spoken communication and exhibits serious behavior problems (including hitting himself) that occur more often when he is asked to complete work, treats such as mints, gummy bears, and small drinks can be used as rewards for working. The incentive system is an important part of his success.

Incentive systems cannot be haphazard. Each incentive or reward system must be designed for the individual student and be based on the level of the problem behaviors as well as on his or her interests, payoffs, and strengths. The team must decide which behaviors will be rewarded, what the rewards will be, how often they will be provided, and exactly what the student needs to do to earn them (Machalicek et al., 2007). It is important to choose systems that can fit into the schedule and demands of the transition plan and the student's daily and weekly schedule. It is also important to be consistent when administering the rewards. These systems require consistent use by all team members over several weeks or longer to achieve behavior change.

Remove Payoffs for the Problem Behavior

One purpose of Craig's self-injury is to get a soda from his mother. Therefore, Craig's behavior change plan needs to ensure that his self-injury no longer serves that purpose (Hieneman et al., 2006; Kincaid et al., 2002; Machalicek et al., 2007; Snell et al., 2005). This means no more sodas for self-injury. This particular strategy is also called *extinction*. Simply put, extinction means that the payoff is removed so that there is no longer any reason to engage in the behavior. This, combined with the other strategies discussed, makes for a very effective plan.

Often, extinction can be achieved by continuing with the schedule or the ongoing activity only when the student is not having an outburst. If Maria starts to scream at her desk, the teacher does not respond directly to the screaming. The teacher might wait several minutes, then simply direct Maria back to the task at hand. The functional behavior assessment has revealed certain purposes to the problem behavior, and the behavior support plan must include procedures to ensure that the problem behavior no longer serves those purposes, or functions.

Specify How a Problem Behavior Should Be Handled

There are times that, to remove a payoff, you might ignore a behavior—for instance, if the function of the behavior is to gain attention. This is an appropriate response as long as the student and others in the environment are safe. If ignoring a behavior could result in injury, teams must develop very consistent ways of responding that keep the person and others safe without giving undue attention to the behavior. Strategies such as blocking or other forms of nonaversive physical management may be needed. Any staff who may need to use these techniques to physically prevent a student from hurting him- or herself or others must receive special training and certification, and the use of those procedures as well as student progress must be carefully monitored by the team.

Provide Social Skills Training

Students with autism generally lack the social skills that other students have (Bellini, 2006; Matson, Matson, & Rivet, 2007). Greeting others, taking turns in conversation, and other social manners often have to be taught and polished as the student makes his or her way through school. Once transition begins, social manners for the workplace and marketplace might also need to be taught, including accepting instructions, accepting feedback, waiting in lines, and sharing workspace. Goals for social skills must be very specific. It may be difficult to teach a young man with autism to hang out with other students, but it is possible to teach him to wait his turn to speak. To be effective, goals must also be tailored to the student's needs and the situations in which the student is operating. Table 2.4 presents a list of social skills that adolescents with autism and Asperger's syndrome often need to be taught.

Using Social Amenities

Students with autism sometimes do not use social amenities. Phrases such as *please, thank you,* and *you're welcome* are simple, short, and easily taught. Although students might know to use these phrases with family members, it might be necessary to teach them to use them at school, at work, in stores, in banks, and in restaurants.

Using Appropriate Greetings

A common complaint about individuals with autism concerns their greeting of other students and co-workers. Some students with autism fail to greet or acknowledge others; others greet the same people over and over again. Teaching the appropriate use of greetings can be helpful, especially as the student in transition strives to fit in at the workplace.

Table 2.4.   Social skill goals that might need to be taught

Using social amenities—*please, thank you, you're welcome, excuse me*
Using appropriate greetings for the context
Terminating conversations
Sharing workspace
Accepting correction
Responding assertively
Accepting suggestions
Asking for help
Revealing a problem
Waiting in line
Taking turns

Terminating Conversations

Some individuals with autism, even if they are intelligent and have good verbal skills, need to learn how to end conversations. A common complaint of peers, supervisors, and co-workers is that the worker with autism walks away while being spoken to.

Sharing Workspace

Workplaces can sometimes require workers to rearrange their space or to share space that was previously their own. This can be irksome to anyone, but it is especially upsetting to a worker with autism who has come to rely on the consistency of his or her area. Social skills training can target learning to share space.

Accepting Correction

Difficulty accepting correction is not limited to individuals with autism. Many people do not like to receive correction or criticism. People with autism, however, often react more strongly. Social skills training may need to focus on teaching the student exactly what to say and do when given correction.

Responding Assertively

People with autism can sometimes be easily taken advantage of. One young woman with Asperger's syndrome was arriving at work each morning quite distraught. The problem was that a strange man had been sitting next to her on the bus and putting his arm around her, and she did not know how to respond. Social skills training was needed to teach her to say, "Leave me alone." Another student attended many general education classes throughout his school day and was often approached by his peers. His gym teacher eventually found out that these students were asking for his money and that he had given away hundreds of dollars over the course of the school year.

Accepting Suggestions

Some students with autism have trouble accepting suggestions. They can be rigid in their outlook. If a teacher or parent provides a suggestion, this can result in refusal to take the suggestion and can even serve as a trigger to acting out behavior. Providing the student with general instructions on the need to accept suggestions, followed by regularly scheduled role playing and the opportunity to practice accepting suggestions can be effective. When a suggestion is provided, the student can be reminded to accept suggestions just as he or she practiced in the role plays.

Asking for Help and Revealing a Problem

One of the most important social skills at work is to ask for help when it is needed. Individuals with autism faced with difficulty at work might become upset, stop working, and even leave. Students with autism might also be reluctant to reveal that they have a problem for which they need help. In either the work or school setting, social skills training can be used to teach individuals how to ask for help or how to talk to others about a problem.

Waiting in Line and Taking Turns

Waiting in line and taking turns can be challenging for anyone. For some people with autism, waiting in line can trigger behavior that is unacceptable in the community, such as cutting in line, pushing, or walking directly up to the counter. Some students with autism may need to be taught how to behave in crowded situations and when waiting in lines.

Once the team has identified the social skills a student needs to learn, team members design an instructional strategy to teach those skills. Chapter 5 provides a thorough review of how to teach skills, including social skills.

Provide Psychological Supports, Counseling, or Psychiatric Help

Psychological supports may be needed to help the student in the areas of social adjustment and self-control. This chapter has outlined a process for helping students with problem behaviors. Often, a psychology professional or a professional with skills in behavior change will be needed to organize and lead the effort to develop the student's behavior change plan. The professional's support may include training the teacher, job coach, and others involved in the transition process to apply the strategies and help the student meet behavioral goals.

Some individuals with autism benefit from counseling. Counseling can be provided by psychologists, guidance counselors, or social workers who are skilled in working with students with developmental disabilities. Counseling can provide assistance on two levels. First, some individuals with autism are aware that they have a disability and strive to understand it and live with it. Counseling can help these individuals come to terms with their diagnosis. Counseling can also help individuals achieve self-control and self-management of their behavior. The therapist, serving as both a role model and a teacher, can also help individuals with autism learn how to negotiate their social world.

Although there is no medication to cure autism, some people may experience relief from persistent medical and psychiatric conditions related to autism by taking medication. Anxiety, depression, compulsive behaviors, rituals, and explosive outbursts can sometimes be helped by medication as prescribed by a psychiatrist. Medication can be especially helpful when it is paired with a psychological approach and educational interventions that seek to help the individual learn more acceptable ways of dealing with problems. Not all individuals can be helped by medication, and most medications have side effects. The individual, the family, and a psychiatrist who is competent in dealing with individuals with developmental disabilities need to discuss potential medications, their benefits, and side effects (Schall, 2002).

JEFF'S POSITIVE BEHAVIOR SUPPORT PLAN

Jeff's team selected strategies for behavior change based on the functional behavior assessment they completed. These strategies were using an individual schedule, teaching Jeff a better way to cope with triggers, teaching him a better way to achieve the function of problem behaviors, and responding differently to new behaviors and problem behaviors.

Using an Individual Schedule

To help Jeff make the transition from one task to another more easily, the team provided him with a written schedule of start and stop times for each task. He slowly learned to adhere to the start and stop times and not become so upset if the task was not finished by the stop time.

Teaching a Better Way to Cope with Triggers

Part of Jeff's plan included instruction on how to interact with girls now that he was an adolescent. His health teacher provided him with a list of dos and don'ts when seeing women to whom he was attracted. This list helped him learn a better way to respond to the trigger of seeing a woman in sandals or open-toed shoes.

Teaching a Better Way to Achieve the Function of Problem Behaviors

As noted previously, social skills training was a critical piece of Jeff's plan. Specifically, Jeff's team taught him to accept instructions and correction. This training was done each day at school by his instructional aide. Once he started a part-time job, the transition teacher dropped by his worksite once per week and did the training there. Social skills training was also used to teach Jeff to greet others in more acceptable ways than stepping on their toes or punching their arm.

Responding Differently to New Behaviors and Problem Behaviors

Jeff's plan for responding differently to new behaviors and problem behaviors had two parts: providing incentives for new behaviors and responding to problem behaviors.

Incentives

Jeff's team decided to use incentives to encourage more cooperative behavior. A checklist was designed with the following behaviors on it: *works quietly* (no screaming or stomping), *respects others* (no incidents of stepping on toes or other unwanted physical contact), and *respects women's privacy* (no incidents of staring at feet or commenting on shoes).

At the end of each day, Jeff's instructional aide rated him on each category. He was given a 1 if he successfully demonstrated the behavior in a category and 0 if he had a problem. If he earned all 1s for the week, his instructional aide would take him on an outing of his choice. Favorite destinations were the airport to watch the planes take off and the used bookstore. An incentive was added that encouraged longer periods of good behavior. If Jeff earned all 1s for a month, he was able to go out to a restaurant of his choice with his instructional aide or with peers, in addition to an outing of his choice. If he was successful for 3 consecutive months, he was allowed to plan a party at home or school and invite several people of his choice. The longer he successfully exhibited the behaviors, the greater his rewards were.

Response to Problem Behavior

Jeff's plan also included a strategy for dealing with his outbursts when they occurred. The team decided that if he began to yell or was verbally abusive, no offers of help or breaks would be provided. Rather, the teacher would repeat the instruction or feedback and walk away. Jeff would be left alone with his outburst. He needed to learn that verbal abuse was not the way to get help or relief. Jeff began to improve in this area, and his verbal abuse virtually disappeared.

Jeff stopped staring at women's feet once he realized that it was just not acceptable. Prior to discussing this behavior with his teacher and having it put on his checklist, he was unaware that it was a problem.

Over time the checklist was turned into a self-management strategy, meaning that Jeff, rather than the instructional aide, began to rate his behavior. Social skills training sessions were cut back from daily to once per week and finally to once every 2 weeks. Jeff continues to hold his transition job, and both Jeff and his behavior support team are pleased with his progress.

CRAIG'S POSITIVE BEHAVIOR SUPPORT PLAN

Craig's team developed his behavior support plan based on the triggers, payoffs, and functions of his behavior. The selected strategies were using a picture schedule, eliminating triggers, and responding differently to new behaviors and problem behaviors.

Using a Picture Schedule

Craig's plan included a picture schedule depicting his tasks and activities. Opportunities to obtain his favorite objects and tools were included on his schedule. Because his schedule was presented in pictorial form, Craig could see when he could have access to his favorite objects and activities.

Eliminating Triggers

Because speaking to Craig sharply was a trigger, his plan included new strategies for giving him instructions and feedback. All instructions and feedback were to be given in calm, quiet tones. Staff were to avoid harsh tones and harsh phrases, such as *no* or *stop that*. Instead, Craig was to be told what he should be doing rather than what he should not be doing.

Responding Differently to New Behaviors and Problem Behaviors

Craig's plan for responding differently to new behaviors and problem behaviors had three parts: providing incentives for new behaviors, being alert to problems, and responding to aggression or self-injury.

Incentives

Craig enjoyed frequent access to small snacks and drinks, and his outbursts were often related to his attempts to get these items. A reward plan was developed that allowed Craig to earn access to small amounts of food and drink. About every hour throughout the school day, Craig was rewarded with a small amount of a favorite food or favorite drink for cooperative, productive behavior. He was rewarded for cooperating with academic tasks as well as with job tasks. The only exception to this hourly reward was if Craig hit himself. In those cases, there would be no reward for at least 2 hours. The purpose of this delay was to ensure that Craig did not have access to rewards too soon after an outburst.

Craig's incentive plan gave him the opportunity to relearn how to obtain favorite snacks. Rather than bang his head for these snacks, he learned that he could have them through cooperative behavior.

The incentive plan was easily used at Craig's new job site. When he was given a job at a local pizza restaurant assembling pizza boxes, his job coach would give him a small snack, such as a few chips, about every hour of assembling pizza boxes. Also, Craig was well aware that soda, one of his favorite drinks, was sold at the pizza restaurant. He was allowed to have one at the end of the work period if he worked cooperatively without any incidents of self-injury.

Alertness to Problems

Staff remained alert to situations in which Craig needed assistance or attempted to ask for something. If possible, Craig was given what he asked for or was told when he could have it. By responding to his few verbal demands, staff members were teaching him that words were an effective way to get what he wanted and that he did not need to resort to hurting himself or others.

Response to Aggression or Self-Injury

Craig's plan included strategies for how adults would respond if he should try to hurt himself. His school staff were trained in the use of approved blocking procedures, which they would use without comment to prevent him from hurting himself. If he tried to hurt himself or someone else, he would also be calmly redirected to his ongoing task. Once Craig had calmed down enough to respond to instructions, staff would once again present the ongoing task. No longer did staff attempt to find out what was wrong or give him snacks or favorite items to calm him down. This strategy enabled Craig to learn that hurting himself or others no longer served a good purpose.

Over time, Craig did come to learn that words were effective for attaining what he wanted and that cooperation paid off. He also learned that hitting himself and others no longer served a purpose for him. These behaviors declined from about twice per day to about once per month.

MARIA'S POSITIVE BEHAVIOR SUPPORT PLAN

Behavior support strategies for Maria were chosen based on the information obtained about her triggers, payoffs, and purposes. The selected strategies were using an individual schedule, cushioning the impact of triggers, teaching Maria a better way to achieve the function of problem behavior, and responding differently to new behaviors and problem behaviors.

Using an Individual Schedule

Like Craig, Maria functioned best with a schedule. She was able to adjust much more successfully to changes in her routine by using her schedule. Because of Maria's level of reading skills, she used a written schedule rather than a picture schedule.

Cushioning the Impact of Triggers

The kinds of events that triggered Maria to throw objects, such as disappointments and schedule changes, typically could not be avoided. Because of this, her plan included strategies for cushioning disappointments and schedule changes, such as giving Maria as much advance notice as possible and carefully explaining a change to her. If an activity that she had looked forward to was canceled, an alternative pleasant activity would be provided. For example, when a lightning storm closed the pool and Maria could not go swimming, a trip to the bowling alley was substituted, and this was explained to her before she could become upset.

Because corrective or negative feedback often triggered Maria's movie dialogues, the plan included strategies for error prevention and correction. Changes were made to the way her more difficult tasks were taught so that she would be less likely to make mistakes. Reprimands and negative feedback were limited as much as possible; when correction was necessary, it was provided in a more positive way. A staff member might say, "Maria, make sure to fold it evenly" rather than "That's wrong; it's too crooked." All feedback was given in gentle, calm tones.

Self-scratching was often triggered by peer teasing. This teasing was minimized as much as possible by having the instructional aide be more alert to Maria's interactions with others. Also, social skills training and reminders were provided to teach Maria to say "hi" to her peers rather than to initiate interaction with a movie dialogue.

Teaching a Better Way to Achieve
the Function of Problem Behavior

There were two ways Maria's team achieved her plan for teaching a better way to achieve the function of problem behavior. First, they taught her to repeat movie dialogue at predetermined times. Second, they taught her to ask her mom to provide more comfort to her when she was very disappointed.

Scheduled Dialogues

Because Maria did appear to enjoy her movie dialogues, time was included twice per day in her written schedule for her to recite movie dialogues. Generally they were scheduled before lunch and at the end of the day prior to leaving for home.

Asking for Sympathy from Mom When Disappointed

Using a Social Story (see Chapter 5), Maria's team coached her and modeled ways for her to ask for sympathy and comfort when she was disappointed. For example, Maria often became very distraught during thunderstorms. She learned to go to her mother during a thunderstorm and tell her mother she was afraid and wanted company. This was a much better alternative to screaming when she heard thunder.

Responding Differently to New Behaviors and Problem Behaviors

Maria's plan for responding differently to new behaviors and problem behaviors had two parts: providing incentives for new behavior and responding to problem behavior.

Incentives

Maria enjoyed attention from her teacher and instructional aides. Her behavior support plan therefore included a schedule of praise and positive feedback for working on tasks and assignments and completing them. In addition, she received a special reward at the end of the day if she had been cooperative; followed her dialogue schedule; and had no incidents of throwing items, tearing her clothes, or scratching herself. The reward was special time with one of her favorite staff or the opportunity to buy a snack from the school vending machine. Once she started a part-time job, the vending machine snack reward occurred at the end of her work hours.

To diminish Maria's self-scratching, the staff used lotion as an incentive. At the end of the school day, if Maria's skin was clear and had no new scratches, she would be told how beautiful and clear her skin was and given scented lotion to rub on her arms. Her mother did the same thing at the end of the evening at home. If there were new scratches or marks, staff and her mother made no comment and provided no lotion.

Response to Problem Behavior

If Maria had an outburst, such as throwing an object, scratching herself, or tearing her clothing, staff continued to provide instructions on what she should be doing instead, such as "Follow along with the article the teacher is reading." During an outburst, Maria was given no reassurances, no counseling, and no attempt to solve her problems or remove her from the situation. Walks, drinks of water, and explanations were no longer provided after problem behavior. Similarly, if she engaged in a movie dialogue outside of the scheduled time, her teacher avoided eye contact, said nothing to her about the dialogue, and continued presenting the task or instruction when Maria was done.

After several weeks of these behavior support procedures, Maria's behaviors began to improve. Most days she was able to limit her movie dialogues to the scheduled time, and she looked forward to her reward at the end of the day. As time went on, incidents of tearing her clothing, scratching herself, and throwing objects declined noticeably. Her mother used the lotion strategy at home, and Maria came to take pride in her clear skin. With the help of her instructional aide, she learned to say "hi" to boys in the hallway rather than to recite *Finding Nemo*. Other students began to say "hi" back, and their teasing decreased.

Several months into the school year, Maria landed a part-time job stocking shoes at a local department store. She worked 3 hours per day, 3 days per week. Her support strategies were used at work. She was given lots of help to reduce the number of errors she made. Feedback was positive and gentle. She was taught to greet her co-workers by saying "hi," and time to recite her dialogues was scheduled at the end of her work hours. If she was cooperative at work and had no behavioral outbursts or unscheduled dialogues, she was allowed to purchase a snack of her choice from the vending machine in the employee's break room at the end of each day. The few times she had outbursts, co-workers would look the other way and her job coach would direct her back to her task. As Maria's behavior and work skills improved, she became a valued worker.

PULLING IT ALL TOGETHER

Because individuals with autism frequently display problem behavior, transition teams supporting them will need to assess the function of problem behavior and develop positive behavior support plans. As demonstrated in Jeff's, Craig's, and Maria's cases, teams can and frequently do experience success in decreasing problem behaviors and increasing positive behaviors. This occurs when team members meet regularly, discuss problems openly and work together to solve them, and call for help from other professionals when necessary. By taking this approach, teams are able to proactively address the problem behaviors of transition-age students with autism.

3

Educational and Transition Planning

Carol Schall

Much of the research on autism is focused on early intervention for children 6 years and younger (Iovannone, Dunlap, Huber, & Kincaid, 2003). There is a growing body of investigations, however, of educational outcomes in individuals with autism and Asperger's syndrome (Howlin, Goode, Hutton, & Rutter, 2004; Jennes-Coussens, Magill-Evans, & Koning, 2006; Schall et al., 2006). In the latter area of research, there is mixed news for those who are interested in good outcomes for individuals with autism. Teachers and caregivers naturally hope that students graduate with the skills necessary to live personally satisfying lives. That is, they hope that students have friendships with people they care about and who care about them, work in jobs that provide them with a sense of contribution and satisfaction, live interdependently with people who care about and for them, pursue higher education courses, and report that they are basically happy with their lives. The research that looks at whether these conditions are attainable indicates that, by and large, people with autism *can* work and achieve a quality life but that they need support to do so (Howlin et al., 2004; Jennes-Coussens et al., 2006; Schall et al., 2006; Schaller & Yang, 2005; Tsatsanis, 2003). Therefore, teams supporting students with autism must learn how to plan and implement the most effective supports in high school to guarantee that students achieve a successful transition from school to a rich and satisfying adult life. To do this well, teams must first explore the assessment process so that the plan created for students is as effective as possible. Once each individual's needs are identified, teams must develop a sound education plan. The rest of this chapter describes the important assessments and educational and transition planning processes that will assist teams in creating transition IEPs that result in positive outcomes for students with autism.

ROLE OF ASSESSMENT FOR TRANSITION-AGE STUDENTS WITH AUTISM

The purpose of transition assessment is to assist the team in identifying priorities and developing a transition IEP. The development of a sound, comprehensive transition IEP that leads to employment or postsecondary educational options for students with disabilities is one of the most important activities that middle and high school teams can do for students with autism. In this chapter, we will use the term *transition IEP* when referring to the transition plan included in the student's IEP. This document (see the appendix at the end of this chapter for examples) includes the student's postsecondary goals and needed transition services. This document should be a part of a student's IEP, and parts of this document may replace the same sections in the IEP. Regardless of the language used to describe the plan, students with autism require individualized planning that matches current educational activities to the student's desired educational outcomes. Without this kind of planning and preparation, students with autism are at risk for lifelong dependence on others. IDEA 2004 defined transition services as follows:

> The term "transition services" means a coordinated set of activities for a child[1] with a disability that:
>
> • Is designed to be within a results-oriented process, that is focused on improving the academic and functional achievement of the child with a disability to facilitate the child's movement from school to post-school activities, including postsecondary education, vocational education, integrated employment (including supported employment), continuing and adult education, adult services, independent living, or community participation;
>
> • Is based on the individual child's needs, taking into account the child's strengths, preferences, and interests; and
>
> • Includes instruction, related services, community experiences, the development of employment and other post-school adult living objectives, and, if appropriate, acquisition of daily living skills and functional vocational evaluation. [34 CFR 300.43 (a)] [20 U.S.C. 1401(34)]

For the purposes of this discussion of transition and educational planning for students with autism, the important aspects of this definition are the words "results-oriented process" and "based on the individual child's needs . . . strengths, preferences, and interests." To ensure a results-oriented process that takes into account the student's needs, strengths, preferences, and interests, the transition IEP

---

[1]*Author's note:* The 2004 reauthorization of IDEA changed the term *student* to *child.* Throughout the rest of this chapter, I will refer to transition-age individuals as *students* rather than *children.* In this case, however, I am quoting the regulations as written.

team must review and update a transition assessment at the rewriting of every transition IEP. Prior to discussing the unique assessment needs of individuals with autism further, however, it is important to review some basic information about assessment processes in general.

Basics of Assessment

In education, all instructional activities begin and end with assessment. There are many different kinds of assessment. Most students are familiar with assessment for the purposes of assigning a grade or evaluating their knowledge or skill. Whereas this is the type of assessment most used by general educators, it is not the type of assessment most used by special educators. In special education, assessment measures are used for four purposes (Brown & Snell, 2000; Scott, Clark, & Brady, 2000):

1. *Eligibility*—to determine whether a person is eligible for special education services under IDEA 2004

2. *Evaluation of educational practices*—to evaluate the effectiveness of educational practices and adjust them to meet the student's needs

3. *Reporting*—to document and report a student's progress toward the achievement of standards or IEP goals

4. *Curriculum and program development*—to identify a student's needs for the purpose of planning the IEP

Whenever team members need more information to adequately serve a person with autism, they should complete an assessment. The type of assessment is determined by the questions the team wants to answer. For example, if a school- or community-based team wants to determine whether a person has a disability, members should complete an eligibility assessment. If team members want to identify the knowledge or skills a person should learn over the next school year, they should complete a curriculum and program development assessment. Table 3.1 lists the types of assessments, the questions that are answered by each type of assessment, and the purpose for that assessment.

Once team members have identified their questions about a student's educational performance, they must identify the methods they will use to gather the information to answer their questions. Assessment questions can be answered via 1) formal assessment measures, such as published tests or behavioral checklists; 2) informal measures, such as interviews, review of past records, teacher-made tests, or person-centered planning tools; or 3) clinical observations of the student in different settings, such as the classroom, community, or a job. Most teams use formal and informal measures and clinical observation for almost every assessment. Table 3.2 lists the tools used for four types of assessment, when they are used, and who usually completes them.

In theory, these four types of assessments are discrete, that is, they are distinct from one another. In reality, however, there is some overlap between the types. Thus, assessment is ongoing and cumulative. Although assessment is a very robust

Table 3.1.   Types of assessments, purposes, and questions answered

Type of assessment	Purpose for assessment	Questions answered by assessment
Eligibility	To determine the presence, if any, of a disability that affects the student's education and qualifies the student for services under IDEA 2004	Is a qualifying disability present? How does that disability manifest itself in the educational environment? What are the student's strengths and needs related to that disability? What related services are likely needed to give the student access to the educational environment?
Evaluation of educational practices	To determine whether the teaching methods used have resulted in student progress	How much progress has the student made toward mastering particular IEP goals and objectives? Is the teaching method resulting in enough progress? Will the student master the IEP goals or objectives during this school year? Should the educational team change the way instruction is provided to increase the student's progress toward the goals or objectives?
Reporting	To determine whether the student has acquired the necessary skills as determined by state standards and the student's IEP	Has the student mastered the state curriculum or alternative curriculum for his or her age and grade level? What grades has the student earned based on his or her work for this grading period? Has the student mastered the given IEP goals and state standards for this year?
Curriculum and program development	To determine a student's educational needs and desires for his or her IEP and school curriculum; to recommend IEP goals and objectives for the coming year	Is the current program meeting the student's current and future needs? What are the student's long-term goals for his or her life? How can the educational team assist the student in achieving those goals? With the limited time and resources available, what are the priorities for this student for the coming educational year? What should we teach this student in the coming year?

Key: IDEA 2004, Individuals with Disabilities Education Improvement Act of 2004 (PL 108-446).

topic with much attention in the literature, the brief overview here provides most readers the necessary basic information. What is most germane to the topic of transition assessment and autism is the student's response to testing and the essential elements of a transition assessment for the purposes of planning a transition and educational program. Each of these topics is discussed in the following sections.

Assessing Students with Autism

Although the assessment process itself is fairly well defined, assessing students with autism can be complicated. Just as every student with autism has unique learning characteristics, each also has unique responses to assessment. These responses can be challenging to members of the education team. First, students with

Table 3.2. Types of educational assessments used in special education

Type of assessment	When it is performed	Who usually completes the assessment	Assessment tools typically used
Eligibility	Prior to entering special education services and at least every 3 years after a student is first found eligible (the exact elements of the eligibility can and frequently do change over time)	An interdisciplinary child or youth study team, which can include a school, child, or adolescent psychologist; a social worker; an educational diagnostician or special education teacher; a general education teacher; related services therapists; school administrators; parents; and caregivers	*Formal assessments:* Standardized intelligence testing, standardized and criterion-referenced learning, and achievement tests; parent and teacher behavioral questionnaires *Informal assessments:* Clinical observation; review of the youth's medical, social, and educational records; person-centered planning
Evaluation of educational practices	Regularly throughout the school year in all curriculum areas	Classroom special or general education teacher	*Formal assessments:* Textbook-published tests, published curriculum assessments *Informal assessments:* Teacher-made tests, ongoing data collection
Reporting	Regularly throughout the school year in all curriculum areas and yearly during the evaluation of state standards	Classroom special or general education teacher	*Formal assessments:* Textbook published tests, state standards evaluations *Informal assessments:* Teacher-made tests, graded projects, graded classwork or homework
Curriculum and program development	At least yearly but more often when current program is questioned	Whole team for student, including teachers, parents, caregivers, other staff from different agencies, and related services therapists	*Formal assessments:* All previously noted assessments *Informal assessments:* All previously noted assessments, review of the student's educational records, review of the student's response to the current program, person-centered plans and tools

autism have difficulty generalizing skills between settings, materials, and other people. Skills that appear to be mastered in one setting with certain materials and specific people may not be demonstrated at all in different settings with different materials and new people. An examiner may therefore conclude that a student with autism has lower skills and abilities because the student does not perform a task in a new setting, although the student is quite independent at the skill in familiar settings.

Second, many students with autism can become prompt dependent. That is, they do not perform a task, even one that they can complete fairly well, unless they are prompted in the same way they have always been prompted. Again, a team member might miss the skills that the student can perform because the examiner has not used the exact words that the teacher does when asking the student to perform a task. Thus, an examiner who is not familiar with the student might conclude that the student is unable to perform certain skills when actually the student is not able to perform the skill without particular prompts. This error can make it difficult to make sound educational decisions on behalf of that student.

Students with autism also can exhibit *stimulus overselectivity*. This characteristic of learning means that students with autism tend to focus on irrelevant stimuli instead of on the important aspect of a stimulus. For example, if a teacher used a green block to teach a student how to identify a square, the student might only recognize something as square if it is also green. Likewise, if a teacher teaches a student to fold towels for a hotel at a table in the classroom that has a yellow mat on it, the same student might not be able to fold towels if there is a red mat on the table (Janzen, 2003; Scott et al., 2000; Siegel, 2003).

In general, students with autism respond poorly to changes in their routines. Students with autism who experience a testing situation as a change in their routine will probably not perform at their highest abilities. A student in such a situation may refuse to do anything for the examiner. This frequently leads to evaluators reporting that an individual student with autism is uncooperative or unable to be tested when in fact the disruption in routine simply caused a reaction characteristic of individuals with autism. Such students should be observed in their everyday setting to assess the true presence of skills and abilities.

Finally, students with autism, especially those with Asperger's syndrome tend to have difficulty imagining themselves in different situations, which affects their response to test questions that ask them to do so (Attwood, 2006; Siegel, 2003). Many vocational interest inventories and tests ask individuals to imagine themselves in situations and respond to questions about those situations. If a student with Asperger's syndrome is not able to imagine him- or herself in such situations, the responses he or she gives to that test must be viewed cautiously.

Under controlled and contrived assessment conditions, all of the learning characteristics discussed here will result in a performance that is less than the student's best. Therefore, in addition to identifying the questions they may have about a student, teams supporting individuals with autism must also discuss the best way to elicit a productive student response. Figure 3.1 displays a short worksheet that teams can use when planning assessment for a student with autism.

Imagine that Jeff's team decided to have Jeff complete a vocational interest inventory that asks him to respond to situations and select preferred work settings. If Jeff is unable to imagine the conditions of a job, he may respond favorably to jobs

Student's name: _____ Date: _____

Team members present:

_____

_____

I.   What questions do we have about the student?

1. _____

   _____

2. _____

   _____

3. _____

   _____

II. What type of assessment will help us answer these questions?

☐ Eligibility   ☐ Evaluation of educational practices

☐ Reporting   ☐ Curriculum and program development

III. What learning characteristics will adversely affect these assessment results?

☐ Difficulty with imagining   ☐ Prompt dependence

☐ Difficulty generalizing skills   ☐ Stimulus overselectivity

☐ Difficulty with changes in routines   ☐ Communication difficulties

IV. What assessment methods will we use to triangulate the information?

Assessment method	Team member responsible	Modifications needed
1.		
2.		
3.		

Figure 3.1.   Assessment planning guide for students with autism.

Autism and the Transition to Adulthood: Success Beyond the Classroom by Paul Wehman,
Marcia Datlow Smith, & Carol Schall © 2009 by Paul H. Brookes Publishing Co., Inc. All rights reserved.

that would actually be very poor matches for him and unfavorably to jobs in which he could be very successful. Results on this interest inventory have to be measured against other information the team has about Jeff and his performance in different situations. Jeff is able to complete some skills independently but may not perform those skills in new situations. Again, the team will have to supplement formal assessment methods with their everyday knowledge of Jeff's abilities.

Given these assessment challenges, teams often must *triangulate* the information to have as full a picture as possible about the student's needs and abilities. During the process of triangulation, the team gathers information in three or more different ways and compares that information across all of the assessment methods. Imagine that the team notes that on the vocational interest inventory, Jeff identified jobs requiring a lot of customer service and customer contact as preferred careers. Team members also know that Jeff tends to be abrupt, even rude at times, when he is challenged or interrupted. These are not characteristics that indicate success in customer service and contact with customers. Also, the team acknowledges that Jeff has not had a lot of experience with work situations. He has not had the typical experiences that other students his age have had, such as cutting grass during the summer or helping a neighbor clean out the garage for extra spending money. Because Jeff is naive about what sort of jobs would be a good fit and has never worked in a job setting, the team concludes that more information is needed about Jeff's interests, strengths, and needs to assess what the team should do next. Therefore, team members decide to complete some *situational assessments,* in which Jeff gets to work in a few different jobs while they assess his performance on each job. They also incorporate the knowledge that his teachers have about his work in school to further consider the best types of careers for Jeff.

These three tools—the vocational interest inventory, the situational assessment, and the information from observation in his current school placement—will provide a fuller picture of his interests, skills, and abilities. By using information from three different sources, the team is engaging in triangulation to fully understand Jeff's career interests and strengths. Using triangulation often helps teams supporting students with autism to consider the person from many different perspectives and increases the strength of the assessment information they collect.

Assessment to Inform Transition Planning

Students with autism entering middle school have already experienced multiple assessments across their education. At this critical time, however, the focus must shift from what is missing in a student's developmental profile to what skills are necessary for the student to be successful in the next stage of life. This shift in focus necessitates a shift in assessment priorities. That is, instead of measuring how well a student has mastered lower grade-level skills, team members must now measure the student's interests, preferences, strengths, and work habits and describe supports and modifications necessary for the student to be successful in the future. In fact, Sitlington, Neubert, Begun, Lombard, and Leconte (2007) defined *transition assessment* as "an ongoing process of collecting information on a student's strengths, needs, preferences, and interests as they relate to the demands of current and future living, learning, and working environments" (p. 2). Furthermore, Sitlington and Clark (2007) identified eight areas that compose minimum compliance with the charge to assess academic and functional performance:

1. Interests

2. Preferences

3. Cognitive development and academic achievement performance

4. Adaptive behavior

5. Interpersonal relationship skills

6. Emotional development and mental health

7. Employability and community skills

8. Community participation

Considering the unique needs of transition-age students with autism, this list is helpful as long as the student's unique communication and social skill needs are assessed under the areas of adaptive behavior and interpersonal relationship skills. This shift toward a future-oriented focus can be measured by a change in questions the team seeks to answer through the assessment process. At the end of Chapter 1, Jeff's, Craig's, and Maria's case studies each presented a set of questions. Those questions could be used to develop a transition assessment for each student. These students' case studies, along with the questions, will be revisited in this chapter.

Table 3.3 presents some of the questions that should drive assessment as students enter high school and prepare to make the transition into the community. These questions will guide the team to use assessment methods that move beyond an update on the student's current reading and math scores toward the develop-

Table 3.3.   Questions that individualized education program teams should consider for transition-age students with autism

To what degree is the student self-determined, that is, able to make personal decisions and accept responsibility for those decisions?

What is the student's or caregiver's vision for the student's future?

Where does the student want to live and work as an adult?

What elements would create an enviable life for this student?

What skills and abilities does the student currently possess that would match his or her vision?

Will this student need additional training or education after high school to be able to realize his or her vision?

What resources are available to the student to help him or her achieve this vision?

Is this student able to live independently, that is, does the student have the ability to care for him- or herself, live independently in an apartment or a house, get around in the community, and/or budget money wisely?

What is the depth of this student's experiences in the world of work and adult life?

What skills and abilities will this student need to learn between now and high school graduation that will assist in achieving his or her vision?

What experiences does this student need to better inform his or her decision making to prepare for life beyond high school?

What experiences, resources, and new agencies will increase the likelihood of a smooth transition into work or postsecondary education and adult life?

ment of a plan to move from school to adult life with mindfulness and efficiency. In fact, the answers to these questions will assist the team in prioritizing the skills that will help ensure the individual a smooth transition to adulthood.

TRANSITION ASSESSMENT

The purpose of transition assessment is to develop and update a transition plan, embedding skills into the transition IEP that move the student toward his or her desired career and adult life (Leconte, 2006). The elements included in such an assessment vary based on the student's age and needs. Some elements are career awareness assessment, vocational evaluation and assessment, assessment of independent living and community skills, and assessment of self-determination. Each of these elements will be described in turn.

Career Awareness Assessment

By elementary school, all students begin to become aware of workers around them. The first stage of career awareness begins as early as kindergarten, as many social studies lessons explore the roles that workers play in the lives of youngsters. These youngsters begin to imagine themselves as workers in their pretend play. Children with autism of the same age typically do not engage in pretend play. That is, they do not pretend to be a store clerk, firefighter, or parent. Thus, they do not begin to role-play adult life. In addition, they do not seem to notice the jobs happening around them as they go to the store, doctor, or other places of community service (Frith, 2003).

In middle school, students without disabilities engage in career exploration. They might shadow workers to learn about job requirements and duties. This usually happens in both formal and informal ways. Formally, career exploration occurs in the context of academic coursework. For example, students learn about scientific careers as they also learn science. Some students also pursue some kind of paid work experience that allows them to earn extra money and begin learning about possible career paths. Informally, students form friendships with older siblings, coaches, club sponsors, or their friends' parents, who occasionally discuss their careers. These informal mentoring relationships with adults allow students to explore successful employee characteristics while considering desired employer characteristics. At this same age, students with autism may engage in some, but usually not all, of these experiences. Generally because they are socially less mature than their peers without disabilities, their parents are sometimes reluctant to allow them to hold a job (Schall et al., 2006). When students with autism do engage in some of these experiences, they typically do not connect what they learn from the experiences to possible future jobs or career decisions.

The last stage of career awareness, during a student's high school career, can be considered career preparation. For some students, this stage culminates in employment; for others, this stage is prolonged by pursuing additional courses of study in postsecondary settings, such as vocational/technical training or coursework at a community college or university. In the career preparation stage, students without disabilities typically continue targeted academic training in preparation for their identified careers. They also acquire related work experience that

Table 3.4.   Stages of career development

Stage	Setting	Goal of stage	Transition activities
Career awareness	Elementary school	Develop image of self as worker	Odd jobs, informational field trips, formal school-work
Career exploration	Middle school	Learn about the characteristics of various types of employment settings	Informational field trips, formal and informal mentoring experiences with adults, job internships, situational assessments
Career preparation	High school, vocational training programs, community college, university	Learn the skills required in a particular job	Job internships, situational assessments, part-time work
Employment search	After graduation from programs	Believe that one can work and learn the skills necessary to market oneself and secure a job	Apply for jobs, write résumé, learn social and communication skills specific to interviews and work environments, accept employment, begin work

further assists them in confirming their career choice. During this stage of career development, most students are narrowing their choices to a select few using the information they have collected throughout their education. Table 3.4 provides an explanation of each stage of career awareness and the types of activities in which students engage that promote the goals of each stage.

It is easy for high school teachers, guidance counselors, and other transition team members to assume that at least some stages of career development have been attained by students with autism. Unfortunately, these students may not have had the same exposure to job exploration or part-time work as their peers without disabilities. When teachers and transition team members begin to ask questions about career interests and successful job experiences, students with autism and their parents may not be prepared to answer these questions. Thus, before asking these types of questions, transition teams need to assess students' career awareness. Figure 3.2 provides an example of the information about which the team should inquire.

Collecting information about a student's career awareness will assist the team in identifying the types of career awareness experiences a student needs in order to make decisions about desired jobs or postsecondary education. Regardless of a student's prior experiences, it is important to consider the student's career awareness needs and identify goals, objectives, and educational experiences that will increase his or her ability to achieve the ultimate goal of a job or continued education or training.

Vocational Evaluation and Assessment

The purpose of a vocational evaluation and assessment is to identify a student's employability and vocational skills and to identify potential job matches. There are many published, formal tools that assess this information (for a review of these tools, see Sitlington et al., 2007). As noted previously, however, due to unique

Student's name: _____ Date: _____

Name of individual completing this form: _____

Relationship to student: _____

Sources of information for this form (check all that apply):

☐ Review of educational records   ☐ Interview with student

☐ Interview with previous teachers   ☐ Interview with student's parent

☐ Personal knowledge of student's experiences

1. Describe experiences in which the student learned about or observed others at work:

   _____

   _____

2. Has the student expressed interest in any particular careers? If so, which ones, and how did the student express interest?

   _____

   _____

3. Has the student performed odd jobs or chores for extra money? If yes, describe the student's experiences and performance:

   _____

   _____

4. Has the student ever volunteered in an internship or other nonpaid regular position? If yes, describe the student's experiences and performance:

   _____

   _____

5. Has the student ever worked in part-time or full-time employment? If yes, describe the position the student held, the support the student required, the rate of pay, the length of employment, and the student's experiences and performance:

   _____

   _____

6. What types of learning experiences would assist this student in better understanding the world of work and his or her career preferences and interests?

   _____

   _____

7. List the individualized education program goals and objectives that will address these learning experiences:

   _____

   _____

Figure 3.2. Sample questions and information review about a student's career awareness.

Autism and the Transition to Adulthood: Success Beyond the Classroom by Paul Wehman,
Marcia Datlow Smith, & Carol Schall © 2009 by Paul H. Brookes Publishing Co., Inc. All rights reserved.

learning challenges individuals with autism may not perform well on such assessments; it is therefore important to consider using other, more natural methods of vocational evaluation and assessment.

The three types of assessments that allow for observation of skills in natural environments are performance samples, behavioral observations, and situational assessments. Each of these allows the student to practice and perform a skill in a natural environment while the evaluator observes and collects information on the student's performance. One advantage of this for an individual with autism is that he or she frequently has the opportunity to adjust to the changes in routine prior to the collection of assessment data. Another is that the student's regular staff can implement the assessment procedures. If these assessments are provided by an outside evaluator, that person can spend time with the individual in the assessment setting to build rapport and become familiar to the student. Finally, because these assessments frequently occur in natural settings, the person with autism will likely give authentic responses; therefore, the quality of information collected is usually representative of the person's abilities.

For performance assessment, the teacher or evaluator sets up a simulated task or assesses the student's performance in an actual job-related task. A *performance sample* usually occurs in the context of a vocational lab or in the classroom. Perhaps one of the best ways to collect performance samples is to find and assess jobs within the student's natural environments, such as the school or community. This will decrease the amount of materials and settings a teacher or vocational counselor must simulate and increase the soundness of observations. For example, if a team wanted to assess Craig's ability to assemble items in a job situation, they could set up a performance sample at the local pizza shop where Craig works during midday hours. There they could measure his productivity, problem-solving abilities, and accuracy at assembling pizza boxes.

Such assessments, however, may not give enough information on work behaviors that are important. Therefore, a teacher or vocational evaluator may decide to complete a *behavioral observation*. One of the challenges Maria presents at work is repeating dialogue from her favorite movies and television shows. Although Maria works well in the department store stockroom unpacking shoeboxes, she occasionally repeats dialogue from movies at times other than the agreed-on time at the end of her shift. Because Maria's team had previously concluded that the repetition of movie dialogue signaled that Maria was stressed or unhappy, the vocational counselor observed Maria at work and used a scatter plot to identify potential triggers for this behavior. Figure 3.3 shows the scatter plot for Maria's repeated dialogue at her part-time job.

The scatter plot indicated that Maria's behavior occurred mainly when she was unloading boxes from pallets and during her break at the end of her work day. After watching her more carefully during this task, the counselor wondered if Maria did not have adequate lifting skills, making the task of unloading the pallets too difficult for her. The vocational counselor was able to identify an important area in which Maria required direct instruction and also recommended a redesign of Maria's job to limit the amount of heavy lifting she had to do. Specifically, the counselor suggested leaving the pallets on the hydraulic dolly so that Maria could lift the plane of the dolly to the height of the shelves she was to place the shoeboxes on. This way Maria could take the individual shoeboxes out of the larger box instead of lifting the larger box from the floor to another surface first. In this case, the

Directions: Leave the box empty for no repeated dialogue. Mark "/" for repeated dialogue that stopped within 1 minute of starting. Mark "X" for repeated dialogue that lasts longer than 1 minute.

Time	Activity	Jan. 24	Jan. 26	Jan. 28	Feb. 1	Feb. 3
10:00	Unloading pallet	/	X	/	/	X
10:30	Unpacking boxes, stacking shoeboxes					
11:00	Unpacking boxes, stacking shoeboxes			/		
11:30	Moving display shoes to front of store	/				
12:00	Unpacking boxes					
12:30	Taking break in break room	/	/	X		/

Figure 3.3.   Scatter plot of Maria's repeating dialogue. (*Source:* Touchette, MacDonald, & Langer, 1985.)

behavioral observation resulted in identifying skills for Maria's transition IEP (e.g., proper lifting technique) and work station redesign.

The final method of assessment allows the teacher or vocational counselor to design a brief experience for the student to try out a job, then systematically record observations of the student in that situation. These *situational assessments* can occur in contrived or real settings. As noted previously, the best setting for assessment is a natural setting because this provides excellent information about students' preferences and interests as well as their abilities and skills. This type of assessment was mentioned previously in reference to Jeff's vocational interest inventory. During summer school, Jeff's teacher contacted a business in which Jeff could work for a brief period of time. Figure 3.4 presents the results from the situational assessment completed during this experience at a local video game store, where Jeff worked the counter, completed data entry, and worked with stock inventory tasks. This information assisted the team in identifying Jeff's strengths, interests, and needs related to work and helped them prioritize social skill targets for his IEP.

Assessment of Independent Living and Community Skills

As noted at the beginning of this chapter, IDEA 2004 addresses independent living and community skills as well as career and academic skills. To assess a student's independent and community living skills, the team must gather information outside the school setting by consulting with parents and caregivers and observing the student in community-based settings.

Although independent living and community skills are not typically the domain of teachers, it is an important domain to consider. For example, parents frequently do much more for their children than is necessary. For students without autism, having a parent do their laundry does not mean that they cannot learn how

Jobs assessed

Job 1—Jeff worked in the stock room with an inventory reader. He was required to systematically scan each item with the inventory reader, then put all items back on the shelves in an organized fashion, making sure that like items were stacked in the same place.

Job 2—Jeff worked in data entry by uploading the stock information from the inventory reader to the computer. He then tabulated the stock and tracked sales over the week. He also verified cash register receipts against the data in the the stocking database and developed a report of sales for the week of July 5–9.

Job 3—Jeff worked the counter selling video games, answering customer questions, and assisting customers in finding stock.

Work performance

Jeff came to the video store on the dates of the assessment properly groomed and dressed. He reported that his mother assisted him in picking out clothes and reminded him to shower each night. His hair was neatly combed, and he was ready on time. His mother dropped him off and picked him up each day. He reported that he does not like to ride the public bus and preferred that his mother pick him up because she would be on time. He entered the store enthusiastically but was frequently distracted by the stock, especially when he was completing inventory. He picked up the games and read each game, then commented on how he did when he played the game. The manager frequently had to remind him to continue recording the stock.

He displayed similar behavior when customers bought games, particularly games he liked. He would frequently engage them in one-sided conversations about the game, his abilities with the game, and how much he liked the game. When one customer returned a game he did not like, Jeff asked the customer what was wrong with him. The manager had to intervene and complete the transaction because Jeff was a bit upset that the customer did not like a game he liked.

Jeff was most successful when preparing the report of sales. For this task, he worked in the back of the stockroom at the small desk and displayed consistent effort in completing the task. His only challenge with this task occurred when he made a mathematical error and got up and left the desk, muttering to himself. He went to the break area and ate a snack, then returned to his work about 10 minutes later.

When he was first learning tasks, Jeff asked an excessive amount of questions and wanted frequent reassurance that he was completing the task correctly. Once he learned each task, however, Jeff's work was very accurate and thorough. His only difficulty, as mentioned previously, was off-task behavior related to his interest in the video games and inappropriate interactions with some customers.

Job skills

Jeff was accurate when handling money, completing the report of sales, and shelving items. As noted above, his intense interest in video games contributed to a slow rate of work. It is difficult to tell whether he would have this problem when handling items that were not of interest to him. He was easily frustrated when he made a mistake. He was also a bit argumentative when corrected by the teacher and supervisor.

Productivity

As noted previously, Jeff completed inventory slower than other staff due to his reading many of the video game boxes. After an initial period of frequent question asking, Jeff completed the sales report faster than any other staff member. He was quite successful in the task and was able to complete most of the mathematical aspects of the report without a calculator. Finally, his productivity at the counter was slow and hampered by his long conversations with customers.

Self-determination

Jeff is able to make personal choices but did not demonstrate an understanding of his work choices as a part of an overall plan for his life. Rather, he seemed to respond to situations

Figure 3.4.   Report of Jeff's situational assessment at the video game store.   *(continued)*

Figure 3.4.   *(continued)*

presented as if they were disconnected from each other. He was dependent on his mother and his manager to direct him. He also had difficulty understanding his role in events around him during his work at the video store. For example, when he made a mistake on the sales report, he blamed the calculator and the fact that the desk was rocking instead of considering his role in inputting the numbers into the calculator. He was able to identify his strengths at work, especially his mathematical skills and his knowledge of video games. He did not identify times when he talked too much or displayed a poor attitude. He did not understand his disability or how to advocate for the supports that would increase his success in that environment. Finally, he did not see his participation in this situational assessment as a part of an overall plan to understand his interests, preferences, and abilities related to his transition to adulthood. Instead, he reported that he expected his parents to take care of him as an adult.

Jeff's interest in the jobs

Jeff reported that he enjoyed his work at the video store but did not like being corrected. He reported that he especially enjoyed completing the sales report, although he could not understand why so many people bought a particular game that he thought was "stupid." He also reported that he did not like standing on his feet for so long when he worked the counter.

Recommended goals for Jeff

Overall, Jeff's experiences in this situational assessment were successful and informative. Jeff's challenges in this environment were mainly related to his excessive interest in video games. Although he chose this environment, it might not be the best fit for a long-term career. His interest in video games made it difficult for him to remain on task and accept customer feedback without argument. It may be possible, however, for Jeff to learn to manage his impulse to disagree with customers who do not like his favored games so that he could work in a personally stimulating environment. Following are recommended goals for Jeff as he continues to explore potential careers. The individualized education program team should work with Jeff to narrow his priorities over the next year and assist him in selecting goals and objectives that will help him achieve his priorities.

1. Jeff will self-monitor his production speed and increase speed when distracted with 75% independence.

2. Jeff will accept customer feedback with minimal comment for 80% of opportunities.

3. Jeff will ask for help when he makes a mistake for 100% of opportunities.

4. Jeff will respond to every customer's requests for help with a smile and kind comment for 100% of opportunities.

5. Jeff will remain calm and ask for a break when he makes a mistake or receives correction for 75% of opportunities.

6. Jeff will accept his own mistakes by identifying personal errors that could have contributed to his mistakes and listing ways he can avoid such mistakes in the future with 75% accuracy.

7. Jeff will identify personal strengths and discuss how they relate to his future plans.

8. Jeff will identify the characteristics of his disability and the ways he is affected by them at school, in the community, and at work.

9. Jeff will continue to explore jobs and develop his career goals and interests through further community- and school-based work experiences.

to do their laundry on their own. Students with autism, however, may not do their own laundry because they tend to have poor problem-solving skills and may not consider it problematic to go to work wearing dirty clothes. Thus, it is important to consider the personal skills that students with autism need to be successful in adult life and discuss how to teach those skills during high school. A formal standardized assessment that may help the team achieve this goal is the Vineland Adaptive Behavior Scales (Sparrow, Balla, & Cicchetti, 1984).

Assessment of Self-Determination

Self-determination is the ability to make choices, select goals, and develop a plan to achieve those goals (Field & Hoffman, 2007). This is a critical set of skills for transition-age students with autism. Without being able to choose, plan, and act for the benefit of their own future, students with autism will lack the required investment necessary to follow their own transition plans to fruition. Thus, teams must assess and plan for increasing a student's self-determination skills.

Self-determination is a set of skills that results in an individual's being the "causal agent" in his or her life (Wehmeyer, Gragoudas, & Shogren, 2006). This definition does not imply that a person is entirely independent of any other supports. Rather, self-determination implies that when a person needs supports, he or she selects when and by whom those supports are provided. This is an important point when considering the needs of individuals with autism (Held, Thoma, & Thomas, 2004). Self-determination is not just a concept that is relevant for individuals who, like Jeff, are able to speak for themselves and make detailed choices about their lives; it is just as relevant for students who, like Craig, do not use words effectively to communicate (Wehmeyer, 2002).

Figure 3.5 shows a model of self-determination, which contains the following components (Field & Hoffman, 2007):

1. Know yourself and your environment

2. Value yourself

3. Plan

4. Act

5. Experience outcomes and learn

This model shows each skill required for each step in the process of planning for the future. Table 3.5 lists the component elements of self-determined behavior described by Wehmeyer et al. (2006).

Although most of the literature on self-determination is not disability specific, it is clear from the discussion of autism thus far that teams supporting students with autism must pay close attention to the communication and social interaction skills required for a student to become self-determined (Field & Hoffman, 1999). Teams must ensure that relevant, measurable goals that increase a student's self-determination are included in the transition plan.

Because the components of self-determination touch on every aspect of transition, this is arguably one of the most important aspects of transition assessment for students with autism and can serve as the centerpiece for the transition IEP. It

56   Schall

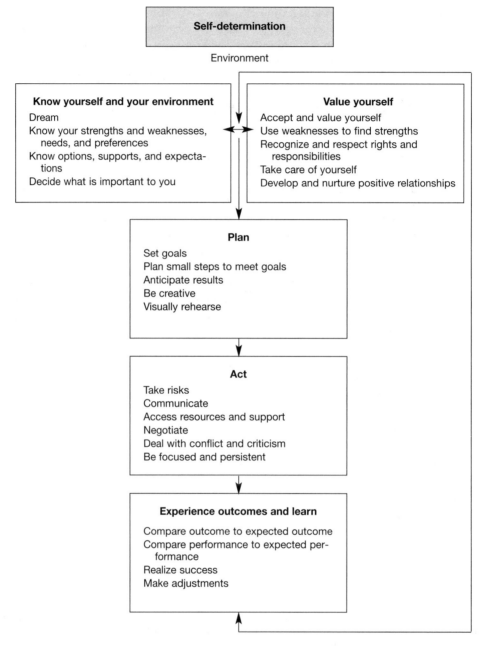

Figure 3.5. Model of self-determination. (From "Development of a Model for Self-Determination," by S. Field and A. Hoffman, 1994, *Career Development for Exceptional Individuals, 17*(2), p. 165. Copyright 1994 by the Hammill Institute on Disabilities. Reprinted with permission.)

is common for all adolescents to change their minds often and head in different directions throughout the transition years. A student may identify one career option, then choose another as he or she gathers more information about other career options, and then decide to pursue a degree at the local college. Thus, it is critical that a transition assessment identify and support a student's ability to be self-determined so that he or she is well prepared for life out of school. In many ways,

Table 3.5.   Component elements of self-determined behavior

Choice-making skills

Decision-making skills

Problem-solving skills

Goal-setting and attainment skills

Independence, risk-taking, and safety skills

Self-instruction skills

Self-advocacy skills

Internal locus of control

Positive attributions of efficacy and outcome expectancy

Self-awareness

Self-knowledge

From Wehmeyer, M.L., Gragoudas, S., & Shogren, K.A. (2006). Self-determination, student involvement, and leadership development. In P. Wehman, *Life beyond the classroom: Transition strategies for young people with disabilities* (4th ed., p. 43). Baltimore: Paul H. Brookes Publishing Co.

being self-determined becomes the bedrock on which students can personally guide their own lives.

There are two types of formal assessments of self-determination: independent, standardized assessments and pre- and postcurriculum assessments that are a part of a published curriculum. Among the best known of the independent standardized assessments is The Arc's Self-Determination Scale (Wehmeyer & Kelchner, 1995). This 72-item, self-report scale is designed for students who are able to read or respond to questions to assess their own level of self-determination. (In addition to the student version, there is an adult version available from the publisher.) For students who are not able to respond to written or verbal questions, teams might use the American Institutes for Research Self-Determination Scale (Wolman, Campeau, DuBois, Mithaug, & Stolarski, 1994). This scale has a student, parent, and educator version that enables teams supporting individuals who are nonverbal to gather information about self-determination from key team members.

There are a few curricula that include pre- and posttest criterion-referenced assessments. Some examples of these are

- *Steps to Self-Determination: A Curriculum to Help Adolescents Learn to Achieve Their Goals* (Field & Hoffman, 1996)

- *Next S.T.E.P. (Student Transition and Educational Planning) Curriculum* (Halpern, Herr, Doren, & Wolf, 2000)

- *ChoiceMaker: A Comprehensive Self-Determination Transition Program* (Martin & Marshall, 1995)

The assessments associated with each of these curricula allow teams to assess students' self-determination skills initially and then periodically as students participate in the curriculum. These assessments provide teams with specific goals, objectives, and strategies to address the self-determination needs of students with autism.

Despite careful attention to the needs of individuals with intellectual disabilities, these curricula still may not meet the needs of students with autism, particularly those who have additional disabilities or severe communication deficits. Consequently, all formal assessments must be used along with informal methods, such as behavioral observations, to assess students' abilities across the skills listed in Figure 3.5 and Table 3.5. For example, Craig's team identified assembling pizza boxes as a possible skill of interest from their ongoing observations that Craig remained on task and focused best when he was building things. From this observation, they surmised that Craig liked to build things. Behavioral observations such as these provide students with severe communication challenges a voice in their own transition process.

EDUCATIONAL AND TRANSITION PLANNING

After assessing a student's career awareness, vocational skills and abilities, independent living and community skills, and self-determination, many teams will have a long list of skills to address in the student's transition IEP. How can these skills be prioritized? What are the most important skills for any given student? The fact that Jeff struggled with some aspects of his job at the video game store does not mean that he has to work on every skill necessary to be successful as a clerk in a video game store; perhaps Jeff is not interested in being a clerk in any store. The process of transition assessment should identify not only the skills on which the student should work but also the skills on which the student *wants* to work. Thus, teams must identify the student's preferences as well as his or her strengths and weaknesses. Whereas an assessment of self-determination will explain the degree to which a student can make such a choice, a person-centered plan will assist teams in identifying the student's interests, goals, and desires. The next section describes person-centered planning and how it informs the transition IEP planning process for students with autism by capitalizing on self-determination and identification of preferences.

Person-Centered Planning

Person-centered planning, also known as *personal futures planning,* is a team process in which a person with a disability and his or her chosen support network meet and discuss their vision for a positive future. The team also compares that vision to a measure of the person's life now and develops an action plan to take steps toward achieving that vision. This plan then acts as a guide for all future actions and choices. In the context of transition planning, the person-centered plan allows the team to personalize and prioritize goals and objectives in the student's transition IEP so that they reflect a course of action that will be personally satisfying for the student.

Although the topic of person-centered planning follows assessment in this chapter, this is not the case in practice. The best time to complete a person-centered plan is when the team feels a need to clarify a person's desires and thereby achieve clarity in their own planning on behalf of that person. For Maria's team this is a must. They really do not know how to plan her high school career and are wondering where to go next. Therefore, they may postpone some assessments until they complete a person-centered plan for her. The few studies on person-centered planning for people with autism reveal significant improvements in outcomes for people when they are empowered to voice their preferences and participate fully in the development of their transition IEP (Held et al., 2004; Kincaid et al., 2002; Smith, McDougall, & Edelen-Smith, 2006).

The essential components of a person-centered plan include a process led by a neutral facilitator and a team that is chosen by the person and is not necessarily representative, but additive (Kincaid, 1996). For example, a person may not want to include the school psychologist in his or her person-centered plan because the individual has little contact with the psychologist on a regular basis, but he or she may consider the clerk at the local convenience store to be an essential member of the team. The process of creating a person-centered plan usually incorporates group graphics, such as large chart paper, markers, and pictures to record the group's work. Not only does this meaningfully include individuals with disabilities, but it also creates an atmosphere that promotes creative thinking. Kincaid also identified "five essential goals, outcomes, or valued accomplishments" associated with the plan:

- Being present and participating in community life

- Gaining and maintaining satisfying relationships

- Expressing preferences and making choices in everyday life

- Having opportunities to fulfill respected roles and to live with dignity

- Continuing to develop personal competencies

Clearly, these goals are in perfect alignment with the goals discussed previously regarding transition assessment.

Completing a Person-Centered Plan

There are many different processes that a team could select to complete a person-centered plan, such as Personal Futures Planning (Mount, 2000), Planning Alternative Tomorrows with Hope (PATH; Pearpoint, O'Brien, & Forest, 1993), Making Action Plans or MAPs (also known as McGill Action Planning System; Forest & Pearpoint, 1992), and Essential Lifestyle Planning (Smull, 2005). Figure 3.6 presents a sample MAP for Craig.

As is evident in Craig's MAP, there is a lot of information for his team to use in the development of his transition IEP. Another planning tool that works quite well in a school context is Mount's (2000) Personal Futures Planning. In this person-centered planning tool, teams select the frames through which they can explore a student's preferences, desires, and vision. Following is a partial list of the frames from which a team can select:

- Person's history

- Relationship map

- Places map (a map of all the places the person goes)

- Dreams versus nightmares

- What works versus what does not work

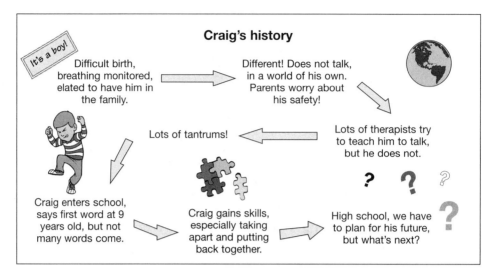

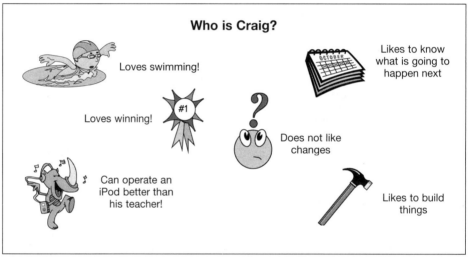

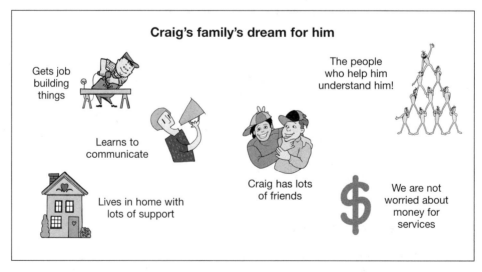

Figure 3.6. Sample McGill Action Planning System (MAP) for Craig.

Craig's family's fears for him

 Too many changes in staff or schedule

Being told NO! or STOP!

 Having nothing to do

 Being alone without friends

 Being abused or taken advantage of

Craig's needs

- Structure
- A schedule
- Preparation for changes in his routine
- Help with his daily living routines
- Reminders to take a bath
- Help with money

- A chance to work
- A way to say what he needs and wants to say
- Help from community services
- A PBS Plan
- More people for rehabilitative services on his team

Craig's strengths

- Has a loving family
- Loves to keep moving
- Can operate an iPod
- Loves to build things

- Is never sick or out of school
- Follows his schedule
- Is a good swimmer
- Likes to work and be busy

Craig's ideal day (after high school)

- Listens to music every morning after he wakes up, about 10 minutes
- Wakes up around the same time every day—about 7:00 A.M.
- Goes to work around 9:00 A.M., where he stays busy and does basically the same things every day; has a regular schedule

- Has a break about every hour
- Goes to the YMCA to swim after work before coming home
- Listens to music before dinner
- Plays with Legos
- Goes to bed around 10:00 P.M.

- What earns this person respect versus what does not earn this person respect

- Choices made by the person versus choices made by others

Using information from person-centered planning meetings helps the transition team identify meaningful, reasonable long-term goals for a student with autism. It also helps the team create goals and objectives for the transition IEP so that the student can achieve his or her life goals.

The overarching goals of a person-centered plan are to 1) coordinate the team's efforts to support the person in achieving his or her own dream and following his or her own path and 2) view the person in the context of his or her life experiences and not in the context of the disability. For individuals with autism who are limited in the ways they can communicate their dreams and vision, family members and caregivers who are closest to the person and know this person's preferences would be best able to present a vision on his or her behalf. As depicted in Figure 3.6, Craig's family talked about their dreams and fears for Craig. This process is not dependent on intellectual or communication ability; rather, this process is dependent on a team of committed individuals who are willing to ask the student with autism what he or she wants and really listen to him or her. Teams who have used this tool and experienced the outcomes related to person-centered planning strongly praise the process (Held et al., 2004; Sax, 2002). They report that, by using person-centered planning tools, they are more creative in the activities used to support students and in the skills they include in the transition IEP. In other words, person-centered planning changes the way team members think about the student, which in turn changes their day-to-day interactions with the student.

Moving from Vision to Plan

Although many teams find that the creativity of the person-centered planning process enriches the transition IEP, some have trouble moving from the visioning stage to the planning stage. Therefore, it might be helpful to make that step in the process a little more clear. When putting a vision into action for a transition-age student, it is important to address the following year's work in a transition IEP but also to keep a more long-term view. Figure 3.7 shows the Transition Planning Map, a tool that teachers can use to work backward from a student's vision to plot out year-by-year goals for the transition IEP.

A team uses this map by writing the post–high school vision in the last column on the right. Then, the team works backward from that point. For example, imagine that Craig's dream is to work in a job that involves building something. The team would plot that dream in the far right column in the row titled *Work*. By working backward, the team might plot Craig's transition years as demonstrated in Figure 3.8.

In this example, Craig's team moved from his family's vision for him to work in a job in building to the present school year, when they will complete a thorough transition assessment. They will also look for internships and additional work experiences for Craig outside of the pizza restaurant. This type of planning enables the team to help Craig move toward his goals sooner and avoids the rush at the end of high school to teach work skills and behaviors in too short a period of time.

Age Domain	16–17	17–18	18–19	19–20	20–21	21–22	Vision
			Work backward from vision to current school year →			↓	
Work							
Academic							
Independent living							
Community/recreation/leisure							
Self-determination							
Transition activities							

Figure 3.7. Transition planning map.

Age	16–17	17–18	18–19	19–20	20–21	21–22	Vision
Domain				Work backward from vision to current school year			
Work	Complete transition assessment, including career awareness assessment, vocational evaluation, person-centered plan, and self-determination evaluation; identify job preferences; work in additional internships at school or community-based jobs	Identify skill strengths	Complete job training in at least four different jobs that interest Craig 3 days per week for at least 3 hours	Complete job training in at least four different jobs that interest him 5 days per week	Identify specific jobs that interest him, apply for those jobs, work part-time through work study	Work in a paid job related to building or other area of interest to Craig	Work in a job that involves building

Figure 3.8. From Craig's vision to individualized education program goal planning

Again, by aligning the transition IEP with Craig's long-term vision, it is more likely that Craig will accomplish that vision.

Maria's Person-Centered Plan and Her Ocean Voyagers

Maria's team gathered to complete her person-centered plan using the PATH model (Pearpoint et al., 1993). Maria's actual PATH is quite colorful and full of hand-drawn pictures; following is a synopsis of each area in the PATH in the order in which the team developed them.

The Team

Maria worked with her mother and her teacher to develop the invitation list for the PATH meeting. Maria invited her general and special education teachers, the para-professionals from her classes, and her supervisor at her part-time job. She wanted to invite the manager of the department store where she worked, but her mother did not know that person at all. They also planned the snacks for the PATH meeting. Maria's preferences were honored even in this. The way the meeting was planned made it clear that this was truly Maria's meeting.

Touching the Dream

As Maria began to talk about her vision, at first she talked about what she liked, including her favorite DVDs and television shows. Shortly after Maria's mother described Maria's part-time job, Maria began to talk about typing. It became clear that Maria really enjoyed typing and might be interested in an office job in which she could use her considerable spelling skills by typing or transcribing notes. Thus, Maria's dream began to take shape. Other aspects of her dream included living in her own home, having a saltwater fish tank, taking trips to the ocean, and having more friends. Maria was also very adamant that she go to college. Maria's mother dreamed of Maria having support in her adult life. She shared that she worried about Maria constantly and dreamed of a day when Maria could sleep in her own home and be well cared for. Maria's mother also dreamed of Maria enjoying reading and watching videos.

Sensing the Goal

From that vision, the team collaborated in identifying the positive and possible goals they could accomplish in 1 year to help Maria move closer to her vision. Maria's teacher knew about a community college program called the AVE program—Adults in Vocational Education. They had a clerical skills program that fit well with Maria's vision for herself. The AVE program required students with disabilities to read on at least a third-grade level, so one of the goals Maria and her team added to her PATH was to continue to work on her reading and math skills so that she could apply for that program and be accepted.

Another goal related to Maria's vision to live in her own home. The team identified the importance of improving Maria's budgeting and money skills: If she wanted to live in her own home, she would need to pay her own bills. The team also identified the importance of independent living skills for Maria, such as preparing meals and keeping the house clean. Another area where the team saw the importance of goal setting was related to Maria's dream of having more friends. Team members felt that it was important to discover ways to increase the number of friends she had by identifying other students who shared her interest in saltwater fish and movies. That discussion led to the final goal: The team would get a saltwater fish tank for Maria's house and teach Maria to care for her fish. They also decided to find some other students who liked movies and set up a regular movie-of-the-month club in the neighborhood. They hypothesized that, although they could not find friends for Maria, they *could* find people who shared her interests and develop opportunities for them to interact. Perhaps, when Maria and the other individuals in her movie club got to know each other better, Maria would make friends with them.

Now

The PATH process requires that the team take a quick snapshot of the individual's current status. When Maria and her team described her "now," they felt the disparity between Maria's vision and her current reality. Although they were excited that some aspects of Maria's previous education had prepared her well for adulthood, they recognized that more work had to be done. For example, Maria really wanted to be accepted into the AVE program, but the reading and math requirements could prove to be a barrier. Through discussion and a review of Maria's previous records, it was noted that Maria did not retain her reading and math skills over long breaks from school, such as holidays and summer vacations. The team also noted that Maria had no close friends, and though team members were saddened by this, they were confident that the PATH process would enable them to facilitate some new relationships for Maria. Finally, while discussing Maria's life at present, they noted how much she relied on her mother for everyday tasks. Everything Maria did, from showering to making her lunch, was completed under her mother's watchful eye. In other words, Maria was not very independent. The team felt most challenged by Maria's desire to be independent, living on her own.

People

The team members took stock of their skills and the types of skills they were missing and would need in order to help Maria accomplish her PATH goals. Some of them even signed up to do unusual tasks. For example, one of the paraprofessionals agreed to try to find someone who knew how to take care of a saltwater fish tank. Maria's work supervisor agreed to take her to the movies with one of her friends once per month. Together the team members identified the people they had and the people they needed to reach their goals. Maria's teacher agreed to be the PATH coach—the person who would encourage the team and also hold the members accountable for what they had agreed to do.

Getting Stronger

By this point in the process, the team members were becoming a cohesive unit, united for the purpose of supporting Maria. One of the ways they identified to make themselves stronger as a team was to meet at a local coffee shop once every other month. There they continued their work on Maria's behalf over coffee and donuts.

Action Plan

The final steps of Maria's PATH process involved writing a solid action plan. The team accomplished this by "walking backward," starting with the ultimate goal and setting realistic interim goals that Maria could take to achieve her dreams. The team identified some immediate tasks for Maria to do to begin working toward her long-term goals. Each person left the PATH meeting with a reasonable to-do list of actions to support Maria. For example, her teacher set up an informational interview at the community college for Maria and her mother to learn about the AVE program. Her supervisor delivered the movie section of the newspaper to Maria on Wednesdays so that she could plan the movie they would see. The paraprofessional called a friend who had a saltwater fish tank to find a pet shop that could help them set one up for Maria. Each action led to other actions—all for Maria.

Maria's team revisited the PATH at their meetings at the coffee shop. They named themselves "Maria's Ocean Voyagers." Over time, some of the team members changed. When Maria graduated, her teacher remained on her team, but her paraprofessional did not. Instead, one of the people working at the department store with Maria joined her team. Together they were a part of Maria's success.

Maria's team used this PATH to frame their work with her in her remaining years in school. They selected academic and functional skills based on Maria's vision for herself. Thus, her transition IEP included the following goals, which the team will revisit at least annually:

1. Maria will read and comprehend third- to fourth-grade high-interest material with 95% accuracy and 95% comprehension.

2. Maria will add, subtract, multiply, and divide at the third-grade level with 90% accuracy.

3. Maria will complete mathematical operations using money, time, and measurements at the third-grade level with 90% accuracy.

4. Maria will describe the food chain in three different saltwater environments and prepare a report on the care of saltwater fish tanks with 85% accuracy.

5. Maria will work in a clerical job in the community with support at least 10 hours per week while in school.

6. Maria will develop a budget and manage her own money with 85% independence.

7. Maria will describe her strengths and make goals and plans with 85% independence.

8. Maria will complete her daily personal hygiene routine with 100% independence.

9. Maria will clean her room, make dinner, clean the kitchen, and clean her bathroom with 95% independence.

DEVELOPING A TRANSITION INDIVIDUALIZED EDUCATION PROGRAM

As Maria's team discovered, once a team has completed a transition assessment and has used a person-centered plan to prioritize the areas most in need of direct instruction, the team is primed to create the person's transition IEP. Although a person-centered plan is not required, nor should it be completed for every IEP, such a plan is the best way to find direction for a student's future while the student is in high school. Although a person-centered plan may be completed only once during a student's high school career, the IEP must be completed yearly. In addition to yearly completion, the IEP during the transition years must include a transition plan (i.e., transition IEP) that focuses specifically on the student's transition goals. This plan is intended to reach beyond the school environment and set a course for the student's future. According to IDEA 2004, for students who are in their last years before their transition out of high school, transition teams must also write a *summary of performance,* a document developed by the IEP team that describes the person's skills and needs at graduation. The summary of performance is designed to be shared with other agencies who will provide services to a person with autism after high school. The components of the transition planning process are described in the following sections.

Transition IEP Team

As noted in Chapter 1, the IEP team expands during transition from school to adult life and may include current or potential employers, community agency personnel, and—if he or she is not already involved—the student. In fact, the transition IEP team often includes any of the following individuals:

- *Student*—In many states, once a student reaches the age of majority, he or she is required to participate and sign the IEP unless the parents have been granted guardianship by a court (this age varies from state to state, but is generally on or around the student's 18th birthday).

- *Parent*—Although not required to be members of the transition team, parents are very necessary and helpful to the process, especially when the student is under the age of majority.

- *Special education teacher*—The special education teacher's membership on the transition team is required.

- *General education teacher*— If the student receives or may receive any portion of his or her education in a general education environment, the general education teacher's membership on the transition team is required.

- *Vocational educator*—The vocational educator is not required to be a member, but he or she can be very helpful regarding the availability of vocational training services.

- *Case managers from adult services agencies*—Although membership is not required for case managers, they can provide helpful information on adult services.

- *Vocational rehabilitation counselor*—The participation of a vocational rehabilitation counselor may vary depending on the student's age and the availability of services.

- *Other community members with relevant information for the student and the team*—Not every student has community members on the transition IEP team, but occasionally the transition IEP team decides to include such members.

Each of these team members plays a very important role in transition IEP planning. Again, not every team will have representation from all members at meetings. If the team needs expertise from a particular professional, however, it is important to include that individual. Following are some of the skills the team members can bring to the meeting.

Student

Over time, students can and should learn to lead their own IEP meetings; it empowers them and can help improve their social and communication skills and self-determination. After several years of running her transition team meetings, Maria mastered many of the self-determination skills necessary to succeed in the community and achieved other goals that were set for her.

Parent

Parents of students with autism frequently have a wealth of information about their children and their learning and behavioral history. Many also have personal contacts in the community that could be beneficial to students. For example, Maria's mother knew the movie theatre manager in their town from her high school days, and she was able to connect with that person on Maria's behalf. Jeff's parents talked at length at one of his meetings about strategies they used to motivate Jeff to complete tasks such as cleaning his room and taking a bath. This helped his team think of new ways to motivate Jeff in school.

Special Education Teacher

The special education teacher's role in leading the transition IEP team changes during transition planning as the student takes on more responsibility. First, the special education teacher must make sure the list of invitees is complete and includes relevant agency personnel. Second, the teacher must ensure that new team members have adequate information to participate fully in the meeting. Finally, and most important, the special education teacher must make sure that the student and his or her family are fully supported so that they can take an active role in the meetings.

General Education Teacher

The general education teacher can provide the transition team with information about the general education curriculum and how best to include students with autism in that curriculum. They also can share information about their experiences with the student and their observations of the student with peers without disabilities. These observations can help the team address the student's social and communication skills.

Vocational Educator

Vocational educators offer an important perspective on students with autism. Their knowledge of careers and the skills required for success in those careers are invaluable as teams plan for a student's future. Vocational educators should participate in the transition IEP meeting and offer the team guidance about careers and skill development opportunities.

Case Managers from Adult Services Agencies

Case managers from adult services agencies frequently perform assessments that assist the team in addressing the student's personal, home care, and community needs. They also can offer or refer the person to funding sources and services outside the school that can assist the person in achieving his or her goals for independence. Finally, such team members often can refer individuals to self-help or support groups, where they can meet and learn from others who also have autism.

Vocational Rehabilitation Counselor

Vocational rehabilitation counselors can offer the team additional assessments and services. For example, vocational rehabilitation counselors often provide funding for situational assessments (like the ones Jeff experienced over the summer) and summer vocational programs. In addition, vocational rehabilitation counselors bring a perspective regarding the world of work that other team members might not have. Vocational rehabilitation counselors frequently have previous experiences and know about work options. They frequently are able to make suggestions that other team members might not have considered, such as *self-employment*, *job carving*, or *job sharing*. (All of these terms will be defined and explained in Chapter 7.)

Other Community Members

The transition meeting offers an important opportunity for community members and other professionals to get involved and learn about a student. These members will vary depending on community resources and the student's needs. Maria's local pet store owner became involved in her meeting to support Maria's interest in fish, as the owner had several saltwater fish tanks of her own. Jeff required intensive preparation from tutors to help him learn to improve time management and planning and study on his own so he could attend college, so his team included these tutors. Craig's team included community services providers who assisted his parents in exploring independent living options for Craig.

Written Transition Individualized Education Program

According to IDEA 2004, the transition IEP should include a statement of the student's post–high school goals, but it must also include the academic and other goals that need to be accomplished during the current school year. IDEA 2004 changed the requirement for the age by which a transition plan must be completed from 14 to 16. From the point of view of career awareness and development, however, starting to plan a student's transition at 16 may be a little late. Because there is no prohibition against writing a transition plan earlier, it remains a good idea to begin the transition planning process when the student is 14 years old.

The following sections will demonstrate transition IEPs for Jeff and Craig. As these two students have very different needs and goals, their cases will provide examples of how this process is implemented for students with varying needs.

Transition Individualized Education Program for Jeff

After their initial assessments (described previously in this chapter and in Figure 3.4), Jeff and his team identified the many skills and domains in which Jeff required ongoing special education and direct instruction. The team felt that Jeff's social skill needs were as important to address as his strong academic skills. After enrolling him in an Education for Employment class; continuing with speech therapy; developing a social skills class; referring him to the vocational rehabilitation agency in his state; preparing him for community college; and formulating a plan (which included his parents) for the development of personal hygiene, banking, and job skills, the team knew that Jeff could not also maintain a full academic load. Thus, out of his schedule of seven classes per semester, his team created a plan that allowed two classes per semester for his special education needs—education for employment and social skills for success. This meant that he would graduate from high school in 5 years instead of the traditional 4. Table 3.6 presents the curriculum plan that Jeff's team proposed to assist him in meeting his personal goals, achieving an honors diploma, and acquiring the social and job skills he needed to continue his education and become a successfully employed adult.

This is, of course, a tentative plan and subject to change based on Jeff's ability to complete all classes successfully. Also, as Jeff learns more about his chosen career, he may change his focus, which would change this plan as well.

Table 3.6. Jeff's planned high school curriculum

High school year 1	High school year 2	High school year 3
English 9	English 10	English 11
Social studies 9	Algebra II (He completed Algebra I in the middle school honors class)	Calculus
Earth science		Chemistry
Physical education and health	Computer programming	Computer animation
Basic computer programming elective	Biology	Elective
Education for employment 1	Physical education, health, and driver's education	Work study—two periods
Social skills for success 1	Education for employment 2	
	Social skills for success 2	

High school year 4	High school year 5
Trigonometry	English 12
Computer elective—dual enrollment at the community college	Math elective—dual enrollment at the community college
Science elective—dual enrollment at the community college	Computer elective—dual enrollment at the community college
Western civilization	Science elective—dual enrollment at the community college
Elective	Work study—three periods
Work study—two periods	

Jeff's team also developed a transition IEP for him. The chapter appendix presents Jeff's transition IEP. This transition IEP is a living document and may be reviewed and changed at every IEP and transition meeting, but it includes the critical goals and activities that Jeff and his team have determined are necessary for him to achieve his goals of graduating from high school, attending community college, and securing employment involving computers.

Craig's Transition Assessment and Transition Plan

Like Jeff and Maria, Craig's team used person-centered planning, self-determination assessments, and vocational and adaptive behavior assessments to help shift the focus from Craig's disability to his future. In some ways, this was a more important task for Craig than for Jeff or Maria because of his age (he was 17 when he transferred schools, and his previous school had never approached transition planning) and his support needs. Once the team realized that Craig had at most 4 years left in his public school career, the team members felt the urgency of their task. After completing their transition assessment, Craig's team noted that there were many basic skills to address. Specifically, Craig's communication challenges made it difficult for him to make choices, express preferences, and be self-determined. Building a viable, functional communication system became one of the highest priorities. Another very high priority was to build Craig's independent work skills. The team knew that he could work as a result of his success at his part-time job putting together pizza boxes, but team members also knew that they needed to increase his independence in work environments. Craig had many strengths on which they could capitalize. For example, the fact that they had been able to identify the function of his self-injurious behavior and address that function successfully meant that Craig was communicating some important things with his behavior. The next step for them was to find a symbolic communication system that would be easily understood by the people around Craig.

As a result of the transition assessment and the development of Craig's MAP (see Figure 3.6), the team's first task was to complete an assistive technology assessment to identify any possible high-technology or low-technology communication devices that might increase Craig's ability to communicate. That assessment indicated that there was an electronic device that could be used to increase Craig's ability to use symbolic communication. Also, his team discovered that Craig related well to picture representations of the things he wants, so the assistive technology team recommended teaching Craig to use a picture system to communicate. Craig's transition IEP, along with his summary of performance, is in the chapter appendix.

Incorporating State Standards Documentation into Functional Activities and Instruction

Since the No Child Left Behind Act of 2001 (PL 107-110), no discussion of educational planning is complete without consideration of statewide assessment programs. Although this type of assessment does not directly inform the development of a transition IEP, it is now a regular, required part of every student's education (Kohl, McLaughlin, & Nagle, 2006). Because educators must prepare students for

Table 3.7.   Alternate standards and functional activities for teaching standards

Statewide standard	Functional activities during which the standard can be taught
Reading: The student will read and demonstrate comprehension of a variety of informational selections.	During a lesson on cooking, the student will read from a picture recipe and follow the instructions to prepare the food.
English: The student will describe and appropriately use formal and informal English.	On the job site, the student will address co-workers, customers, and supervisors accordingly.
Mathematics: The student will identify representations of a given percent and describe orally and in writing the equivalence relationship between fractions, decimals, and percents.	While delivering the middle school's newspapers, the student will calculate the percentage of newspapers delivered and yet to be delivered using fractions, decimals, percents, and simple ratios.
Science: The student will investigate and understand different sources of energy, including renewable and nonrenewable sources.	While completing community-based training, the student will identify how different environments are heated, including buildings, cars, outdoor areas, and homes.
History and social studies: The student will identify and compare changes in community life over time, in terms of buildings, jobs, transportation, and population.	While completing community-based shopping tasks at various times of the year, the student will note changes in the number of stores and restaurants open, the number of people working, and the merchandise for sale at the stores.

these progress assessments, they sometimes assume that they do not have the time to support students with autism in community-based instruction or work experiences, even though they are required by law to do so. In fact, teachers can and frequently do teach standards-based skills in everyday functional experiences. When students read a bus schedule, they are using basic reading and math skills. Thus, a teacher can teach reading and math while helping students with autism learn to ride the bus. In this example, a teacher is addressing students' functional skill needs—bus riding—while also teaching the reading and math state standards.

As noted previously in this chapter, students with autism can have very poor outcomes when their specific transition needs are not addressed. A program that focuses on basic academic skills, such as learning the alphabet and counting to 10, instead of work skills, such as riding a bus or counting the number of towels in a hotel room, may result in these poor outcomes. Functional, social, and communication skills are as important for students with transition IEPs to learn as academic skills. What matters to employers is that their employees are qualified to complete their jobs. Educators should therefore embed reading, math, social studies, and science into the IEP of every student with autism in the context of individual functional skill needs. Table 3.7 presents some typical alternate state standards and functional activities during which a special educator could teach those standards.

In short, teaching standards-based skills through functional activities is very important for all students with disabilities. To do this, teachers should identify the functional skills that are included in a student's IEP or transition IEP and then identify the standards that can be addressed in the context of those activities. The steps for embedding standards into the functional activities from a student's IEP are presented in Figure 3.9.

Student's name: _____   Date: _____

Individualized education program (IEP) year: _____

1. In column 1 of the table below, list the functional activities, skills, or tasks included in this student's transition IEP.
2. In column 2, list all of the possible academic skills from the state's standards that can be demonstrated in the context of performing each activity, skill, or task listed in column 1.
3. In column 3, identify the curriculum area and number for each standard listed in column 2.

1. Functional activities, skills, or tasks from student's IEP or transition IEP	2. State standards that are or can be demonstrated with each functional activity, skill, or task	3. Curriculum area and standard number for each standard listed

4. Look at your state's requirements for skill inclusion. Have you addressed all skills required by your state's assessment program? If not, list those skills that are not included above in column 4.
5. List some functional activities that would meet those standards in column 5.

4. State standards required by the state's assessment program that are not addressed in the list above	5. Functional activities that would allow student to learn and demonstrate the state standards listed in column 4

Figure 3.9. Steps for embedding standards into functional activities.

Autism and the Transition to Adulthood: Success Beyond the Classroom by Paul Wehman, Marcia Datlow Smith, & Carol Schall © 2009 by Paul H. Brookes Publishing Co., Inc. All rights reserved.

Development of a Summary of Performance

The transition assessment process culminates with the development of a summary of performance. As described in IDEA 2004, this document is the guide that will provide information about a graduating student's current needs, strengths, preferences, and interests. The summary of performance should incorporate information collected through the transition assessment process and should assist students in achieving their postsecondary goals. Craig's team prepared his summary of performance as a part of his transition IEP (see the chapter appendix). The team members decided to do this in case Craig graduated earlier than expected from high school. They also acknowledged that, if Craig did not graduate early, they would have to update that summary every year.

To further foster self-determination and maintain a person-centered planning approach, Martin, Van Dycke, D'Ottavio, and Nickerson (2007) recommended that students themselves direct the development of the summary of performance. For students with autism, such a student-directed process empowers them to view themselves as the causal agent in their own lives. This in turn assists families and educational staff in stepping back to allow the student to make life decisions on his or her own.

PULLING IT ALL TOGETHER

The process of completing and updating a transition assessment may seem overwhelming. Remember that there are a number of ways to complete this assessment, and not every team supporting students with autism will use every single assessment method. Table 3.8 shows how this process might be implemented for Maria beginning at the age of 16 and carried throughout her high school program. The transition IEP team hopes that their extensive assessment and planning over time will help Maria achieve her goals as a self-determined young woman who can speak for herself.

The point of transition assessment and planning is to assist the team in developing an effective transition IEP that reflects the student's personal goals, interests, and strengths. The assessments chosen should provide the answers a team needs to improve their plan for the student with autism. The plan should then be the driving force to actualize the student's future.

Transition assessment and planning are powerful processes because they enable the person with autism and the transition team to plan the person's transition to adulthood mindfully and with purpose. Transition planning provides a new focus for the remaining years of a student's education. This process must be updated yearly with a variety of different tools to identify the student's needs, strengths, preferences, and interests. For students with autism, it is particularly important to develop and continually revisit the transition plan so that they lead personally satisfying and enriching lives. It is only with a sound plan, informed by assessment, that teams can truly assist students in accomplishing their goals.

Table 3.8. Transition assessment across Maria's high school years

Maria's age	Career awareness	Vocational evaluation and assessment	Self-determination assessment	Person-centered planning
16	Informal review of Maria's records and discussion with her parents	Behavioral observation of Maria at school jobs; performance assessment in school- and community-based jobs	Formal assessment using The Arc's Self-Determination Scale	Completion of MAP; development of Transition Planning Map (see Figure 3.7)
17	Completion of a vocational interest inventory	Completion of situational assessments at six different jobs across the school year	Ongoing assessment using a published self-determination curriculum	Discussion of dreams and nightmares in the context of the self-determination curriculum
18	Maria's development of her own summary of performance	Formal vocational assessment in selected careers through the local rehabilitative services agency; initiation of job-finding services	Goal of working part time achieved by end of school year; continuation of job over summer	Maria's invitation to her team to complete a PATH with her
19	Continued development of her own summary of performance	Regular job evaluations at her part-time job	Development of a long-term career goal and regular measurement of progress on that goal; meeting with rehabilitative services case manager to discuss career plans	Record of accomplishments from her PATH
20	Graduation from high school with awareness of her own strengths, needs, preferences, and interests; presentation of her own career plan and summary of performance to agencies that continue to support her at work; full-time job and attendance at community college to continue developing work skills			

Appendix

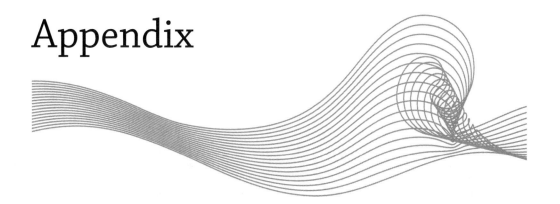

Transition individualized education program

Student's name: _____ Townley _____ (last) _____ Jeff _____ (first) ___ T. ___ (middle initial)

Age: 15 years old _____   School: Middleboro High School _____

Student's identification number: 876543 _____

Participants

Name	Position
Mrs. Richmond	Special education teacher
Mrs. Keswick	Speech pathologist
Mr. Harris	Algebra teacher
Mrs. Jacesko	English 9 teacher
Mr. Titus	Principal
Mr. Cheswick	Community service board case manager
Mrs. Townley	Mother
Jeff Townley	Student

Present level of performance
(Note: Include recent transition assessments and student's postschool vision.)

Student profile and postschool vision

Jeff is a ninth-grade student with Asperger's syndrome. He is an energetic young man who enjoys socializing with others as long as the conversation is one of his choosing. Jeff enjoys playing video games and writing simple computer programs. He has stated that he wants to go to college and eventually work in the computer gaming industry. He is an excellent student and takes advanced coursework in math and science. He is taking college-track regular classes in English and social studies.

Jeff's Asperger's syndrome is characterized by significant pragmatic communication and social skill deficits. Specifically, he tends to be abrupt in his communication with others and sometimes offends peers and teachers with his comments. Although he does not intend to offend, he does not seem to be aware when his comments might be too blunt. In addition, Jeff struggles with the social aspects of communication. For example, he frequently talks very loudly, sometimes does not respond when others talk to him, continues to talk without listening to others in the conversation, and at times is argumentative when he disagrees with others.

At home Jeff needs reminders to shower, shave, and use deodorant regularly. He relies on his parents to transport him to activities and events. He currently takes the bus to school but has never used public transportation. Jeff does not earn an allowance or have a bank account, although with his excellent math skills it is likely he would be good at keeping track of his money.

Jeff struggles when he confronts a problem or must make a choice. He has not demonstrated sufficient self-determination skills in the areas of problem solving, goal setting and attainment, self-advocacy, self-awareness, and self-knowledge.

Employment and vocational training

Jeff does not have any work experience in or out of school. A brief situational assessment was completed at the local video game store, during which Jeff demonstrated strengths in inventorying and preparing stock reports. He struggled with social aspects of the job, including interacting with customers, co-workers, and his supervisor. More specifically, Jeff has difficulty accepting criticism and correction from his supervisor and listening to others.

Postsecondary, career, or technical education

Jeff has excellent computer skills and has begun to learn basic computer programming. He is disorganized in his academic classes and often gets a lower grade than his work would earn because he loses assignments, turns them in late, or does not complete them fully.

Community, financial, self-determination, social, and life skills

Jeff does not currently initiate his own personal hygiene regimens. His mother reminds him daily to shower, shave, and use deodorant. Jeff is dependent on his parents to take him to after-school activities and job sites. He does not currently use public transportation or know how to get a bus schedule.

Figure A.1. Jeff's transition individualized education program.

Also, his parents expect him to get a driver's permit and complete driver's education when he reaches the appropriate age. Although Jeff has excellent math skills and can complete financial operations; he does not currently have a bank account or receive a regular allowance. Jeff has not attended his own IEP or transition meeting yet. He also has not demonstrated the following self-determination skills: problem solving skills, goal-setting and attainment skills, self-advocacy skills, internal locus of control, self-awareness, and self-knowledge. Jeff has displayed problem behaviors in the past. A positive behavior support plan was developed to meet his needs. Although this plan (see Chapter 2) has been very successful, Jeff is dependent on an individual assistant to implement the plan, rate his behavior, and deliver his incentives.

I. Career outcomes

1. Long-term employment goal (may include integrated employment and supported employment):

Jeff will work in a job in the computer gaming industry.

Yearly goals to accomplish long-term goal:

Jeff will work in at least two different jobs in the school and community. He will also identify characteristics and behaviors of successful employees in the context of his Education for Employment class by June of next year.

Person(s) responsible for implementation:

Special education teacher, Jeff, speech pathologist

2. Long-term vocational/technical training goal:

Jeff will attend a college of his choice and study computer programming (see next goal for details).

Yearly goals to accomplish long-term goal:

See next goal area.

Person(s) responsible for implementation:

See next goal area.

II. Postsecondary education and training outcomes

3. Long-term higher education goal:

Jeff will attend a college of his choice and study computer programming.

Yearly goals to accomplish long-term goal:

1. Jeff will use his personal digital assistant to record and check off all assignments when he completes and turns them in to his instructors by June of next year.
2. Jeff will ask for clarification and help on assignments he does not understand by June of next year.

Person(s) responsible for implementation:

Jeff, special education teacher, speech pathologist

4. Long-term continuing and adult education, career/technical education goal (may include public or private technical school):

Since it is Jeff's goal to attend college, he does not currently have a career or technical education goal.

Yearly goals to accomplish long-term goal:

None

Person(s) responsible for implementation:

None

5. Long-term residential goal:

Jeff will live independently in an apartment or a home of his own, manage his own money, and advocate for himself.

Yearly goals to accomplish long-term goal:

1. Jeff will complete regular chores and odd jobs at home for allowance by June of next year.
2. Jeff will follow and complete a daily personal hygiene checklist with 100% accuracy by June of next year.

Person(s) responsible for implementation:

Mr. and Mrs. Townley, special education teacher, Jeff, physical education and health teacher

6. Long-term transportation/mobility goal:

Jeff will learn to drive and/or use public transportation.

Yearly goals to accomplish long-term goal:

Jeff will take public transportation to and from desired locations by June of next year.

Person(s) responsible for implementation:

Special education teacher, Jeff, Mr. and Mrs. Townley

7. Long-term financial/income needs goal:

Jeff will open a bank account, develop a budget, and manage his own finances.

Yearly goals to accomplish long-term goal:

Jeff will open a bank account and balance his own statements on a regular basis. He will also budget and purchase his own personal supplies and entertainment items by June of next year.

Person(s) responsible for implementation:

Jeff, Mr. and Mrs. Townley, special education teacher

8. Long-term self-determination goal:

Jeff will make choices and decisions about what he would like to participate in and do. He will also ask for modifications and accommodations when teachers forget to provide them for him.

Yearly goals to accomplish long-term goal:

Jeff will complete education in self-determination in his Social Skills for Success class. He will ask for accommodations and modifications from teachers who forget to provide them to him. He will also develop a personal profile of his strengths and goals by June of next year.

Person(s) responsible for implementation:

Speech pathologist, Jeff, Mr. and Mrs. Townley, special education teacher

9. Long-term social and communicative competence goal:

Jeff will monitor his own behavior and deliver his own rewards based on his current positive behavior support plan.

Yearly goals to accomplish long-term goal:

Jeff will monitor his own positive behavior support plan and report to his teacher at the end of each class with his own rating to ask for his own incentives by June of next year.

Person(s) responsible for implementation:

Special education teacher, Jeff, speech therapist

10. Health/safety goal:

See long-term residential goal.

Yearly goals to accomplish long-term goal:

See long-term residential goal.

Person(s) responsible for implementation:

See long-term residential goal.

Student's career preference:

To work in the computer gaming industry

Student's major transition needs:

1. Participate in job try-outs
2. Explore community living options
3. Self-monitor personal hygiene and behavior
4. Participate in community-based instruction activities
5. Increase social skills related to interacting with others
6. Make contact with local rehabilitative services agency through a referral
7. Explore potential college programs and their requirements
8. Plan his high school curriculum (subject to change on a yearly basis) to ensure that his schedule allows for the communication and social skills training he will need as well as the academic preparation that will result in his achieving his goals
9. Provide direct instruction in self-determination

Transition individualized education program

Student's name: _____Barnes_____ (last) _____Craig_____ (first) __J.__ (middle initial)

Age: 17 years old

School: Coolidge High School

Student's identification number: 946048

Participants

Name	Position
Mr. Baskins	Special education teacher
Mrs. Samson	Speech pathologist
Ms. Tams	Occupational therapist
Mr. Lowsinski	Health and physical education teacher
Dr. Baskerville	Principal
Mr. Henry	Community service board case manager
Mrs. Barnes	Mother
Mr. Barnes	Father
Craig Barnes	Student

Student profile
(Note: Include recent transition assessments and student's postschool vision.)

Student profile and postschool vision

Craig Barnes is a 17-year-old student with severe autism. He is an active young man who enjoys being busy and living a routine daily schedule. Craig enjoys swimming, putting together puzzles, and building with materials like LEGO blocks. Craig also likes the activities he does in Special Olympics, especially swimming and other water sports. During his free time, Craig enjoys doing puzzles and watching animated DVDs.

Craig's autism is characterized by a significant communication deficit, severe sensory abnormalities, and challenging behavior. He has just been evaluated for assistive technology and has begun to use a picture communication device. When the device is not available, Craig also uses a few pictures to request food items, free time activities, and a break. Recently, the speech therapist has introduced additional pictures to increase Craig's expressive and receptive vocabulary. The team has noticed that with an increased ability to communicate, Craig's inappropriate behavior has decreased. He has also begun to use a daily picture schedule.

Craig has a negative reaction when he is denied something he wants or is spoken to in a harsh manner. Specifically, Craig will hit his head and bite his wrists. On rare occasions, these behaviors have been directed at other people. These behaviors have decreased significantly over the past few months with the introduction of his positive behavior support plan.

Craig has a limited wardrobe. He only likes soft cottons against his skin. He prefers to go barefoot, but he has been able to tolerate some shoes. The occupational therapist works with the team to make sure that Craig's sensory needs are met through regular, age-appropriate sensory activities.

At home, Craig walks around his yard, goes on some community trips with his family, and sporadically helps out with chores around the house. He will assist with taking out the trash, but most of the time he is not interested or does not understand the expectation. Craig needs reminders to dress and groom himself but is independent in navigating his environment. He will get his own snack from the cupboard but does not cook or prepare any foods beyond opening a package. He keeps busy by looking at magazines, playing by himself, or watching DVDs.

With the support of the local resource center, Craig's team completed a MAP and is planning to do a PATH, a person-centered approach, this year to identify goals the family, school, and community may have for him. Craig's family is anxious to begin developing community supports and plans for Craig when he finishes school. They would like to see him living in another supported environment, being involved in the community, and working.

Employment and vocational training

Craig has a job assembling pizza boxes at a pizza restaurant several hours per week. His family would like to see him continue to work and try additional jobs. They would also like to see him involved in the community following his public education.

Figure A.2. Craig's transition individualized education program.

Postsecondary, career, or technical education

Craig's family does not elect for him to attend postsecondary or technical education. The severity of his disability precludes this option at this time.

Community, financial, self-determination, social, and life skills

Craig currently lives at home. His family would like to explore supported community living options for him. While at home, Craig occasionally helps with chores, such as taking out the trash and cleaning the bathroom; however, he needs to be reminded to complete these weekly chores as he does not seem to understand the importance of doing them on a regular basis. Craig sometimes needs reminders to participate in proper, regular self-hygiene. Although Craig cannot cook, he can pick out prepared snacks for himself. He enjoys watching movies, looking at magazines, and playing alone.

Craig goes on community trips with his family. Most of these include going to the park, out to eat, and to the mall, and he is taken there by his parents. Usually these trips are infrequent and short in duration. Craig's family would like him to develop the skills to take the bus into town to attend more community sites, such as the grocery store, movies, and festivals.

Craig is dependent on others to buy things for him. He is not able to make a simple transaction in a store to purchase a desired item, which caused embarrassment for his family when he started eating donuts at a local grocery store.

Craig has begun to follow a daily picture schedule at home and at school. He does not participate in selecting the routine but would most likely benefit from making some of those decisions. Recently, he has been using pictures to improve his ability to communicate. This is helping to alleviate challenging behavior and seems to give Craig a more effective way to tell the team what he wants or needs.

As mentioned in the student profile and postschool vision, Craig's problem behavior manifests in hitting and biting himself and sometimes others. The functional behavior assessment has shown that the behaviors are most likely to occur when Craig has been denied a desired item or is being talked to with a harsh tone. The team is working with Craig on a plan to reduce antecedents that cause this behavior; to teach Craig to communicate his feelings, needs, and wants; and to support him when he is in crisis.

I.   Career outcomes

1. Long-term employment goal (may include integrated employment and supported employment):

   Craig will work in a supported environment in a job that interests him.

   Yearly goals to accomplish long-term goal:

   Craig will try out different jobs in the school, including delivering the morning announcements to the teachers in the school and sorting the teachers' mail by matching the names on the letters to the names on the teachers' mailboxes. He will also try out additional community jobs, such as stocking shelves in a local grocery store, managing shopping carts at a local department store, helping assemble furniture at a local furniture store, and completing odd jobs at a local coffee shop by June of next year.

   Person(s) responsible for implementation:

   Special education teacher, Craig, speech pathologist

2. Long-term vocational/technical training goal:

   Craig has not identified a postschool vocational goal.

   Yearly goals to accomplish long-term goal:

   None

   Person(s) responsible for implementation:

   None

II.   Postsecondary education and training outcomes

3. Long-term higher education goal:

   Not applicable

Yearly goals to accomplish long-term goal:

Not applicable

Person(s) responsible for implementation:

Not applicable

4. Long-term continuing and adult education, career/technical education goal (may include public or private technical school):

Not applicable

Yearly goals to accomplish long-term goal:

Not applicable

Person(s) responsible for implementation:

Not applicable

III. Community, financial, self-determination, social, and life skills outcomes

5. Long-term residential goal:

Craig will live in a supported living environment.

Yearly goals to accomplish long-term goal

1. *Craig's family will explore community living options for him with his community services board case manager by June of next year.*
2. *Craig will complete simple chores including dusting, vacuuming, washing dishes, and making his bed by June of next year.*

Person(s) responsible for implementation:

Community services board case manager, family, special education teacher, speech pathologist, Craig

6. Long-term transportation/mobility goal:

Craig will have access to the community for leisure and basic living needs with assistance from the community supports available.

Yearly goals to accomplish long-term goal:

1. *Craig will fasten his own seat belt in all cars and vans by June of next year.*
2. *Craig will participate in weekly community-based leisure activities by June of next year.*

Person(s) responsible for implementation:

Special education teacher, Craig, family, speech pathologist, occupational therapist, community services board case manager

7. Long-term financial/income needs goal:

Craig will purchase desired items.

Yearly goals to accomplish long-term goal:

1. *Craig will select an item, present money, and wait for his change in community stores by June of next year.*
2. *Craig will present money for admission to movies and other community activities by June of next year.*
3. *Craig will carry his own wallet with his identification card and money by June of next year.*

Person(s) responsible for implementation:

Special education teacher, Craig, family, speech pathologist, occupational therapist, community services board case manager

8. Self-determination goal:

   Craig will make choices and decisions about what he would like to participate in and do.

   Yearly goals to accomplish long-term goal:
   1. Craig will increase his use of receptive and expressive vocabulary by increasing his picture card repertoire by June of next year.
   2. Craig will use these new picture cards in conjunction with his object system to express choice and make simple decisions by June of next year.
   3. Craig will participate in developing his daily schedule by June of next year.

   Person(s) responsible for implementation:

   Speech pathologist, Craig, family, special education teacher

9. Long-term social and communicative competence goal:

   Craig will identify the triggers that cause him to react inappropriately and learn coping skills to exhibit appropriate behavior.

   Yearly goals to accomplish long-term goals:

   Craig will request desired items and activities using his picture communication system by June of next year.

   Person(s) responsible for implementation:

   Speech pathologist, Craig, family, special education teacher

10. Health/safety goal:

    Craig will monitor his sensory needs.

    Yearly goals to accomplish long-term goals:
    1. Craig will identify sensory activities that are effective for him by June of next year.
    2. Craig will request the sensory activities in which he wants to engage by June of next year.

    Person(s) responsible for implementation:

    Speech therapist, Craig, occupational therapist, special education teacher, family

Student's career preference:

None has been determined.

Student's major transition needs:
1. Participate in job try-outs
2. Explore community living options
3. Complete simple chores and prepare a simple meal
4. Participate in community-based instruction activities
5. Increase receptive and expressive communication
6. Identify triggers to behavior and learn coping skills when in crisis situations
7. Identify sensory activities and communicate requests to others

Summary of performance

Student's name: _Craig J. Barnes_

Disability: _autism_

Student's address: _317 Key Circle, Verona, PA_

School's address: _719 Eighth Street, Verona, PA_

Student's identification number: _946048_

Phone Number: _777-555-2320_

Phone Number: _777-555-4658_

Postsecondary goals

Employment:

Upon graduation, Craig will be employed in a community-based, supported-employment setting.

Education/training:

Upon graduation, Craig will have received the training and support needed to be successful in his job.

Independent living/community participation:

Upon graduation, Craig will live in a supporting living arrangement (group home, supported apartment, or other such community-based arrangement).

Current academic achievement *(include courses of study)*

Craig currently receives all of his education in a special education environment. In the next school year, Craig will go to physical education with a 10th-grade class. He also will complete jobs around the school with peers without disabilities. Craig is in a functional skills program and will graduate with an IEP diploma. Craig can identify basic signs, such as the men's room and "closed" signs. He has extremely limited math skills but is learning to exchange money for goods when making a purchase in stores. Craig is learning to use an electronic picture communication device. He is also able to use pictures alone to communicate basic wants and needs.

Craig's greatest strength is his ability to take things apart and put them back together. In addition to puzzles, he also has taken apart and put his school desk back together. As a part of his school curriculum, Craig will attempt a number of community-based jobs in addition to his current job of putting pizza boxes together. Additional jobs may include stocking shelves in a local grocery store, managing shopping carts at a local department store, helping assemble furniture at a local furniture store, and completing odd jobs at a local coffee shop.

Current functional performance

At home, Craig walks around his yard, goes on some community trips with his family, and sporadically helps out with chores around the house. He will assist with taking out the trash and cleaning the bathroom, but most of the time is not interested or does not understand the expectations to do these tasks regularly. Craig needs reminders to dress and groom himself. He will get his own snack from the cupboard but does not cook or prepare any foods beyond opening a package. He keeps busy by looking at magazines, playing by himself, or watching DVDs.

Recommendations for achieving postsecondary goals

Employment:

Craig should participate in a functional vocational assessment to determine jobs at which he may excel and in which he shows interest. It would be best for Craig if he could try some jobs out prior to employment. Craig will need a written schedule and task list to help him understand the transitions and expectations within the work environment. Although Craig will be an exceptional employee given a job and environment that is structured and nurturing, others in the workplace will need to understand Craig's behavior challenges and positive behavior support plan so that they can support him.

Figure A.3. Craig's summary of performance.

Education/training:

Craig does not plan to go to college at this point, but he will need to increase his communication skills so that he can ask for help and training in his work environment when he becomes confused or needs assistance.

Independent living/community participation:

When Craig moves to his supported living arrangement, he will continue to need support from others to be successful. He will also continue to need assistance in identifying different community activities in which he can participate. Because he likes to be active and is athletic, Craig will need support to join a gym and pursue the activities that interest him.

Transition individualized education program

Student's name: _____ (last) _____ (first) _____ (middle initial)

Age: _____   School: _____

Student's identification number: _____

Participants

Name   Position

Present level of performance
(Note: Include recent transition assessments and student's postschool vision.)

Student profile and postschool vision

Employment and vocational training

Postsecondary, career, or technical education

Community, financial, self-determination, social, and life skills

Figure A.4.   Transition individualized education program.

Autism and the Transition to Adulthood: Success Beyond the Classroom by Paul Wehman,
Marcia Datlow Smith, & Carol Schall © 2009 by Paul H. Brookes Publishing Co., Inc. All rights reserved.

I. Career outcomes

1. Long-term employment goal (may include integrated employment and supported employment):

    Yearly goals to accomplish long-term goal:

    Person(s) responsible for implementation:

2. Long-term vocational/technical training goal:

    Yearly goals to accomplish long-term goal:

    Person(s) responsible for implementation:

II. Postsecondary education and training outcomes

3. Long-term higher education goal:

    Yearly goals to accomplish long-term goal:

Person(s) responsible for implementation:

4. Long-term continuing and adult education, career/technical education goal (may include public or private technical school):

Yearly goals to accomplish long-term goal:

Person(s) responsible for implementation:

III.   Community, financial, self-determination, social, and life skills outcomes

5. Long-term residential goal:

Yearly goals to accomplish long-term goal:

Person(s) responsible for implementation:

6. Long-term transportation/mobility goal:

Yearly goals to accomplish long-term goal:

Person(s) responsible for implementation:

7. Long-term financial/income needs goal:

Yearly goals to accomplish long-term goal:

Person(s) responsible for implementation:

8. Long-term self-determination goal:

Yearly goals to accomplish long-term goal:

Person(s) responsible for implementation:

9. Long-term social and communicative competence goal:

   Yearly goals to accomplish long-term goal:

   Person(s) responsible for implementation:

10. Health/safety goal:

    Yearly goals to accomplish long-term goal:

    Person(s) responsible for implementation:

Student's career preference:

Student's major transition needs:

Summary of performance

Student's name: _____

Disability: _____   Student's identification number: _____

Student's address: _____   Phone Number: _____

School's address: _____   Phone Number: _____

Postsecondary goals

Employment:

Education/training:

Independent living/community participation:

Current academic achievement *(include courses of study)*

Current functional performance

Recommendations for achieving postsecondary goals

Employment:

Education/training:

Independent living/community participation:

Figure A.5.   Summary of performance.

4

Meeting Transition Goals Through Inclusion

Carol Schall and Jennifer McFarland-Whisman

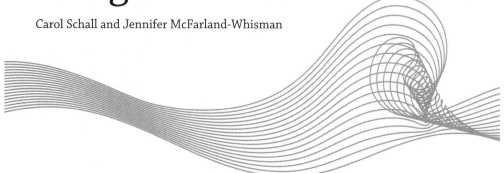

Many youth with autism have significant communication and social challenges. Like Jeff, Craig, and Maria, most students require direct instruction in communication and social interaction. They also need to learn from and with peers who do not have autism. In Chapter 3, you read about the decision made by Jeff's team to provide him with direct instruction in employment and social skills. Although Jeff is a bright student and ultimately plans to seek a college degree, he and his team recognize the importance of providing direct instruction in these very important life skills.

Unlike Jeff, Craig spends all of his time in a special education classroom, where his team has been able to decrease his challenging behavior and increase his work skills. Craig seems safe in this environment, but it will not result in his learning the social and communication skills he needs to be successful in the job market. As his team members attempt to implement his person-centered plan, it is painfully obvious that to be able to work in the community, Craig must learn to interact with people without disabilities now, while he is still in high school. Jeff, although at the other end of the autism spectrum, risks the same outcome: having job skills but not the social skills to be successful as an adult worker. Supported inclusion is therefore an important aspect of both young men's transition preparation. Because the ultimate goal for Jeff, Craig, and Maria is full inclusion in community-based living and work environments, it is very important to increase inclusion wherever feasible while meeting their individual direct instruction needs.

INCLUSION AND AUTISM

Goals and Objectives for Inclusion

Inclusion is the practice of placing individuals with disabilities into classroom and community settings and situations with their peers without disabilities. This is a very important aspect of education for individuals with ASD. Inclusive experiences enable individuals with ASD to learn social and communication skills with other students in the very place they will use these skills. In inclusive classrooms and settings with their peers, students with autism experience the same sort of preparation for life after high school that students without autism experience. Thus, through inclusive experiences, a team is able to address the most difficult aspects of autism, the two areas students with autism need to work on to make the most of their postsecondary life: social and communication skills. For individuals with autism, the objectives of inclusion are to

1. Help students gain the knowledge and skills taught in the general education classes

2. Provide peer models for communication

3. Provide skilled peers to practice new communication skills with and receive guidance from peers and adults about communication

4. Provide peer models for social interaction

5. Provide skilled peers to practice new social skills with and receive guidance from peers and adults about social interaction

6. Provide opportunities for natural friendships to occur

7. Foster independence and self-determination

8. Provide opportunities to become members of the school community

When students with autism go to class and interact with peers without disabilities, they have much to gain that will enrich their lives and give them opportunities to learn new skills (Harrower & Dunlap, 2001). Judging from the objectives of inclusion, Jeff, Craig, and Maria have not had successful inclusive experiences. Jeff's social skills are not improving, and he has not increased his level of self-determination. Craig has never had a chance to reap the benefits of interaction with peers without disabilities. Maria has had some inclusive experiences, but the focus of those experiences has been to address her educational needs, not to increase her participation in the school community. It is very important that the teams for these three students identify the goals and objectives the students will meet through inclusion and communicate those goals with all teachers who will teach them. This is particularly important because Jeff, Craig, and Maria are getting ready to make the transition from school to adult life. Without these essential

Table 4.1.   Inclusion goals and objectives for Jeff, Craig, and Maria

Student	Jeff	Craig	Maria
Goals	Jeff will learn the social skills necessary to establish and maintain positive social interaction with peers and teachers by receiving a rating of 90% or higher on the objectives listed below.	Craig will receive a rating of 80% or higher on his projects and on objectives listed below.	Maria will improve her social and computer skills and receive a rating of 90% or higher on the objectives listed below.
Objectives	Jeff will ask for clarification from a teacher or peer when he does not understand assignments. When given social scenarios and a list of statements, Jeff will identify socially inappropriate statements and socially sensitive statements. Jeff will increase the number of socially sensitive statements he makes in class. Jeff will join activities with peers in small groups and complete assigned projects with their input. Jeff will ask for assistance and direct instruction when he identifies conflict within small groups in inclusive settings. Jeff will contribute to the community of his classes by identifying ways he can help individuals in the class or the class as a group.	Craig will prepare visual reports on selected classroom topics. Craig will answer questions using an augmentative device in all inclusive environments. Craig will ask for help using his augmentative device. Craig will contribute to group projects by gathering necessary equipment and materials. Craig will greet his peers. Craig will complete at least one project and master at least one concept per lesson. Craig will follow two-step directions as part of the classroom routine.	Maria will position the paper in the printer and refill it when it runs out of paper. Maria will touch-type letters, numbers, words, sentences, and paragraphs using the QWERTY keyboard, including standard punctuation, with 90% accuracy. Maria will type at 40 words per minute when provided with a visual sample of information. Maria will name, save, spell-check, and correct her files with 90% independence. Maria will set up and save her work in two or more organizational folders on a flash drive with 90% independence. Maria will ask for help when she encounters a problem with her computer or word processing program.

skills and experiences, they will leave school without the necessary abilities to network with peers. Table 4.1 shows the inclusion goals and objectives for Jeff, Craig, and Maria.

As vital as inclusion is, providing it without meeting the individual needs of the person with autism is not a sound educational practice. It is important, then, to identify the individualized goals of an inclusive experience for each person and to ensure that each person's vision for his or her future is addressed in the everyday experiences in school. A successful inclusive experience is one in which the individual with autism

- Acquires the necessary knowledge and skill from the class

- Improves communication

- Improves social interactions

- Interacts with others in the context of the inclusive experience

- Makes informed choices in the inclusive environment

- Is a member of the classroom community

Through careful planning and collaboration, general and special education teachers can meet the needs of students with autism in inclusive settings while optimizing learning for all students. The student and the IEP team must consider the impact of the disability and prepare both the environment and the student for inclusion.

Impact of Autism in Inclusive Environments

Students with autism experience many benefits from learning in inclusive settings. For example, individuals who are included receive greater social support from their peers and have a higher level of engagement in educational activities than students who are in self-contained settings (Harrower & Dunlap, 2001; Simpson, de Boer-Ott, & Smith-Myles, 2003). Students with autism and severe intellectual disabilities frequently have more advanced IEP goals and make significantly greater gains in independence and social interaction than students who receive their special education services in self-contained settings (Fisher & Meyer, 2002). Students who are included and have social support also have a larger circle of friends than those who are in self-contained settings (Ochs, Kremer-Sadlik, Solomon, & Sirota, 2001; Paul, 2003). These benefits make transition into postsecondary education, the workforce, and the community easier for students with autism. Although these outcomes are impressive and desired, they do not occur simply because the student with autism is present in a general education setting. Such outcomes require careful planning, monitoring, and implementation. When considering an inclusive experience, teams must understand the impact of autism and plan to address that impact in the inclusive setting in a proactive way.

Some of the challenges faced by students with autism in inclusive settings include difficulty adjusting to new people, environments, and activities; communicating effectively; and interacting with others in formal and informal ways. They may also display challenges related to sensory sensitivities, sequencing tasks, and organization of materials (Janzen, 2003; Prelock, 2006; Scott et al., 2000; Siegel, 2003). Navigating these challenges prepares students for transitions that will occur as they move to postsecondary education, the workforce, and the community. Transition IEP team members play a key role in monitoring how students with autism adjust to the people, routines, and settings in the inclusive classroom. Discovering the reasons for a student's negative reaction to change in the inclusive school setting can help the team target how to make future transitions go more smoothly, which will help the student live a more inclusive life outside of the secondary school setting.

Jeff's challenges related to Asperger's syndrome were most apparent in his social studies and English classes. The social studies teacher frequently asked the class to move between a textbook, newspaper and newsmagazine articles, other books, and the students' notebooks to take notes, find information, and discuss current events. Jeff seemed to be several steps behind the rest of the class when making transitions between these materials and keeping up with his notes. When he was behind, or lost, he frequently shouted out rude comments in frustration. In English class, Jeff could easily identify details in the books the class was reading,

but he had more difficulty inferring meaning and discussing themes within literature. He was not at all shy when disagreeing with other students and frequently
called their ideas stupid.

As Craig had never been in an inclusive classroom, his team was unsure how
he might react to the situation. Team members worried that he would not be able
to keep up with the pace and that his sensory sensitivities might lead to challenging behaviors. For example, they worried that the movement of students in inclusive classrooms might disturb Craig's sense of order and his desire to maintain a
stable environment. They also worried about how the general educators would
communicate with Craig. Despite these concerns, they ultimately decided that it
was in Craig's best interest to pursue an inclusive class for him.

Maria had difficulty making the transition from her special education classes
to her inclusive classes. She relied on a one-to-one paraprofessional to walk her to
and from class and would not go to class without the paraprofessional next to her.
Even as she became more independent in the classes, she would not go unless the
paraprofessional accompanied her. She also refrained from any interaction with
other students. When one of her peers in a typing class asked her what page they
were on, Maria giggled and looked away from the student.

STRATEGIES TO SUPPORT SUCCESSFUL INCLUSION

As noted, successful inclusive experiences are dependent on thoughtful planning
and implementation. Every aspect of inclusion must be considered and discussed
regularly among team members. It is particularly important to consider the best
environment for inclusion, how to balance direct instruction and inclusion, how to
foster open communication among team members, and how to implement classroom strategies and supports to increase students' independence in the environment. These topics are discussed in the following sections.

Selecting the Best Environments for Inclusive Experiences

Traditionally, individuals with severe disabilities have been included in classes
such as physical education, art, or music. These classes do not necessarily offer the
best opportunities for inclusion, particularly for students with autism. Classes
such as these are characterized by less structure and more noise and movement
than academic or vocational classes, and they frequently involve many transitions.
For example, middle and high school gymnasiums often have squeaky floors,
noisy crowds, and unpleasant smells from sweat. Students with autism might
resist or be overwhelmed by these sensory experiences. Placing students with
autism in these environments without taking into account individual needs may
be counterproductive and result in a negative experience for all—the students with
autism, teachers, staff, and peers. Inclusive placements should be carefully considered and individualized to capitalize on a student's strengths and abilities.

Inclusive experiences result in the most growth when they are carefully
planned to coordinate with the student's transition IEP. Adolescents with autism
should go into inclusive environments to develop skills that increase their independence and self-determination and move them closer to their personalized
goals, as described in Chapter 3. For example, Maria is in an inclusive computer/

Table 4.2.   Questions to consider when selecting an inclusive environment

Will this class result in skills the person needs to achieve his or her personal goals as identified in the person-centered transition plan?

Is this environment a match with the person's sensory, visual structure, and organizational needs? If not, can you alter the environment to meet this person's needs?

Are the teachers in the environment flexible in their expectations? Will you be able to modify the content and assignments so that the person with autism will have meaningful instruction, be able to demonstrate what he or she has learned, and access the material fairly?

Are you able to provide supports in this environment to match the person's needs?

Will the person need greater access to an adult in this environment? If so, what training does the adult need that will enable him or her to offer the appropriate amount of adult support?

Do the peers in this environment need instruction about inclusion or any other special information? If so, what is needed, and how and when will you meet their needs for information?

Do all of the adults who are a part of the inclusive experience communicate well? Do they have ways to communicate effectively and efficiently to ensure the person's success?

Do team members have the information they need to support this inclusive experience? If not, who else does the team need to make this experience successful?

typing class not only because she is interested in typing and the class is relatively inclusive friendly but also because she wants to someday work in an office setting. In an office she will work with computers and people without disabilities, so it is beneficial to her to take a class in high school that provides this same environment. Table 4.2 lists some criteria that should be considered when selecting an inclusive experience for a student with autism.

Balancing Inclusion and Direct, Specialized Instruction

As mentioned previously, determining a student's level of participation in inclusive settings should be individualized. Inclusion will not look the same for every person. It is important to have a balance between inclusive experiences and the direct, specialized instruction that a person might need to accomplish specific goals set by the team, the person, or the person's family. In addition, inclusion for students like Craig may look different from elementary school to middle school to high school. His inclusive experiences might be centered on his interests. Because Craig has an interest in putting things together, he might take an industrial arts class with his peers at the vocational/technical center in his school district. As he ages, his inclusive experiences might shift from the school building to the community, where he might have an internship at a local business. Maria has expressed an interest in typing and going to the AVE program at the local community college. She needs inclusive experiences to prepare her for community college classrooms and classwork. Jeff, on the other hand, has already had a fair amount of inclusive experiences, and he is prepared for postsecondary education as far as completing schoolwork with minimal accommodations. He still has difficulty controlling his temper, however, so his team has determined that what he needs now is direct instruction to acquire proper social skills, and the team would like him to practice these skills in inclusive settings.

To balance inclusion and direct, specialized instruction, adults must be available to facilitate social interaction and provide direct instruction when needed. Students with autism need the Goldilocks Rule of adult support—that is, *not too much* adult support (in which case the adult hovers over the student and does not allow for independence); *not too little* adult support (the student makes mistakes without learning from them); but the *just right* amount of adult support so that the student receives instruction when needed and has enough independence to learn the necessary social skills.

For Jeff, the Goldilocks Rule of adult support resulted in his speech therapist increasing her time with Jeff during his inclusive classes and decreasing her one-to-one sessions with him during study hall. Initially, she was providing 60 minutes per week of speech therapy, divided into two sessions during study hall. When she began delivering services in Jeff's inclusive classes, she provided more coaching in his English and social studies classes because these classes used small-group instruction and large-group discussion. Jeff was more prone to making social errors in these classes than in his math and science classes, where the teachers relied more on lecture and individual projects. The speech therapist mostly provided direct instruction during the classes. She developed hand gestures to cue Jeff to talk less, change the way he said something, or stop to listen to the others in his group.

The speech therapist also developed some checklists and "dictionaries" that she uploaded to Jeff's personal digital assistant (PDA) to remind him the rules of conversation on which they were working. Figure 4.1 shows an example of one of these dictionaries. The therapist found the PDA checklists and reminders to be helpful because she could pull up the screen in Jeff's inclusive classes without drawing a lot of attention to her direct instruction. She also met with Jeff twice per month in study hall to discuss his progress on his objectives and to help him practice new social skills to use in his classes.

Maria experienced very successful inclusive experiences that focused on increasing her independence in going to and from class and completing class assign-

Jeff, if you see any of these kinds of faces
on the person you are speaking to:

Stop what you are saying!
Ask, "I'm sorry, did I say something wrong?"
Listen to the answer.
Change what you are talking about.
Pick one of your safe topics.
Excuse yourself from the conversation.
Remember to tell me (your speech therapist) about the interaction.

Safe topics:
Say 2 things you like about the person.
Say 2 things you like about the class you are in.
Say 2 things about the weather.

Figure 4.1.   Jeff's facial expressions dictionary uploaded to his personal digital assistant (PDA).

ments in her typing and reading classes. These experiences will prepare Maria to be successful in an administrative job, where she will be expected to complete assignments independently and conduct work, such as filing, in different areas or departments of an office building. The biggest challenge her team faced was developing a plan to decrease the paraprofessional's tendency to hover over Maria in her classes and to increase Maria's interaction with other students. They accomplished this by pairing her with a peer helper during her transitions and seating her near this person during class. Thus, team members were able to meet the Goldilocks Rule by substituting a peer for a paraprofessional.

For Craig, the Goldilocks Rule of adult support resulted in the placement of a paraprofessional with him in his industrial arts class. The paraprofessional was not assigned to Craig only; he also assisted other students. Prior to being placed in this class, the paraprofessional learned about Craig and a few other students who needed support in the classroom. He learned about Craig's augmentative communication system and how to modify assignments so that Craig could complete them with his communication system or by using pictures. With assistance from a supervising teacher, the paraprofessional consulted with the special education teacher to simplify tests for Craig so that Craig had fewer questions to answer and could answer them with his communication device. The paraprofessional also brought materials to Craig's special education teacher to be modified so that others could communicate with Craig through pictures and words. Figure 4.2 shows an example of a picture sequence the paraprofessional used to teach Craig how to clean up his area after using the industrial arts equipment.

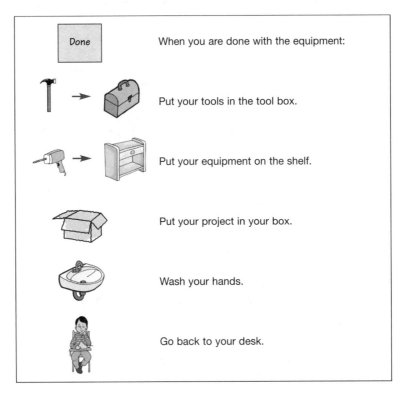

Figure 4.2.   Craig's picture schedule explaining how to clean up after he uses the industrial arts equipment.

The paraprofessional's success with the picture sequence was in large part because the special education teacher, the industrial arts teacher, the paraprofessional, and Craig's parents developed clear communication about the goals for the inclusive experience and ways to achieve those goals. Craig benefited by being in this inclusive setting because his ability to communicate with his industrial arts teacher and other students in the class gave him confidence that he rarely experienced outside of his special education classroom.

Fostering Open Communication Among Team Members

We cannot understate the contribution of communication to the success or failure of an inclusive experience. As Jeff's, Craig's, and Maria's stories illustrate, communication and collaboration between special and general education teachers—as well as with parents—are key for setting up successful inclusion experiences that will enable students to learn, gain confidence, and succeed in any postsecondary environment. If Craig's team does not know his interests or goals for the future, team members might place him in a class that does not address his interests and that will possibly be boring for him. If the special educator does not know how Craig is responding to the supports provided in the industrial arts classroom, she will not be able to help the paraprofessional modify the instruction or materials to make Craig's experience a successful one. If the industrial arts teacher does not understand why Craig is in his class or what expectations he should have for Craig, he is likely to provide assignments that are either too easy or too hard for Craig. Craig's reaction to either of these scenarios might cause the industrial arts teacher to become frustrated at having Craig in his classroom. If the paraprofessional does not know how best to modify the environment and assignments for Craig, Craig is likely to become frustrated or bored. All of these situations may result in difficult behavior that could lead Craig's team to conclude that inclusion, rather than lack of communication, was the reason the experience was not successful. This situation would result in dramatically different outcomes for Craig. To ensure positive outcomes, Craig's team must communicate in efficient and effective ways so that they can plan for success.

Figure 4.3 shows a simple participation checklist that Craig's team used to document any difficulties he experienced in the inclusive environment so that they could be shared with all team members and addressed early on. This form was completed daily by the paraprofessional and shared with Craig's general education teacher and special education teacher. At one point, when the industrial arts class was completing a lot of classroom lecture and not working in the shop, the paraprofessional noted that he did not know how to modify the materials and Craig was becoming loud and distracting. Craig's special education teacher observed in the classroom and made some targeted modifications to the materials. These held Craig's attention, and his behavior improved. The team also made accommodations so that Craig could work in the shop to practice using the equipment he was learning about in the classroom. These changes made the class a much more enriching and successful experience for Craig.

Because Maria's team was working to increase her independence in the inclusive classroom, they had to develop a way for her general educator to effectively but quickly communicate Maria's successes and needs to her special educator. Maria's special educator modified the form used by Craig's team to make commu-

Week of: _____ September 15 _____

Class: _____ Industrial Arts _____

Time: _____ 8:00–9:30 A.M. _____

Teacher: _____ Mr. Hughes _____

Paraprofessional: _____ Mr. Thomas _____

Type of class

1 = Lecture

2 = Interactive whole-class discussion

3 = Activities in groups with peers

4 = One-to-one modified instruction from paraprofessional

Level of participation

0 = Left class because of behavior challenge

1 = Remained in class but unable to participate because of behavior; made a lot of noise; distracted other students

2 = Distracted but on task; made noises but returned to task once directed by paraprofessional; completed work with a lot of prompting from paraprofessional

3 = On task; completed work with minimal assistance from paraprofessional; generally quiet

Date	Type of class	Level of participation
9/15	2	2
9/16	3	3
9/17	1	1
9/18	1	1
9/19	3	3

Figure 4.3.   Craig's daily class participation checklist.

nication more effective and efficient for the general educator. Figure 4.4 shows the weekly communication form Maria's team developed.

By using this checklist, Maria's special education teacher was able to help the typing teacher develop strategies for increasing Maria's independence and peer interaction. Initially, Maria was shy about asking for help from the paraprofessional. When she encountered a problem or question, she would simply stop her work and pull out a notepad to draw. Maria's special education teacher gave her typing teacher feedback on how to redirect Maria and encourage her to ask the paraprofessional for help. Over time, Maria not only learned to ask the paraprofessional for help, but she also began to ask questions of the students sitting around her. Instead of not asking questions, and therefore not completing her work, Maria learned how to surmount obstacles by asking for help and continuing her work. In this situation, team communication led to strategies that will help prepare Maria for requesting help from peers in classes she will take at the community college and in an office setting.

Month(s): _____September–October_____

Time: _____10:00–11:30 A.M._____

Class: _____Typing_____

Teacher: _____Ms. Schlicker_____

Paraprofessional: _____Mrs. McLeod_____

Level of independence

1 = Required frequent adult prompting to complete most transitions and tasks

2 = Required minimal adult prompting to complete most transitions and tasks

3 = Required peer support to complete most transitions and tasks

4 = Completed most transitions and tasks independently

Level of interaction

0 = Did not respond to interaction attempts from teacher or peers

1 = Responded to interaction from teacher but not peers

2 = Responded to but did not initiate interaction with teacher or peers

3 = Responded to and initiated interaction with teacher but not with peers

4 = Responded to and initiated interaction with teacher and peers

Date	Independence	Interaction
9/15	1	2
9/22	2	2
9/29	2	3
10/6	3	2
10/13	3	3

Figure 4.4. Maria's weekly independence and interaction checklist.

Implementing Classroom Strategies and Supports to Increase Students' Independence

Independence in an inclusive school environment is a skill that will prepare students with autism to be independent in postsecondary education, work, or community settings. Following are specific accommodations and modifications that increase the success and independence of students with autism in inclusive settings.

Minimizing Sensory Irritants

As mentioned previously, many students with autism have sensory issues that directly, and often negatively, affect their inclusive experience. Students may find particular sensory stimulation to be not only irritating but also painful and disruptive to their ability to learn and participate in typical activities. For example, Jeff is uncomfortable around fluorescent lighting and often cannot concentrate on what others are saying under such lighting conditions. Craig has difficulty with the clicking noise made by the heat register when it comes on, and he becomes extremely anxious when the bell rings between classes. Maria requires a large personal space and does not like to be touched or bumped by others. Although Jeff, Craig, and Maria have the potential to benefit from their inclusive experiences, they will not be able to maximize their experience if these environmental issues are not addressed.

As you can see, Jeff, Craig, and Maria have different sensory issues that need to be addressed individually. Each student with autism will respond to sensory input differently. The team needs to be aware of each individual's sensory issues and any accommodations or adaptations that will assist the individual in fully participating in inclusive experiences. This means gathering information about how the individual responds to various sights, sounds, smells, levels of touch, and textures. The best way to gather such information is to ask the individual, parents, teachers, and support staff who know the individual well.

Modifying a classroom environment to address sensory issues is often a complicated and difficult task. Many schools are unprepared or unable to make widespread environmental changes (e.g., changing all the lighting in a school building to incandescent, changing the heating system). Simple adaptations and accommodations, though, can lessen the impact of sensory issues on the student with autism. When accommodations for sensory issues are being considered, three key questions apply:

1. *Can the source of the sensory input be eliminated or avoided?* For example, avoid placing a student who gags at the smell of certain foods in a cooking class or in the cafeteria when these foods are being prepared.

2. *Can the source of sensory input be modified?* For example, reduce the amount of material posted on a classroom wall for a student who has difficulty with excessive visual stimulation.

3. *Can the student be taught a new response?* For example, teach the student to recognize the problem and ask to leave the area.

To address Jeff's difficulty with fluorescent lighting, his team might consider incandescent lighting when feasible or allow him to wear a baseball cap or light sunglasses in class. In Craig's case, he could have access to headphones or a CD player to block out the clicking sound of the heat register and bell. He could also be taught to ask (through his augmentative communication system) to take a break and leave the room if the noise becomes too irritating, or he could be seated as far from the register as possible. To accommodate Maria's need for more personal space, her team might consider allowing more space between desks, enrolling her in smaller classes with fewer students, and dismissing her from class 5 minutes early so that she avoids a crowded hallway. They can also teach Maria to back away slightly from others if they invade her space.

Taking the time to make adaptations and accommodations for students' sensory issues will benefit everyone involved. Teachers will be able to focus on teaching rather than on dealing with problems that occur when sensory issues are not addressed. Students with autism will be better able to learn and participate in inclusive settings, and their skills at managing potentially irritating sensory stimulants, or being able to identify them to others, will prepare them to navigate future environments that contain these irritants.

Providing Visual Supports

All people learn differently—some learn aurally, others visually, others through hands-on experiences. Most typically developing students learn through some combination of these modes. Most, but not all, individuals with autism learn best visually and through hands-on experiences. Unfortunately for these students, the school day is typically filled with verbal input. In traditional lecture-style teaching, for instance, most lessons are delivered verbally. Students are also provided with verbal directions and expectations throughout the day (e.g., "Get out your text-book and turn to page 72"). Such instruction is difficult for many students with autism, who may have a heightened sensitivity to auditory input that interferes with their ability to understand spoken language completely.

Providing supplemental visual supports can help students with autism better understand classroom content and routines. Many students, for instance, benefit from having a visual schedule of their day. The format of the schedule should be individualized; students might use a picture schedule or a written schedule. As students enter middle and high school, they should use more complex, socially appropriate scheduling systems. Rather than post picture or written schedules on the wall, for instance, teams might place them in a student's binder or agenda. Teams might also teach the student to use a PDA or other electronic scheduling device. If possible, students should be taught to arrange their own daily schedule and independently check it throughout the day. Teachers may be responsible for notifying a student or modifying the schedule should a schedule change occur on any particular day (e.g., early release or a pep rally).

Sometimes it is beneficial for students with autism to have access to mini-schedules or checklists that depict specific classroom routines or assignments. For example, Jeff occasionally forgets to do his daily "bell-ringer assignment" in his first-period class, which he is supposed to work on at the beginning of class. His teacher developed a checklist of each step of the activity for Jeff to follow on an index card, laminated it, and placed it on the first page of his agenda book. Now Jeff comes to class and completes the bell-ringer assignment without prompting. Minischedules also can be constructed from pictures, as they are for Craig; he uses his to help him put away materials in his industrial arts class (see Figure 4.2).

Students who have difficulty understanding when tasks will begin and end benefit from visual supports that provide this information. Although teachers can refer to the classroom clock to tell students approximately how long they will have to work on lessons; some students with autism benefit from having an individual, visual timer. One brand is called a Time Timer; these visual timers can be purchased at http://www.timetimer.com and include individual desktop, electronic, and wristwatch versions. Maria has difficulty reading silently for long periods of time, so her reading teacher has her set the Time Timer wristwatch for the amount of time Maria is expected to read.

Some students benefit from a visual representation of what they are working for and how many activities they have to complete before they are finished. Before his reading class begins, Craig chooses a picture card of what he is working for, such as a puzzle, and attaches it to a Velcro strip. The paraprofessional attaches four tokens to the strip, showing Craig that he must complete four activities before he can work on the puzzle. This system is illustrated in Figure 4.5.

The presentation of curricular content can also be enhanced through the use of visuals. Many students with autism respond well to lectures that are supple-

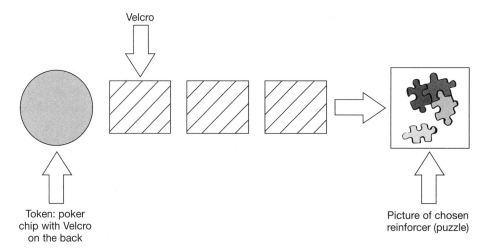

Velcro

Token: poker
chip with Velcro
on the back

Picture of chosen
reinforcer (puzzle)

Figure 4.5.   Craig's token board. The number of tokens indicates how many activities Craig must complete before obtaining his reinforcer.

mented with PowerPoint presentations, videotapes, pictures, or overhead transparencies to outline key points. Graphic organizers such as Venn diagrams and word webs can assist students in understanding concepts, particularly abstract concepts and the relationships among concepts. Graphic organizers can also help students organize their thoughts and ideas for writing papers.

Structuring Tasks and Classroom Routines

As is true for most people, individuals with autism learn best when expectations are clear, materials are prepared ahead of time and organized, and classroom routines are structured. A cluttered, unorganized classroom, expectations that are unclear or inconsistently followed, and ever-changing classroom routines will make learning in an inclusive environment difficult if not impossible for a student with autism.

From the beginning of the school year, classroom rules and expectations should be provided to students and consistently reinforced and enforced. Conveying a few key expectations clearly and in a manner consistent with a student's needs and abilities will help the student behave in an appropriate way. For some, this means having visual supports (e.g., pictures, videotapes, checklists). For example, Craig requires a good deal of visual support, role play, and reminders to understand the safety rules in his industrial arts class. His team provides pictures of the rules (e.g., always wear your safety glasses during projects), role-plays necessary steps (e.g., practicing putting on the safety glasses), and provides verbal and visual reminders (e.g., a picture of his safety glasses is placed on his schedule when the class is about to start a project, the paraprofessional prompts Craig to put on his safety glasses when he forgets). Jeff needs classroom expectations written down and occasionally requires a verbal or visual (e.g., written on a sticky note) reminder from his teachers. Maria requires visual routines to assist her in asking for help and in responding to other students when they ask her questions.

Daily lessons should be prepared ahead of time, and materials should be organized and easily accessible. Labeling the location of materials and organizing materials in cabinets, bins, or clear plastic shoeboxes can help students find and return materials independently. File folders and file cabinets can be used to organize written materials. Many students with autism respond well to color-coded organization systems. For example, a red file folder might be used for all work turned in to the teacher, and a blue file folder might contain written materials for the class to use for that day's lesson.

Considering Other Environmental Issues

The layout of the classroom can indicate the way in which various spaces are to be used. Group activities can be conducted at tables; desks can be used for quiet, individual activities. An area for quiet study time can provide students with autism the opportunity to move to a different part of the classroom if they find noise or movement distracting or if they just need time alone.

Providing space for movement also can be helpful for students with autism who have difficulty paying attention for long periods of time. For example, Craig has difficulty sitting for more than 15 minutes. Some of his teachers provide him with space, marked off by masking tape, to pace at the back of the room. Other teachers, who are not able to provide similar space, allow Craig to run an errand, get a drink, or sharpen his pencil when he needs to move.

Students with autism may need a quiet place to relax or get away when they feel overstimulated or overwhelmed. If not provided with a place to cool down, some students will become overly anxious, engage in challenging behavior, and become disruptive in the classroom. Providing calming activities and materials in a designated area will help students relax and return to class. For example, beanbag chairs and calming music might be provided. This space could be located at the back of the classroom, in a corner of the library, or in a special education room. Some schools have set up specially designed rooms with calming sensory materials. These rooms often contain relaxing chairs, lava lamps, and calming music and lighting. Maria's school has such a room. When she becomes overwhelmed, she asks to go to her quiet room where she can listen to music or page through a magazine. This room is located in one of the small prep rooms just off the stage in the auditorium. Because it is only occupied during assemblies and plays, it is available at most other times of the day.

Providing Behavior Supports

A major obstacle to successful inclusion for students with autism is challenging behaviors. Whereas learning issues and environmental issues can generally be accommodated, challenging behavior can be more daunting. If Jeff curses at his teacher, if Craig becomes upset and starts to bang his head against the wall, or if Maria launches loudly into a recitation of *Finding Nemo* during a class lecture, the continuation of the inclusive experience can be threatened.

If a student engages in challenging behavior that could disrupt the peace of the classroom or threaten the safety of the student or others, behavior supports should be put into place. Although the goal of such behavior supports is the prevention of behavioral outbursts, the behavior support plan must include procedures for dealing with these behaviors when preventions fail.

Chapter 2 provided extensive coverage of behavior support plans, including specific plans for Jeff, Craig, and Maria. Inclusion planning should include a careful review of behavior support planning and adaptations of the behavior support plan for the inclusive environment. Teams must decide which behavior supports are needed in the inclusive environment and who will be responsible for providing them. Teachers, paraprofessionals, and other staff who will be involved in the inclusion process must be trained in a student's behavior supports and in their own role in providing those supports.

PULLING IT ALL TOGETHER

To be successfully included, Jeff, Craig, and Maria required careful selection of classes to match their person-centered transition plans; consideration of how to address their direct instruction needs in inclusive settings; increased communication across team members; and structured classroom supports, routines, and spaces. This level of support increased their independence, communication skills, social skills, and knowledge of the subjects they studied. The skills they learned in inclusive settings will help them make successful transitions from secondary school to postsecondary education, work, and the community.

5

Teaching Youth for Success

From Classroom to Community

Dawn R. Hendricks, Marcia Datlow Smith,
and Paul Wehman

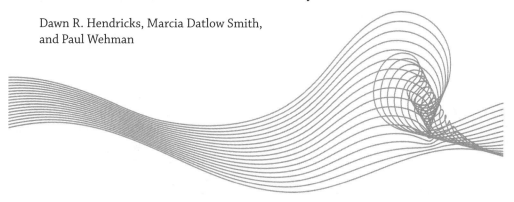

The previous two chapters contained discussions about planning and assessment for transition; how students with autism should be included in schools; and how collaboration among students, IEP and transition teams, teachers, and community members might occur, resulting in successful transitions for students. We now turn to how to teach skills that will help further integrate students with autism in the community, using systematic instruction.

Systematic instruction is the set of learning strategies and techniques that can empower young people with autism to be more competent and capable (e.g., Snell & Brown, 2006). These learning strategies need to be evidence based; that is, they need credible empirical research as a foundation. Systematic instruction is based on a plan, with changes and revisions made after a careful review of student progress. More is known today than ever before about how to help children and youth with autism learn (e.g., Kluth, 2003; Myles, Grossman, Aspy, Henry, & Coffin, 2007). Those students with more severe forms of autism, who years ago would have languished in state institutions or sat at home all day, and those students with milder forms of autism, who years ago would not have had the opportunity to participate in postsecondary education, now have the opportunity to learn and use skills that are essential for a good quality of life in postsecondary education, the workplace, recreation sites, home, and the community.

Teaching students with ASD, however, requires two major considerations. First, what skills are going to be taught (Collins, 2007)? Will they have meaning and be naturally occurring over time? Do they have relevance? To ensure relevance, work skills such as entering data, folding laundry, or stocking shelves should be taught in a work setting rather than in a school classroom. Shopping and money skills should be practiced with actual money in a drugstore, not with pretend money in a special education classroom. Students who intend to pursue postsecondary education can prepare by taking a community college class while in their last year of high school.

The second major consideration is how skills will be taught. In other words, which learning techniques and strategies are the most effective with students with autism? If the goal is to teach students specific skills to help them navigate specific situations, teams need to figure out the best way to teach these skills to each student. For example, teaching Jeff, who is verbal, to take the bus would require a different approach than teaching Craig, who is mostly nonverbal, how to ride the bus. If effective techniques are not used to teach competency in any type of functional skill, students with autism might not retain what was taught.

As noted in Chapter 2, young people with autism often present challenging behaviors that can interfere with learning, and this should be considered when planning to teach a student a specific skill. Only by finding ways to eliminate or manage challenging behaviors while teaching skills to a student will team members ensure that the student will learn and retain those skills. Given the learning and behavioral characteristics of youth with ASD, it is essential that students receive regular, frequent instruction in community settings if they are to make a successful transition to independence in their own communities. As students move through adolescence, in addition to inclusion experiences in school, teaching must occur in the community (Weiner & Zivolich, 2003). Community-based instruction provides genuine experiences and practice in participating in community settings. It also gives teachers an idea of how students will react to environments and situations outside of the classroom, which will help them teach their students to be successful in the community.

In this chapter, we approach teaching with these issues in mind. To know what to teach, teams must know what environments the students will be in (Brown & York, 1974). Hence, in the first half of this chapter we describe how community-based instruction services are best delivered (Dymond, 2004) and discuss typical types of community settings where teaching can occur. There is good evidence supporting functional community-based instruction as a strategy (Collins, 2007; Wehman & Kregel, 2004). In the second half of the chapter, we provide an overview of the basic instructional techniques that, when applied correctly and consistently in community settings, are successful with individuals with autism.

WHY SHOULD TEACHERS PROVIDE INSTRUCTION IN THE COMMUNITY?

In community-based instruction, educational objectives are taught in natural community environments, such as community college classes, worksites, shopping malls, and restaurants. Increasing numbers of educators are accepting that community-based instruction is best for implementing transition programs for young adults with autism (Dymond, 2004; Weiner & Zivolich, 2003). Whenever possible, instruction should be provided in the community where the student lives and in the businesses and other locations frequented by the student and his or her family, or in locations the student plans to frequent (e.g., community college). This will ensure that the student has opportunities to socialize in the community and learn skills that will be applicable to his or her natural environments.

A major advantage of community-based instruction is that it enables students with autism to generalize what they have learned. Students often do not carry over classroom instruction into the community, which makes instruction nonfunctional (Wehman, 2006). For example, Craig learned to take his wallet out of his pocket and remove a dollar bill in his classroom. When asked to remove his wallet in a store, however, he became confused and refused to do so. The skill taught in the classroom did not generalize to the store. It is beneficial, therefore, for students to be increasingly exposed to community-based training as they progress through school. The more difficulties displayed in skill transferal by an individual, the more he or she can benefit from instruction in the community environment, regardless of the type or severity of autism the student has.

A second advantage of community-based instruction is its functionality. Regardless of the student's disability or its severity, community-based training experiences appear to be the most functional. The skills taught at job sites are the very skills that will earn these future workers wages in community businesses.

It is recommended that teachers identify sites for community-based instruction for at least 50% of their curricula. These sites can encompass vocational or educational training, home living skills instruction, recreational instruction, and community skills development.

Creative teachers who understand that leaving the school grounds to go to community sites may not always be possible will identify sites and tasks on the school grounds that can approximate natural environments for students. Lessons in such settings should ideally begin when students are 10–13 years of age. Possible sites for work experience in school include the following:

- Main office
- Attendance office
- Library
- Audiovisual room
- Athletic office
- Teachers' workroom
- Nurse's office
- Counselor's office
- Cafeteria
- Physical plant and grounds

Dozens of tasks can be identified for experience and specific instruction at school sites. For example, students can enter attendance information or semester grades on a computer in the attendance office. In the main office, students can deliver faxes, photocopy documents, and serve as runners, delivering documents and messages to classrooms. They can even take telephone messages if they have the requisite communication skills. In the library, students can file check-out cards, put protective covers on new books, repair old book covers, and check in and reshelve books. In the nurse's office, students can enter health status information on the computer. In the multimedia room, they can maintain records and deliver audiovisual equipment to appropriate classrooms. Students can assist with cleaning and landscaping the grounds.

Maria participated in various administrative jobs at school for part of her day, including filing paperwork in the main office and typing postcards in the counselor's office. Behavioral observations, performance assessments, and situational assessments were completed for each of these jobs. Because these administrative jobs related to the type of work Maria hoped to do after community college, Maria's team was able to get more accurate feedback on her job performance and behavior in these environments than they were in classrooms teaching functional skills or in Maria's typing classes. Maria would ask the paraprofessional for help in her typing class, but when initially working in the counselor's office, Maria would freeze up if she encountered a problem. Teaching Maria to ask for help in a work environment was important because learning to ask for help in the classroom did not automatically translate to her work environment. Over time Maria learned to successfully ask for help when she encountered a problem in any of her school-based administrative jobs.

DESIGNING COMMUNITY-BASED WORK PROGRAMS FOR STUDENTS WITH AUTISM

To successfully implement any community-based instruction program, teams must make a philosophical commitment to the training. This commitment involves identifying specific program objectives and the target age and populations of students who will participate. From this identification process, team members can select different types of jobs, community activities, and resources for specific students. Potential training sites where initial contacts can be made with business owners or employers will then become apparent. Teams should visit these sites to determine whether a sufficient array of skills and activities could be acquired by a student. Once it appears that the site is appropriate, team members should be ready to negotiate to use the site for training. This usually entails writing a training agreement and asking the employer to sign it. School personnel should be familiar with U.S. Department of Labor laws pertaining to the hiring, training, and compensation of students, as well as any local laws that might pertain. These laws also need to be explained to employers. A detailed listing of the steps and activities involved in developing community-based training sites is provided in Table 5.1.

Conducting a Job-Market Analysis

Initially, school officials may want to identify a task force of teachers to develop procedures for completing a community job-market analysis (Pumpian, Shepard, & West, 1988). The task force may appoint the transition coordinator to complete business contacts, or a special education teacher at the secondary level may take the lead. In any case, a plan of action should be developed to prevent duplication of effort.

Table 5.1.   Steps and activities for developing a community-based vocational training program

Steps	Activities
1. Conduct a community job-market analysis.	1. Identify a school task force and/or individual(s) who will be responsible for completing the analysis. 2. Survey the telephone directory yellow pages. 3. Read the classified section of the newspaper. 4. Contact local business organizations (e.g., Chamber of Commerce). 5. Survey school graduates to determine jobs held by individuals with disabilities in the community. 6. Create a list of potential jobs, by job type, that are available to students with severe disabilities.

2. Identify businesses with the targeted jobs and contact the personnel director or community-based training sites and employer.	1. Establish a school policy for contacting employers/businesses.
	2. Identify school personnel responsible for business contacts.
	3. Review and revise (as needed) school insurance/liability policy to cover transportation.
	4. Outline school policy for meeting labor law regulations.
	5. Develop a contract for meeting the labor law requirements.
	6. Contact the business by letter and/or telephone.
	   a. Briefly describe the school's community-based program.
	   b. Discuss jobs that may be appropriate for training.
	   c. Schedule a time to visit and explain the program further.
	7. Visit the business in person.
	   a. Describe the purpose of vocational instruction.
	   b. Discuss the employer, teacher, and student responsibilities on the job site.
	   c. Explain the labor law regulations for nonpaid work experiences.
	   d. Discuss liability issues.
	   e. Develop a community-based training agreement.
	   f. Identify possible job tasks for training.
	   g. Schedule a time to observe the identified tasks to develop task analyses.
	   h. Send a thank-you note.
	8. Compile a file for each business visited.

3. Select and analyze appropriate jobs for community-based training.	1. Visit the job site. 2. Discuss the identified jobs with the site supervisor. 3. Discuss the job-site rules and regulations. 4. Observe the coworkers performing the job duties. 5. Select the tasks best suited for students with severe disabilities. 6. Develop a job duty schedule and task analyses for the activities selected. 7. Identify available times with the employer or department supervisor for training. 8. Request at least 1- to 2-hour blocks of time for each site identified. 9. Agree on a start date.

4. Schedule community-based training.	1. Identify students to receive vocational training.
	2. Hold individualized education program/individualized transition plan meetings for students.
	   a. Identify student training needs.
	   b. Discuss purpose of community-based vocational training with transition team members.
	   c. Write vocational goals/objectives.
	3. Match students to available sites.

(continued)

Table 5.1.   *(continued)*

Steps	Activities
4. Schedule community-based training. *(continued)*	4. Sign community-based training agreements (student, parent(s), employer, school representative).
	5. Develop a daily schedule.
	6. Develop a transportation schedule.
	7. Send a copy of the schedule to the school principal, special education supervisor, parents, employers, etc.
	8. Provide parents with information on individual insurance coverage for liability.
5. Design individual systematic instruction programs.	1. Modify job duty schedules and task analyses based on student characteristics.
	2. Select a data collection procedure.
	3. Take a baseline of student performance on all tasks to be taught.
	4. Select an instructional procedure.
	5. Select a reinforcer.
	6. Implement the training program.
	7. Take probe data on student performance.
	8. Routinely review student data and modify program format as needed.
	9. Review student goals and objectives for training and update as needed.

Note: From Inge, Wehman, and Dymond (2005). Community-Based Vocational Training. In *Intellectual and Developmental Disabilities: Toward Full Community Inclusion* (3rd Ed.) (p. 368–369), by P. Wehman, P.J. McLaughlin, and T. Wehman (Eds.), 2005, Austin, TX: PRO-ED. Copyright 2005 by PRO-ED, Inc. Reprinted with permission.

Once school personnel have been identified to complete the market analysis, they may begin by surveying their local chamber of commerce or economic development office, looking in the telephone directory, reading the newspaper want ads, interviewing potential employers, completing follow-up contacts with school graduates, and contacting adult service agencies and supported employment programs to determine job placements for individuals with disabilities. Teachers can also knock on the doors of local businesses to find out what they do and whether they might be potential job sites for students.

Matching Jobs

Once the local economy has been assessed to determine the possible job types for students with autism, team members must determine a student's interests, match these interests to available jobs, and decide where instruction before and during the job will occur. Each student should have the opportunity to experience a variety of jobs in a number of different settings to help the student develop a work history, continue to determine his or her job preferences, identify future training needs, and determine skill characteristics for future job matching.

Finding Appropriate Jobs for Community-Based Instruction

Jobs for students with autism must be selected based on the suitability of the tasks as well as the feasibility of the job setting. The challenge with students is not limited to teaching them the job tasks; challenges also lie in teaching them to adapt to the social demands of the worksite. Jobs must be chosen with a student's challenging behaviors in mind. For example, if a student talks excessively, it might be best to avoid job sites in which it is essential to work quietly. Because of the vast individual differences in youth with autism, as noted in Chapter 1, each student's challenges should be carefully matched to the needs of the workplace and its environment.

Setting Up a Community-Based Site

Often, the initial contact made with a business is with an employer or management-level individual who will not be able to specifically assist the teacher in identifying jobs for training. The teacher will be referred to a supervisor, who will be the actual contact person for community programming.

Activities for the teacher during this phase of setting up a community-based training site include observing the co-workers as they perform the job duties available, selecting tasks that would be appropriate for students, and actually working the selected job duties. A tentative schedule of the activities that the student(s) will be performing should be developed, as well as task analyses for skills targeted. Both the schedule and the task analyses may need modification once specific students are assigned to the worksite. The teacher should negotiate with the manager the times for the student(s) to be on site and a start date, and the teacher should also gain permission from the student's parent or guardian for the student's participation.

A training schedule needs to be developed that specifies days of the week and times that job training will occur at the various student worksites. Table 5.2 presents a schedule of student training at job sites. The instructor identified in the schedule provides job training to students each time they go to the job site.

Developing a Schedule of Job Duties

A job duty schedule outlines the specific work tasks students will perform as well as the time the tasks will be performed and productivity expectations. In addition to job duties, the teacher should determine if there are any special requirements the employer has for students on the job site. Questions such as the following should be asked:

- Does the employer/supervisor want the students to wear a uniform or specific clothing (e.g., white shirt with black pants)?

- Is it important that students report to the supervisor or to a co-worker upon arrival?

- Do employees have assigned lockers, and will students have one?

- Is there an identified break area and employee bathroom?

- Are there specific break times for employees?

- Are there any company benefits that may be available to students (e.g., free lunch or soda)?

- Are there any restricted (hazardous) areas or activities?

- Is there a company policy or procedure for reporting accidents on the job?

Table 5.2.   Student training schedule

Student	Location	Time	Instructor
October 22–December 7			
R.M.	Shoney's	7:30–9:15 A.M.	Curtis
J.G.	Shoney's	9:45–11:45 A.M.	Curtis
L.R.	Shoney's	12:45–2:45 P.M.	Curtis
M.L.	Hechingers	7:30–9:15 A.M.	Chris
G.A.	Hechingers	9:45–11:45 A.M.	Chris
H.R.	Hechingers	12:45–2:45 P.M.	Chris
C.S.	Howard Johnson's	9:45–11:45 A.M.	Stacy
P.P.	Howard Johnson's	12:45–2:45 P.M.	Stacy
December 10–January 8			
P.P.	Shoney's	7:30–9:15 A.M.	Stacy
J.A.	Howard Johnson's	9:45–11:45 A.M.	Stacy
H.R.	Howard Johnson's	7:30–9:15 A.M.	Curtis
M.L.	Howard Johnson's	12:45–2:45 P.M.	Curtis
L.R.	Hechingers	7:30–9:15 A.M.	Chris
R.M.	Hechingers	9:45–11:45 A.M.	Curtis
J.G.	Hechingers	12:45–2:45 P.M.	Chris
C.S.	Shoney's	9:45–11:45 A.M.	Chris
January 18–March 8			
J.A.	Shoney's	7:30–9:15 A.M.	Stacy
M.L.	Shoney's	9:45–11:45 A.M.	Chris
H.R.	Shoney's	12:45–2:45 P.M.	Chris
J.G.	Howard Johnson's	7:30–9:15 A.M.	Curtis
L.R.	Howard Johnson's	9:45–11:45 A.M.	Curtis
R.M.	Howard Johnson's	12:45–2:45 P.M.	Curtis
P.P.	Hechingers	9:45–11:45 A.M.	Stacy
C.S.	Hechingers	7:30–9:15 A.M.	Chris

Note: From Inge, Wehman, and Dymond (2005). Community-Based Vocational Training. In *Intellectual and Developmental Disabilities: Toward Full Community Inclusion* (3rd Ed.) (p. 377), by P. Wehman, P.J. McLaughlin, and T. Wehman (Eds.), 2005, Austin, TX: PRO-ED. Copyright 2005 by PRO-ED, Inc. Reprinted with permission.

All of this information should be recorded and placed in a file that can be accessed by all school personnel. Accessibility would be particularly important during teacher absences, when another school employee must supervise the site. Once all of the issues have been discussed, a written agreement should be worked out with the employer that includes students' duties, productivity requirements, hours, number of students placed there, rotation schedules, and other pertinent arrangements.

Writing a Task Analysis

The teacher should complete a thorough task analysis of each activity listed on the job duty schedule prior to bringing students to the worksite. He or she should observe other employees performing the task; identify each step that is completed; and perform the job, modifying the steps as necessary. Finally, the teacher should

Table 5.3.   Task analysis for rolling newspapers

1. Gather supplies: newspapers, rubber bands, plastic bags.
2. Lay the newspaper flat on the table with the fold facing the worker.
3. Grasp the folded edge of the newspaper.
4. Roll upward four complete rolls.
5. Holding the rolled paper in one hand, pick up a rubber band with the other hand.
6. Slide the rubber band halfway down the newspaper.
7. Place the rolled newspaper into the receptacle or bag.
8. Pick up the next newspaper and continue with Steps 2–7 until all newspapers are rolled.

Note: Task analysis contributed by Jan Miller Vogel, Director of Support Services, Community Services for Autistic Adults and Children (CSAAC), Montgomery Village, Maryland.

check with the supervisor to ensure that the teacher is performing the task as students will be expected to perform it.

Each step in a task analysis should consist of one observable behavior that can be taught individually. The steps should be worded in the second person so that they can be used as verbal prompts during instruction (e.g., "Roll the newspaper"), and they should refer to things that are observable (e.g., "Pick up the rubber band"). A good task analysis assists the teacher in organizing instruction, providing consistent training, and evaluating the student's performance.

Completing a job to production standards and in a timely manner often will be an issue with students with severe disabilities. For instance, students may continue to perform a step in a task even though it is not necessary (e.g., continuing to wipe the table long after it is clean, rolling a newspaper over and over). A task analysis can help eliminate this problem. For rolling newspapers, for instance, the teacher could write the task analysis to provide structure to the steps that the student is repeating (e.g., "Roll the newspaper four complete turns"). Most students with autism are visually alert and will quickly grasp the details of a task (e.g., how many revolutions to roll the newspaper); for them to do so, however, the task must be consistently presented, which a task analysis allows for. Table 5.3 shows a sample task analysis for rolling newspapers in preparation for delivery to customers.

Scheduling and Providing Transportation to Community-Based Instruction Sites

Creative use of school personnel to schedule and transport students for community-based instruction will clearly be the greatest challenge for administrators and team members working with students with severe disabilities. Staffing solutions include team teaching; use of volunteers, paraprofessionals, peer tutors, graduate students, and student teachers; heterogeneous grouping of students; staggered student training schedules; and integrated therapy services provided by support personnel. Transportation options may include using volunteers' and parents' cars with mileage reimbursement, coordinating training schedules with regular school bus schedules, using public transportation, using school district vehicles, and walking to sites within short distances. Using public transportation is especially encouraged, as this travel training provides additional life skills needed for transition.

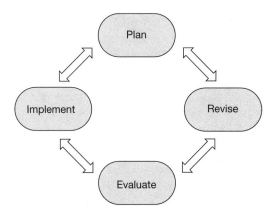

Figure 5.1.   Four-step instructional process.

DESIGNING AND IMPLEMENTING INSTRUCTION

Once community sites have been identified and a schedule for student placement determined, the teacher must design instructional programs outlining how each student will be taught the job and other related life skills. Included in the design should be 1) specific training objectives, 2) individualized task analyses, 3) data collection guidelines, 4) instructional strategies, and 5) reinforcement procedures. Instruction should include ongoing evaluation resulting in necessary program modifications that will lead to student success.

Because individuals with ASDs are a heterogeneous group, making implementation decisions is often a difficult task for educators; there is no single practice that is effective for all students. This requires educators to be knowledgeable of a range of practices (National Research Council, 2001). Instruction must be individualized and guided by the student's specific needs and characteristics. Educators have a responsibility to ensure that instruction is appropriate, effective, and results in continued learning. This requires critical evaluation, with ongoing modifications made as the student's needs change, progress is made, progress ceases, or problems arise. To provide effective instruction that results in sustained learning, educators should implement four steps: plan, implement, evaluate, and revise. See Figure 5.1 for a visual representation of this model. Note the double arrows in the figure, which indicate that an instructional plan may involve going back through the planning process as well as forward. For example, during implementation, a glitch might arise, requiring the instructor to return to the planning stage.

Plan the Instruction

Well-planned instruction is an essential component of any educational program. This is especially true for adolescents with autism. These students face critical time limitations for learning life skills required in adulthood. Instruction must be intensive and provide sufficient opportunities for practice, generalization, and maintenance of learned skills (Chin & Bernard-Opitz, 2000). This requires careful planning.

The student's goals and objectives should determine the specific target skill to be taught. As discussed in the first section of this chapter, a thorough task analysis, identifying each step of the target skill, must be completed prior to beginning instruction. Determining where and when instruction is delivered ensures that teaching conditions are optimal for learning. Whenever possible, instruction should be provided in natural community settings where the skill will be used and at a time the skill would naturally be performed. The time of day provides another motive for students, as learning can be maximized by teaching more difficult skills when the student is alert and focused and easier skills when the student may be fatigued.

A number of other factors must be considered when determining how to deliver instruction. The teacher must ensure that individual objectives can be effectively implemented. Instruction should provide sufficient opportunities for repeated practice and include both small- and large-group instruction and direct, one-to-one contact with teaching staff for adequate individualized attention. Because many adolescents with autism have difficulties generalizing the skills they learn, staff must consider carefully the person who will provide instruction and how materials will be used. It is not unusual for a student to successfully carry out a skill for one person or with one set of materials but not another. The teacher therefore needs to ensure that instruction is generalized across teachers and materials to the maximum extent possible.

Decisions for instructional delivery should be made on an individual basis. Results of ongoing program evaluations should influence instruction and direct needed modifications. Evaluation will be discussed in detail later in this chapter.

Consider Maria's desire to work in an office. As this will require good typing skills, her teacher outlined the steps for systematic instruction to improve Maria's typing and computer skills. Figure 5.2 presents the task analysis, teaching procedures, and evaluation methods used by Maria's teacher for these skills.

Implement Instruction

It is necessary to ensure that instruction is delivered where and how it was designed to be. Instructional practices have a better chance of being successful if they are implemented consistently and accurately. All individuals involved with a student's educational program—including paraprofessionals, related service providers, and of course the student's parents—must receive training to ensure quality implementation and precision of instruction.

The manner in which instruction is implemented is, again, dependent on the student and the learning techniques that have proven to be successful with the student. As described previously, most students with autism learn better by being shown how to do something and by trying it out themselves than by being told verbally how to do it. It is important to find out which instructional methods work for certain students; the manner of instruction may have to be modified from the way an employer typically teaches his or her employees to complete a task. For instance, when Craig began working at the pizza restaurant, the owner gave him only a verbal explanation for how to assemble the boxes. Craig became frustrated, which could have led him to have an outburst and potentially be fired from his job, but his teacher quickly stepped in and modeled how to assemble a box for him.

Student: *Maria*	Program: *Computer skills*

Target behavior

Maria will open a document in Microsoft Word, type a five-sentence paragraph by copying prepared text, proofread her work, correct errors, and save the document.

Task analysis

1. Maria will retrieve her work folder located in the classroom filing cabinet.
2. Maria will walk to her designated computer, sit down, take out the report found in the folder, and place the report on the desktop document stand.
3. Maria will open Windows Word by double-clicking the desktop icon.
4. Maria will name the document and save it by clicking on *File,* clicking on *Save As,* choosing *My Documents* from the drop-down menu, typing the name of the report in the window, and clicking on *Save.* The name of the document can be found at the top of the report in bold letters.
5. Maria will type the entire paragraph exactly as it is typed in the prepared report.
6. Maria will click on the *Save* button.
7. Maria will proofread her work and correct any errors.
8. Maria will click on the *Save* button.
9. Maria will close the document.
10. Maria will return the report in the folder to the filing cabinet.

Procedures

Setting: Typing class on Monday, Wednesday, and Friday, 9:00–10:30

Staff: Instructional assistant—Jordan

Materials: Computer station, desktop document stand, work folder containing report

Instructional opportunities: 3–4 opportunities per class

Instruction delivery: Task analysis using total task presentation

Prompting type: System of least prompts using the following prompts

- Specific verbal instruction
- Specific verbal instruction paired with gesture
- Partial physical guidance
- Full physical guidance

Consequence correct: Staff will provide verbal praise to Maria upon correct completion of each step. As independence increases, delivery of verbal reinforcement will be provided intermittently. Upon complete independence, a verbal reinforcer will be provided upon completion of the entire sequence.

Consequence incorrect: Staff will provide prompting using a system of least prompts.

Measurement

Criterion: The skill will be considered mastered when Maria completes the entire sequence with no prompts, typing the entire paragraph exactly as it is typed in the prepared report 4 out of 5 opportunities.

Data collection frequency: Data will be collected on the first and second trial of each class.

Data collection description:

- Record number of prompts delivered during the entire session.
- Record number of words typed correctly and the number of words typed incorrectly prior to Maria's proofing her work.

Teacher's initials: _____

Figure 5.2. Planning systematic instruction for Maria.

Evaluate Instruction

Once instruction is implemented, the teacher must conduct ongoing evaluation of the student's performance. Evaluating instruction is important because it not only demonstrates whether the student has made progress but also allows the educator to make objective decisions about the effectiveness of instruction. Without evaluation, ineffective instruction may continue for lengthy periods, resulting in a waste of the student's precious time. It is tempting to provide subjective thoughts and feelings about student progress; however, this results in poor decision making. Evaluation should involve objective data collection measures that allow for an accurate analysis of the student's performance.

The type of evaluation will vary depending on the student, the skill, and the instructor. Data collection methods can range from checklists to sophisticated computer analysis. Before data collection occurs, the following questions must be addressed:

- What behavior will be evaluated?
- Where will data collection occur?
- When and how often will data collection occur?
- What type of data collection will be used?

What Behavior Will Be Evaluated?

A primary component of data collection is a precise definition of the skill being taught. The definition should describe the skill based on observable behaviors or events. For example, Maria is to clean the kitchen after preparing a meal. This goal may evoke different images and meanings for different people. For one person, this may mean clearing the counters. For another, it may mean clearing the counters and washing the dishes. For another, it would involve clearing the counters, washing the dishes, and also drying the dishes and putting them away. The lack of a precise definition results in ambiguity for both teaching and student progress. With a clear definition, the student as well as the teacher will know the precise expectations for a behavior.

Where Will Data Collection Occur?

It is critical to ensure that the student is able to demonstrate the skill in the environment where it will be performed. This requires that data collection occur in the natural environment without being cumbersome, disruptive, or taking away from instructional time. Craig assembles pizza boxes at the local pizza restaurant. His teacher collects data at the job site two times per week. Jeff is learning to increase his ability to take turns during conversations. His main opportunities for conversation are with peers in the school cafeteria. His teacher records data during lunch, in the school cafeteria, when Jeff has an opportunity to interact with a number of classmates in a social environment.

When and How Often Will Data Collection Occur?

Data collection should begin prior to implementing instruction. A baseline measure indicates the student's level of performance prior to delivery of any instruction. This baseline is then compared with the student's performance after the implementation of instruction to determine its effectiveness.

As mentioned in Chapter 2, it is not necessary to collect data every time a skill is taught. Evaluation is an ongoing process that allows the educator to make objective decisions using data collected over time. Data may be collected on a sample basis. This requires setting up an unbiased system by collecting data at regular and planned intervals. For example, when Maria is working on cleaning up the kitchen, it is not always possible to take data, so her teacher has set up a system for collecting data three times per week.

What Type of Data Collection Will Be Used?

There are several basic ways to measure a given skill. The type of measure depends on the student, the skill to be evaluated, and the instructional setting. *Frequency data* provide the number of occurrences of the skill. While Craig is working on assembling pizza boxes, his educational team keeps a frequency count of the number of boxes he is able to put together in a 5-minute period. *Duration* is the amount of time it takes to complete a skill. Maria's educational team is keeping duration data on the amount of time it takes her to type a paragraph. *Latency* refers to the amount of time it takes for a person to respond to an instruction or a cue. Jeff's educational team is evaluating the latency between Jeff's supervisor at the video game store providing an instruction for Jeff to do something and Jeff actually beginning the task. *Quality* measures the condition of the skill. Maria is to greet classmates when arriving at lunch; however, she speaks in a soft voice that is difficult to hear, so her educational team has created a 5-point scale to rate the quality of her greetings.

During evaluation, the teacher should naturally look at the accuracy of the student's performance. Other considerations are equally important, however. The rate of student performance indicates whether the student is fluent with the skill. For instance, Maria has a goal to brush her teeth independently. If it takes her 10 minutes to complete the steps to do this, it will be necessary to alter instruction to help her perform this task at a faster rate. Factors that may impede performance include inattention due to physical discomfort, fatigue, overstimulation, or lack of reinforcers; presence of difficult behaviors; or instructor characteristics.

Revise Instruction

If the instructional method is flawed, accomplishing a goal is that much more difficult. For this reason, it is important to review and revise instruction based on the outcome of putting a taught skill into practice.

Maria has been learning how to manage her own money by practicing the skills involved in community settings. When Maria made a purchase, she was taught to write the amount of the purchase in a checkbook ledger. After a week of instruction, her teacher realized that the space provided in the ledger was too small for Maria to use neatly. As a result, the numbers were often illegible. Maria's teacher altered the instruction by replicating the ledger in a large spreadsheet. Although this change helped, yet another revision was soon needed. Maria's teacher found that Maria often made mistakes when entering the purchase amount. Her teacher felt that the community setting was too overstimulating and distracted Maria from doing this correctly. She altered instruction by having Maria collect her receipt after a purchase, place it in her purse, then enter the amount in the spread-sheet when she returned to school. These minor revisions in instruction allowed Maria to be successful and learn the skill in a timely manner.

INSTRUCTIONAL STRATEGIES: TEACHING, MAINTAINING, AND GENERALIZING NEW SKILLS

To adequately prepare for adulthood, individuals with autism will require instruction in a variety of areas. Instruction will likely be needed in academics, vocational exploration and training, hygiene, personal management, community-based life skills, and recreation and leisure. To further complicate the situation, manifestation of the core characteristics of autism will continue into adolescence and adulthood for most individuals (Seltzer, Shattuck, Abbeduto, & Greenberg, 2004). Instruction specifically designed to develop communication, socialization, and appropriate behavior may be needed.

This section describes instructional strategies that have been empirically demonstrated to be effective with adolescents with autism. Although we cannot discuss every instructional method purporting to be beneficial, we provide essential strategies for transition planning. Some of the strategies may be used to teach a variety of skills, while others may be used to teach a specific skill. Still others may emphasize the development of relationships and appropriate behavior.

Applied Behavior Analysis

Among the most researched strategies for working with individuals with autism are those based in applied behavior analysis (ABA; Simpson, 2005). ABA refers to a set of principles that evaluates the interaction between antecedents and consequences; this information is then used to systematically provide instruction. This set of principles provides a broad range of instructional strategies that can be tailored to match an individual's specific learning needs (Dunlap, Kern, & Worcester, 2001). It is beyond the scope of this book to provide a comprehensive description of ABA and how it may be used with individuals with autism; however, many of the instructional strategies reviewed in this chapter are based on the principles of ABA. Teams using ABA for instructional purposes will need to coordinate the instructional plans with the behavior support plan, as discussed in Chapter 2, as there may be overlapping procedures.

Reinforcement

A central component of ABA, and a strategy in itself, is the effective use of reinforcement to influence and motivate learning. Reinforcement is a process for strengthening behavior and, as such, provides motivation. Motivation is an important component of learning for all students. This is especially true for adolescents with autism, who have been fraught with learning challenges their entire educational careers. To maximize participation and learning, it is critical that students receive reinforcers that provide motivation to engage in instructional activities, attempt new tasks, and continue building skills.

A variety of reinforcers can be used to motivate students. Some students may be intrinsically motivated to learn, whereas others may respond to adult recognition of efforts and successes. Still others may require other types of reinforcers. For example, students can earn access to breaks or specific privileges for engaging in a work task, participating in cleaning activities, or completing a reading assignment. Ultimately, natural reinforcers—those that occur naturally as a result of a specific action (e.g., a paycheck after 40 hours of work; a good grade on a book report)—should be utilized. This will help maintain the behavior and ensure that the student does not become dependent on items or events that would not normally occur (e.g., getting candy for working well on a group project). Because the goal of reinforcement is to increase the rate of learning, the educator must determine whether the student's learning rate is sufficient or if additional reinforcers are needed. When designing a reinforcement system, consider the following questions:

- Are naturally occurring reinforcers enough to strengthen learning?

- What motivates the student to learn?

- How often are reinforcers needed to strengthen learning?

- Once a skill is learned, can I systematically reduce the level or type of reinforcer to ensure maintenance of the skill, and if so, how?

Consider how reinforcement plays a role in Maria's community skills instruction. Maria is working on counting money and purchasing items independently. She practices this skill at the school store. Maria is motivated by this activity and enjoys picking out an item and paying for it. Because of her high level of motivation, she does not require additional reinforcers to learn this task. The purchase itself serves as a reinforcer for the skills of counting money and purchasing items. She is less motivated to work on filing, which is a skill she is learning while working in the school's main office. To encourage her work on this skill, Maria's teacher provides a 5-minute break after every set of 30 reports Maria files for her to look at her favorite magazine.

Prompting

A critical component of any instruction is the application of prompting procedures. A prompt is a cue or an instruction that is given before or during a student's action or response. It increases the likelihood that the student will emit a correct response and reduces the possibility of errors (Billingsley & Romer, 1983). Effective instructional prompts will vary depending on the individual as well as the specific task. The goal is to select the least intrusive prompt needed to help the student perform the correct response. Table 5.4 provides a hierarchy of prompts.

Planned, systematic delivery and fading of prompts is essential. There are a variety of prompt delivery and fading methods that have been used successfully with individuals with autism.

System of Decreasing Prompts

A system of decreasing prompts provides diminishing levels of assistance. It uses two or more prompts that are arranged from the most intrusive to the least. The

Table 5.4.   Hierarchy of prompts

Prompt	Description	Example
1. Full physical guidance	Gentle guidance is provided to help the student complete the entire step or activity. The instructor's hand is placed over the student's hand and guides the student through the motion.	Physically guiding the student through all steps involved in washing a plate or folding a pair of jeans
2. Partial physical guidance	Gentle guidance is provided to help the student complete a portion of the step or activity.	Physically guiding the student to place the plate in the dish water and pick up the sponge, then discontinuing the prompt
3. Shadowing	The instructor holds his or her hand several inches above the student's and shadows the student's movements. If an error is made, the instructor immediately stops the action and provides physical guidance.	Physically mirroring a student's actions as he or she folds a pair of jeans
4. Gesturing	The instructor uses gestures, such as pointing, tapping, or nodding head, to motion toward an item or location.	Tapping the sponge after the plate has been placed in the dish water and pointing to the second pair of jeans that are to be folded
5. Specific verbal instruction	The instructor gives a verbal instruction that tells the student exactly what to do.	Pick up the sponge. Now wash the plate.
6. Nonspecific verbal instruction	The instructor gives a verbal instruction that provides a hint about the next step or reminds the student to move on to the next step.	What do you do next? Now what? Keep going.
7. Independence	No guidance is needed.	

student is given high levels of assistance when the task is first introduced, and the support is slowly faded by moving systematically through the prompting hierarchy. When using this approach, it is not necessary to provide all the levels of prompting shown in Table 5.4. Only those that benefit the student and provide the support needed to learn the specific skill are used.

System of Least Prompts

Some students benefit from a system designed to provide little or no prompting initially, with a gradual increase in assistance. A system of least prompts helps to prevent too much prompting from being provided by allowing the student the opportunity to perform the skill before assistance is offered. The educator applies the least intrusive prompt needed to be successful and allows approximately 5–6 seconds for the student to respond. If the student does not respond correctly, then the educator repeats the step using the next most intrusive prompt. Prompting continues to be increased until the student demonstrates the target behavior.

Maria is learning to file reports in the main office to prepare for a clerical job after community college. Her teacher decides to use a system of least prompts to teach this skill, starting with a nonspecific verbal instruction. Maria picks up a report and looks at it. The teacher says, "Where does it go?" and waits 5 seconds. Maria does not respond. Her teacher then says, "Maria, look at the name on the report" (specific verbal instruction). Maria looks at the report, reads the name aloud, and opens the appropriate file drawer. Maria's teacher is prepared to provide a gesture prompt if Maria is unable to follow the specific verbal instruction within 5 seconds.

Time Delay

Another prompting procedure is time delay. With this approach, the amount of time provided between the instruction and the prompt is gradually increased. During the original presentation of the instruction, the student is immediately prompted and provided a reinforcer for a correct response. As the student demonstrates compliance with the task (e.g., the student performs the target behavior with the delivered prompt on 8 out of 10 trials for 2 consecutive days), the type of prompt delivered does not change. Instead, the instructor delays the delivery of the prompt slowly and systematically. For best results and more efficient teaching, the delay should be increased in small increments. According to Walls, Haught, and Dowler (1982), 1- to 2-second intervals should be used to ensure accuracy of responses. The delay between the instruction and the prompt is slowly increased until the student is able to perform the skill independently before a prompt is delivered. For example, Craig's teacher is using time delay to teach him to put on his coat when the school bell rings. She has slowly built the delay and is now waiting 4 seconds before providing the gestural prompt. Craig is now consistently putting on his coat before the 4 seconds are up. Time delay is an evidence-based technique that can also be used in a work setting for teaching students like Craig how to punch a time card.

Goal: Craig will punch his time card upon arrival at work.

Instructional strategy: After working for several months at the pizza restaurant, Craig started a job placement at a local department store. His job was to unpack boxes in the receiving area in the back of the store. His first task was to punch his time card. His teacher decided to use time delay to teach him this task. First, the teacher provided demonstrations of how to slide his time card into the punching machine. Upon Craig's arrival to work, she initially gave the instruction "Slide the card in." For several trials, she gave the instruction immediately upon his arrival at the machine. Once Craig was able to respond to her verbal instruction, she would take him to the machine and wait 2 seconds before giving him the verbal prompt. Craig's teacher continued to expand the amount of prompt delay until he was successfully sliding the time card into the machine before she could provide a prompt.

Discrete Trial Teaching

Discrete trial teaching is an instructional strategy that uses the principles of ABA. Skills are broken down into small, independent steps, and each step is taught individually in a discrete unit and is practiced until mastered. For example, identifying the value of coins can be broken down into five steps: identifying the value of a penny, a nickel, a dime, and a quarter and discriminating between the value of all four coins. This strategy can be used to teach a variety of new skills, including discrimination, receptive language, expressive language, conversation, grammar and syntax, and alternative communication systems (Smith, 2001).

A discrete trial consists of five parts:

1. *Instructional cue*—This cue can be in the form of an instruction, a question, an activity, or another environmental event. The cue indicates to the student that a response is required. The instructional cue should be something that occurs naturally in the environment, such as a school bell or an instruction to the group.

2. *Prompt*—A prompt is given to the student, in any form described previously.

3. *Student's response*—The student may respond correctly, incorrectly, or not at all. The instructor should allow an appropriate amount of time for a response. If the student begins to respond incorrectly, the trial is terminated, and the instruction is presented again.

4. *Consequence*—Based on the student's response, the instructor provides a consequence. If the student performed correctly, a reinforcer may be delivered. If the response was not correct, the instructor presents the trial again with additional prompting to ensure a correct response.

5. *Short pause between the consequence and the presentation of the next instructional cue*—A short interval helps to define the skill being worked on by providing a clear beginning and end.

Task Analysis

The components of a task analysis were described previously. Due to the complexity of many skills, it is often necessary to break them down into small, teachable steps (Cooper, Heron, & Heward, 1987). In a task analysis, each step of the skill is identified and taught in sequence with related steps. Task analysis is a valuable strategy because it enables the teacher to determine the content, sequence, and starting point of instruction and allows skills to be taught in a meaningful series (Axelrod, 1983).

Once the steps in a task analysis have been constructed, the teacher determines how to teach the sequence of behaviors. All steps of the sequence may be presented at once, or they may be presented one at a time depending on the student's learning capability. There are three teaching options when using a task analysis:

1. *Total task presentation*—The student receives training on each step in the task analysis during every session. Prompting is provided for any of the steps the student is unable to perform independently. The entire skill is worked on until the student is able to perform all steps independently.

2. *Forward chaining*—The first step in the task analysis is specifically targeted and taught. The student is physically guided through the remaining steps in the sequence. The first step continues until mastered, at which point the second step is targeted. This procedure is repeated for each remaining step until the student can perform the entire sequence independently.

3. *Backward chaining*—Teaching begins with the last step of the sequence. The student is physically guided through the initial steps. When the final step is reached, instruction is provided by prompting or allowing the student to complete the step independently. When the final step is mastered, the second-to-last step is targeted. This process continues for each remaining step until all steps in the task analysis have been introduced.

Chaining instructional techniques were used to help Jeff learn how to budget for and purchase his supplies.

Goal: Jeff will budget and purchase his own personal supplies.

Instructional strategy: This is a complicated task with many steps, so Jeff's teacher picked one area to teach initially. Jeff enjoys a variety of snacks and is very motivated by food. Because of this natural motivation, Jeff's teacher felt that having him shop for a snack to eat during his break at the video game store would be a good way to start teaching him how to budget and make purchases. Jeff's teacher discussed this with him and his mother, and they both agreed. Jeff's mother agreed to give him $10 per week to buy snacks and drinks for work.

Prior to delivering instruction, Jeff's teacher created a *task analysis.* There were many steps involved. The sequence started with Jeff's evaluating the snacks in the cupboard at home and concluded with Jeff's purchasing items at the grocery store and putting them in the cupboard when he returned home. Jeff's teacher used *total task presentation* to teach the sequence of steps. This meant that Jeff received training on every step of the task each time it was presented. She used a *system of least prompts* as each step was taught. Jeff learned this skill very well; however, he had difficulty with one step of the task. While shopping, he was unable to efficiently find the items he wanted to purchase as he was unable to determine the appropriate aisle to search. Jeff's teacher used *discrete trial instruction* to help him learn to categorize food items. She wished he could have worked on this skill in the grocery store, but due to transportation limitations, she set up a program in the resource classroom. She created a list of categories used to label the aisles as they appeared in the grocery store where Jeff and his mother shopped. During resource class, Jeff spent 10 minutes each day matching snack items to the appropriate category. After 2 weeks of working on this skill, Jeff showed good progress.

Modeling

Modeling consists of providing a demonstration of a skill or task. It provides an opportunity for the student to observe or hear a specific behavior in the context where it is to occur. For that reason, it is effective for teaching a skill in a natural environment setting (Charlop-Christy, Le, & Freeman, 2000). Modeling can be provided live or on video.

Live Modeling

With live modeling, an adult or a peer demonstrates the behavior in real time. When using this method, the person providing the model should exaggerate the behavior and ensure that the student is attending. It may also be helpful to demonstrate the behavior at a slower pace than it would normally be performed. Live modeling may not be useful for all students with autism or with all types of skills, as the model is transient and may not be readily imitated.

Video Modeling

In recent years, video modeling has proven to be an effective strategy for teaching a number of skills (Charlop-Christy et al., 2000). Many individuals with autism enjoy watching movies, television, or animated computer screens. Video modeling combines this motivating activity with instruction. In video modeling, a target skill or task is videotaped and the student watches the video and immediately imitates the model. Video modeling allows for the teaching of a relatively long sequence of steps (Lasater & Brady, 1995). It provides a permanent record of the behavior and capitalizes on the visual strengths found in many students with autism. The video should be short and contain only relevant information that focuses on the skill to be learned (Charlop-Christy & Daneshvar, 2003). The entire sequence may be watched at one time, or the instructor may choose to break the tape into clips and show them one at a time to a student.

Social Scripts and Social Stories

Social scripts and Social Stories are strategies that have only recently been applied to adolescents with autism. *Social scripts* are written or auditory prompts that outline what to say or do in a particular social situation. Most people have social scripts they use throughout the day. For example, they may use a specific script when greeting a co-worker on arrival at work or when making a telephone call. Individuals with autism benefit from having scripts they can use under a variety of circumstances. Students who read can use a written social script (Krantz & McLannahan, 1993). The student reads the script and practices the exchange with an adult. Eventually, the script is memorized and used in appropriate social situations. If the student does not read, a recorded script can be used in a similar manner (Stevenson, Krantz, & McClannahan, 2000). When creating the social script, it is helpful to identify situations when social exchanges should be increased and to identify context and age-appropriate conversation. Social scripts can be used, for instance, to facilitate a job interview. The following describes Jeff's teacher using a social script to prepare him for his interview for a job at the video game store.

Goal: Jeff will complete a job interview.

Instructional strategy: Jeff had never been on a job interview before. His teacher wanted to provide detailed, thorough instruction for this skill, so she chose to use a social script to help him learn appropriate responses. She created a list of questions he was likely to be asked during the interview. She then sat down with Jeff and read the questions, and together they created answers. Jeff's teacher let him lead much of this activity; however, she helped guide and shape the content and encouraged him to expand his ideas. After all the questions were answered, Jeff spent time each day reading the script and practicing the exchange with his teacher.

After a week, Jeff's teacher decided to have a mock interview. During the mock interview, Jeff was able to answer many of the questions and was even able to expand from the social script; however, his teacher was concerned about his body language. He spent much of the time fidgeting in his chair, touching items on the teacher's desk, and looking at the floor. Jeff's teacher felt that more instruction was needed. The social script had worked well, but Jeff needed to work on his nonverbal communication skills.

The teacher decided to use video modeling for this next step. She videotaped a senior in high school completing the interview, using the same script Jeff had created. Each day Jeff watched the videotape, then practiced imitating the nonverbal behaviors as he completed a mock interview with his teacher. After 5 days of watching the tape and practicing the interview, Jeff's behavior improved greatly. His teacher felt that he was ready for his first interview. Jeff interviewed for and was subsequently offered the position at the video game store, where he now works.

Social Stories are similar to social scripts. Social Stories are short narratives that describe a particular situation, including the environment, relevant social cues, and appropriate behavior to be demonstrated (Gray & Garand, 1993). The story is designed to ameliorate a specific problem or situation, and the focus is on the behavior the student is to learn or increase. The story's language is positive, and behavioral expectations are stated simply and clearly. The story is written from the student's perspective and should contain the following: two to three descriptive sentences describing the situation and setting, at least one perspective sentence that describes the feelings of the student as well as others involved in the situation, and one directive sentence that succinctly tells the student the appropriate behavior to demonstrate.

The teacher should introduce the story by reading it with the student several times. Eventually, the student reviews the story independently. Once the student is familiar with the story, the teacher prompts the student to use the new skill in the natural environment. As the student demonstrates mastery of the skill, review of the story is faded.

During lunch, Jeff constantly wants to talk to his peer buddies about maps, even though they are not interested in this subject. Jeff's teacher has written a Social Story to help him refrain from talking about maps and to engage in appropriate conversation. Jeff's Social Story is shown in Table 5.5.

A word of warning: Because social scripts and Social Stories have received little attention by researchers, the exact benefits of such strategies have not been

---

Table 5.5.   Jeff's Social Story for talking about maps at lunchtime.

I think maps are very fun to talk about. (Perspective)

At lunch, I like to tell my friends about maps. I especially like to tell them the names of states and their capital cities. (Perspective)

My friends like to talk to me about other things. They like to talk about cars, football, or movies and a lot of other topics. (Perspective)

It is important that I listen to them talk about these other things. When I listen, I should look at my friends and say one thing about the topic. (Directive)

It makes my friends happy when I listen to them. (Perspective)

demonstrated. Educators should take extra effort in evaluating the effectiveness of these strategies.

Peer-Mediated Strategies

Peer-mediated approaches can provide social companionship for an individual with autism as well as help strengthen and expand skills needed for social improvement (Haring & Breen, 1992). Typically, peer mediation involves identification of a student or a group of students who act as peer supports. These students are taught to initiate, model, prompt, and reinforce specific social behaviors. A specific behavior can be targeted, or a broad goal can be set. Peer mediation provides a natural method for addressing social and emotional needs. Students with autism may be more motivated to work with a peer than an adult. Furthermore, the peer may provide a more appropriate model for the student, making learning and generalization more likely.

Circle of Friends is one peer-mediated strategy that has been demonstrated to be effective with adolescents with autism (Haring & Breen, 1992). With this method, typically developing peers identify themselves as interested in supporting the teen with autism. Social interventions and activities are planned, and peers are taught how to effectively interact with the individual. Peer tutoring is another valuable method (Kamps, Barbetta, Leonard, & Delquadri, 1994). Typically developing students are paired with a student with autism and are taught how to deliver instruction on both academic and social skills. With either Circle of Friends or peer tutoring, planning and practice are important.

Maria's teacher has chosen to use Circle of Friends to enhance Maria's social opportunities. After she met with Maria's physical education class, four of the students in the class indicated an interest in being a part of Maria's social network. Maria's peers are to help her increase the number of social interactions she has each day. They approach her during physical education as well as when they see her in the hallway. Two of her identified friends eat lunch with her each day. The group has also invited her to attend the Friday night football games. Maria's teacher also uses peer resolution to increase Maria's ability to take turns in conversation.

Goal: Maria will take turns in conversations.

Instructional strategy: Maria's teacher felt that this skill should be worked on during naturally occurring social situations using peer mediation. She identified three students from Maria's physical education class who were interested in being her peer buddies. Maria's teacher scheduled a time to meet with the peer buddies during lunch. At this meeting, she outlined Maria's social goal of taking turns in conversation. As part of this goal, Maria would talk no longer than 3 minutes, then stop so that someone else could speak. The peers were instructed on how to provide opportunities for interaction, allow Maria to talk, then interrupt her if necessary if she spoke for more than 3 consecutive minutes. If Maria gave someone else a turn without being prompted, the student would express appreciation, then take his or her turn. The peers brainstormed the times and places they encountered Maria and would be able to interact with her socially. Together, the peer buddies provided four to five opportunities for interaction each day, including the entire lunch period.

REACHING INDEPENDENCE

Although most individuals with autism will continue to need some level of support into adulthood, independence to the maximum extent possible should be encouraged. The educator should employ instructional strategies that foster independence and allow the student to take responsibility for his or her own behavior. Although the strategies discussed in the preceding section can be used to teach independence in a variety of skills, more support may be needed to ensure that the individual learns to integrate skills, manage behavior, and deal effectively with the emotional stress of everyday life. Over time, these skills will help ensure successful transitions to postsecondary education, work, and the community.

With a self-management strategy, students learn to recognize, monitor, and evaluate their own behavior over time (Koegel, Talebi, Koegel, & Carter, 2006). Self-management promotes independence because it shifts responsibility from the teacher to the student. It has been successfully used to increase a variety of skills in individuals with autism, including communication, social interaction, and time on task, as well as decrease disruptive behavior (Koegel, Koegel, Harrower, & Carter, 1999). There are three primary components of self-management:

1. *Self-monitoring*—The student is taught to recognize his or her target behavior and learns to determine the occurrence or nonoccurrence of that behavior. Initially, the student is taught to monitor his or her behavior over a short duration of time. For example, after 3–5 minutes the student is cued to determine whether the behavior occurred. As the student gains competency, time is gradually increased.

2. *Self-evaluation*—The student determines whether the target behavior occurred and records the presence or absence of that behavior. The student records behavior incidents on a device that is easy to use and tailored to fit his or her needs.

3. *Self-reinforcement*—Once the student learns to recognize and record the occurrence of a target behavior, the student learns to determine whether a reward was earned for appropriate behavior. For this step, the teacher creates a goal or designated criteria. For example, a student working on making comments to others may have a goal of making three appropriate comments per hour. When the student makes a comment, the student records it, and at the end of the hour he or she counts the number of comments made. If the predetermined goal is met, then he or she receives a reward for reaching the goal.

It can be challenging to teach self-management to students with ASDs, but as with all skills, systematic instruction paired with ample opportunities to practice can result in success. It is often helpful to teach each component of self-management separately. It should start with the student learning to identify his or her behavior and end with self-reinforcement. Upon introduction of each component, a high level of supervision is often required. As the student gains mastery, supervision can be gradually faded. To maximize the likelihood of success, goals should be realistic and attainable. Requirements for meeting the goals can be expanded as the student demonstrates success.

Jeff often had trouble doing his assigned work, especially homework. An assessment of the problem revealed that although he was capable of doing the assigned tasks, he often forgot to bring the necessary books home, or he forgot the assignment altogether. His team hoped to increase independence in this area by teaching him to use a PDA to track assignments.

Goal: Jeff will use his PDA to record assignments and to check off all assignments when he completes them and turns them in to the instructor.

Instructional strategy: To initially teach the skill, Jeff's special education teacher modeled how to enter the assignment into the PDA and how to mark it as completed. She modeled this sequence three times throughout the school day, once during math class and two times during resource class. On the second day, she modeled the sequence one time during math. For the remainder of the day, she used a system of least prompts to ensure that Jeff was able to complete the task independently. By the end of that day, Jeff was demonstrating independence on this task. Jeff's teacher was concerned, however, that he might not enter the information consistently, so she set up a reinforcement system to motivate him to track his assignments. The special education teacher worked with his general education teachers to determine assigned tasks. Every Friday afternoon during lunch, Jeff's teacher reviewed his PDA. If he had tracked his assignments with 90% accuracy during the week, he was able to purchase an item from the vending machine with money given to him by his mother. This reinforcer motivated Jeff to use his PDA consistently and accurately.

Craig learned how to use self-management strategies in the pizza restaurant, where he was gradually becoming more independent at box assembly.

Goal: Craig will work in three different community-based jobs in assembly or packaging.

Instructional strategy: Craig has worked in a pizza restaurant assembling boxes and at a department store unpacking boxes in the receiving department. Craig's teacher recently found him a new job assembling display stands at a book and music store, making use of Craig's skill and desire to put things together. His teacher used video modeling to teach the assembling skill. She videotaped a co-worker putting together the display stands. When Craig arrived at work, he watched the video two to three times. He then practiced putting together the stand. His teacher also used a system of least prompts to provide further support. A rein-

Table 5.6.   Self-management procedures

1. Operationally define the target behavior.	A concrete definition of the target behavior is necessary so that the student and teachers can identify and agree upon the occurrence or nonoccurrence of a behavior.
2. Identify functional reinforcers.	Effectiveness of the self-management system is contingent upon reinforcement, as the student must be motivated to consistently and accurately use the system. The best way to ensure that the reinforcer is meaningful is to let the student select it.
3. Design or choose a self-management method or device.	The student should have a quick, clearly defined way to record the occurrence of the behavior. This could involve writing numbers, making tally marks, placing stickers on a chart, or using a counter.
4. Teach the individual to use the self-management device.	Modeling and prompting are effective strategies to teach the student to accurately recognize and record the target behaviors. Reinforcement can encourage accurate recording. Careful monitoring by the teacher will ensure that the student understands the procedure and is not cheating to gain the reinforcer. It is important that such instruction take place in the natural environment so that the student learns to self-monitor in the real world.
5. Teach self-management independence.	The teacher gradually withdraws from the process and allows the individual to conduct the steps independently. Fading should be a gradual, methodical process. Ongoing evaluation will help ensure that the student continues to be successful as support is decreased.

From Koegel, R.L., Koegel, L.K., & Parks, D.R. (1995). "Teach the individual" model of generalization: Autonomy through self–management. In R.L. Koegel & L.K. Koegel (Eds.), *Teaching children with autism: Strategies for initiating positive interactions and improving learning opportunities* (pp. 67–77). Baltimore: Paul H. Brookes Publishing Co; adapted by permission.

forcer—a can of soda from the break room soda machine—was provided after Craig correctly assembled a designated number of display stands.

Once Craig learned to assemble the display stands independently, his teacher taught him to self-manage his work behavior. She provided a target number of stands to assemble in a 20-minute time period. She made a chart with a number of circles corresponding to the number of stands Craig was expected to assemble and placed the chart on the wall. Each time Craig completed a stand, he made a check in one of the circles. He wore a watch that timed the 20-minute interval. When his watch alarm sounded, Craig looked at the chart to determine if all the circles contained a check. If they did, he could go to the soda machine and buy a can of soda. Craig was very motivated by soda and was easily able to learn the self-management strategy. This allowed him to be independent in the work setting. In addition, the reinforcer of buying a can of soda was quite typical for the setting, as Craig's co-workers often bought cans of soda as a perk of their employment.

Koegel, Koegel, and Parks (1995) outlined the procedures for teaching self-management. These steps can be found in Table 5.6.

Maria's educational team put together a comprehensive plan to address her IEP goals. For each goal, they selected instructional methods based on her individual characteristics, including learning style, interests, and level of motivation. An outline of Maria's school day is provided in Table 5.7. The table lists the skills Maria is working on as well as the instructional method employed to teach each skill. It shows a new job Maria started at a doctor's office doing clerical work.

Table 5.7. Maria's instructional day

Time	Location	Skill	Instructional method
8:00–8:15	Locker in school hallway	Unpacking	Task analysis using forward chaining Prompting using system of least prompts Reinforcement (verbal praise)
	Locker in school hallway	Social interaction with peers	Peer mediation Social script Prompting using system of least prompts (peer delivered) Self-management
8:15–8:35	Special education classroom	Making meal (breakfast)	Task analysis using forward chaining Prompting using system of least prompts Reinforcement (eat breakfast)
	Special education classroom	Reading (recipe instructions)	Task analysis using forward chaining Prompting using system of least prompts Reinforcement (eat breakfast)
8:35–8:45	Special education classroom	Using a napkin while eating	Live modeling Prompting using time delay Reinforcement (eat breakfast)
8:45–9:00	Special education classroom	Cleaning up kitchen	Task analysis using forward chaining Prompting using system of least prompts Reinforcement (earn points toward school store)
9:00–9:15	Special education classroom	Personal hygiene skills (brushing teeth)	Video modeling Prompting using system of least prompts Reinforcement (earn points toward school store)
9:15–10:05	Typing classroom	Computer skills	Task analysis using total task presentation Prompting using system of least prompts Reinforcement (verbal praise)
	Typing classroom	Social interaction with peers	Peer mediation Social script Prompting using system of least prompts (peer delivered) Self-management
10:10–10:40	Main office	Filing	Task analysis using forward chaining Prompting using system of least prompts Reinforcement (5-minute break to look at magazine)
	Main office	Asking for a break	Social Story Reinforcement (5-minute break)
10:45–12:15	Special education classroom	Math	Modeling Discrete trial instruction Prompting using system of least prompts Reinforcement (earn points towards school store)
	Special education classroom	Reading	Modeling Prompting using system of least prompts Reinforcement (earn points towards school store)
12:20–12:35	School store	Math	Modeling Prompting using system of least prompts Reinforcement (purchased item)

(continued)

Table 5.7.   *(continued)*

Time	Location	Skill	Instructional method
12:20–12:35 *(continued)*	School store	Reading	Modeling Prompting using system of least prompts Reinforcement (purchased item)
12:40–1:10	Cafeteria	Social interaction with peers	Peer mediation Social script Prompting using system of least prompts (peer delivered) Self-management
1:15–2:00	Science class	Science report	Modeling Prompting using system of least prompts Reinforcement (verbal praise)
	Science class	Social interaction with peers	Peer mediation Social script Prompting using system of least prompts (peer delivered) Self-management
2:05–3:00	Community work setting (doc-tor's office)	Clerical tasks	Modeling Prompting using system of least prompts Reinforcement (5-minute break to look at maga-zine)
	Community work setting (doc-tor's office)	Social interaction with peers	Social script Prompting using system of least prompts Self-management

PULLING IT ALL TOGETHER

When providing instruction, the educator must consider where, when, and how to teach new skills so that they will have meaning to students and be naturally occurring over time. Whenever possible, instruction should take place in community environments at naturally occurring times. Educators must be knowledgeable of a range of educational practices that have been empirically demonstrated to be effective with adolescents with autism (National Research Council, 2001). This will allow educators to create an educational plan that maximizes learning and results in student success.

6

Navigating the World of Adult Services and Benefits Planning

Grant Revell and Lucy Axton Miller

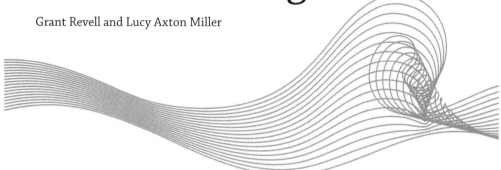

Effective transition from school to the adult community and employment for youth with autism requires knowledge of an array of local and state agencies and organizations. Not only do students with autism need to explore and plan for employment after high school, but they also must develop an understanding of the many services available to them in the community. This chapter focuses on coordination with key community agencies and organizations that are potential resources for employment and related services for youth with autism, including those agencies that provide disability benefits planning.

The move from the public education system to the adult service system during the transition process involves learning about a new set of community resources, each with unique rules, regulations, eligibility guidelines, and procedures. For individuals interested in entering competitive employment, there are a variety of opportunities and potential challenges in working with the adult service system (Wehman, Revell, & Brooke, 2003). In the public education system, special education services are an entitled service for eligible individuals; local school systems are the single agency that coordinates education services. It is critically important to note that this single point of service coordination does not exist in adult services.

Once students with autism reach age 22 or have completed high school with a regular diploma, they no longer have a legal right to the variety of services covered by IDEA (U.S. Department of Education, 2005). For the most part, services in the adult system are not entitlement based. Most postsecondary employment and related service agencies have their own eligibility systems that must be met prior to acceptance into an individual program. Different laws and policies govern each of these programs. Families of individuals with autism report that identifying, accessing, and paying for needed adult-oriented services involves working through a complex public and private service system (Sullivan, 2001). Therefore, students with autism and their family members must gain a strong understanding of these community programs to ensure a smooth transition to adult services that help achieve student-driven outcomes.

Because there is no specific program or agency that serves individuals with autism in the adult service system, transition-age youth and their families have the potential to receive services and support from a variety of public and private programs. The exact combination of programs will vary depending on the needs of each student and his or her transition goals, the nature of the student's disability, the economic resources of the community, and the eligibility requirements of the various potential community resources (Wittenburg, Golden, & Fishman, 2002). Examples of community organizations and programs that are important transition resources are state vocational rehabilitation (VR) programs, community rehabilitation service providers, Centers for Independent Living (CIL), One Stop Career Centers, community service boards, and Work Incentives Planning and Assistance (WIPA) projects. Many of these agencies and programs have entrance eligibility and prerequisite criteria.

There is evidence that youth with autism have difficulty gaining access to the services in the adult system they need in order to successfully make the transition to employment. For example, in 2005 fewer than 2,000 individuals with autism received services through the VR system, and only 1,200 of those receiving services were successfully employed (Dew & Alan, 2007). Of the youth with autism who had been out of school for 1 year or more, only one in five reported receiving ser-

Table 6.1.   Community service programs and services in the adult system

Community service program	Potential services for youth in transition
Work Incentives Planning and Assistance (WIPA)	Provides financial analysis and information on work incentives and disability benefit programs operated under the Social Security Administration
State vocational rehabilitation (VR) services	Primary nationally available employment service support for individuals with disabilities. For eligible individuals, VR agencies provide vocational assessments leading to development of an individual plan for employment (IPE). Variety of employment-related services can be provided under an IPE, including training, counseling, job placement, and supported employment.
Community rehabilitation programs (CRPs)/ employment service organizations	Community programs working with state VR agencies and other case management agencies, frequently on a fee-for-service basis, to provide employment assessments, job placement, and follow-up services
Local community service boards	Provide service coordination and assistance for counseling, family planning, nutrition, health care, and transportation. Eligibility guidelines vary from state to state for individuals with autism-related disorders.
Centers for Independent Living (CILs)	Provide information on self-advocacy and understanding one's rights as well as training programs dealing with money management, sexuality, leisure activities, socialization, and many other aspects of independent living
One Stop Career Centers	Local centers operating under the authority of the U.S. Department of Labor. Assist with career and vocational counseling, occupational training, and job placement and follow along

vices from a state VR agency. Also, youth with autism were less likely to be employed than youth with other disabilities, and employed youth with autism worked fewer hours than employed youth with other disabilities (U.S. Department of Education, 2005).

Table 6.1 shows a variety of typical community programs and organizations and the purpose of each. Each of these is discussed in this chapter. There are potentially many other local resources, such as social service agencies for individuals needing public assistance utilizing Temporary Assistance for Needy Families (TANF; *Temporary Assistance for Needy Families*, 2008). Also, universities and community colleges, covered in detail in Chapter 8, can provide information and referral assistance through their resource and support centers for students with disabilities. These offices can assist with arranging potential accommodations, identifying potential benefit opportunities, and linking students to internship and job opportunities. It is important to involve these community agencies early in the transition process so that the individual, his or her family, and the entire transition team can become familiar with the resources that are available from the specific agencies (Wehman, 2006). Without continual involvement, planning, and collaboration with key community agencies, the potential for a successful transition from secondary education to the community will be greatly diminished for students with autism.

EMPLOYMENT SERVICES AND SUPPORTS

Youth in the transition process have potential access to a variety of community training, employment, and support programs. These programs offer an array of service coordination assistance, employment services, and funding possibilities; however, they operate under different federal, state, and local laws; regulations; policies; and service arrangements. The key to a successful transition outcome is early involvement with these programs during the planning process.

Becoming fully educated about the resources and service relationships that characterize community training, employment, and support programs available to individuals in transition is a critical first step for students, families, and transition teams. Next, team members should identify the primary community agencies and work to incorporate these programs into the transition plan (i.e., transition IEP). The primary case management/service coordination resource among the agencies should be identified. This role might be taken on by different agencies depending on the nature of an individual's disability and core service needs and/or local eligibility requirements. Early transition planning can help to establish these key relationships with community agencies and establish the primary- and secondary-level participation needed by each to support a successful employment outcome.

State Vocational Rehabilitation Services

The Rehabilitation Act of 1973 (PL 93-112), as amended in 1998 (PL 105-220), provides federal grants for states to operate comprehensive programs of VR services for individuals with disabilities. VR is a cooperative program between state and federal governments that exists in all 50 states, the District of Columbia, and the U.S. territories. It should be a core transition resource for youth with disabilities throughout the transition process. VR provides an array of services and supports focusing specifically on achievement of an employment outcome, including but not limited to the following:

- Assessment for determining eligibility for VR services

- Vocational counseling, guidance, and referral services

- Vocational and other training, including on-the-job training

- Personal assistance services, including training in managing and directing a personal assistant

- Rehabilitation technology services

- Job placement services and supported employment services

A VR agency also provides direct services, such as counseling and guidance and job placement assistance, and it will usually arrange with other community providers to obtain services such as rehabilitation technology and supported employment. The ability of a VR agency to reach into the community for individualized services is one of its key strengths. VR agencies are well positioned to serve as the service coordination hub for employment-oriented community services for eligible youth with disabilities.

Before any VR services can be obtained, a young adult with autism must complete an application that is reviewed and approved by a VR counselor. Qualification for VR services is based on the following eligibility criteria: 1) the presence of a disability that is an impairment to employment and 2) the expectation that the provision of VR services will result in the achievement of an individual's employment outcome.

Once eligibility for VR has been determined, an individualized plan for employment (IPE) is developed by the VR counselor. The IPE identifies both the employment goal chosen by the individual and the services needed to achieve that goal. The IPE is developed in close cooperation with the individual, the individual's family, and the transition team. It can serve as a roadmap for making the transition to employment. Rehabilitation counselors can be a helpful resource when planning and implementing the transition plan. Counselors provide case management and service coordination and often have extensive connections with other community agencies and employers. Case management through VR continues until case closure occurs. Case closure can occur after a minimum of 90 days of employment in a job consistent with the employment objective established in the IPE. Case closure can also occur if the individual is not making progress toward achieving an employment outcome. Because of limited previous work experience and the employment challenges associated with autism, some youth benefit from a more extended period of support and training to become acclimated to the demands and expectations of the competitive job site. The case closure provisions of the VR system sometimes work against the employment support needs of these individuals by limiting the period of time after employment that VR will participate in providing services.

VR counselors also have access to case service funds that can be used to purchase services from authorized vendors, such as postsecondary education and training, supported employment, transportation, and tools and uniforms. These services must support the employment goal established in the IPE. VR counselors are also usually familiar with other funding sources that can be used to complement VR funding.

During the early stages of planning for transition, VR counselors can serve as an information resource about community services for transition teams. This information and referral resource would be of value for students ages 15–16. Some youth considered higher functioning with a diagnosis of Asperger's syndrome may not meet the eligibility requirements for VR services, as VR is required by law (PL 105-220) to place a priority on those individuals with the most significant disabilities. As noted previously, determination of eligibility for VR services is done by the VR counselor. Even if a youth with a disability is not found eligible for VR services, the counselor could still be a source of information and referrals, either informally as part of a school-based transition resource team or formally through meetings with the student and his or her family.

As a youth with autism nears completion of his or her secondary education program, the rehabilitation counselor can become actively involved so that an IPE could potentially be in place as the student prepares to exit the school program. IPEs are frequently done during the final year of a student's secondary program to ensure that VR services are in place at the time of completion of the secondary program.

The disabling conditions related to autism could potentially meet the requirements for eligibility for VR services based on a significant or most significant disability. As noted previously, however, many youth with disability profiles related to autism are not being served by VR agencies at present. These youth and their families might encounter resistance on the part of VR to providing services. This may be related to concerns over the ability of youth with autism to achieve an employment outcome based on the employment services available in their community. As more community programs become skilled in providing employment supports for individuals with autism, the opportunities for these individuals through VR should improve.

The community link between VR and any individual seeking services is so important. Although VR agencies work under federally mandated guidelines, there are variations from state to state in how VR eligibility guidelines are interpreted and applied that have a substantial impact on the extent to which VR services are available in a specific state and community. Each state has a Client Assistance Program (CAP) that is set up to provide information, protection, and advocacy services for individuals with disabilities. Youth with autism and their families who have questions or concerns about the experience they have with a VR agency should consider using the CAP in their state for information and assistance regarding the VR program. A national directory of state VR agencies and their associated CAPs can be found online (see Small Business and Self-Employment Services [SBSES], 2008).

Community Rehabilitation Programs

Community rehabilitation programs (CRPs) are usually not-for-profit or for-profit private agencies that assist people with disabilities in obtaining and maintaining competitive employment. Specific services offered by providers will vary; many offer career counseling, assessments, benefits counseling, job placement, and supported employment services designed to assist individuals with disabilities to live and work in the community. Since many CRPs obtain much of their funding through contractual arrangements, access to their services can require a funding authorization from an agency such as VR.

CRP staff occasionally work cooperatively through contracts with school systems and offer work experience programs while youth with autism are in school. There are limited potential opportunities for CRPs to be involved with students like Jeff and Maria, who will look for work as part of their education programs. Rather, CRPs, for the most part, are linked closely to the adult service community because they derive their funding from agencies such as VR. CRPs might be referred to as a future potential resource during early transition planning and exploration for younger students. Their more immediate impact is for students who, like Craig, are nearing their actual transition into the community.

The employment support staff at CRPs are usually called employment consultants or specialists, job coaches, or another similar title. As a component of an employment plan for an individual, an employment consultant might work, for example, in cooperation with a referring VR counselor to seek out benefits counseling assistance, child care options, mental health services, or other supports needed.

CRPs can provide a variety of employment-related services, such as assistance with exploring potential job and career options, job preparation, job development, and job placement services. Staff might assist individuals with job interview practice, job-seeking skills, résumé preparation, guided job searches, and negotiations with employers. For example, perhaps an employer has an available job that includes multiple duties. Some of these duties match well to the abilities of the job applicant with a disability; others are a poor match for the applicant. The employment consultant, with the permission of the applicant, might work with the employer to negotiate a customized job carved out of the original job description that is a good match for the individual with a disability (Virginia Commonwealth University [VCU], 2008b). Once the job match is completed, the employment consultant can assist with training at the job site, help the worker with a disability adjust to job demands, and provide ongoing support as needed to help maintain the job or assist with a job change.

State Developmental Disabilities Agencies and Local Community Service Boards

In some states individuals with autism may be eligible for services administered through a state developmental disabilities administration (DDA) or a local community services board (CSB). Maryland, for example, has a state-administered DDA (http://www.ddamaryland.org/services.htm); Virginia is an example of a state with a community services board system (http://www.dmhmrsas.virginia.gov/SVC-CSBs.asp). Unlike state VR agencies, CSBs do not operate under a specific set of federal laws and are known by a variety of names, such as intellectual disabilities, mental health, developmental disabilities, or substance abuse services, any of which potentially covers some individuals with autism. A state-administered DDA that includes some individuals with autism within its eligibility guidelines potentially offers reasonably consistent statewide access to services, as compared with the wide variations in potential services found in community-administered programs.

With both state-administered DDAs and locally administered CSBs, eligibility for services is based on the presence of a disability that meets specific guidelines, and these guidelines vary considerably from state to state and community to community. Individuals with autism, their families, and transition teams need to learn early on about the eligibility requirements and service opportunities in their specific state and community. Parent groups, VR, community rehabilitation programs, and other members of the adult service system network are good resources for this. Since there are times that even eligible individuals are placed on a waiting list because of lack of funding (Braddock, Hemp, Parish, & Rizzolo, 2002), early contact in advance of the actual transition point will potentially allow a youth with autism to work through the eligibility and waiting list steps in time for services to be available when actually needed.

When available, service coordinators within the local CSB/DDA program are excellent resources for the transition planning team. Generally, service coordinators are available to serve as a coordination hub with very specific knowledge of services for youth as well as for family members. Service coordinators can attend transition meetings, both as resources for information and referral and also to help plan for specific transition support services needed by an individual, including employment and employment-related services. The knowledge that these service coordinators have to offer is more likely to benefit older students (e.g., those closer to graduation), but their inclusion on the team can certainly still benefit younger students as they become aware of the opportunities available in their community.

Service coordinators from CSBs also have access to a variety of funding resources to assist with the acquisition of employment supports. A primary funding source is the Home and Community-Based Services (HCBS) Medicaid waiver. The purpose of this waiver is to provide services for individuals who, without these services, would need to live in an institutional setting because of the significant nature of their disability. For eligible individuals, the HCBS waiver can provide access to supports for community living and employment (West et al., 2002). The HCBS waiver might be a resource for some individuals with autism with more significant support needs; however, it is important to emphasize that Medicaid waiver applications are made at the state level, and the content of waiver programs varies considerably from state to state. Each waiver defines a specific target population and specifies the services that will be available (Braddock et al., 2002), so it is important for transition teams to understand the waiver program in their state and to determine how it might provide additional support for students.

Centers for Independent Living

CILs are a strong potential resource for local transition teams and can provide a wealth of information for transition-age youth and their families. CIL staff can assist in helping to build self-advocacy skills, can provide general information about community resources, and will also offer classes in areas such as financial management, socialization, sexuality, leisure activities, peer counseling, and self-advocacy. CILs frequently serve as a community hub for information, services, and support for individuals with disabilities, including those with autism, and can help significantly in planning and implementing transition plans.

Employment services available through CILs can vary substantially from program to program. The service most frequently available is training in job-seeking skills. Some CILs do provide direct employment support by helping consumers locate jobs. CILs place a premium on self-advocacy and independence, so part of the peer counseling service is to help job applicants represent themselves effectively to employers. Peer education might also involve information and guidance on how to approach self-disclosure to an employer about the presence of a disability, particularly in situations where there is a need to negotiate a job accommodation.

Youth with autism and their families should contact the center in their community to learn how it might be of help. The ENDependence Center of Northern Virginia (ECNV; 2008) emphasizes that it is a community-based resource and advocacy center managed "by and for people with disabilities" and that it promotes the independent living philosophy and equal access for all people with disabilities. Specific services offered include

- Peer counseling services
- Advocacy and outreach services
- Independent living skills training
- Information and referral services
- Personal assistant services
- Support group services

These services might be of particular interest to older youth with autism who are preparing for a transition to community living and who are in need of training (e.g., independent living skills training) and/or independent living supports (e.g., personal assistance services).

One Stop Career Centers

The Workforce Investment Act (WIA) of 1998 (PL 105-220) created One Stop Career Centers (or "One Stop Centers") as a key employment resource in the community. The One Stop Centers have core services that are available to anyone in the community who needs help in locating employment. These core services mainly involve access to self-directed job searches through an information center that contains information on available job openings in the community. For those individuals who are eligible for more intense services through the One Stop Center, a variety of individualized services are potentially available, including access to vocational training and assistance with job placement.

Youth and young adults with disabilities are targeted for services through One Stop Centers. Therefore, One Stop Centers can serve as a significant resource for youth with disabilities and transition teams in the development of the transition plan. One Stop Center staff, such as plan managers and disability program navigators, can assist in planning employment-related services, including reaching into the community to identify and acquire other needed transition services. By design, One Stop Centers frequently serve as a home base for many community partners, such as VR and representatives of community rehabilitation programs that co-locate staff within the One Stop setting.

One Stop Centers have job listings identifying available employment opportunities. Information from interest inventories can help guide a job search. For individuals who need accommodations to access job information through, for example, computerized job search resources, One Stop Center workstations are frequently equipped with accessibility kits that accommodate a variety of disabilities (Gervey, Gao, & Rizzo, 2004). One Stop Centers offer job clubs, where an individual looking for employment can get support and information from peers and a group facilitator. Some One Stop Centers have employment resource staff who will represent the job interests of an individual with a disability to a potential employer and help negotiate a job opportunity (Targett, Young, Revell, Williams, & Wehman, 2007). Additional employment services of potential value to youth in transition include paid and unpaid work experiences, occupational skills training, job placement, and follow-up services after employment to help with job retention and career development. Funding for employment services through a One Stop Center occurs frequently through the center's direct links with the other community agencies that fund employment services, such as VR and CSBs.

Career exploration labs at the One Stop Center can be used for career awareness and exploration, including taking interest tests and accessing web-based links to job information. Career exploration may also include planned visits to job sites to review employment opportunities, meetings with employer representatives, and summer job programs. As youth near completion of their school program, exploration may include more extended internships or part-time employment built into the individual's school program and transition plan. One Stop Centers are an evolving community resource. Youth with autism, their families, and their transition teams need to become thoroughly familiar with the resources and services available from the One Stop Center in their community early on in the transition process.

As is true with all the community programs and resources described in this chapter, youth, families, and transition teams must determine the specific services available in their locale. Consider the various ways that community agency staff are involved in the transition planning process for Jeff, Craig, and Maria. Service coordination for Jeff might come through a service coordinator at a CSB; the main contact on Craig's team might be from VR; and because Maria's goals include going to college, the plan manager at a One Stop Center might be the hub for her transition planning.

ROLE OF DISABILITY
BENEFITS PLANNING IN TRANSITION

Effective transition planning includes a review of the critical issues surrounding disability benefits provided by the Social Security Administration (SSA). For many students with autism, the monthly cash payments provided by SSA disability programs represent an important source of monetary support. Associated public health insurance benefits, such as Medicaid and/or Medicare, frequently pay for essential medical equipment and services. Although Social Security disability benefits offer youth with disabilities significant financial resources that can facilitate transition, fear of potential benefit loss caused by paid employment is a major barrier to seeking employment (Miller & O'Mara, 2006).

Work and receipt of disability benefits are not mutually exclusive. The SSA disability programs include numerous provisions, known as *work incentives*, that are designed to ease the transition from dependence on benefits to greater economic self-sufficiency. These work incentives offer transition-age beneficiaries exciting opportunities to participate in postsecondary education and to obtain the workplace services and supports necessary to fully accommodate disability in the workplace. Receipt of Social Security disability benefits should be viewed as a potential advantage that can be used to achieve transition goals, including paid work in community businesses.

Although Social Security disability benefits play a significant role in promoting successful transition to adult life, the impact of these benefits on youth with disabilities is seldom considered during the formal transition planning process. Although this oversight is attributable to numerous factors, it represents a significant missed opportunity to educate students with disabilities and their families. Social Security disability benefits may be a valuable resource to eligible students as they make the transition from school to adult life, as they not only offer cash payments and health insurance but also include numerous provisions specifically designed to increase employment and earnings capacity during and after secondary education. Furthermore, in some cases failure to focus on Social Security disability benefits during transition is not just a missed opportunity; it may cause harm to students and family members who are neither educated about nor prepared for the changes that earned income may have on cash benefits and medical insurance (Miller & O'Mara, 2003).

UNDERSTANDING BENEFITS PLANNING SERVICES

If work incentives associated with Social Security disability benefits are to be used strategically to achieve goals, such as maintaining paid employment or pursuing postsecondary education, beneficiaries and their family members need to understand how the benefit programs function and how employment affects these benefits. Unfortunately, the SSA disability programs and Medicaid and Medicare are terribly complex. Few beneficiaries or disability professionals understand the SSA work incentive provisions and how these provisions can be used to facilitate successful transition planning. Furthermore, Social Security disability benefit expertise is generally not available within the special education system, the state VR system, CRPs, or the larger disability services community. Although SSA personnel certainly understand how the disability benefits function, they simply do not have the time to counsel individual beneficiaries on how to best utilize work incentives to achieve an employment or community living goal. To help address the need for effective benefits planning, the SSA established a new program called the Work Incentives Planning and Assistance (WIPA) project in September 2006 and currently maintains cooperative agreements with 104 WIPA projects. In most communities, the only available source of reliable benefits planning services are from the designated SSA–funded WIPA project. The benefits counselors who work in WIPA projects are referred to nationally as Community Work Incentive Coordinators (CWICs). To locate the WIPA provider in a particular area, visit the SSA's (2008a) web site.

The WIPA initiative funded by the SSA has created a national network of benefits planning. Some states have chosen to expand on SSA–funded services by providing additional resources for benefits planning. Some state VR agencies, for instance, have become actively involved in funding and/or providing additional benefits planning assistance. States therefore vary significantly in terms of the availability of WIPA; some states will only have SSA–funded WIPA projects, whereas others may have multiple options for obtaining benefits or work incentives planning services. To find the options available in a given community for benefits planning or work incentives advisement, the best place to start is with the designated WIPA project. The CWICs will be familiar with any additional sources of assistance with benefits, what these services consist of, and any eligibility requirements.

The benefits counseling services available from WIPA projects are limited to individuals who are already receiving Social Security benefits based on disability and are focused exclusively on work or work-related issues. Students who are not already receiving Social Security disability benefits and those who are not considering employment would typically not receive anything from WIPA projects beyond initial information and referral services. To receive WIPA services, a beneficiary does not have to be working, or even actively seeking work, although these individuals would be considered a high priority. Students and their family members who are just starting to think about work also need accurate information about work incentives and the effect that working will have on public benefits. Transition-age youth with disabilities who are in the initial stages of exploring the possibility of employment are very appropriate WIPA referrals, and some WIPA projects prioritize this population.

Eligible youth can expect to receive the following services from WIPA projects, depending on their presenting needs and preferences:

- Analysis of current benefit status, verification of all benefits received, and identification of other available benefits the individual might be eligible for

- Assistance with identifying, selecting, and/or clarifying career goals as well as assistance with determining what specific services, supports, or accommodations may be necessary to achieve the desired career goal

- Explanation of the SSA's Ticket-to-Work program and the full array of vocational services and supports available to individuals with disabilities in the local WIPA service area

- Thorough explanation of how paid employment will affect all public benefits received

- Individualized work incentives planning and assistance designed to promote achievement of employment and other transition goals

- Counseling on wage reporting requirements for Social Security disability benefits

- Counseling on available health insurance options and advisement on how health insurance is affected by paid employment

- Proactive follow-up services to ensure that work incentives are properly applied or to resolve problems related to employment and benefits

- Long-term work incentives management provided on a scheduled, continual basis as needed to support employment efforts

- Assistance with resolving problems related to work efforts, higher education, occupational skills training, and work attainment or continuation of work

SOCIAL SECURITY DISABILITY BENEFITS APPLICABLE TO TRANSITION-AGE YOUTH

There are a host of specific issues regarding Social Security disability benefits that may affect transition-age youth with disabilities; some of these issues are related to employment or postsecondary education, and others are not. All of these issues, however, are important to transition planning, and most will require intervention from trained, experienced benefits specialists to reap the maximum advantage for the student. Although all of these issues cannot be explored in detail in this chapter, we will identify the most critical ones and summarize them according to age—under 18 and over 18.

There is a common misconception that all students with disabilities receiving cash benefits from the SSA are getting a type of benefit called Supplemental Security Income (SSI). Although the majority of students with disabilities would be receiving SSI payments funded under Title XVI of the Social Security Act of 1935 (PL 74-271), by no means does this apply to all students. A small percentage of transition-age youth will be receiving Social Security disability benefits authorized under Title II of the Social Security Act, such as Social Security Disability Insurance or Childhood Disability Benefits, which are not available until an individual turns 18. To further complicate matters, some youth receive both SSI and a Title II Social Security disability benefit.

Because the Social Security system can be very confusing, it is critical that the transition coordinator assist students and family members in verifying which type of benefits are being received so that correct advice on work incentives may be provided. There are clearly many different Social Security benefit programs available, and these benefits vary widely in how they function. Families and transition teams are strongly advised to enlist the help of a benefits specialist or CWIC to get this information from the SSA.

Social Security Disability Benefits for Youth Younger than Age 18

If a school transition coordinator asked parents of transition-age youth with severe disabilities to identify their main concern regarding transition into employment, many would express frustration with trying to establish or maintain eligibility for the SSI program and Medicaid. Although the need for an SSI cash payment is of paramount importance to some of these families, most will say that Medicaid coverage is their most critical need. Some children with autism have significant medical expenses, including costly treatments, services, and medications. Often these medical interventions are not covered by private insurance, or the existing coverage involves high premiums, co-payments, or deductibles that families can ill afford. The quest for affordable health insurance that covers needed services is often the driving force behind the desire to establish SSI eligibility for youth.

SSI is a means-tested program, meaning that there are financial eligibility considerations based on parental income or resources. Many children with severe disabilities are not eligible for SSI for this reason. This practice, called *deeming*, is based on the notion that those who have a responsibility for one another share their income and resources, meaning that a parent's or guardian's income and assets are taken into consideration when determining eligibility. The portion of parental income or resources shared with the child is deemed by Social Security as being available to that child for the purposes of SSI eligibility and when calculating the amount of the SSI payment. Determining how much of the parental income and/or resources to count against the child is a process called *parent-to-child deeming*. If deemed parental income and/or resources exceed the limits established by the SSA, the child is found to be ineligible for SSI and the associated Medicaid coverage (VCU, 2005). In other cases, families have trouble obtaining the evidence needed to facilitate a positive disability determination. For example, a student with Asperger's syndrome may function well enough in school that he or she is not eligible for Social Security disability benefits.

It is essential to recognize that a great deal of time, energy, and effort may have been expended to secure a student's SSI benefit. Parents who have fought a long, exhausting battle to establish SSI eligibility are particularly loath to risk benefits by having their child pursue paid employment.

To illustrate how work incentives built into the SSA disability programs can help younger students achieve employment and other transition goals, we discuss Jeff's and Maria's stories first. Because Craig will soon turn 18, we will focus on his situation in a later section.

Jeff's Disability Benefits

At 15 years old, Jeff receives a reduced SSI payment due to the impact of deemed parental income. His SSI payment is $450 per month, and he also receives Medicaid coverage. Jeff's transition plan includes an employment goal, but his plan indicates that perhaps self-employment might eventually be best in light of Jeff's vocational preferences and capacities. Jeff's parents think he might like to own a plant business some day because he enjoys helping his mother with her flower and vegetable gardens and is a member of the school horticulture club. In addition, Jeff has the ability to participate in postsecondary education. He would like to study computer programming at the community college, and his parents hope to save enough money over the next few years to make that goal a reality.

Consider how SSA work incentives would apply to Jeff. First, as long as Jeff remains in school and is younger than 22 years of age, he would be able to apply the Student Earned Income Exclusion (SEIE). SEIE is an SSI special work incentive for young people who are attending school and are trying out paid employment in preparation for adult life. In 2008, the SEIE allows SSI recipients who are younger than age 22 and regularly attending school to exclude up to $1,550 of gross earned income per month, up to a maximum annual exclusion of $6,240. (The SEIE exclusion amounts are raised every year in January; visit http://www.ssa.gov for more information.)

For the purposes of the SEIE, "regularly attending school" means that the student takes one or more courses of study and attends classes according to one of the following schedules:

- At least 12 hours per week in Grades 7 through 12

- At least 8 hours per week in a college or university

- At least 12 hours per week in a training course to prepare for employment (15 hours per week if the course involves shop practice)

- For less time than indicated above for reasons beyond the student's control (e.g., illness)

The SEIE is applied to a student's gross earnings before any other allowable exclusions. The annual SEIE maximum applies to the calendar year, from January through December. It is not possible to apportion the amount of the SEIE applied in a given month. All earnings received in a month up to the current monthly maximum will be excluded as long as the individual remains eligible for the exclusion and the annual maximum has not been reached.

Assuming Jeff works in a part-time job at which his monthly gross earnings are under $1,550 per month and do not exceed $6,240 for the whole calendar year of 2008, he would be able to keep his full $450 monthly SSI payment and all of his take-home pay. He could continue to work like this throughout his high school years and experience little if any reduction in his SSI payment and no change to his Medicaid coverage.

Jeff has some additional issues to address because of the possibility of eventually owning his own business and pursuing postsecondary education. There is another SSI work incentive that can be used to help Jeff and his parents bring one or both of these goals to fruition: a work incentive the SSA calls a Plan to Achieve Self-Support, or PASS.

A PASS allows a person with a disability to set aside income and/or resources for a specified period of time to pay for items or services needed to achieve a specified work goal. These services include education or training, job coaching or other support services, transportation, job-related items, equipment needed to start a business, or just about anything else needed to achieve an occupational goal.

Income and/or resources set aside in a PASS are not counted when determining SSI eligibility or when determining the amount of SSI payment. This means that a student whose income or resources are too high to qualify for SSI may develop a PASS to set aside the excess income and/or resources for his or her work goal, thus establishing initial SSI eligibility. For someone like Jeff who has already been found eligible for SSI, a PASS may be used to set aside income or resources that would otherwise cause ineligibility or reduced benefit payments.

For Jeff, a PASS could be used to set aside the deemed parental income that is currently causing his SSI payment to be reduced below the 2008 federal benefit rate (FBR) of $637, which is the maximum federal SSI payment an individual may receive. In Jeff's case, the SSA has valued the deemed parental income at $187 each month. By using a PASS, Jeff could identify a specific occupational goal, set aside the deemed income of $187 each month in a special PASS account, and save this money to pay for the items or services he needs to achieve his goal of small business ownership. The SSA would disregard this income and increase his monthly SSI payment to the 2008 FBR of $637.

The PASS plan would also allow Jeff to accumulate more than $2,000 in his PASS account and not have this money cause him to be ineligible for SSI. The SSI program is strictly means-tested. Individuals who have countable resources (e.g., bank accounts) of more than $2,000 will be found ineligible for the SSI program. Excess resources will cause loss of both SSI cash payments and Medicaid coverage. Consultation with a qualified benefits specialist can provide more information about what counts as a resource and what does not.

There is currently no limit to how much an SSI recipient can accumulate under an approved PASS. Jeff's plan would need to describe how the saved money would be spent to help him achieve his occupational goal. The expenditures might include paying for plant care training, covering the costs of inventory, and purchasing the tools and equipment he would need to start his business. In addition, if Jeff works at a part-time job while he was in school, he can put his earnings from this job into the PASS account. Without a PASS, the SEIE would reduce his countable earned income so that it would not cause any loss of SSI cash payments. However, Jeff cannot save the earnings from his part-time job for future use because resources of more than $2,000 would cause ineligibility for SSI. With an approved PASS, Jeff can save his earnings in the PASS account, and they will be disregarded by the SSI program.

Using a PASS allows individuals with disabilities to leverage their own Social Security disability benefits to pay for the items or services they need to become successfully employed or self-employed. A distinct advantage of a PASS is that it allows individuals with disabilities to direct their own career plan and secure the necessary items or services to reach their work goal. Although developing a PASS plan is somewhat complicated and time consuming, the advantages of this powerful work incentive make it well worth the effort. Jeff and his parents would need the services of a trained benefits specialist to help them develop the written plan and handle the PASS submission, approval, and management process.

Jeff is an excellent candidate for using a PASS for several important reasons. First, he has deemed income from his parents to set aside in a PASS. The SSA does not allow a person to set aside SSI cash payment in a PASS—only other forms of income. Second, Jeff has a clear occupational goal: to establish a plant business. Third, Jeff's occupational goal will require a fairly substantially investment to attain. He will need to purchase a variety of items and services to start his business and may need specialized items or services to accommodate his disability in operating the business.

Although the age of 15 might be a bit young to actually submit a PASS in most cases, it is not too young to begin planning for an occupational goal and mapping out the steps for accomplishing this goal. Assuming Jeff will graduate from high school at the age of 18, it would not be premature to start developing the PASS as early as 16 years of age. There is no requirement that individuals be a certain age to submit a PASS, only that they have a feasible occupational goal, income or resources to set aside in a PASS, and a clear and reasonable plan with time lines for how the occupational goal will be achieved using PASS funds (VCU, 2008a).

Maria's Disability Benefits

At 16 years old, Maria receives a monthly SSI payment of $300 and has Medicaid coverage. Her SSI payment, like Jeff's, is reduced from the 2008 maximum FBR of $637 because of deemed parental income. Maria's transition plan currently contains a goal of employment, and Maria's teacher would like to refer her to the high school community-based vocational education program in hospitality training. Maria's mother is very concerned that participation in this program, which involves trying out a variety of paid jobs in a hotel, will cause Maria to lose her SSI and Medicaid coverage.

The good news for Maria and her mother is that the SEIE will significantly reduce how much earned income the SSI program will count for Maria. Because SSI payments are reduced by countable income, applying the SEIE will allow Maria to keep more of her SSI check when she goes to work. In many cases, the SEIE allows students to test their ability to work without experiencing any reduction in the SSI check at all. In other words, Maria would have to get a job paying more than $1,550 per month before she would experience any reduction in her SSI cash payment. As long as she does not earn more than $6,240 in calendar year 2008, she can work each month and still keep all of her SSI check and her Medicaid.

Maria would remain a student for the purposes of the SEIE when classes are out for the summer if she attends classes regularly just before the time classes are out and also does one of the following:

- Tells the SSA that she intends to resume attending regularly when school reopens

- Actually does resume attending regularly when school reopens

This means that Maria could even benefit from the SEIE if she got a summer job while school was not in session. When Maria graduates from high school, she can continue to apply the SEIE over the summer months if she intends to resume school (e.g., college) after summer break—as long as she is still younger than 22. If she changes her mind and decides not to pursue postsecondary education, she will no longer be considered a student, effective with the month her intent changed. That would be the last month in which the SEIE could be used to reduce her countable earnings.

Although the SEIE is an extremely useful work incentive, it is not the only exclusion available to reduce countable earned income for SSI recipients. Even if Maria got a job that paid more than $1,550 per month or she earned more than $6,240 in calendar year 2008, she still would not be likely to lose all of her SSI cash benefit. After the SEIE is exhausted, the SSI program still allows a $20 per month general income exclusion and a $65 per month earned income exclusion to be subtracted from earnings. After these additional exclusions, the SSA only subtracts $1 from the SSI check for every $2 left as countable income. Maria will still come out ahead by working even after she is no longer eligible to apply the SEIE. More detail on the specifics of the SEIE can be found on the SSA's (2008b) web site.

A note of caution: Even if Maria is working and keeping all of her SSI cash payments, she still needs to be careful not to accumulate countable resources of more than $2,000. As mentioned previously, individuals who have countable resources of more than $2,000 will be found ineligible for the SSI program.

Unlike in Jeff's case, a PASS would not be pursued for Maria. Although Maria has deemed income from her mother to fund a PASS and has an interest in attending community college, she does not have a specific occupational goal and does not need to purchase any items or services to achieve an occupational goal. Therefore, Maria would not be a candidate for a PASS at this time. Although a PASS is a powerful work incentive, it is not useful or applicable to all beneficiaries.

Supplemental Security Income Recipients and Postsecondary Education

Because SSI is a means-tested program that imposes strict limits on income and resources, many youth with disabilities and their family members assume that there is no way to retain SSI eligibility and save for postsecondary education. In fact, this is not the case. Although a PASS offers an excellent way to save for postsecondary education without risking benefit loss, it is not the only way, and it may not be the best way for some SSI recipients. Benefits specialists can counsel families on how they can receive assistance in paying for postsecondary education as well as on how they can save money for educational purposes without risking loss of SSI benefits due to excess resources and parental deeming.

Social Security Benefits After the 18th Birthday

The 18th birthday is a turning point for all youth in the United States because it marks the beginning of legal adulthood. This is also true for youth with disabilities, of course, and there are some profound changes in the way the SSA handles disability benefits for those 18 and older. These changes will vary greatly depending on an individual's circumstances. In most cases, students, families, teachers, and transition specialists have no idea that this milestone can cause such upheaval in students' benefits. They are often completely blindsided by the events that take place.

The year before a student turns 18 must be spent by carefully examining all of the relevant benefits issues that may arise and planning how to deal with them. A special process for conducting this review has been developed, called the *age-18 benefits checkup*. It is considered to be a recommended practice in work incentives counseling for transition-age youth. The age-18 benefits checkup can be thought of as a wellness approach—somewhat like an annual medical checkup—that is focused on promoting positive benefits outcomes and avoiding potential problems. An age-18 benefits checkup guide can be accessed online (see VCU, 2008a).

SSI recipients who turn 18 must have their eligibility reviewed as if they were applying for SSI for the first time, without consideration of previous disability determinations. This process is known as the age-18 redetermination. In the SSI program, the definition of *disabled* changes when a person turns 18, and all SSI recipients are reassessed under the new, tougher adult disability standard. A substantial proportion of these youngsters fail to meet the new adult disability criteria (Auxter, Halloran, Berry, & O'Mara, 1999). Students who are not determined to be "disabled" as adults are often terminated from SSI cash benefits and generally lose Medicaid coverage.

Another critical age-18 event is the beginning of eligibility for a type of Title II Social Security disability benefit called *Childhood Disability Benefits* (CDB). Students who become eligible for CDB when they turn 18 often lose eligibility for the SSI program. CDB payments are viewed as unearned income by the SSI program, and they may exceed the allowable limit for SSI benefits. Sometimes these students mistakenly lose their Medicaid coverage, even though laws do exist to prevent this from happening.

Fortunately, not all Social Security changes that occur at the age of 18 are negative. In fact, some very positive changes can occur. For example, there are many students who fail to qualify for SSI benefits as children because of excess parental income or resources. Once an individual turns 18, the SSA views the person as an adult and no longer counts the income from his or her parents. This is true even when the parents have obtained legal guardianship of the individual through the court system. It is not uncommon for the 18th birthday to mark the beginning of SSI eligibility, if the student applies for benefits. We will explore this issue further by using Craig as an example in a later section.

Understanding the Supplemental
Security Income Age-18 Redetermination Process

The age-18 redetermination process may occur at a regularly scheduled continuing disability review or at another point as determined by the SSA. The redetermination usually occurs within 12 months after the 18th birthday, although this is not required by regulation. Individuals who are not determined eligible for SSI benefits as adults will receive a written notice that they are no longer qualified to receive benefits. These individuals are entitled to receive 2 more months of payments after the date of this notice. Overpayment will occur if an ineligible individual continues to receive payments after the 2-month grace period, so families should be prepared to pay back the overpayment amount. Individuals found ineligible under the adult rules are not required to pay back *all* SSI payments received after the birthday month; the SSA will only seek to recover those payments received after the determination has been made and the 2 grace months are over. It is important to help families understand this point, as it causes a great deal of needless worry when the redetermination is conducted some months after the 18th birthday.

The most difficult aspect of the age-18 redetermination is that SSI cash payments and Medicaid will stop if the student is not found eligible under the adult disability standard. It is bewildering for students and their families, who may have received benefits for many years, to suddenly be declared ineligible even though there has been no change in medical condition or ability to function since eligibility was originally determined. Although there is nothing an SSI recipient can do to avoid the age-18 redetermination process, there are ways to minimize any potential adverse impact this process may have. Involving a skilled benefits specialist or CWIC the year before redetermination to plan and prepare for it is a crucial first step. The benefits specialist can provide information about the redetermination process and dispel many of the myths that transition specialists, teachers, parents, and even disability professionals may have about this critical transition issue.

Many people are under the mistaken impression that SSI recipients must not be working at all when the age-18 redetermination occurs. Normally, when an adult first applies for SSI, the SSA examines whether the person is working and, if so, whether earnings are over a specified limit referred to as *substantial gainful activity* (SGA) (in 2008, the SGA guideline is $940 per month of gross earnings for an individual who is "disabled" and $1,570 for an individual who is blind). This is because the SSA defines disability for adults in terms of an individual's ability to work at SGA, the minimum level necessary for basic self-support. Individuals 18 and older who are earning more than the current SGA guideline are not considered to be "disabled" under the SSA's rules, no matter what diagnoses or impairments the individual may have. Under normal circumstances, individuals who are working at a level that would count as SGA would not be eligible for SSI or any other form of Social Security disability benefits.

During the age-18 redetermination, however, the SGA test of the adult eligibility determination process is waived. Transition-age youth may have countable earnings above the current SGA guideline and still be found eligible for SSI under the adult rules as long as the medical disability standard and all other SSI eligibility criteria are met. Because the SGA test is waived for these individuals, there is no reason to hold back on paid employment until after a student successfully completes the age-18 redetermination. In fact, there is no reason not to engage in paid employment before, during, or after the redetermination (VCU, 2003)!

Students Who Are Vulnerable During Age-18 Redeterminations

The SSA (2007b) reported that more than 40% of all young adults who were redetermined at the age of 18 in 2006 initially failed to meet the adult disability standard. The redetermination process affects individuals with particular disabilities more negatively than those with other disabilities. Here are some examples of individuals who historically have experienced heightened vulnerability during the age-18 redetermination process:

- Students with respiratory, endocrine, and cardiovascular disabilities

- Students who had to appeal their initial SSI determination due to failure to meet the childhood disability standard (these individuals would logically be assumed to be at risk during redetermination, as they struggled to meet even the less stringent child's standard)

- Students who have experienced an improvement in their medical condition

- Students with certain behavioral disorders, such as attention-deficit/hyperactivity disorder or Asperger's syndrome, who may have difficulty meeting the adult disability standard without additional disabling conditions or secondary diagnoses

Continuing Supplemental Security Income Eligibility for Students with Disabilities Under Section 301 Provisions

Although the SSA usually discontinues an individual's benefits if he or she is found to be ineligible at the age-18 redetermination, the SSA may continue to provide cash disability payments and medical insurance (Medicare and/or Medicaid) to certain individuals even though they no longer actually meet the SSA's definition of disability. These individuals must be participating in approved educational or training programs that may enable them to become self-supporting. This important provision is known as Section 301 because the statutory authority for these continued benefits first appeared in Section 301 of the Social Security Disability Amendments of 1980 (PL 96-265).

For an individual to continue to receive disability benefits under Section 301, the following three basic requirements must be met:

1. The individual has to be participating in an appropriate program of vocational rehabilitation services, employment services, or other support services, including participation in special education services.

2. Participation in the program must have begun before the date as of which the individual no longer meets the SSA's disability criteria. For transition-age youth, this means before the 18th birthday, since this is the point at which the disability standard changes and the age-18 redetermination occurs.

3. The SSA must find that continued participation in or completion of the program will increase the likelihood that, once participation ends and benefits stop, the individual will not need disability benefits again in the future.

Current SSA regulations for the Section 301 provision include changes that are highly beneficial for students with disabilities receiving special education services. For example, an "appropriate program" for Section 301 purposes now includes participation in secondary school for students 18–22 as long as the student receives services under an IEP or an individualized transition plan (ITP). Participation in an educational program is defined as taking part in activities or services outlined in the IEP or ITP. This means that students who are found not to meet the adult definition of disability after the age-18 redetermination may continue to receive SSI benefits up to the age of 22 as long as they continue to receive special education services under an IEP or ITP.

In addition, under Section 301 rules, the SSA will *assume* that continuation in or completion of the special education program will increase the likelihood that there would be no future need for an individual to receive disability benefits. This means that students who cease to be eligible for SSI due to an adverse age-18 redetermination avoid having to pass case-by-case "likelihood" determinations that are otherwise part of the Section 301 approval process. In effect, the SSA is making a general policy statement, based on current research, that completing an educational program is assumed to lead to positive outcomes that are beneficial to the disability programs.

Continuation of SSI benefits under Section 301 is a critically important option for transition specialists to be aware of. Students with Asperger's syndrome in particular may be at risk of benefit loss after an age-18 redetermination, and they should be informed about Section 301 protections in the year before this redetermination. In most cases, a trained benefits specialist or CWIC from a WIPA project will need to act as a coordinator to facilitate a successful Section 301 determination; the local SSA field office may not have experience with these cases, and the other involved parties (state VR agency, private VR provider, and school) may not know that this provision exists (Miller, 2006).

Establishing Entitlement for Childhood Disability Benefits

As mentioned previously, turning 18 can also have implications related to eligibility for Social Security disability benefits authorized under Title II of the Social Security Act. The most common form of these benefits provided to transition-age youth is CDB. Individuals who receive CDB payments are adults with disabilities who do not have sufficient work credits of their own to establish insured status for Social Security disability benefits but who receive a Title II benefit based on a parent's insured status.

This program was previously referred to as Disabled Adult Child benefits, and some SSA employees may continue to use this phrase when referring to CDB payments. A benefits specialist or CWIC can explain the critical provisions income and medical benefits for the CDB program and may need to provide support to families to make certain the provisions are applied properly. In some states and locales, the agency administering Medicaid programs routinely fails to identify eligibility for this special category of Medicaid coverage. For more information about the work incentives that apply to the CDB program, refer to SSA's (2007a) *Redbook: A Summary Guide to Employment Supports for Individuals with Disabilities under the Social Security Disability Insurance and Supplemental Security Income Programs*. It can be accessed from the SSA's web site.

Transition-age youth with disabilities are poised at a critical juncture in their lives unlike any other they may experience. This juncture presents some unique challenges as well as opportunities related to work incentives planning and assistance. The challenges include facing the upheaval of the SSA disability program changes that occur at age 18 and experiencing the turbulence of simply planning for adulthood. The technical benefits information provided in this chapter may seem a bit overwhelming, but the most important concept to grasp is that Social Security disability benefits planning does play an important role in facilitating successful transition from school to adult life for students with disabilities. Although parents, transition specialists, and teachers may be confused about all the different disability benefits, their associated work incentives, and how they may be used to achieve transition goals, there is a reliable source of help available for many students. It is up to special education professionals, such as transition specialists, to avail themselves of this assistance in the transition planning process.

Introducing work incentives planning early on has tremendous benefits for both students and teachers. It can help students avoid some of the fear and inertia that can ensnare older beneficiaries into a lifetime of dependency on public benefits. It offers teachers the chance to focus on teaching and mentoring to build long-term benefits in literacy and independence. Delivering work incentives planning and assistance to youth in transition is a preventive measure that, if performed competently and consistently, will pay dividends far into the future.

Craig's Disability Benefits

Craig is approaching his 18th birthday and will soon be facing some very critical transitions related to any disability benefits he receives from the SSA. Craig's situation is very different from both Maria's and Jeff's in that he was denied SSI benefits due to excess parental income and resources when he first applied after receiving a diagnosis of autism. Craig currently receives no benefits from the SSA and is not covered by Medicaid.

At this juncture, Craig's transition team is recommending that he participate in the school's community-based employment program. His longer-term transition goals include obtaining services from a local supported employment provider and moving into a supported apartment program. Craig's parents are concerned about his ability to support himself financially without any public disability benefits. They are also worried about helping Craig find appropriate health insurance because soon he will not be covered under his father's employer-sponsored insurance plan.

Craig's transition specialist was baffled by the fact that Craig does not seem to qualify for SSI benefits, and she recommended that the transition planning team get some help from a benefits specialist. She contacted the local WIPA project and found that Craig did not qualify for their services because he was not already an SSI recipient. However, the CWIC she spoke with from there provided her with some important information about establishing SSI eligibility when Craig turns 18, which the teacher shared with the team at the next transition meeting.

The CWIC told Craig's transition specialist that the 18th birthday marks the end of deeming parental income and/or resources. As mentioned, Craig's parental deemed income was so high that it had completely precluded Craig's eligibility for the SSI program when he initially applied. Once a student turns 18, however, parental income and resources are no longer considered in making SSI eligibility determinations or in calculating the amount of the SSI payment. At this point, only the income and resources of the individual with the disability are considered. The

CWIC explained that Craig's family should reapply for SSI as soon as Craig turns 18 as it is highly likely that he will now be found eligible. Craig's transition specialist was excited to hear this because SSI benefits can greatly aid in the transition process by providing students with cash resources, Medicaid coverage, and access to valuable work incentives.

Craig's transition specialist was concerned, however, that if Craig continued to work his part-time job assembling display stands at the book and music store, he would not be found eligible for SSI when he turned 18. The CWIC assured her that Craig's part-time job would not result in gross earnings of more than the SGA guideline of $940 per month. This low level of employment was highly unlikely to adversely affect Craig's ability to establish eligibility for SSI, although it would probably cause a reduction in the amount of SSI he would receive each month.

Based on this helpful information, Craig's family agreed that continuation of his part-time employment would be acceptable. Craig worked 10 hours each week at an hourly rate of $7.50. On his 18th birthday, Craig and his parents went to the local SSA field office and applied for SSI. After 3 months, Craig received a notice that he was found eligible for SSI and would receive a monthly payment of $424.67 and Medicaid coverage.

Although Craig's parents were pleased with this outcome, they were confused about the amount of the check, as the award letter did not mention anything about deducting for Craig's job or his wages. Craig's transition specialist referred Craig to the local WIPA project, and Craig was found eligible for work incentives planning and assistance services because he now was SSI eligible. After verifying Craig's benefits and performing a detailed benefits analysis, the CWIC informed the family that Craig's SSI reduced payment was not due to his wages, as he was eligible for the SEIE and all his earnings were being discounted by that work incentive. Instead, Craig's check was being reduced because the SSA had determined that his parents were providing him with in-kind support and maintenance (ISM), which begins at age 18. ISM is unearned income attributable to the eligible individual in the form of food or shelter that is given to the individual or received because someone else pays for it. ISM may be provided by someone who resides in the same household as the recipient (e.g., parent) or by someone outside of the household. ISM can cause a person to be ineligible for SSI benefits and can reduce the amount of benefits paid. An SSI recipient who pays nothing toward the cost of his or her food and shelter is considered by SSA to be receiving full ISM. In this case, the SSI recipient will receive a one third reduction in the current federal benefit rate (FBR), which is $637.

Craig was not paying anything out of his SSI check for the cost of his food and shelter, so SSA was reducing his check by one third of the current FBR for a base monthly SSI payment of $424.67. The CWIC counseled Craig and his transition team on ways that Craig could pay for some or all of his food and shelter costs in order to increase his base SSI payment. Craig's parents were very interested in learning about this process because Craig's long-term goal is to live in a supported apartment. The higher monthly SSI payment would help him to be more economically self-sufficient, greatly facilitating independent living (Miller, 2007).

Craig continued to participate in the community-based work transition program through his last year of high school. In that last year, when Craig was 21, he started to receive services from the state VR agency. His VR counselor referred him to a private employment service agency for supported employment. The agency helped him secure a customized job at a manufacturing company (discussed further in Chapter 7). Upon completion of high school, Craig was offered the opportunity to continue working for the manufacturing company on a full-time basis at an hourly wage of $8.50. Craig's parents had maintained contact with the CWIC from the local WIPA project and, when full-time employment became a possibility, they asked for help in understanding how this would affect Craig's SSI benefits and Medicaid.

The CWIC advised Craig and his parents that SSI recipients always come out ahead financially by working; the more a person works, generally the better off the individual will be. Although Craig would lose access to the SEIE when he stopped attending school or turned 22, he would still receive the other work incentives available in the SSI program. This includes a $20 general income exclusion, an additional $65 earned income exclusion, and half of remaining earnings. Only the portion remaining after all of the deductions are applied will be subtracted from Craig's SSI payment. In addition, if Craig incurs any expenses due to his disability and because he is working, he could claim additional deductions known as impairment-related work expenses (IRWE) to further reduce his countable earnings (SSA, 2007a).

Because Craig will be working full time at a relatively high wage, the amount of his countable income will be high enough to cause his SSI cash payment to be reduced to zero. The CWIC assured Craig and his parents that this would not mean the loss of Medicaid coverage. Craig will be able to retain his Medicaid coverage under another work incentive referred to as 1619(b) Extended Medicaid Coverage. As long as Craig's earnings remain under a certain annual threshold and he continues to meet all of the other SSI eligibility requirements related to unearned income and resources, he can keep his Medicaid indefinitely. Because the manufacturing company offers an excellent health insurance package to their full-time employees, however, Craig will not need Medicaid. The CWIC worked with Craig and his family to determine which benefit package was most advantageous (VCU, 2002, July). Craig and his parents continue to contact the CWIC whenever benefits questions or problems arise.

PULLING IT ALL TOGETHER

For youth with autism and their families, making the transition from the education system to the adult services community is truly a mix of opportunities and challenges. The opportunities come from the array of services and resources that are potentially available. VR offers a national network of state agencies and community services that are specifically designed to help individuals with disabilities achieve and maintain employment outcomes. CRPs can offer more prescriptive, localized services that apply to local cultures and economies. CSBs can combine a variety of community living supports, such as service coordination and supported living with access to funding for employment through, for example, a prescriptive HCBS waiver. One Stop Career Centers and CILs both offer a variety of potential resources and services that directly support transition to community living and employment. Timely and effective WIPA can provide families with an understanding of the relationship between employment and receipt of disability benefits.

The challenge faced by youth with autism and their families is that these many resources vary considerably at the state and local level. Some do not exist in certain communities or are bound by limited funding and waiting lists. Eligibility requirements vary from state to state and program to program. Limited funding that does not fully meet the needs of individuals with disabilities, including those with autism, is a universal and ongoing concern. Being well informed about resources at the community and state level *and* learning how to network effectively among these resources are the keys to planning and implementing an effective transition program for a student with autism. The transition team can reach out to important community resources both formally, with an invitation for them to join the transition team for specific youth, and more informally, as sources of general information and referral for families.

7

Integrated Employment

Pamela Sherron Targett and Paul Wehman

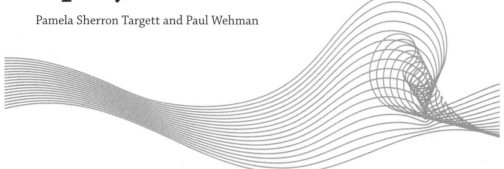

Chapter 6 provided a review of the array of adult services that may be available in different communities for young people with autism. These services vary from state to state, and some young adults will not be able to obtain services. This is one major reason that real work for real pay has eluded individuals with autism, many of whom continue to be unemployed (National Organization on Disability, 2004; Wagner et al., 2005).

The good news is that research has shown that with the right support, individuals with autism can work in a variety of jobs in their community (Hillier, Campbell, et al., 2007; Moore, 2006; Schall et al., 2006; Wehman, Targett, et al., 2007). In this chapter, we explain how to support individuals with autism so that they can be successful in the workplace, something many of them want. We also examine some of the work challenges they face and the types of supports that may help them be successful. In addition, different types of work styles, from close and traditional to distant and innovative, are explored. We look at employment in the community as well as some less traditional options, such as working from home and self-employment.

UNEMPLOYMENT AMONG INDIVIDUALS WITH AUTISM

In the past, whereas many people with other types of severe disabilities went to work in the community, many individuals with autism attended vocational workshops and activity centers (García-Villamisar, Wehman, & Diaz Navarro, 2002; Howlin, 2000). Other people with autism never even ventured out that far, remaining at home or in institutional care (Howlin et al., 2004; Hurlbutt & Chalmers, 2002).

There are a number of reasons people with autism historically have not worked and have not been eligible for support services. First, some individuals with autism face learning, social, and behavioral challenges on a daily basis. Due to these challenges, they frequently require intensive support to perform various activities in the home, school, and community (Smith, 1994). This support must be carefully planned (Wehman, 2006). For example, the level, type, and intensity of support a job seeker with autism may require must be reviewed before the individual finds a job, before he or she accepts an offer, and after being hired. Sometimes a workplace support that is available to all workers, with or without disabilities, is all the new employee with autism will need. At other times, the new employee with autism may need on-the-job support from an outside source, such as a VR service provider, often called a *job coach* (Schall et al., 2006; Wehman, Inge, et al., 2007).

Second, as noted in Chapter 6, it is critical for students with autism to start working with the adult vocational service provider (e.g., the state VR agency) years before leaving school. Failure to make timely contact with the vocational service provider may result in a student's underemployment or lack of employment. According to Cameto, Levine, and Wagner (2004), only 25% of teachers surveyed contacted job placement agencies on behalf of students, and only 35% contacted supported employment programs. Almost as many contacts were made to sheltered employment programs (30%). Moxon and Gates (2001) reported a significant lack of service provision and multidisciplinary support for individuals with autism.

To obtain or retain a job, many individuals with autism need a network of family, friends, and service and support personnel (Fast, 2004; Hillier, Campbell, et al., 2007; Howlin, 2000). However, at age 21, entitlement to services provided by the school system ends, and reliance on adult service providers starts. A lack of skilled service providers and unstable funding is a primary barrier to obtaining needed vocational services (Smith, Belcher, & Juhrs, 1995).

Another factor that has influenced employment for individuals with autism is the public's opinion about whether people with severe disabilities should work in the community. Negative perceptions spill over into the world of business. For example, some employers may have concerns about the costs associated with hiring someone with autism, safety issues, or what will happen if the new employee is not successful in the position (Peck & Kirkbride, 2001). Sometimes an individual with autism will need to have a job created (Griffin & Targett, 2006). A created job is designed to use the individual's vocational strengths and abilities and minimize his or her disability.

Many people with disabilities hesitate to go to work for fear of losing their financial and medical benefits. Individuals with autism and their families are often concerned about how a paycheck will impact Social Security disability benefits, health care, and other disability-related benefits (Kregel, 2001). Changes in SSA work incentives and benefits counseling have reduced these concerns for some (Miller & O'Mara, 2006). For more on these issues, see Chapter 6.

FACTORS LEADING TO SUCCESS IN THE WORKPLACE

Experience has shown that with the right instruction and supports, individuals with autism can work in a variety of places (Smith et al., 1995). They can learn skills that lead to success at work, such as communication, interpersonal skills, and management of problem or unusual behaviors (Burt, Fuller, & Lewis, 1991). Verbal instruction, demonstration, graduated guidance, a system of prompts, written cues, and adaptations are strategies that can be used to teach individuals with autism vocational skills in the workplace (Smith et al., 1995).

Several studies have looked at the unique needs of individuals with autism in the workplace and how to meet those needs. Most of these studies have involved the use of behavior management strategies to reduce difficult behavior, including aggression, self-injury, pica (the persistent craving and compulsive eating of nonfood substances), and property destruction (Berkman & Meyer, 1988; Kemp & Carr, 1995; Smith, 1986; Smith, 1987; Smith & Coleman, 1986). Foley and Staples (2003) showed effective use of augmentative and alternative communication interventions to reduce these types of behaviors. Lattimore, Parsons, and Reid (2006) found that multistimulus assessments were an effective way to predict work preferences in adults with autism. Lattimore et al. found that job-site training paired with simulation resulted in a more rapid and higher level of skill acquisition than did job-site training alone for adults with autism. These studies offer a good start, but much more research is needed to find the best ways to help individuals with autism acquire work skills. It would be helpful if future research looked at workplace strategies such as applied behavior analysis (Wehman, 2006).

In addition to learning specific job and related skills in a real-work setting, workers with autism are likely to need some level of vocational support services, regardless of ability level (Hagner & Cooney, 2005; Hillier, Campbell, et al., 2007; Nuehring & Sitlington, 2003). Vocational service providers, such as job coaches, can assist a person with autism with finding and retaining a job. Effective job coaches are skilled in a number of areas. For example, job coaches who work with a person with autism who has severe intellectual disability and/or behavioral problems must know how to teach the person necessary work skills and how to reduce challenging behaviors. Job coaches should also be able to establish relationships with workers at the job site to build co-worker support for the employee with autism. These are not easy tasks, and many job coaches themselves need training and ongoing guidance to provide these supports.

Job coaches can assist individuals with finding and retaining a job by following several steps. First, they should find out what the person with autism likes and dislikes by watching him or her perform job tasks at a business (Nuehring & Sitlington, 2003). Providers should also learn about the individual's social and communication needs (Müller et al., 2003). Second, they should make a careful match between the person and the workplace by learning about a job in advance and considering the support the person with autism may need to succeed (Hillier, Campbell, et al., 2007; Smith, 1990; Wehman, Targett, et al., 2007). Third, job coaches should be ready to make changes to the way a job task is done or, when possible, to the workplace to support the person with autism (Hagner & Cooney, 2005). With these practices and other advances in the field of disability and employment, more and more individuals with autism are being encouraged to work in the community (Moore, 2006; Schall et al., 2006; Wehman, Revell, Brooke, & Parent, 2005; Wehman, Targett, et al., 2007).

EMPLOYMENT PRACTICES

Many individuals with autism, including those with the most severe challenges, express an interest in working. Although finding a job and staying employed are not easy for these individuals, working full or part-time in the community earning minimum wage or higher should be an option for all who want to work (Luecking & Gramlich, 2003; Wehman, Inge, et al., 2007; Wehman et al., 2003).

In 1971, when Kanner provided a follow-up report on 96 individuals he first studied as children, only 11 had jobs. At the time, many people felt that individuals with autism were not able to work. Since that report, more attention has been focused on improving employment for individuals with autism. Although more research is needed to find the best practices to assist individuals with autism in the working world, a number of practices are now generally recognized as effective. In the following section we review two practices that help people with disabilities work: supported employment and customized employment. (The definitions for these terms are provided in Table 7.1, and differences are explored in Table 7.2.)

Supported Employment

Supported employment consists of a VR professional, often an employment specialist or a job coach, providing or arranging supports to help the person with a disability meet his or her employment goals (Brooke, Inge, Armstrong, & Wehman, 1997; Wehman, Targett, et al., 2007). Supported employment can occur concurrently

Table 7.1. Definitions of employment practices

The Federal Register 34 *CFR* 361.5(b)(53) states that *supported employment* means

(i) Competitive employment in an integrated setting, or employment in integrated work settings in which individuals are working toward competitive employment, consistent with the strengths, resources, priorities, concerns, abilities, capabilities, interests, and informed choice of the individuals with ongoing support services for individuals with the most significant disabilities—

   (A) For whom competitive employment has not traditionally occurred or for whom competitive employment has been interrupted or intermittent as a result of a significant disability; and

   (B) Who, because of the nature and severity of their disabilities, need intensive supported employment services from the designated State unit and extended services after transition as described in paragraph (b)(20) of this section to perform this work; or

(ii) Transitional employment, as defined in paragraph (b)(54) of this section, for individuals with the most significant disabilities due to mental illness. (*Source:* http://www.ed.gov/legislation/FedRegister/finrule/2001-1/011701a.html)

The U.S. Department of Labor, Office of Disability and Employment Policy (ODEP), states that

   "*Customized employment* means individualizing the employment relationship between employees and employers in ways that meet the needs of both. It is based on an individualized determination of the strengths, needs, and interests of the person with a disability, and is also designed to meet the specific needs of the employer. It may include employment developed through job carving, self-employment or entrepreneurial initiatives, or other job development or restructuring strategies that result in job responsibilities being customized and individually negotiated to fit the needs of individuals with a disability.

   "Customized employment assumes the provision of reasonable accommodations and supports necessary for the individual to perform the functions of a job that is individually negotiated and developed." (*Source: Federal Register*, June 26, 2002, Vol. 67. No. 123, pp. 43154–43169)

Table 7.2. Similarities and differences between customized and supported employment

Similarities	Differences
Both benefit people with disabilities so they can use their skills to earn wages, be productive, and make a meaningful contribution to the economy. Fundamental to each practice is the individualization of services to address the unique needs and desires of the person with the disabilty. Each requires a careful assessment of the job seeker's job preferences and vocational strengths (social, communication, and job skills) prior to starting a job search. Each involves a careful analysis of how the workplace and job requirements match the job seeker's preferences and vocational strengths. The work environment is modified or adapted as needed to match the worker's social or communication skills. Existing job duties may need to be restructured or negotiated or a new job may actually need to be created for the job seeker. Each provides various levels or intensity of support to promote success at work.	Supported employment is recognized as a service delivery option and has exclusive funds (Title VI-C) and authorization of case service dollars (Title I). Customized employment requires a blend of general funds and other resources. In customized employment the support person is referred to as a *personal agent*. In supported employment an *employment specialist* provides services. Customized employment results in a completely personalized job description. In supported employment, sometimes work descriptions are modified or new work is created. At other times, the worker performs an existing position with little or no employer negotiations. In supported employment, the employment specialist provides direct support to the worker throughout the various phases of employment, including ongoing follow-up services. In customized employment, direct support varies as needed to help promote success at work. Supported employment is primarily intended for individuals with severe disabilities. Customized employment may benefit someone with a mild, moderate, or severe disability. In a customized approach, the job seeker's disability may not be revealed depending on support needs. In supported employment, upfront disclosure is essential.

with a student's high school experience, or it can occur after a student leaves high school or a postsecondary school. It has been proven as an effective way to help people with intellectual and other disabilities work (García-Villamisar & Hughes, 2007; García-Villamisar et al., 2002; Howlin, Alcock, & Burkin, 2005; Smith et al., 1995). The practice of supported employment has increased employment rates, raised earnings (Howlin et al., 2005), and improved the quality of life for many individuals with autism (García-Villamisar et al., 2002). García-Villamisar and Hughes (2007) noted that adults with autism had better cognitive skills after engaging in supported employment. The average length of time in community-based employment for these individuals was 30 months.

The job coach's first task in supported employment is to get to know the job seeker. Two ways to do this are to talk to the people who know the job seeker best, such as family members, and to spend some time with the job seeker in the community. In addition, the coach may observe the job seeker performing various job tasks in different work settings. Sometimes the pair may spend some time doing other things together, such as shopping or going out for a meal. This is called a *functional assessment*. A great deal of valuable information can be gathered through a functional assessment, such as the job seeker's work strengths, interests, and potential support needs. This information will help the job coach find or create suitable

Table 7.3.   Information gained through functional assessment activities

What activities does the person prefer?

What activities does the person dislike?

What does the person excel in (skills and knowledge)?

Does the person over- or underreact to certain stimuli (visual, auditory, tactile)? If so, give an example of type and under what circumstances.

How does the person communicate basic needs (asking for help or getting information)?

Does the person present and communicate in a way that would usually be perceived as socially appropriate to others (e.g., maintains good hygiene, initiates interactions, responds to others' social interactions, respects personal space, takes turns)?

What are some examples of the type of things the person can do independently?

What are effective strategies for teaching the person a new skill (e.g., prompts, correction, level of supervision)?

Does the person manage down time (find something new to do without being prompted) once a task is completed?

How does the person respond to changes in routine?

Does the person show any emotions or behaviors that might negatively affect employment? If so, how are these managed in various settings?

How does the person solve a problem?

Does the person generally stay focused on the task at hand?

work options for the individual. Information gathered through talks and observations should help the job coach answer questions such as those listed in Table 7.3.

After getting to know the job seeker, the job coach meets with employers to try to identify work opportunities. The job coach must learn about the job tasks and the work environment and then decide if there may be a suitable match between the job seeker and employer. If a match seems likely, the job coach discusses the work with the employer, job seeker, and his or her family. Then, if all parties are interested, the job coach helps him or her complete an application and an interview and follows up afterward.

It is critical to note that the job seeker will likely not possess the skills necessary to perform a particular job, and *this is not essential to a match.* The person should not have to prepare for the position before he or she can be hired. The individual will learn the job and other work-related skills once employed. Thus, a good match, in addition to meeting certain personal preferences, is one where it appears likely that with the right support, including intensive on-the-job skills training from a job coach, the person with autism will be able to learn and eventually perform the job duties. The supportiveness of the workplace is thus another factor to take into consideration. Prior to the introduction of supported employment, people with severe disabilities spent a lifetime getting ready to work. The result was that most never went to work in the community as they were never fully ready to work.

From the first day of employment, the job coach provides workplace support to help the new hire succeed at work. Workplace supports vary from one person to the next. A typical support is on-the-job skills training. For example, the job coach may learn the job duties alongside the new employee. Once the employer's formal training stops, the job coach keeps teaching the new hire how to do the job and other work-related tasks, such as signing in or purchasing snacks in the breakroom. This continues until the new employee is able to work without assistance.

Some individuals with autism may have difficulty communicating and interacting with co-workers. In some cases these difficulties can be resolved with simple instructions. For example, the job coach may model appropriate behavior while providing a signal such as a finger over the mouth to relate a need to lower one's vocalizations. In other cases, individuals may need a behavior support plan, as described in Chapter 2. The goal is to provide the right type and combination of supports to help the person with autism learn how to meet the employer's standards and get along with others in the workplace.

Prior to searching for and beginning a job, the transition team, job coach, job seeker, and family collaboratively make decisions about ways to support the person with autism at work. Later, with the help of the employer, data should be collected to decide if the supports that were put in place were indeed effective, and if not, new ones are tried. Data may be collected and reviewed to see if the worker with autism is learning how to do the job, performing the work fast enough, or interacting effectively with others, among other things. Program guidelines related to putting key work supports in place at job sites are provided in Table 7.4.

Over time, as the new employee with autism performs the job to meet the employer's standards, the job coach begins to gradually fade his or her presence from the job site. However, as long as the person is employed the job coach should be available to provide more support if needed. This is often the case, especially for those with severe challenges. This ongoing, long-term support is a unique feature of supported employment. Supported employment funding from the state VR system, however, is time limited (up to 18 months). This means that the long-term funding to provide continual or intermittent on-the-job support throughout the person's employment must be obtained from another source, such as the HCSBS waiver program referred to in Chapter 6. Long-term support allows the employee with autism and the employer to be supported for as long as needed.

After the intensive on-the-job training by the job coach, a couple of monthly job site visits may be all that is needed by some workers with autism until circumstances require additional support (e.g., a change in job duties, change in management). Other workers may require the job coach's support more often, perhaps weekly or daily. Sometimes an employer will feel that co-workers can sufficiently support the employee with the disability.

It is interesting to note that employment results for individuals with higher functioning autism are not as good as might be expected. They experience frequent unemployment and underemployment; switch jobs frequently; have difficulty adjusting to new job settings; make less money than their co-workers; and are much less likely to be employed than typically developing peers, individuals with less severe language disorders, or individuals with learning disabilities (Cameto et al., 2004; Howlin et al., 2004; Hurlbutt & Chalmers, 2002; Jennes-Coussens et al., 2006; Müller et al., 2003). Even those individuals with postsecondary educational expe-

Table 7.4. Guiding principles for effective on-the-job skills training techniques and strategies for workers with autism

Based on proven state-of-the-art practices

Initially developed from functional assessment outcomes (including input from the family and others who know the person best and observations in real, not clinical, settings) and continually evaluated and adjusted if needed

Includes a variety of individualized approaches

Implemented by trained personnel

Evaluated by measurement of outcome-based progress

rience commonly face employment difficulties (Howlin, 2000). According to self-reports, vocational success relies not on the completion of job duties but on the person's ability to handle the social aspects of employment (Hurlbutt & Chalmers, 2002; Müller et al., 2003).

While in high school, both Craig and Maria, with the help of their transition planning teams, decided to use a supported employment approach. A job coach worked with each of them. Craig's job was created specifically for him, whereas Maria's job already existed. Both received on-the-job support and long-term follow-up services. The following section offers a closer look at how supported employment was used to help these two students. A description of how their jobs were developed is included along with some of the challenges each faced.

Craig's Supported Employment

As mentioned in Chapter 6, during his final year of high school, Craig was referred to a private employment service agency for supported employment services. Craig's job coach visited Craig and his family in their home. She asked a number of questions, including what types of things Craig liked and disliked doing around the house and in his spare time. During the visit, she also observed Craig's behaviors and the family's interactions. She noted that Craig seemed very excited, running around the house and spinning around and around. His mother told her that this behavior was more frequent when he met new people. The job coach also noted that Craig's parents were very supportive and wanted him to go to work. They spent time discussing a possible work schedule, transportation possibilities, and potential job duties and places of employment for Craig. Prior to leaving, the job coach set up a time to meet Craig the following week at the community pool. There, she talked to family members again and watched Craig swim and interact with others.

Next, the job coach set up situational assessments so that Craig could try some job tasks in the community. One assessment took place at a department store. There, Craig helped process (e.g., unpack boxes, put security and price tags on items, sort items into carts) and stock merchandise. Craig was very distracted throughout this assessment. For example, instead of remaining on the task at hand he wanted to process only things for the toy department. He was also very interested in items used in the swimming pool, such as floats, face masks, and flippers. After several attempts to get him to stay on task, Craig began to hit his head and run around the processing area. He was quickly out the door and onto the main floor, running up and down the store aisles. The job coach could not keep up with him; however, she had a good idea about where he was going and found him sitting in an aisle of the toy department.

The second situational assessment was conducted at a hotel. Craig tried out some work tasks in both the laundry and housekeeping departments. Craig seemed to enjoy performing some tasks in housekeeping. For example, he seemed to like restocking the soaps, shampoo, lotion, and other products in the bathrooms. He also seemed to like making the beds. He did not seem to like operating the vacuum or dusting furniture. When asked to vacuum, Craig sat on the floor and started hitting his head with his hand. He refused to return to work when asked. When given the option to return to replenishing bathroom supplies, he did so. Craig was very shy about knocking on a door to announce his arrival and request permission to enter a guest room. He told the job coach, "No, no, strange."

Table 7.5. Craig's vocational strengths, interests, and support needs

Craig preferred work that required him to put things together (e.g., put missing amenities into guest basket, make the bed).

Craig liked to work around others. He learned several tasks by observing other workers performing a task.

When Craig was engaged in a task requiring use of his hands, his arm-flapping behavior decreased.

After Craig had tried out the various work tasks, the job coach was able to identify many of Craig's vocational interests, strengths, and potential support needs. (Some examples are listed in Table 7.5.) This information was shared with Craig and his parents during an IEP meeting. At this time, his parents requested that the job coach try to find a job near the mall or at a business located about 10 minutes from their home.

The job coach went to the mall and approached more than 30 businesses about hiring Craig. No one seemed interested. Time and time again, she was told that business was too slow and they were not hiring. A couple of employers said they might consider some seasonal help but would not be hiring for a month or two.

The job coach met with Craig and his family to discuss the preliminary results of the job search and to identify other ways to network with potential employers. Through these talks she learned, among other things, what area businesses they frequented and where some of their friends and family members worked.

The next day, she took a drive around a nearby office park to find out what types of businesses were there. There were a number of places she had never heard of. There was a company that recycled ink jet cartridges and a distributor of screws, fasteners, and other hardware. She also saw a manufacturing company. The job coach went inside to inquire about the nature of the business and to make an appointment with the hiring manager. The receptionist explained that the company manufactured packaging products, such as boxes, liners, and bubble wrap, and she recommended that the job coach call the owner and manager before 8 A.M. or after 5 P.M.

As the job coach was leaving, the hiring manager returned early from lunch and said he had a little free time if the job coach would like to briefly meet with him. The job coach explained the concept of supported employment services, including on-the-job support from a job coach. The hiring manager said he had hired people with disabilities in the past and that a couple had turned out to be great employees while others had not. The job coach went on to explain that the young man she represented, Craig, was very good working with his hands and loved to put things together. She told him about the time Craig took apart a desk and put it back together with no directions. The hiring manager said he was going to need a new production worker in a week or so to replace an employee who would be retiring from work. He warned the job coach that the work was fast paced and anyone hired who did not carry his weight would slow things down and be fired. The job coach stated again that she sensed that this could be a great match for Craig. She also said that she would have a better idea if she could spend a little time learning more about the job duties. She asked if she could come to the job site and observe the work. The hiring manager told her to be there the next morning at 7 A.M.

The next day the job coach observed the job. She learned that the production line employees rotated among five positions. Position one kept the line stocked with materials; position two operated the machine, including loading materials; positions three and four took the end product off the line and inspected it; and position five, the *boxer/packer*, packed the orders to be shipped. In addition to working on the line, all employees had to pull orders and load trucks and vans as needed throughout the day. Large truck loading was completed from the docking bays, but smaller shipments were hand trucked and loaded onto vans parked in the busy parking lot.

The job coach knew that Craig had a history of not paying close attention to moving vehicles in parking lots. As a matter of fact, it was not unusual for him to bump into a moving car. She began to think about ways this might be able to be managed at the workplace.

The job coach met with the hiring manager again the following day and told him again that she thought it would be a great match for Craig. She explained her only reservation—having Craig learn to load the vans in the busy parking lot. She asked the hiring manager if he would consider allowing Craig to perform some other duty instead of loading the trucks and vans. The hiring manager said that he might consider her request but not until he met the applicant. He asked her to bring Craig in later that afternoon.

When Craig walked in to meet the hiring manager, they immediately recognized each other as being from the same neighborhood. Craig and the hiring manager's son attended the same high school. The hiring manager also recalled seeing Craig and his family at various sporting events and even at the grocery store.

After meeting Craig, the hiring manager offered him a job as a production worker. He would work 20 hours per week for minimum wage. After 90 days, he would be up for a review to increase his hourly rate. In addition, the hiring manager agreed to negotiate the truck and van loading duties out of the job description. He assigned Craig to a boxer/packer position, the fifth worker, in one of the processing lines. As needed, Craig would be pulled to work in this same spot in different production lines while the boxer/packer for that line would load the truck or van. A description of Craig's negotiated job duties and the work setting are provided in Table 7.6.

Table 7.6.   Boxer/packer job and worksite description

Job description

The boxer/packer is the last employee in a five-person processing line and is responsible for packing orders to be shipped. This position requires the employee to fold cardboard into boxes. There are five different box sizes. Box making requires the same basic procedure each time. Each box is lined with a plastic bag. Next, bundles of cardboard inserts are packed into the box. When the box is full, the top flaps are closed and sealed by feeding the box through an automatic tape machine. As needed, the roll of adhesive is reloaded in the dispenser. Sealed boxes are loaded onto a pallet using a specific configuration that is predetermined by the method of shipping to be used, such as air, ship, truck, and so on. Loaded boxes are then labeled for shipment to the appropriate customer. During slow periods, the employee will construct extra boxes, sweep, and straighten his or her work area.

Worksite description

The position is located on the second floor of a mid-sized, dimly lit packaging material distribution company. The floor is concrete. Indoor temperature is subject to daily outdoor temperatures, and fans are available. The noise level is high, and ear plugs are provided. Task completion is highly dependent on other co-workers. The employees continuously work side by side. The majority of employees frequently interact with one another during work. Supervision is moderate. Casual clothing is worn. The majority of work and break areas are accessible.

Maria's Supported Employment

In addition to taking classes to prepare her for the community college AVE clerical skills program, Maria took part in several situational assessments while in high school. Her school had a community-based vocational education program in hospitality training, through which she got to try out many different job tasks in a hotel during her junior year. For instance, she worked in the sales and banquet department, where she learned how to set up tables and chairs for events by following a written diagram. She also spent some time in the grounds maintenance division. There she worked as part of team that picked up trash from the grounds, emptied trash cans, and cleaned the outdoor breezeways and stairwells. She also learned about maintaining flowering beds and cleaning the swimming pool.

While Maria participated in these work activities, her teacher took notes about the tasks Maria seemed to like and dislike. She noted that Maria much preferred working in an office setting than in a hands-on work environment. The teacher also noted Maria's skills and some possible support needs; some of her findings are shown in Table 7.7.

In her senior year, Maria was referred to the school's supported employment program and met with a job coach. The job coach reviewed Maria's work profile and talked to her teacher about her school and community-based work experiences. He also set up a time to meet Maria and her mother in their home. While there, he learned more details about Maria's likes and dislikes. He also learned about the things she did at home, possible support needs, and her availability to work. This would be used to help the job coach make a good job match for Maria. For example, the job coach would be looking for work that offered health benefits, paid above minimum wage, and would not require work on Sundays. He would also try to find a job that would allow Maria to learn a new skill. Some of Maria's behaviors, such as throwing things or scratching herself, would need to be addressed. The job coach familiarized himself with her behavior support plan and decided to try to find work in a supportive environment to minimize Maria's possible self-injury.

The following week, the job coach met with a couple of event-planning businesses. One employer expressed some interest in having Maria work there but stated that the job would require work on weekends as needed. The next day, the job coach headed to his office to set up some more employer meetings. On the way to work, he stopped for coffee at a local shop that also offered catering services. Previously, the shop had only been open in the morning. Now they were also open for lunch and dinner. The atmosphere seemed friendly and upbeat.

The job coach got his coffee, returned to his car, and drove to work. Later that day, he returned to the shop after the morning rush had passed. He asked the woman at the counter if he could talk to the manager. The shift supervisor agreed to speak with him.

The job coach complimented the business and then briefly explained to the shift supervisor that he was trying to help a young lady with a disability find a job doing administrative tasks in this line of work. He asked if they were looking to hire anyone. The shift supervisor said he might need another worker, so the job coach went on to explain supported employment services in more detail. He also spoke highly of Maria's strengths and her interest in working. The shift supervisor said he was open to hiring anyone as long as the person could get the job done, but the job coach would have to contact the owner.

Table 7.7.   Excerpts from Maria's vocational profile

Work factors	Skills and support needs
Availability	Maria can work part time Monday through Saturdays. She prefers to have Sundays off but will consider working them on occasion.
Transportation	Maria's mother will help transport her to work if the job site is on the way to her place of employment. Maria must get to work by 8 A.M. and end by 6 P.M. Monday through Friday. Saturday hours are flexible.
Endurance	If the work pace is steady and manageable, Maria does not need a break until after about 4 hours. If working at a faster pace, she may need a break sooner.
Orienting	Maria was able to learn how to get around the building and grounds without assistance and would prefer to work alone.
Appearance	Maria has difficulties with hygiene. She recently learned how to use antiseptic wipes to wash her face and arms if she gets sweaty on the job. Her mother is having her bathe nightly. Her clothes are usually clean but often not pressed.
Communication	Maria uses short phrases to express her basic needs and wants. For example, she will say, "Maria eat" when hungry or thirsty and "Maria sit" when she is ready to take a break or end her shift.
Social interactions	Maria often seeks out social interactions by repeating movie dialogue. Generally, she keeps in her personal space when she does so. On occasion she has invaded another's space. For example, she is attracted to colorful jewelry on other people and may attempt to touch it.
Unusual behavior	Maria recites dialogue she hears elsewhere. For example, she may recite the words of a song heard on the radio until a new song starts and holds her attention. She may invade others' personal space (see comment under "Social interactions"). If she becomes frustrated, she will scratch her arms and rip her clothing. This was observed once during the assessment when she became upset because she could not take a break.
Attention to task	Once she learns a routine, Maria needs few prompts and low supervision to stay on task.
Sequencing of job duties	Maria follows a schedule written in simple language to perform up to three tasks in a sequence.
Adapting to change	When told that change will occur, Maria adjusts with less difficulty.
Functional math	Maria can count from 1 to 30 and up to 1,000 in increments of 10.
Functional reading	Maria recognizes many words and is able to alphabetize quickly, which helps her file, type, and organize paperwork.

A few days later, the job coach met with the owner and explained supported employment and Maria's abilities. Afterward, the owner invited the job coach to see the administrative office located behind the storefront and take a closer look at what the job would require. Not only would Maria be in charge of filing purchase orders and typing up quotes for the catering business, but she would also be required to help prepare and serve food in the storefront when it got busy. The job coach felt that this could be a good job match for Maria. It involved a skill set she liked and was familiar with (administrative duties) but also introduced a new skill set, preparing and serving food, something Maria had not yet learned to do even at home. His big concern was how to reduce Maria's recitation of phrases while in the storefront with customers and make sure she did not get upset and throw things or scratch herself. Another behavior support plan was drafted to help reduce these behaviors.

Later the next day, the job coach met with Maria and her mother in their home to discuss the advantages and disadvantages of the job. The following week Maria interviewed for the job. After meeting with the owner and shift supervisor, she was told to report to work the following day.

Maria was hired to work 20–30 hours per week for the catering company. The office job duties included typing and filing; in the storefront, Maria would be slicing and plating pies and cakes, making pizzas to be cooked, making salads, and giving customers their orders. The pay was $8.00 per hour. Partial medical benefits with an employee contribution of $20.00 per pay period and a 20% discount on food were also included. The job required working on Saturdays and at least one Sunday per month, which Maria and her mother found agreeable.

Customized Employment

In more recent years, a customized approach to work emerged when the Office of Disability Employment Policy was created within the U.S. Department of Labor (Wehman, Inge, et al., 2007). Customized employment involves finding creative ways to identify and use the strengths and abilities of individuals with significant disabilities by actively negotiating job tasks or duties with businesses (Inge & Targett, 2006). This process individualizes the employment relationship between an employee and employer in a way that meets the needs of both. It is based on a match between the strengths, needs, and interests of the job seeker with a disability and the identified business needs of the employer or the self-employment business.

Like supported employment, customized employment requires learning about a person's strengths, interests, and support needs before helping the individual find a job. In a customized employment approach, however, jobs are actually created through employer negotiations. The negotiations result in a personalized job description for the new employee. This job description may result from negotiating new work from an existing job, or it may be completely new. This process has been referred to as *job carving, job creation,* or *job restructuring.* This is different from a supported employment approach. In supported employment, a job description is sometimes modified or a new one is created, as in Craig's case, but it is not thoroughly *customized.* Much of the time, job seekers using a supported employment model apply for and are hired to perform existing jobs with little or no up-front employer negotiations, as in Maria's case.

In customized employment situations, it is assumed that the individual with the disability will receive any needed supports to perform the job that was individually negotiated and developed. For instance, the job seeker may be represented by a *personal agent,* a VR specialist who can help negotiate a job. After hire, additional support on the job may or may not be provided. For example, the personal agent may simply assist the new hire with locating some special equipment to help perform the job duties or talk to the employer about a suitable work schedule; afterward, no other help may be provided. In other instances, on-site job coach services, like those described for supported employment, may be required. For example, a job coach may be needed to teach the new worker how to use a picture book to see what task should be done next. The job coach may help the new employee build relationships with others at work. Sometimes support is needed off the job site, like training in riding the bus to and from work. There are many different ways in which job coaches can work with individuals, even in customized employment. All of the services mentioned, however, take place for a limited amount of time.

Customized employment starts with a process called *discovery*. Discovery is not planning; it is an assessment process that seeks to answer the questions "Who is this person?" and "What are the ideal conditions of employment for this person?" (Callahan, 2004). After the discovery process, the job developer or personal agent should have some ideas about where to go look for possible work; instead of an identified job goal or description, he or she will have a review of the person's work interests and strengths. This helps the job developer create or develop a job.

One useful approach that may be used during discovery is MAPS and personal futures planning (see Chapter 3). Generally, a group of people get together to share information about the job seeker's background and history, dreams, fears, needs, and what is important to him or her. This information is used to help make plans for the person's future, including goals for working and living in the community. In a customized approach, the job developer may not tell the employer about the person's disability unless necessary. In supported employment, letting the employer know that the job seeker has a disability is required. This way the employer will see why a job coach or other supports may be needed. Whether customized employment or supported employment is pursued, the planning team, job seeker, and the family should decide in advance what to tell the employer about the person's disability and support needs.

Jeff's Customized Employment

In Jeff's junior year of high school, he was referred to his local VR agency for a vocational services. Discovery activities revealed a number of Jeff's vocational abilities, interests, and possible support needs. These are listed in Table 7.8. Based on this information, Jeff's personal agent worked with him to locate and negotiate a self-employment contract incorporating his interest in plants.

The personal agent went to a large greenhouse that sold plants to the public and offered services to area businesses by maintaining plant accounts around town. For example, for a monthly fee live plants were placed in local businesses and maintained by greenhouse staff. This involved making weekly visits to water and care for the plants, rotating old plants out of the site, and replacing them with new ones. When the plants were returned to the greenhouse, they received a routine cleaning and additional care to ward off disease and prevent parasites.

During a meeting with the greenhouse owner, the personal agent learned that although the business had grown in public service, expansion in the private accounts was slow. Further questioning revealed that the owner did not have enough

Table 7.8.   Jeff's vocational strengths and challenges

Strengths	Challenges
Excels in math	Invades others' personal space when meeting/talking
Excels in science	Speaks in very loud monotone voice
Enjoys being around others	Sometimes makes inappropriate comments to women
Has full physical abilities	Adapts to change with great difficulty
Can lift more than 50 pounds	May wander when left unattended
Tells time	
Sticks to a task	
Communicates clearly	

skilled staff to further develop this part of her business. Senior staff, who managed the accounts, also maintained the plants. It had taken many years for them to gain the skills needed to care for the plants; some were very rare and expensive.

The job required workers to identify the plant and then follow the proper cleaning process. This included removing dead or dying leaves, using a steamer machine, and applying solutions to clean and shine the plants. The plants also needed to be examined for disease and parasites. The workers had to be able to recognize these problems and use the right treatment and/or pest control procedure. This involved treating plants with carefully mixed solutions and monitoring their progress.

The personal agent thought about Jeff's interest in science and how it might be applied in this setting. Later that evening, he met with Jeff and his parents to discuss his ideas. Together they came up with an idea for Jeff to care for the plants brought in for maintenance. Jeff seemed interested, and it appeared that it might be a good job match because it would capitalize on his interest in science and gardening. In addition, he could work alone most of the time and be supervised by two people. The workstation would be located in an area that did not have a direct exit to the outdoors, which would limit Jeff's tendency to wander around outside.

The next day the personal agent called the owner and asked if she would review a job proposal for Jeff to contract plant care services. She was agreeable. The personal agent wrote up the proposal and presented it to the owner the following week. After the meeting, the owner told the personal agent that she would have to discuss the idea with the staff and would let him know her decision in a few days. After a week passed with no word from the owner, the personal agent called to see if she had made a decision. She told him that she was not really sure about the idea but would at least like to meet Jeff. Jeff met the owner a couple of days later. She liked him from the start, although she was a bit put off by his interest in her shoes. He kept staring at her red pumps and one time reached down to touch them. After meeting Jeff, the owner told the personal agent to call her back the next day.

The following day she agreed to contract with Jeff as a plant health care specialist with one rule. The contract would need to specify that she could stop services at any time for any reason with a 2-week written notice. Jeff would be hired to work 25 hours per week and be paid a set monthly fee that worked out to be about $8.25 per hour. The job proposal is presented in Figure 7.1.

PLANNING FOR SUCCESS AT WORK

No matter whether supported employment or customized employment is pursued, individual vocational supports must be planned and put into place to support the worker with autism. Preemployment supports include helping the job seeker identify his or her abilities and preferences, support needs, and a work style option, such as employment in the community, telework, or self-employment. This information should be used to help the job seeker find, develop, or customize a job in the community or start a business. After the job seeker begins working, new supports are put into place. Again, the type of support needed will vary. Some workers may need simple supports, such as a modified break schedule or rearrangement of the workstation so that work materials are easier to reach. In other instances, more support will be required. Job coaches may be needed on the job to

Position: *Plant health care specialist*

Job description

The specialist will clean plant foliage, remove dying foliage, identify plant disease and parasites, treat plant disease and parasites, and prune plants if needed. The specialist will also assist with picking up account plants on Saturday mornings.

Benefits to business

Contracting with a plant health care specialist will free up time for management to develop new accounts and expand this part of the business. It is anticipated that additional accounts will increase annual revenues by at least 25% without the need to incur additional expenses.

Applicant's experience

Jeff excels in science at school. For the past 2 years, he has been involved in the horticulture club, where he has learned both the common and scientific names for more than 60 house plants. He has started a notebook that has pictures of the plants labeled by both common and scientific names. These two categories are cross-referenced in the back of his guide.

    At home, Jeff is responsible for a number of activities, including yard work. He routinely works with his father to mow the lawn and prune outdoor plants. He also assists his mother with upkeep of a large flower garden year round and a small vegetable garden in the spring and summer months.

    Jeff also excels in math. He is particularly good at measurements and weights. During a work experience in his school's cafeteria, positive comments were made about his ability to follow complex steps when preparing foods.

Hours

The specialist is contracted to work up to 25 hours per week. He prefers to work 1–6 P.M. on Tuesday and Thursday and 9–6 P.M. on Saturdays.

Work area

The work station is set up in the number 6 plant house. The entrance and exits for this area are located at the main building. Casual work attire is acceptable as long as it is neat and clean. The majority of employees at the job site are males. The account manager will oversee the contracted work. Task completion is not usually dependent on other workers. There will be no formal supervision; however, the account manager will meet with Jeff on a scheduled basis to ensure that his work meets standards. As needed, the specialist will accompany the account manager out to retrieve account plants on Saturday mornings. These are located in a variety of office settings around town.

Workplace supports

Jeff will take the bus to the job site on Tuesdays and Thursdays. His parents will transport him on Saturdays.

    During the first week, Jeff and a job coach will receive skills training about plant maintenance from a senior staff member. The job coach will continue to accompany Jeff to work to ensure that he is able to follow the proper procedures to clean and care for the plants as specified by management. As Jeff becomes proficient at following the procedures, the job coach will fade his presence from the job site. No long-term support will be provided.

    Sometimes Jeff speaks in a loud voice. When this occurs, he needs to be reminded to lower his voice. The job coach places a finger over his own lips and tells Jeff to use a soft voice. The job coach will model this for others.

    Once Jeff starts a task, he likes to finish it. Whenever possible, the staff will wait until he completes a task prior to attempting to attract his attention. Staff will know that Jeff has completed a task because he will say, "That is all for today, class" before starting the next one. If an interruption is needed, staff will say, "Jeff, stop; you need a break."

Figure 7.1.   Employment proposal for Jeff.

As an extension activity, Jeff's horticulture teacher and job coach will help him further develop and refine his plant guide, adding procedures for maintaining each plant as dictated by the management. The final product will include pictures of plants and be laminated and bound.

Time keeping

The specialist will keep track of his own time and present a time sheet to the employer on the 1st and 15th of the month. Any variations in the established schedule will be subject to management approval. In the case of illness, the specialist will notify management as soon as possible and prior to the start of the shift.

Pay

A monthly fee for services is to be negotiated.

Length of contract

The contract will begin in June and come up for renewal in December.

provide skills training and behavioral support and/or develop relationships with others in the workplace. Table 7.9 lists several types and examples of supports.

Natural supports may also be developed. Natural supports are those provided by co-workers or management—or, if the person with autism has a home-based job, those in the home—to help the worker carry out his or her job. For example, a co-worker may help the worker with a disability set up his or her work area or tell the individual when it is time for a break.

Support Needs

Assessing the level of support needed to ensure vocational success requires a vocational support specialist to understand the individual's vocational strengths and potential support needs. This knowledge can be gained from a review of the individual's current records, such as behavior management plans and notes about participation in community-based vocational education programs; and interviewing family members, school personnel, and others who know the person best. When using a supported employment approach, a functional assessment, as described previously, can be very valuable.

This information should be used when making decisions about the type and level of supports the person with autism may need to obtain and maintain employment. Behavior, communication, social skills, responses to sensory stimulation, the ability to handle change, and cognitive skills and learning style should be taken into account. Each of these will be looked at more thoroughly.

Behavior

An assessment of behavior problems should be conducted to decide the level of support that will be needed on the job. Behaviors that are harmful to the person and/or others can quickly lead to unemployment. For example, Jeff's exiting a lo-

Table 7.9.   Examples of supports and instructional strategies

Support	Instructional strategy
Applied behavior analysis (ABA)	Use ABA to increase or decrease a given behavior. Training uses a formal and systematic framework. (See Chapter 2 for details.)
Changes in the environment	Minimize visual (light, movement, reflection, background patterns) or auditory (machinery, music, talking) stimuli that are distracting to a worker. Clearly identify work areas, such as workstations and breakrooms, as well as entrances and exits. Clear, physical boundaries will help the worker understand where each area (and associated tasks) begins and ends.
Visual schedule	Create daily schedules that use visual cues to tell the worker when tasks will occur and in what order. Schedules can depict the worker's entire workday, part of the day, or one activity at a time. Students who do not understand verbal directions for where to go and what to do will benefit from this strategy. Also, predictable scheduling can lessen anxiety for some workers, as they can anticipate what comes next. Examples of visual schedules are photographs; labels, hand-drawn illustrations, or pictures on cards; pictures combined with written information; or written words alone. Teach the worker to independently use the schedule.
Structuring of work routine	Whenever possible, structure the way work is done to make sure the worker understands what is to be done, when it is finished, and what happens next. Routines help make work become more familiar. A checklist or flowchart can be used to help keep the worker on track. Sometimes, a schedule can be combined with the checklist. Those who do not read might use a matching system. The system must be designed to ensure that the worker can maintain expected performance standards for quality of work and productivity.
Visual instructions and cues	Train the worker to use existing cues, or create and implement visual instructions that show the worker what to do (including what to do with materials). Capitalizing on visual strengths can help the worker focus on relevant information.
Manipulation or alteration of antecedent events that signal behaviors	To change undesirable behavior, make a change in the routine or environment, teach the worker to request a break or use a relaxation strategy, or explain to the worker how the behavior affects others. Rather than trying to guess what the person wants, let the person use an augmentative and alternative communication device to choose an activity that depicts his or her choice. Verbal directions should be minimal, and it is important to follow through with the action if the behavior does not change.
Reactive strategies that manipulate or alter the consequence of the behavior	To change undesirable behavior, ignore it, interrupt a behavior to stop self-stimulations, or redirect the worker to a task in which the undesirable behavior is not observed. For individuals with higher functioning autism, design and implement a written contract that specifies consequences and rewards for behavior.

cation and wandering around outside may not hurt anyone but himself, but his being absent for the remainder of his workday is not likely to be tolerated by an employer for very long. Behaviors resulting in property damage are also not likely to be tolerated. If Craig went to work at a restaurant, he would be reprimanded or fired if he stopped working and began eating food from the kitchen.

Some behaviors, though they are not dangerous and do not lead to property damage, are socially unacceptable. For example, Maria's loud recitation of movie dialogue after interacting with a customer in the catering office storefront is likely to draw the attention of management and others. Verbal outbursts, noisemaking, and hyperactivity—all of which can be associated with autism—may threaten employment.

Planning enough support for workers with behavioral challenges is very important. Because there is no way to predict in advance all the necessary supports that may be needed, staff should lean toward providing more support with the intent of fading or removing it as soon as possible. In addition, if a behavior is considered dangerous, continuous on-the-job support should be in place until more appropriate behaviors are learned and the dangerous behavior has decreased. See Chapter 2 for more information on supporting appropriate behaviors.

Communication

There is a wide range of communication abilities among individuals with autism. They may exhibit absence of or delayed language and communication skills or have difficulty understanding abstract concepts. Some individuals may be able to carry on a conversation using complex sentences; others may not speak or may use only a few words. A person with autism who is nonverbal or has limited verbal skills will typically need more support than those who have more advanced skills. For example, because Craig speaks only a few words, he will need a job coach to help his supervisor and co-workers learn to communicate with him.

Over time, even if a worker with autism does not use many words to communicate on the job, a manager or co-worker may become comfortable enough with the person to know his or her needs. The manager or co-worker can then help the person with autism communicate with others on the job. Managers and staff might also learn how to communicate with a person who is nonverbal by using the individual's augmentative and alternative communication device.

If the individual with autism has difficulty with abstract concepts, it is important that instructions are clear and concrete. For example, the instruction "Put these flyers in the mailboxes" may be confusing to a worker with autism. He or she would respond better to "You have 15 minutes, from 9:00 to 9:15, to put the letters in the staff mailboxes."

Social Skills

Some individuals may have well-developed social skills and need little support in this area. Others, however, may display disruptive or job-threatening behaviors toward others. For example, consider again Maria's repeating movie dialogue. Soon this behavior may annoy her co-workers. Jeff may invade a co-worker's personal space by touching his or her feet or by punching or tripping the person. These behaviors could lead to warnings or termination from work.

The level of support a worker with autism will need on the job depends on the nature and frequency of the behavior. Disruptive, frequently occurring, inappropriate social behaviors require more support. Less frequent behaviors, although disruptive, may be tolerated in some workplaces. Sometimes, help from worksite personnel may be enough to calm the individual and get him or her back on task.

Response to Sensory Stimulation

Social interactions may also be difficult due to sensory perception problems. A person with autism may be overly sensitive to certain stimuli related to sight, sound, or touch. For example, Maria may not like the texture of raw dough and refuse to make a crust for a pie, or she may get distracted and off task because of background sounds.

Ability to Handle Change

Some individuals with autism have a difficult time with change. For example, in the middle of a shift at the manufacturing company Craig worked for, workers were asked to move to another work area and start another task. At first, this change caused Craig to hit himself, but after being reminded about the move 5 minutes and 2 minutes before each move by his job coach, Craig learned that these changes were coming. The changes themselves became part of his routine, enabling him to work successfully without injuring himself.

Some individuals with autism, such as Craig, may only need increased levels of supports during times of change. This requires advance notice that change will take place so the proper support can be put into place in time to prevent a problem.

Cognitive Skills and Learning Styles

Many individuals with autism have some degree of intellectual disability (Yeargin-Allsopp et al., 2003). This must be taken into account when planning the level of support the person will need on the job; however, other factors should also be considered, such as the tasks to be performed and the existing cues in the workplace. For example, a person with autism and severe intellectual disabilities may require only low to moderate levels of support if the job tasks mirror his or her abilities.

Prompts are often used to enhance instruction for workers with autism. Table 7.10 provides an overview of some types of prompts. It is important to use the least amount of prompting or assistance to elicit the desired response from the worker. The goal is to teach the worker to do the task without a prompt or assistance; therefore, data must be collected to make sure as little prompting as necessary is given. This should help ensure that the worker does not wait for a prompt to complete the next step in a task.

Individual strengths may come in handy in certain workplaces or when customizing a job. For example, Craig loves to build things. He could be very successful in a variety of jobs that allow him to use his hands to either put things together

Table 7.10.   Types of prompts

Type	Description
Verbal prompt	The job coach tells the worker what to do. If the worker does not readily understand words, picture prompts may be provided.
Visual prompt	The job coach provides picture cards or written lists to tell the worker what to do (sequence of job duties, written directions, or steps needed to complete a specific task) or where he or she should be (schedule).
Physical prompt	The job coach guides the worker to perform the task through actions ranging from a simple tap on the shoulder to hand-over-hand assistance. Hand-over-hand assistance may be needed when the worker is learning a task. Assistance can be gradually decreased as the task is learned.
Modeling	The job coach does exactly what the worker is supposed to do while the worker observes. Then, the worker is prompted to do the same. Tasks should be modeled alongside the worker so that he or she does not have to reverse the image of what needs to be done or depend on watching the trainer for a cue. The worker should attend to the naturally occurring cue (e.g., bell, full trash can that needs to be emptied) that should stimulate the response.

or take things apart. Some people with autism have long attention spans and enjoy spending time doing the same task over and over again. Work that is boring to others may be a good match for them. For example, Maria likes to pull tissues out of boxes. She would probably enjoy pulling the packing material out of boxes in a stockroom.

For some individuals with autism, wanting to do the same thing the same way all the time can be troublesome in the workplace. For example, when Jeff first started his plant maintenance job, he wanted to apply the same antifungal product to each plant, but this could have killed the more sensitive plants.

Focusing on unimportant details and failing to see the big picture may also make it difficult for individuals to learn a job. For example, it is hard for Craig to complete the task of putting labels on boxes to be shipped because he spends so much time placing the tag exactly where it should go on the front of each box.

It is important that the worker with autism learn the correct way to perform his or her job duties from the first day. If the worker is taught how to do a task the wrong way, he or she may have extreme difficulty relearning the correct way to do it. Thus, whenever a job coach is providing on-the-job skills training, he or she needs to be familiar with how the worker learns new tasks. Some individuals with autism learn best through verbal instruction and watching someone else do the task; others may need planned instruction using intense prompts, such as physically guided hand-over-hand training. Whenever on-the-job skills training is needed, the job coach should spend time learning the tasks before the person with autism starts work.

Some people with autism may have restrictive, repetitive, or stereotypic patterns of behavior that make it difficult for them to focus on the task at hand. Ways to keep the person's attention should be considered when designing on-the-job instruction. For example, Maria has always liked to line things up. If she went to work in a stockroom, she may enjoy removing the packing material from the boxes, but she may line the pieces up at her workstation instead of throwing them in the recycle bin. As a compromise, Maria's job coach may have Maria focus on lining up the boxes, which may help Maria complete that part of her job successfully.

Level of Support

Most workers with autism will need some type of job coaching or assistance on the job, even if it is only on an occasional basis. Very intensive support can usually be phased out to some degree over time.

Individuals with autism who have dangerous or disruptive behaviors, poor social skills, and/or limited communication skills, even if they do not have an intellectual disability, will likely need ongoing support by a job coach as offered in a supported employment approach. Some individuals may benefit from having a job customized or created specifically for them. A close review of the work supports that an individual may need both on and off the job should help make clear whether or not to use a supported employment or customized employment approach. Following is a look at some of the workplace supports that Craig, Maria, and Jeff used on the job.

Supporting Craig at Work

Craig's job coach went with him on his first day of work at the manufacturing company and began one-to-one on-the-job skills training. The job coach had tried out the job herself first. This allowed her to organize Craig's daily routine and select ways to teach him the job. She developed a task analysis for each task Craig would be performing, such as punching in to work, making boxes, responding to questions, and punching out of work. As discussed in Chapter 5, the steps in a task analysis are stated in terms of observable behaviors, with each step representing one behavior. For example, the first few steps for punching a time card might be 1) look for the time card with your name on it, 2) remove the card from the file, and 3) hold the card with the name at the top facing toward you, and push it into the machine.

After participating in the new employer's training, the job coach continued to teach Craig how to perform the components of his job by having him first observe her performing each task while she talked through the steps. Later, she gave Craig verbal prompts on what to do. By the end of the fifth week of training, Craig had learned how to perform each task associated with his job. He was also taught to switch from one production line to another when told to do so. Overall, he seemed to adjust well to the change from one production line to another. However, one line was near a window, and sometimes when working there Craig would be distracted from his task by staring out the window. The job coach asked if she could put up a blind or curtain in the window to minimize the distraction for Craig. The supervisor said yes. The change benefited everyone on the line, as the sun at certain times of the day would get in everyone's eyes.

Ensuring Maria's Success at Work

Maria's job coach spent time at the catering job prior to Maria's first day of work. He designed a way to teach her each job duty and some other work-related skills, such as saying hello to co-workers and asking for permission to leave her work area. The plan contained training objectives, guidelines for data collection, and prompting and reinforcement procedures.

Each day the job coach collected some data to measure Maria's performance on certain tasks. The data revealed that Maria was gradually decreasing her dependence on the job coach's instruction. By keeping track of the number and types of prompts Maria required, the job coach was able to determine when to gradually begin moving away from Maria during training. When Maria was able to perform 80% of the steps in the task analysis without any prompts from the job coach, he moved farther away from her. Eventually, when she was able to perform all the steps in a task analysis, he left the immediate work area. He continued to fade from the work area and then the job site. After about 4 months, the job coach was only on the job at the start of Maria's shift.

Maria learned her basic job duties well, but she faced challenges with hygiene and getting along with her co-workers. For example, a few times she showed up to work wearing dirty clothing. Each time, the shift supervisor told Maria that she needed to wear clean clothing because at times she would be assisting with customers in the storefront. Once he even left a message for her mother about this. Finally, the shift supervisor called the job coach and told him that Maria could lose her job if she came to work again in dirty clothing. The job coach talked to Maria and her mother about why Maria wore dirty clothing to work. He found out that Maria was dependent on her mother to do her laundry; however, her mother often worked overtime and only did the laundry on the weekend. To help solve the problem, the job coach and Maria purchased four additional outfits for Maria that complied with the store's dress code. That way Maria was more likely to have clean clothes to wear for each shift.

Another problem surfaced when Maria's co-workers tried to change her routine. For example, one day a new co-worker told Maria to stop making pizza and plate some more desserts for the evening shift. Maria got upset and threw a box full of plastic spoons across the kitchen. The spoons went everywhere. Then, she ran back into the office, sat at her desk, and scratched her arms, refusing to return to the storefront. The shift supervisor contacted the job coach. He explained that he really wanted to keep Maria on but that she had to be able to pull her weight up front and stop the outbursts.

The job coach returned to the job site on a full-time basis to work things through with Maria. The first thing he noted was that several of Maria's co-workers were on vacation. In the past, he had worked closely with these staff members, showing them how to best prepare Maria for changes in her daily routine. With many of these co-workers out and the newer workers not familiar with Maria's needs, no one realized that they should be preparing Maria for changes.

After that, when the shift manager knew that people would be out and additional help would be needed in the storefront, he told Maria upon her arrival that she would likely be needed to help out more that day up front with customers. He also gave her a 5-minute and 2-minute warning prior to her having to move to the storefront from the office, and this helped make the transition easier for Maria.

Coaching Jeff at Work

Jeff received time-limited job coach services. A job coach went with him to work on the first day. The job coach helped Jeff organize his plant notebook to make sure all the species of plants to be maintained were included. They took pictures of each plant and included it on the page with the cleaning and other instructions. Then, they made an index and cross-referenced it to include the plants' common and scientific names; this index was put in the back of the notebook.

Jeff's parents had been worried that he might wander away from the job site; however, his workstation is located in an area of the greenhouse that does not have access to the outdoors. His co-workers know that if they see Jeff moving toward a door, they are to remind him to stay inside. So far, Jeff has not attempted to wander. He appears very content staying at his workstation and in the employee break room.

Another problem involved Jeff's behavior toward his co-workers. Whenever another worker was nearby, Jeff would stare at the person's feet and say something like "I want to see [or bite] your pig" (*pig* was Jeff's word for *toe*). The job coach asked the co-workers to ignore him. If Jeff made the comment twice, they were instructed to tell him that what he said made them feel uncomfortable, then ignore him with no further comments or eye contact. Over time this helped reduce the behavior. Jeff still stares at other people's feet, but sometimes he does not make a comment. In addition, most of the staff members wear old tennis shoes or boots to work, so Jeff is rarely interested in their shoes. When he does make a comment, his co-workers simply ignore him.

NONTRADITIONAL WORK

More and more people with disabilities are looking for different work options, such as telework (working from home) and self-employment. Sometimes a person receives supported telework or supported self-employment services, similar to the community-based supported employment approach described previously. VR counselors can use their general case service and supported employment funds for self-employment services. Other individuals with disabilities sometimes use the strategies of customized employment to help negotiate telework or self-employment and to secure additional support on the job. Job coaches should be familiar with these less traditional vocational options so that they can offer sound guidance and counseling to the job seeker.

Telework

Some individuals with autism may be interested in telework. Telework involves working from home and often requires the use of computing and communications technology to perform the job and stay connected to the employer. Some examples of telework jobs are customer service representatives, computer programmers, word processors, debt collectors, and sales or marketing specialists. To be successful teleworkers, individuals should develop self-management skills, computer literacy, organizational skills, dependability, and honesty. Jobs that require good communication or social skills, such as debt collectors and marketing specialists, could be problematic for individuals with autism. Therefore, when telework is pursued, it is very important to consider the likelihood of the job seeker's success on the job with training and support. Even with social skills training, individuals with autism may have difficulty performing jobs that require telephone and/or social skills. For these individuals, other telework options may be more suitable.

There are two types of telework arrangements: The worker is either a home-based employee or a contractor. A home-based employee is on a company's payroll and abides by company rules. A contractor is self-employed. Teleworkers may work full time, part time, or as needed.

There are a number of reasons someone with autism may desire to telework. For example, an individual may need extended rest periods during the workday or alternative scheduling. The person may have limited transportation options, need personal assistance services that are available at home, or perhaps simply prefer to work from home. There are a number of advantages and disadvantages to telework. Its benefits include a barrier-free workplace, lower stress levels, ability to manage work schedule, break times, lack of social contact (for those workers who experience social interaction as stressful or difficult), control over the work setting (e.g., sound, interruptions, temperature), and reduced expenses compared with working in the community (e.g., work clothes, gas, car, coffee, lunch). Disadvantages of telework include lack of social contact, difficulty staying focused or motivated, and having others interrupt the work.

Self-Employment

Self-employment is a growing trend for people with disabilities, especially in rural areas (Griffin & Hammis, 2003). An individual does not have to be able to run a business independently for this to be a viable option. As with the other approaches to employment discussed in this chapter, partial participation with the necessary supports can help the individual be successful. Through the Rehabilitation Act of 1973, its amendments, and the WIA, people with disabilities can get assistance with purchasing business equipment and/or assistive technology, training, and the supports necessary to run a business. For example, a person may need help with business start-up activities or with marketing or accounting. Business ownership may also be promoted under a PASS, as discussed in Chapter 6. This financial incentive provides operating cash to businesses (Griffin & Hammis, 2003).

One way to promote self-employment is through resource ownership. Resource ownership is acquiring materials, equipment, or skills that an employer uses to make a profit (Griffin, Brooks-Lane, Hammis, & Crandell, 2007). Owning resources gives a person with a disability an edge in business start-up, particularly when establishing a small business or a business within a business. For example, say a young man with autism wants to work with animals. The owner of a pet grooming business wants to expand his business to include a mobile pet washing service but does not have the funds to purchase a van. The young man, who has saved money to start his own business, approaches the business owner with a business proposal to purchase the van that can be used to expand the grooming services. In exchange, he asks for a job grooming short-haired dogs in both the store and on the road.

As with other approaches, the support an individual with autism will need to pursue self-employment will range from little to very extensive. The process is much like it is for other individuals engaged in the pursuit of owning their own business. It involves generating business ideas, obtaining financial and benefits counseling, doing cash flow analysis, writing a business plan, and securing funding. The key to this approach is creativity in developing an idea that will use the strengths of the person with autism and appeal to or meet a market niche.

CONTINUED SUCCESS FOR CRAIG, MARIA, AND JEFF

As mentioned in Chapter 6, after graduation Craig was offered a full-time position at the manufacturing company. He is known as a dependable and hard worker. Through work he has made some friends and played on the company's softball team. Craig was able to perform his job and learn new duties with the support of his full-time job coach. On a few occasions, Craig helped the other staff return non-packaged materials back to inventory. He enjoyed this duty so much that he would leave his workstation in the middle of production to perform this task instead. When asked by the production line leader or a co-worker to return to his station, he would look at the staff member making the request, smile, and run to the back of the warehouse. This required the job coach to implement a behavior support plan. She reached a compromise with the manager so that Craig could spend the last 15 minutes of his shift restocking inventory; however, he was only allowed to do this if he had remained on task during his shift. He was also taught that while on the production line he might be asked to get materials needed to restock the line. Craig learned that by staying on task and being near his co-worker, the fourth person on the line, he could increase the likelihood of being asked to perform this activity that he so enjoyed doing.

After a few months at the catering company, Maria's shift supervisor suggested that she also learn how to enter customer satisfaction data on the computer. Her job coach had been visiting her at work three times per week for about an hour per shift but made plans to return to the job site to help her learn this new duty. Maria's mother was pleased that through this job Maria had learned more about preparing foods. Even after Maria stopped working at the catering company, she still helped her mother in the kitchen and sometimes prepared her own meals.

After 18 months, Jeff's small plant maintenance business continues to be successful. His first contract was renewed after 6 months, and he now has a 1-year contract with the greenhouse. Jeff received assistance up front to develop his business and then received time-limited job coaching services. Now, whenever he needs support, it is provided by on-call job coaching.

PULLING IT ALL TOGETHER

With the right type, level, and intensity of support, more and more individuals with autism are working in the community. This chapter described two approaches to help them with this endeavor: supported employment and customized employment. Both practices hold great promise for helping individuals with autism be successful at their work. Some innovative work options, such as self-employment and telework, were also described. All who are involved in helping individuals with autism obtain and maintain meaningful employment are encouraged to refine the options presented here and/or create new solutions.

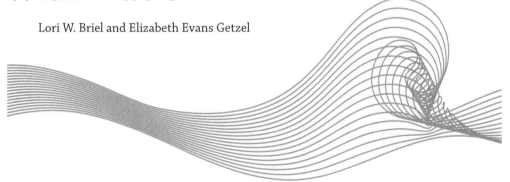

8

Postsecondary Options for Students with Autism

Lori W. Briel and Elizabeth Evans Getzel

Educating young adults with autism in postsecondary education settings is an emerging trend in the field of higher education and disability. Greater numbers of young adults, regardless of their disability, are identifying college as a potential transition goal, particularly 2-year colleges (Wagner, Cameto, & Newman, 2003). As the number of students ages 6–21 who are diagnosed with autism continues to increase, so will the need for further educational opportunities for these students (Volkmar, Lord, Bailey, Schultz, & Kiln, 2004). Based on our knowledge of effective supports for postsecondary education students with disabilities, coupled with the current literature on students with autism and their experiences in college, there are several key areas that emerge as essential in the transition to and retention in higher education programs. These areas include but are not limited to possessing self-determination and self-management skills, using technology, and obtaining internships or other career-related activities (Getzel & Briel, 2006; Getzel & Wehman, 2005; Lipka, 2006; Moon, Grigal, & Neubert, 2001; Moore, 2006; Palmer, 2006; Prince-Hughes, 2002; Zafft, Hart, & Zimbrich, 2004).

It is important to note that few studies have been conducted on the educational attainment of youth with autism and the postsecondary education experiences of these students related to coursework, classroom instruction, accommodations, services, and supports (National Center for Special Education Research

[NCSER], 2007b; Seltzer et al., 2004). On a national basis, information gathered on the educational experiences of students with autism is limited to whether they are in general education or special education classes (NCSER, 2007b). Limited research on postsecondary outcomes is available on students with autism; however, as more is being learned, there is an increasing awareness that these students need postsecondary options to meet their career goals and attain further independence (Rubin, 2007). This chapter presents some of the core elements that are essential for students with disabilities such as autism to make the transition to and remain in college. We also report on what is known to date about the actual experiences of college students with autism.

Research demonstrates that people with disabilities find postsecondary education a means to enhance their chances of 1) obtaining and maintaining employment, 2) earning a higher annual income, and 3) creating a pathway to lifelong independence and a greater quality of life (Fairweather & Shaver, 1991; Wilson, Getzel, & Brown, 2000). Students with disabilities seek further education and training to meet the challenges of today's work environment (Briel & Getzel, 2005; Getzel & Kregel, 1996). The importance of career growth, well-developed technical skills, and successful employment experiences becomes more significant for

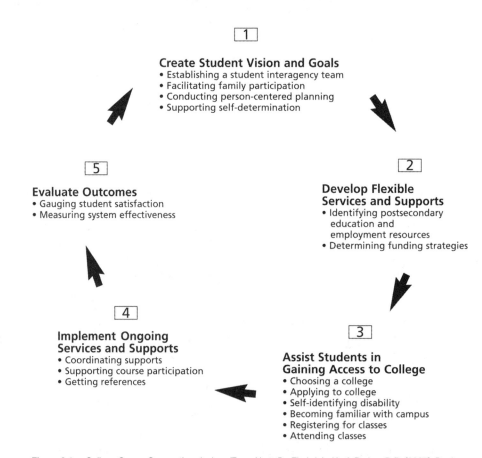

Figure 8.1. College Career Connection design. (From Hart, D., Zimbrich, K., & Parker, D.R. [2005]. Dual enrollment as a postsecondary education option for students with intellectual disabilities. In E.E. Getzel & P. Wehman [Eds.], *Going to college: Expanding opportunities for people with disabilities* [p. 260]. Baltimore: Paul H. Brookes Publishing Co.; reprinted by permission.)

people with high-functioning autism and Asperger's syndrome, who often define themselves by their employment instead of their social network (Grandin & Duffy, 2004). Figure 8.1 is a visual representation of the College Career Connection design, based on a dual enrollment model that was funded by the Office of Special Education Programs from 1998 to 2001. The College Career Connection design is an important model in and of itself in that it was one of the first models that allowed for students with significant disabilities to go to college and participate in inclusive environments. Figure 8.1 has been included because it is a good visual representation not only of the model itself but also of the actions and preparations this chapter suggests that students, their transition teams, and families take to prepare for success in college.

Students with disabilities experience many of the same decisions and preparations for college as other students who are considering going on to postsecondary education. Every student needs to consider the size and location of the college, the programs and majors available, extracurricular offerings, diversity of students, and availability of scholarships or financial aid; however, students with autism also must carefully consider specific factors when choosing an appropriate college or university program. Some of these include the availability of support services, campus accessibility, and documentation requirements to obtain services (Getzel, in press). Although much of this information is available via the Internet and other published sources, parents play the largest role in the college choice and decision-making process for traditional-age students (National Postsecondary Education Cooperative, 2007). Peers, school and college personnel, and mentors also may influence these decisions.

POSTSECONDARY ENVIRONMENTS

Postsecondary education options available for students with disabilities, including students with autism, are increasing as a result of the rising numbers of students with disabilities attending college. Whether students enroll in a 2- or 4-year setting, understanding the challenges of making the transition to a college environment is critical for secondary students with disabilities. Students become fully responsible for managing their college career once they are accepted into a program. In postsecondary environments, the following conditions are present (Brinckerhoff, McGuire, & Shaw, 2002; deFur, Getzel, & Trossi, 1996; Getzel, Briel, & Kregel, 2000):

1. Less contact with instructors

2. Expectations of higher levels of academic capability

3. Fewer tests covering a larger amount of material

4. Changes in the support systems that students previously had in high school

5. Higher expectations to achieve independently

6. Changes in social and independent living demands

The reality of this level of responsibility is often not fully realized until a student is in college. Students with autism face unique challenges entering postsecondary environments, including learning how to act appropriately in classes, how to manage their course load, and how to navigate the social environment unique to college, with roommates and increased independence (Moore, 2006). The more informed students are about the changes in responsibility and the demands of college, however, the smoother the transition will be from secondary to postsecondary education.

It is important that students with autism explore services and supports that will meet their unique needs. There are several postsecondary education options available for students with autism as they consider attending college. Each option must be carefully weighed to determine the environment that best meets students' educational and career needs. The first option is the traditional 2- or 4-year college experience, with supports provided through the disability support services (DSS) office at that college. Some colleges and universities offer specialized programs in conjunction with the services provided by this office. The following three options are considered specialized programs designed for students with disabilities, including students with autism who are in need of more intensive services and supports.

1. *Mixed/hybrid model*—Students with disabilities are involved in social activities and/or academic classes (audited or for credit) with students without disabilities. These students also participate in classes with other students with disabilities, typically life skills or transition classes. Employment experiences are offered both on and off campus.

2. *Substantially separate*—Students are on campus but are in classes only with other students with disabilities. Socializing with students without disabilities is part of the model. Employment experiences are typically offered in preestablished employment settings on and off campus.

3. *Inclusive individual support model*—Students receive individualized services (e.g., educational coach, tutor, technology) and are enrolled in college classes, certificate programs, and/or degree programs (audited or for credit). This model is not program based, but it is integrated into the existing college structure. For example, courses are selected based on students' career goals, and employment experiences include internships, apprenticeships, or work-based learning. (Hart, Grigal, Sax, Martinez, & Will, 2006, p. 2)

Some specialized programs or supports at colleges are offered through for-profit organizations. Others are included as part of a range of services offered on campus. One example of a for-profit company is College Living Experience, which offers extensive supports for individuals with learning disabilities, Asperger's syndrome, and emotional or behavioral disorders. Individuals enrolled in the program receive intensive support to assist them in college, and they live in nearby apartments where independent living skills are taught and reinforced (Lipka, 2006). Other colleges and universities, such as Dowling College and Marshall University, offer their own programs geared to serving students with autism. At a number of colleges and universities, specialized services and supports are provided through the DSS offices on campus or as a separate program in conjunction with these offices (Harding, Blaine, Whelley, & Chang, 2006).

There remains an ongoing need to explore the services and supports that can assist all students; however, information on the effectiveness of these services is limited due to the insufficient research on recommended practices in postsecondary education (Moore, 2006). It is critical when considering postsecondary education services—whether they are for profit or part of a college service support system—that students, families, and transition team members carefully consider what the programs offer and what is a good fit for a particular student with autism and his or her postsecondary education goals.

ACADEMIC CONSIDERATIONS

Students with autism preparing for a more traditional college environment must be able to demonstrate that they meet the academic requirements to enter a college or university. It is important that students are enrolled in college preparatory classes during high school to build a foundation of knowledge, not only to enter college but also to have the academic preparedness to remain in college (Brincker-hoff et al., 2002; Eaton & Coull, 1999; Getzel & McManus, 2005). Transition team members, especially teachers and guidance counselors, should ensure that students are taking the coursework necessary to compete in the college application process. Students with autism must be familiar with the math, science, and language requirements for colleges, especially for the specific higher education programs that they are interested in attending.

If the student with autism has succeeded in college preparatory classes, it is important to thoroughly evaluate how much help the student received from the family and tutors. If that help cannot be duplicated at the postsecondary level, it might be difficult for the student to replicate the academic success he or she enjoyed in high school. As noted previously, however, there are programs that provide extensive services to students with autism.

One academic area that presents challenges for many young adults with high-functioning autism and Asperger's syndrome, and needs to be thoroughly explored by students and family members, is the foreign language requirement for entry into and graduation from the institution (Sicile-Kira, 2004). For students who often have difficulties with communication in their native language, foreign language requirements have the potential to be especially challenging. Colleges vary widely on foreign language requirements. The requirements depend on the school's mission and academic competitiveness (Madaus, 2003). Decisions on secondary foreign language coursework must be carefully weighed with the student's potential career goals and the type of postsecondary education program that would best meet these goals. Specific questions should be asked of college admission offices about their foreign language requirements, such as the following (Madaus, 2003):

1. Is high school foreign language required for admissions? How many years or units are required?

2. If a certain number of secondary units are required, does the university have a policy on waiving or substituting these requirements for students with disabilities?

3. If a foreign language is not a requirement for admissions, does the college prefer that a language be taken in high school?

Students with disabilities admitted into college often face difficulties meeting the language requirement for graduation. Prior to selecting a college, students need to be aware of foreign language policies. It cannot be assumed that because course substitutions for a foreign language were provided at the secondary level or even at another postsecondary program that all colleges or universities follow this same policy (Madaus, 2003). Foreign language requirements for graduation from a university differ even among the programs of studies offered. Careful consideration must be made as to the policies and procedures for course substitutions at a particular college and the requirements for specific degree programs within the college.

FINDING THE RIGHT POSTSECONDARY PROGRAM MATCH

There are several methods for gathering information about specific colleges. The Internet provides a wealth of information through individual college web sites and through web sites that provide information about schools with specialized programs for students with disabilities. There are also resource books that compile information on a number of colleges and universities. It is critical to use several sources to collect information to ensure that the programs are able to best meet the student's learning needs and career goals. Trying to find a campus that meets the unique needs of students with autism can take time and effort. If possible, the students should visit potential schools to learn more about available support services and the staff's experience with providing services to students with autism. Meeting with students who are already enrolled in a particular college or specialized program is one of the best ways to learn about campus experiences, services, and supports. It is helpful to write down the advantages and disadvantages of each college, whether 2- or 4-year, to help in the decision-making process.

The following questions are suggested guidelines for students to ask when visiting a specific school or reviewing information about it (Wilson et al., 2000):

- *Campus climate*—Is the campus atmosphere generally one of acceptance of students with differences in learning styles? Are all students encouraged to participate fully in a variety of campus-life activities?

- *Program philosophy*—Does the college offer a specialized program for students with autism, or are supports offered as part of the college's overall program?

- *Academic adjustments*—How are academic adjustments coordinated? What types of services are typically provided to students with disabilities on campus?

- *Waivers and substitutions*—Are there written policies and procedures for waivers and substitutions? What kind of documentation is required? Who assists in the process of requesting a waiver or substitution? What is the probability that waivers or substitutions are granted?

- *Course load and graduation time*—Is priority registration available for students with disabilities? Is it possible to maintain a reduced course load? Do students with disabilities generally take longer to complete the requirements for graduation?

- *Student support activities or groups*—Are there ongoing groups that meet to talk about issues or concerns related to their experiences on campus? Are there specific activities that are designed to assist students with autism to network with other students on campus? Are there student leadership/mentoring programs to help students feel connected with other students with disabilities on campus?

- *Support services*—What support services are available to all students? Does the campus have support services specifically for students with autism?

- *Orientation*—Are there orientation sessions designed to address disability-specific needs of students prior to entering the college? Are these sessions primarily held during the summer or at the beginning of each semester for new incoming students?

It is essential that students with autism have opportunities to participate in orientation programs on campus or to have individual support to assist them in learning about the campus. An example of the need to assist students is illustrated in the case of a student with autism attending the University of Minnesota. The student would not go into the dining hall, which was filled with large groups of people (Moore, 2006). Instead, he used vending machines to obtain food. The student went the whole semester doing this until his parents notified the DSS office on campus. The disability specialist worked with the student to become accustomed to the dining hall, initially taking him there during times when it was less crowded. The student eventually worked up to obtaining his meals there during busier times.

General Types of Postsecondary Environments

There are a number of reasons to explore different postsecondary programs. Exploring postsecondary options in light of the student's career goals; level and type of support services provided; level of academic preparedness required; and general atmosphere, size, diversity of student body, and campus accessibility are important to the transition and retention of students with autism. One primary consideration is whether to attend a 2- or 4-year college.

Two-year colleges, or community colleges, provide both vocational programs and academic curricula. These colleges offer associate degrees and certificates in various occupational fields. Typically these programs offer students an opportunity to gain skills for employment as technicians, paraprofessionals, and skilled craftsman. Students with autism could attend community college programs through state-supported workforce development and training under the WIA (Rioux-Bailey, 2004). In some states, community colleges play a key role in implementing WIA training programs that offer students with disabilities traditional coursework or customized noncredit training. They also offer programs or transfer courses that prepare individuals to continue their studies at a 4-year institution. Admission to community colleges significantly differs from admission to a 4-year university or college. Community colleges typically enroll individuals who have a high school diploma or the equivalent (GED certificate), or any individual who is at least 18 years old and able to benefit from instruction at the college. It is important to note that the admission requirements for community colleges vary depending on the standards set by the state (Savukinas, 2003). Savukinas described the benefits of attending a community college as gaining college experience taking a few courses at a time; establishing a track record of success; learning a trade; and paying less tuition than at a 4-year institution.

Four-year colleges and universities offer specific coursework to earn a bachelor, master, or doctorate degree. There is great variability among colleges and universities, including their size, the type of degrees offered, the student–professor ratio, and the specific types of services and supports available to students with disabilities.

Once the student is enrolled at a 2- or 4-year college or university, he or she will typically take placement tests to determine if remedial courses are needed. In both 2- and 4-year colleges, documentation is required for students with autism to determine eligibility for support services for the placement tests and in the classroom.

It is also important to consider what type of environment and supports are likely to promote a successful college experience. Most families would want to avoid the experience of Amy. Amy is a young woman with Asperger's syndrome and excellent math skills. She earned high grades in college prep classes and scored well on the SAT, so she chose to attend a 4-year college in another state. Amy did so well the first semester that she stopped using the mentor provided by DSS to help with the transition and orientation process. This mentor had been supporting Amy's success in everyday college life, helping her with social connections as well as coursework. Without this support, Amy fell behind in her studies in the second semester and spent most of her time in her room, avoiding classes and avoiding people. At the end of her freshman year, she withdrew from the college and returned home with a diagnosis of depression. Continuing to work with the mentor likely would have kept Amy on the path to success. In addition, although Amy's secondary academic experiences held promise for success at a 4-year college, the community college close to home might have been a better choice for Amy, with less at stake and an easier transition.

Services and Supports in College

Some of the most commonly requested supports by students with disabilities attending college are textbooks on tape, notetakers, extended time on tests, environments with limited distraction for test taking, use of calculators, and permission to tape lectures (Deschamps, 2004; Getzel et al., 2000; Thomas, 2000). Students with Asperger's syndrome and high-functioning autism may also be eligible to be excused from group projects, receive preferential seating to suit any auditory or visual sensitivity, and receive advance notification for any changes in a schedule (Sicile-Kira, 2004). Students also need to explore services that are available on campus for all students, such as counseling services, writing or math labs, and study skills or time management classes, offered through a counseling center or other entities on campus. Most schools offer a full range of services to assist all students in successfully meeting their academic coursework, and students with disabilities should take advantage of these services along with any specialized services they are receiving.

Students with autism, as well as students with other disabilities, are not automatically entitled to disability-related services and supports; they must meet eligibility requirements through the documentation of a disability. Most, if not all, universities and colleges have a documentation policy or procedure for determining eligibility for services. In many instances, the accommodations provided for students with disabilities do not include all of the services or supports they received in secondary education settings. Students may be unsure how to use or implement these accommodations, as they are now the primary individual responsible for their implementation. Students need to know their rights and responsibilities pertaining to their education in college. Understanding the process of obtaining services and supports on campus is a critical step in determining whether a higher education program can meet a student's unique needs.

Colleges and universities cannot include questions about a disability on their applications; however, students and family members frequently ask whether a disability should be disclosed in the written essay or through letters of recommendation that are included in the application. This is a very personal decision for each student. Some students have disclosed a disability as part of their essay to demonstrate what they have accomplished. Others have used the essay as a means to explain discrepancies in grades or standardized test scores. Harris and Robertson (2001) cautioned that an essay or a letter should focus on such areas as students' academic strengths, college preparatory program, coping skills, motivation, and maturity. In general, college essays or letters are used to provide college admission officers with a more personal view of the applicant. Decisions about what a student with autism decides to include in a letter or an essay should be made carefully. Disclosing a disability at the postsecondary level is only required once a student is accepted and is seeking accommodations from the university.

Most college campuses have a specific office, typically DSS, to handle requests for accommodations and determine eligibility. See Figure 8.2 for a sample eligibility form. If a student is eligible for services, there are no costs associated with the services that the college provides; however, some colleges offer programs that provide additional services beyond what the university or college can regularly provide through their DSS office. Sometimes there is a fee for these additional services or specialized programs. Students and families should find out what is provided as part of the eligibility for services on campus, what additional services are available, and if there are costs to receive these additional services.

Not only must students understand how to obtain accommodations, but they also must understand the importance of utilizing these accommodations while in college. Getzel and colleagues (Getzel, McManus, & Briel, 2004; Getzel & Thoma, 2006) found that college students with disabilities often do not fully utilize their accommodations once they have self-disclosed. Reasons for this include not knowing how to obtain accommodations, being embarrassed about having a disability, trying to be successful without using accommodations, or being newly diagnosed as having a disability while in college (Getzel et al., 2004; Getzel & Thoma, 2006; Smith & Sowers, 2003). Part of the issue is students' lack of understanding of how the supports they received while in high school affected their learning. Many are unable to articulate their learning needs and identify the strategies or supports that assisted them in learning. Transition planning should include a means for ensuring that students take advantage of available and necessary supports in college on an ongoing basis. In Amy's case, presented previously, had there been a system in place that would have ensured that she retained her mentor, it is more likely that she would have continued to be successful.

PREPARING STUDENTS WITH AUTISM FOR COLLEGE

Students with autism need a special set of skills to help them adjust to and remain in college. These skills include time management, studying, decision making, socializing, and independent living tasks, such as maintaining finances, caring for

Disability and Accommodations Assessment for Eligibility Form

Student:

Date:

Accommodation Specialist:

I. DISABILITY/MAJOR LIFE ACTIVITY LIMITATION ASSESSMENT

Limitation is: 1 = Unable to Determine   2 = Mild   3 = Moderate   4 = Substantial

Major Life Activity	1	2	3	4
Caring for oneself				
Talking				
Hearing				
Breathing				
Seeing				
Walking/Standing				
Lifting/Carrying				
Sitting				
Performing Manual Tasks				
Eating				
Working				
Interacting with Others				
Sleeping				

Major Life Activity	1	2	3	4
Learning				
• Reading				
• Writing				
• Spelling				
• Calculating				
• Concentrating				
• Memorizing				
• Listening				
Other:				

Rating Scale:
1 = Unable to Determine   2 = Mild   3 = Moderate   4 = Substantial   NA = Not Applicable

Documentation is Complete	Yes	No					
Impact is:	Current	Potential	1	2	3	4	NA
Impact of Mitigating Measures is:	Positive	Negative	1	2	3	4	NA
Impact is seen in Condition, Manner or Duration:	Yes	No	1	2	3	4	NA
Impact seen in Academic Record:	Yes	No	1	2	3	4	NA

Qualifies as a Disability: Yes No   Unable To Determine

Permanent: Yes No   If NO, duration of temporary disability _____

Disability (Common Description)

Regent Code	Primary: _____	Secondary: _____	Tertiary: _____
McBurney Code	Primary: _____	Secondary: _____	Tertiary: _____

II. ACCOMODATION ASSESSMENT

Duration:

Code: R for *accommodations* determined to be reasonable under the ADA (i.e., they accommodate a substantial limitation to a major life activity).

D for *discretionary* accommodations that would not be required under the ADA (i.e., these accommodations are determined to be helpful for mild to moderate limitations but would not be required under the ADA).

Accommodations

Functional Limitation

Functional Limitation	Accessible Room	Computer	Small Group	Test Alone	Scribe	Doc. Conversion	1.5 Time	Seating	2.0 Time	Other	Braille	Electronic	Audio Tape/CD	Priority Reg.	Lab Assistance	Lib.Assistance	Notetaker	NT Paper only	Red.Course Load	CART	Sign Language Interpreter
						Alternative Testing					Document Conversion			Other						Deaf/HH	
Caring for Oneself																					
Talking																					
Hearing																					
Breathing																					
Seeing																					
Walking/Standing																					
Lifting/Carrying																					
Sitting																					
Performing Manual Tasks																					
Eating																					
Working																					
Interacting with Others																					
Sleeping																					
Learning																					
• Reading																					
• Writing/Spelling																					
• Calculating																					
• Memorizing																					
• Concentrating																					
• Listening																					
Other:																					

Figure 8.2. Disability and accommodations assessment for eligibility form formerly used by the McBurney Disability Resource Center at the University of Wisconsin–Madison. (Reprinted by permission from McBurney Disability Resource Center.) (Note: This form is one example of what a specific university used at one time and should not be interpreted as a model form or information that is widely collected by all colleges or universities.)

clothing, and meeting other personal needs. Schools may have specific programs to help students develop and master these skills. For example, Keene State College in New Hampshire helps students with autism manage the heightened social demands of college by having fellow students serve as social navigators (Moore, 2006). Preparation while students are still in high school, however, will make the transition to college much easier, and the earlier in high school students begin to prepare, the better the outcome. See Table 8.1 for suggested activities to help high school students with autism prepare for college.

Table 8.1. Suggested activities to help high school students with disabilities prepare for college

Year	Activities
Freshman year	Understand your disability and how to explain your learning needs to other individuals.
	Actively participate in the development of your individualized education program (IEP).
	Meet with your guidance counselor to review your schedule and ensure that you are taking the correct college prep courses.
	Understand which accommodations you need to enhance your learning.
	Be involved in school and community activities.
Sophomore year	Continue to be an active member of your IEP team meetings.
	Determine if there are community agencies (e.g., rehabilitative services) that need to be contacted about attending an IEP meeting.
	Visit your school's career center or guidance counselor to discuss college requirements.
	Identify your career interests, and begin looking into possible occupational areas.
	Work on any basic skills that need remediation.
	Be involved in school and community activities.
	Take the Preliminary Scholastic Aptitude Test (PSAT) and consider what accommodations you might need for this test.
Junior year	Identify a possible career goal, and begin looking at colleges that meet your interests and abilities.
	Continue focusing on time management, stress management, and study skills.
	Keep working with your IEP team as you move closer to your transition goal of attending college.
	Identify the academic adjustments that you have found most helpful.
	Make sure to consider your technology needs.
	Take the Scholastic Aptitude Test (SAT) or ACT admissions exams. Think about taking them more than one time.
	Visit college campuses and discuss which services and supports are available through the disability support services office.
	Determine the documentation requirements for the colleges to which you are interested in applying. Make sure your documentation is current.
	Learn about financial aid opportunities and available scholarships.
	Continue contact with community agencies for possible support.
Senior year	Determine the application deadlines for the colleges in which you are interested.
	Work on obtaining letters of recommendation.
	Develop your personal essay. Have a number of individuals review the essay—for example, your English teacher and guidance counselor.
	Complete the college applications, making sure that all directions have been carefully followed. Ask someone to proof your application to make sure you have not missed anything.
	Work with your IEP team and community agencies (if appropriate) to determine your support needs.
	Once accepted, consider attending a preadmission summer program (if the college offers one) to help with your transition into college.

Adapted from Virginia Department of Education, Division of Special Education and Student Services. (2003). *Virginia's college guide for students with disabilities: You know you can do it! Here's how!* (pp. 14–19). Richmond: Author.

Opportunities to develop skills in self-determination and self-management, explore technology, and obtain internships or other career-related experiences give students with disabilities the resources they will need to address the academic and social demands of college. These are discussed in more detail in the following sections.

Self-Determination Skills

Self-determination skills are a set of personal or interpersonal skills that include acceptance of a disability and how it affects learning, understanding which support services are needed, knowing how to describe one's disability and the need for certain supports to service providers, and having the determination to overcome obstacles (deFur et al., 1996; Eaton & Coull, 1999; Getzel et al., 2000; Getzel & Thoma, 2006). There is a great deal in the literature on the critical need for self-determination skills in the transition of students with disabilities from secondary to postsecondary settings (e.g., Getzel & Thoma, 2006; Stodden, Galloway, & Stodden, 2003; Thoma & Wehmeyer, 2005).

Although it can be challenging to help students develop skills to manage their academic program, in particular their services and supports, college service providers use a number of approaches to encourage the development of self-determination skills. These include organizing support groups comprising college students with disabilities, developing training modules on self-determination skills, and using peer mentors during college information sessions to encourage students making the transition to college to understand the support services on campus and the accommodation process (Getzel & McManus, 2005; Getzel & Thoma, 2006).

Self-Management Skills

Closely tied to self-determination skills are self-management skills. Self-management skills in such areas as time management, organizational skills, and study skills for college students with disabilities are common journal topics (Mull, Sitlington, & Alper, 2001). Students with disabilities frequently identify organizational skills, time management, and goal setting as areas in which they need assistance (Getzel & Thoma, 2006; Zwart & Kallemeyn, 2001). Colleges and universities have established a variety of programs to help students in these areas, including having professionals work with students and using peer-based coaching models (Bartlett, 2004; Duffy & Gugerty, 2005; Getzel & McManus, 2005; Zwart & Kallemeyn, 2001). A program developed at Marshall University operated by the West Virginia Autism Training Center enlists graduate students to work with students with Asperger's syndrome to help them review assignments, develop time-management techniques, and work on classroom behaviors (Moore, 2006).

Technology

Students with disabilities often enter postsecondary education programs unaware of existing technologies that can assist them in the academic setting (Getzel et al., 2004). There is an assumption that basic computer skills or general exposure to technology will suffice in college. Exposing college students with disabilities to assistive technologies that can enable them to compensate for their disabilities is critical for helping them meet the academic challenges of college. Some students with autism tend to be visual learners; technologies that could benefit these students include visual planners and schedules, graphic organization software, PDAs, highlighters, color overlays, and graphing papers (Oggel & Palko, 2004). Other beneficial technologies include voice output communication aids, text-to-speech software, word prediction software, and talking calculators. It is important to carefully consider and select with the student the right piece of technology to meet his or her individualized needs. Access to technology that leads to increased success in higher education has the likelihood to improve career outcomes for individuals with disabilities (Burgstahler, 2005; Kim-Rupnow & Burgstahler, 2004).

When possible, college students with disabilities should work with a program or a technology specialist to determine the most appropriate and effective technologies for enhancing their learning capabilities. The steps listed in Table 8.2 are a good starting point for thinking about how technology can be successfully integrated into a student's preparation for college. Background information on the technology and ideas on ways to apply it should be discussed with the student. Students with autism need opportunities to try the technology to learn how to use it and to determine if it is suitable, both for short-term and long-term needs (Burgstahler, 2005). Working closely with someone knowledgeable about technology and the student's needs will increase the likelihood that the student will use the technology and not abandon it should difficulties occur in operating it.

Table 8.2.   Preparing for postsecondary success through technology: Student, family, and transition team action items

Take the initiative and responsibility to explore a student's learning style, disability-related challenges, and the role technology can play in helping the student build on his or her strengths to succeed in college and a career.

Find sources of authoritative, up-to-date information on assistive technology related to the student's needs.

Seek assistive technology solutions that maximize self-reliance and self-determination.

Be willing and prepared to educate teachers and others about assistive technology.

Become acquainted with technology typically used in postsecondary academic and career paths of interest to the student.

Advocate for access to appropriate tools at a student's school and/or find alternate access to technology that supports vocational goals.

Develop the student's skills for using computers, assistive technology, and the Internet.

Employ technology to take advantage of opportunities to participate in classroom activities, such as discussions and interactive projects, at the same level as others.

Become acquainted with academic tools, expectations, and services before making the transition to postsecondary studies.

Learn which postsecondary schools are best at supporting mainstream technology in specific disciplines, assistive technology in inclusive settings, and the design and procurement of accessible technology campuswide.

Connect with role models, mentors, and peers who can assist the student in acquiring and using assistive technology and in learning to advocate for access to programs and resources in education and employment.

Use technology to participate in work-based learning opportunities, such as job shadows, internships, and community service.

Develop independent daily living skills, using technology as appropriate, for life on and off campus.

Source: Burgstahler (2005, p. 195).

Internships and Other Career-Related Experiences

Prior to entering college, students with disabilities typically have limited career development activities and little or no meaningful work experience; this makes it difficult for students to decide on a career (Briel & Getzel, 2005; Hitchings & Retish, 2000). Regardless of whether students plan to pursue postsecondary education, it is important that they consider their career interests and have an opportunity while in high school to try out some jobs that are similar to careers they are interested in pursuing. In addition, college and university career centers and university staff members knowledgeable about students with disabilities need to develop a comprehensive approach to assist students in their career planning. Students need opportunities to understand how their academic accommodations or supports transfer to the employment setting, and they need to learn how to network with professionals in their fields to build a successful résumé of experiences as they move from postsecondary education into their chosen careers.

Some students with autism need more comprehensive career planning support than traditional career planning services offer. For example, some students do not have the grade point average to qualify for an internship through the university, which creates an obstacle to gaining the work experience they need; some students may also need assistance in practicing appropriate behaviors in work environments (Briel & Getzel, 2001, 2005). This is especially important because disclosure of disability in employment settings is less than in educational settings (Greenbaum, Graham, & Scales, 1995; Kakela & Witte, 2000; Witte, Philips, & Kakela, 1998). Internships and other career-related experiences create an important link for students with disabilities to apply the knowledge and skills they acquire in college to a work environment. This link can encourage students with disabilities to remain in school to reach their long-term career goals (Briel & Getzel, 2001, 2005; Getzel & Kregel, 1996).

CHANGING ROLE OF FAMILY MEMBERS

Entering a postsecondary program, perhaps one that is a distance from home, is a major change and adjustment for all students and their families. This is especially true for families of students with autism, who have served as their children's advocates throughout their educational experience. It can be a difficult transition for some families because of their concern for the success and well-being of their children. Postsecondary education has many legal differences from secondary education in what information is shared with parents and the delivery of services and supports. It is important that students with autism and their families work together to better understand these differences and to begin shifting the responsibility of managing the student's education more to the student before entering college.

Students with autism come from all cultural backgrounds, and the values and expectations of their families can play a major role in the decisions made about a particular college. Black, Mrasek, and Ballinger (2003) discussed the individualist and collectivist values of culturally diverse students with disabilities, noting that families may have certain expectations about the type of postsecondary education they believe is appropriate for their son or daughter. Families may wish to see their children attend a specific type of program, for example, a technical college or a specialized program for students with autism. Careful attention to a student's career goals and sensitivity to the family's beliefs and expectations are needed to ensure appropriate planning.

POSTSECONDARY PLANNING FOR JEFF AND MARIA

Goals for both Jeff and Maria included attending college in addition to exploring employment opportunities. The following sections discuss the postsecondary options for these students and their eventual decisions.

Jeff's College Plans

In Jeff's second year of high school, he and his transition team continued to plan for his goal of going to college. Jeff met with his guidance counselor to talk about his potential career interests and skills and to discuss general college requirements. Because of Jeff's interest in video games, Jeff and the counselor explored the growing computer gaming industry and identified coursework and programs in computer programming, animation, and gaming at several universities. In addition to technical skills, it would be important to develop Jeff's communication skills so that he would be able to relate to customers or artists and work on a team. The counselor also informed Jeff about professional organization web sites that he could review, such as the International Game Developers Association, a professional society for video and computer game developers worldwide. Additional research through the Occupational Outlook Handbook showed that over three quarters of computer programmers held an associate's degree or higher, and nearly half held a bachelor's degree. To prepare Jeff for all options, Jeff's guidance counselor recommended that he take the Preliminary SAT to familiarize himself with a real test-taking environment and the kinds of questions he could expect on the SAT.

As noted in Chapter 7, Jeff was referred to his local VR agency for a vocational evaluation in his third year of high school. The purpose was to identify and assess Jeff's vocational interests, abilities, strengths, weaknesses, aptitudes, independent living skills, and functional limitations. Jeff's academic skills were strong, especially in the math and sciences. The rehabilitation counselor recommended additional social skills training and work with a speech pathologist in addition to relevant work experiences in the community to practice appropriate work and communication skills. Assistive technology that helped Jeff with independence and time management included the use of a PDA with alarm settings to schedule daily living tasks and important due dates.

To get a better idea about college requirements, Jeff attended a 1-day college preview event for students with disabilities in his area. Conference sessions included relevant topics, such as learning strategies for college success and organizing life in college using technology, and a panel of students who shared their experiences about navigating college. Jeff enjoyed listening to the students, and after the presentation he asked them questions about how to talk to professors about a disability. Representatives from many colleges in the state were available to answer questions about their programs, admission requirements, and DSS offices. In addition, Jeff was able to visit several colleges in his area that offer beginning coursework in computer programming. Jeff's guidance counselor supported Jeff with registering for and preparing to take the SAT, and his transition team helped him send appropriate documentation well in advance of his scheduled test date to request an accommodation of a separate testing room with appropriate lighting.

Jeff and his team agreed on a long-term higher education goal to complete a bachelor's degree in computer programming. Completion of this degree would qualify Jeff for many positions, and it would lay a great foundation for pursuing the gaming industry. He planned to apply to both a medium-size community college that offers flexibility in course schedules and smaller class size and a large university near his home, well known for its computer programming degree, that offers ample opportunities for work experience through internships and work co-ops. Jeff felt that both options offered different benefits, and he wanted to continue comparing the schools as he proceeded through the application process. With the help of his team, Jeff decided to initially live at home and receive continued support with daily living skills and gain increased responsibility in managing his time, following a college schedule, and meeting deadlines. As Jeff becomes more acclimated to the college setting, he eventually would like to live in a supervised apartment.

Jeff worked diligently on his personal essay for his college applications. He talked with his rehabilitation counselor about how to disclose his disability in a brief, positive way and how his current career goals match his strengths and interests. Late in the year, Jeff found out that he was accepted to both the community college and the 4-year university. He chose the 4-year university.

The summer after high school graduation, Jeff contacted the DSS coordinator to begin the registration process for services and accommodations. He completed an intake form and submitted his current medical documentation. He also requested a separate testing room for the placement tests he would be taking at the summer orientation for incoming freshman. Jeff elected not to participate in the optional overnight stay in the dorm during orientation because he planned to live at home during his first year and continue working at his small plant maintenance business. During the orientation, he took his placement tests, registered for three classes, and met with an advisor. The advisor recommended an orientation class that fosters study skills and career and life planning and provides opportunities to learn about additional support services. For example, the university counseling service offers 1-hour sessions about time management strategies and how to study for exams. In addition, students can go to the university writing center for feedback on improving their papers. Jeff is excited about his future and feels he has many supports in place to be successful in his new environment.

Maria's Community College Experience

Maria and her team moved ahead with plans for her community college experience in a clerical skills program through an on-campus program for students with disabilities. At the informational interview with the AVE coordinator, Maria and her mother learned about the certificate choices that were available and about the admission requirements. The criteria for admission included obtaining a high school diploma or certificate, being an active client of the VR agency, and having the social skills necessary to interact with peers at a college setting. The clerical skills program also preferred that their applicants have prior typing experience.

Maria and her mother both liked the idea that this vocational training program for adults with disabilities was offered through a community college; was located on a college campus with access to peers without disabilities; and focused on functional academics, job skills training, and community-based internships.

During Maria's third year of high school, her team ensured that she completed an introductory computer class that incorporated word processing and file management skills. The team also looked at additional coursework that was required to obtain a high school diploma and planned her schedule for the next 2 years. During this year, a representative from the VR agency became one of Maria's Ocean Voyagers (the group her transition team put together, described in Chapter 3). The team learned about the agency's services, and Maria completed an application. Maria's VR counselor recommended that she participate in short-term work experiences, such as the school's community-based vocational education program in hospitality training (see Chapter 7), to learn about possible career paths. The counselor also recommended that Maria continue to develop her social skills and ability to manage her behavior through participation in community-based instruction. Maria's special education teacher focused on teaching her stress-management strategies.

In Maria's final year of high school, her team assisted her with completing her application to the AVE program. She submitted her required medical documentation and registered with the DSS office on campus. Later in the year, she arranged a meeting with the coordinator to review her application and to talk about potential accommodations for her classes.

Also during her final year of high school, Maria participated in job-shadowing. She met employees and received a brief tour of two work sites. The first was in a doctor's office, where she observed the receptionist answering phones, taking messages, retrieving medical files, and transcribing doctor's reports. The second experience was in the administrative office for a wholesale pet supply chain. Maria observed an employee doing data entry tasks and compiling weekly and monthly reports. The employee gave Maria an opportunity to enter some data. Maria stated that she enjoyed the work observations and especially liked the office setting at the pet supply office. She was subsequently referred to her school's supported employment program and secured a job working with a catering company (as described in Chapter 7).

In the summer after high school graduation, Maria's VR counselor sponsored a new job coach, who assisted Maria in obtaining a job working at a large book and movie store as a floor assistant stocking shelves and assisting with inventory. Her coach continued to work with her on appropriate interactions with customers and strategies to use when Maria feels stressed. Maria expressed an interest in continuing to work there part time on the weekends once college began.

PULLING IT ALL TOGETHER

Educating students with autism in college environments is an emerging trend in higher education. Current college students with autism are providing educators and support service personnel with information and data that will assist and encourage other students with autism to consider college as a viable transition goal. There is still much to be learned about the effectiveness of the services and supports offered to these students. Students, families, and transition team members

Table 8.3.   Resources for exploring
postsecondary education options

http://www.ThinkCollege.net
http://www.transitiontocollege.net
http://www.transitioncoalition.org
http://www.STEPS-Forward.org
http://www.heath.gwu.edu
http://www.professorsadvice.com
http://www.ncset.org
http://www.cns.dircon.co.uk/index.html

must carefully weigh the unique educational needs of students with autism with the type of postsecondary education environment that best meets their needs. Some selected resources to assist in exploring postsecondary education options are listed in Table 8.3.

The transition to college offers exciting opportunities for students with autism, along with specific challenges. Academic preparation, self-determination and self-management skills, and the skills to meet the unique social and independence challenges of college are all factors to consider when pursuing an advanced degree. Students with autism are part of the diversity of learners entering postsecondary education. As the field of higher education and disability learns more about effective methods and techniques for accommodating students with autism, these students, as well as students with other disabilities, will be better able to pursue their educational goals and enter their chosen career.

9

Critical Life Skills

Marcia Datlow Smith and Pamela Sherron Targett

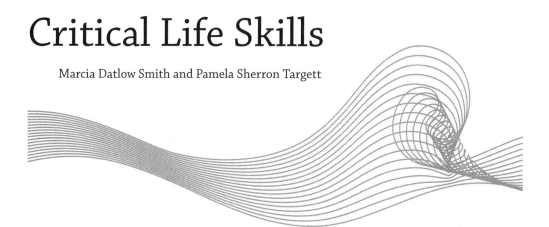

Jeff, Craig, and Maria all have many needs in the area of basic, essential life skills. Spending the time to learn critical life skills now will maximize their independence in the future. When Jeff was 15, his transition team had a planning meeting to discuss assessments and needs in the area of critical life skills. They discovered that although Jeff had no difficulty learning job tasks and household tasks, Asperger's syndrome did affect his ability to handle money, and it also limited his range of interests.

At age 17, Craig had significant needs in *all* areas pertaining to life skills. The challenge for his transition team was to prioritize and choose goals that were reasonable in terms of quantity as well as content. Craig's most pressing problem, his self-injury, was already targeted and addressed in his behavior support plan, as discussed in Chapter 2. For the following year, the team targeted goals in the areas of mobility and recreation.

At age 16, Maria had many needs in the area of critical life skills, so for the following year her team decided to prioritize and focus on two areas. One goal was to increase her independence in hygiene and grooming. In addition, as Maria still slept in bed with her mother, the second goal would be to increase independence by having her learn to sleep alone. Encouraging Maria to sleep in her own bed was a critical life skill that would be addressed with positive behavior supports. Several strategies were selected, including making her room more attractive to sleep in, increasing the attractiveness of her bed by buying *Finding Nemo* linens and a *Finding Nemo* bedspread, playing favorite music prior to bedtime, and providing rewards in the morning if she spent the night in her own bed. In addition, her mother would spend 15 minutes in Maria's bedroom with her with the lights out, as Maria fell asleep. Over time this was gradually shortened to 5 minutes and was finally eliminated.

Although many students without autism enter adulthood lacking some critical life skills, they can often learn what they need to on their own. Many students with autism, however, need specific planning and instruction to learn these skills. High school and the transition years are an ideal time to teach such things to students with autism. Figure 9.1 shows how these skills were addressed in one student's IEP goals and objectives.

Mobility

Current level of performance—Larry can describe the rules for safe street crossing. However, when crossing the street, he often fails to look both ways or attempts to cross against the light. He must be accompanied when out in the community. Larry needs to cross the street twice to get to the stop to catch the bus that takes him to and from work.

Goal 1—Larry will cross a two-lane street at an intersection with a stoplight.

Objective 1.1—When standing at the corner of Main and Harrison streets, where there is a walk signal, Larry will demonstrate with 100% accuracy the steps to safely cross the street on 15 consecutive days.

Objective 1.2—When standing at the corner of Cary and Harrison streets, where there is a traffic light but not a walk signal, Larry will demonstrate with 100% accuracy the steps to safely cross the street on 15 consecutive days.

Recreation and leisure activities

Current level of performance—Larry enjoys swimming and sports; however, he has few recreational or leisure experiences outside of these.

Goal 2—Larry will select and participate in a new recreational activity.

Objective 2.1—When given a choice of new activities (e.g., skating or working out at the fitness center), Larry will choose one to participate in for 5 consecutive days.

Money management

Current level of performance—Larry earns money at his job, but he is dependent on his family to budget and shop for him.

Goal 3—Larry will purchase goods or services.

Objective 3.1—At the grocery store checkout, Larry will use a debit card to make a purchase 5 consecutive times.

Objective 3.2—At the grocery store checkout, Larry will make a purchase with cash by handing the cashier the money, waiting for the change, and putting it in his wallet. He will do this 5 consecutive times.

Socialization

Current level of performance—Larry is very withdrawn. He does not greet others and avoids others due to his poor verbal skills.

Goal 4—Larry will greet others by waving and smiling.

Objective 4.1—While in the grocery store checkout line, Larry will greet the cashier by saying hello (once) for 5 consecutive times.

Objective 4.2—While walking to the bus stop, Larry will greet people he sees on the street by smiling (once) for 5 consecutive days.

Figure 9.1.   Excerpts from Larry's individualized education program for life skills

This chapter explores the many critical life skills that need to be considered in transition planning for students with autism. It offers details on skills needed for community living, including mobility, recreation and leisure, health and safety, money management, personal appearance, social skills, work habits, and maintaining dignity. Most of these skills are also important to home living, which will be further discussed in Chapter 10. In the sections that follow, particular challenges, opportunities, and supports for students with autism will be discussed for each set of skills.

MOBILITY

Mobility, the ability to travel from one point to another, is important to students' independence. Traveling safely by foot, bus, train, or car, however, can present special challenges for students with autism.

Areas in Need of Support

Although students may know the steps involved in safe, independent transportation, they may not actually use those skills during community travel. They may need support and practice with such activities as crossing the street, minimizing disruptive or dangerous behavior when riding in private vehicles, and employing appropriate social skills when using public transportation.

Street Crossings

Failure to pay attention, refusal to follow traffic laws, or the tendency to engage in rituals while walking can all present hazards to students as they attempt to cross streets. Although students might be able to repeat the rules for doing so safely, they might not use them. Larry (see Figure 9.1) can describe the rules for crossing the street safely, but when he is actually crossing the street he often fails to look both ways, crosses against the light, and jaywalks. After several near-accidents, his parents and teachers decided that Larry should be accompanied when out in the community.

Other young people with autism have trouble crossing streets because they engage in rituals while walking. These rituals can be dangerous. For example, a student may have a tendency to spin while walking, which would interfere with his or her ability to pay attention to traffic. Craig requires continuous supervision because of his intellectual disabilities, but he presents an added danger when out in the community because of his tendency to dart away from his caregivers. Because of this behavior, school personnel have been reluctant to take him outside the school. Several times Craig darted into the street, unmindful of the dangers posed by cars speeding by at 40 miles per hour. Fortunately, so far he has stopped traffic before the traffic has stopped him.

Use of Private Transportation

Some students with severe autism display dangerous or disruptive behavior in vehicles. Refusal to remain in the seat and to wear a seatbelt can jeopardize their safety. Mild rocking in a car generally does not pose a problem, but vigorous rocking in a car can shake the vehicle or even break the seat.

Some individuals with autism are very good at geography and know most routes around their community, especially to the places they commonly travel. Unfortunately, if these individuals also tend to insist on regularity and sameness, there can be problems. A student might insist that a certain route be used when going from school to her job site and become extremely upset if the route is varied. Another student might have an aversion to a certain street and become very agitated if the driver drives down it. Other young people with autism will become upset when the driver has to stop at red lights. Such events can result in significant behavior problems in the vehicle.

Some students with autism may act aggressively toward other passengers and the driver. One young man with severe autism has had several incidents of grabbing at the driver of the vehicle when upset, and on one occasion he grabbed the steering wheel, causing an accident. Understandably, people are now reluctant to have him as a passenger in their vehicles.

Use of Public Transportation

Use of public transportation involves logistics and skills that many students with autism can easily learn and master, such as bus numbers, routes, fares, and transfers. The social requirements of public transportation, however, are often more difficult for them to learn.

Talking aloud to themselves on the bus, becoming irate at passengers who accidentally bump into them, and becoming alarmed if the route is changed are not uncommon occurrences for people with autism. One young man, when boarding a subway car, always announced loudly, "Here I am." When debarking, he would announce, "I'm leaving now." A young woman with autism was banned from her bus route after violently shoving a fellow passenger who had accidentally brushed against her shoulder.

Supporting Mobility

A variety of strategies can be used to help students with autism travel safely and comfortably. Some are described in the following sections.

Supervision

Supervision is an obvious solution to most transportation-related challenges. Some students with autism need full-time supervision, especially when using transportation or walking. Others will need time-limited supervision. These students will benefit from training in crossing streets safely and using buses, trains, and subways. Supervision can be faded, although it may be needed occasionally if problems arise.

Instruction

Students with autism may need additional instruction beyond the typical training about routes, bus numbers, and how to pay the fare. For example, Jeff was trained to take the public bus from his school to his afternoon work site. His employer occasionally complained that Jeff was late for work. Jeff's teacher followed him for several days and discovered that Jeff would walk to the bus stop and, if the bus was not immediately there, would then walk to work. On days when the regular bus driver was on duty, he would see Jeff down the road and pick him up. If there was a substitute bus driver, he would continue on his route and Jeff would walk the entire 2 miles to work. On those days, Jeff was late. He needed to be taught how to wait at the bus stop.

Although Craig's team anticipated that he would always have supervision when traveling, the team still felt that he could benefit from street-crossing skills. They identified specific skills to work on, such as waiting at the corner, looking both ways, crossing when it was clear, and staying next to his aide or teacher. The transition team then developed an instructional plan to help Craig learn and practice these skills.

Social Skills

Some students with autism need specific training in appropriate social skills when traveling in the community. For example, a student might need to learn to board and get off the subway quietly, without announcing his or her entry or exit.

Students may benefit from a checklist reminding them of the social rules involved in mobility. One young man was able to walk to school alone, but his vigorous swaying and talking to himself as he walked was not well received by others. He improved his habits when he was given a very short checklist with these rules of behavior: 1) Maintain good posture while walking and 2) walk silently. His mother reviewed these rules with him each morning before he left, and when he arrived at school he would put a checkmark by each rule if he had followed it successfully.

Adaptive Systems

As mentioned previously, a few students with severe autism exhibit dangerous behaviors when riding in a vehicle, such as refusing to remain in their seat, attempting to exit while the vehicle is in motion, or acting aggressively toward the driver or other passengers. Occasionally, adaptive systems are needed, such as a seatbelt system from which students cannot easily remove themselves. These adaptive systems carry the risks of hampering exit in emergency situations, so they need to be carefully thought out and discussed with professionals, such as a psychologist and a transportation director.

Backpacks and Escorts

Darting away from a teacher, a parent, or an instructional aide while walking puts students at risk for running into traffic or becoming separated from their supervisor long enough to become lost. To help reduce these risks for Craig, his transition team decided that he would wear a backpack on outings. That way his aide could casually hold onto the backpack and prevent Craig from darting into the road. A plan for fading the backpack was also to be put into action as Craig demonstrated more cooperation with safe street crossings.

Behavior Support Plan

For students with serious behavior problems that affect mobility, the behavior support plan might need to expand to include those mobility issues. All of the strategies discussed in Chapter 2 can be applied to mobility (e.g., developing a reward system to encourage cooperative behavior on the bus).

RECREATION AND LEISURE

Many students with autism benefit from transition goals in recreation and leisure (Smith & Belcher, 1992). There are many opportunities to become involved in activities; however, some students may be challenged by 1) restricted or intense areas of interest and 2) underdeveloped social skills.

Challenges in Recreation and Leisure

Students with autism have very intense and restricted areas of interest (APA, 2000). Jeff, for example, has been fixated on maps and train schedules since childhood. He spends all his spare time studying maps and atlases. Other students with autism are intensely interested in trains, sports scores, or music trivia. It is not rare for a young man to not want to go out at night because he is absorbed in studying baseball scores. Expanding their range of interests would help these students take advantage of more recreational and leisure opportunities.

Jeff's transition team targeted recreation as an area to work on, hoping that exposure to a wider range of recreational opportunities would provide him with new pastimes that he could come to enjoy. The team planned a rotating series of recreational and fitness activities for him over the course of 2 years. Bowling, swimming, table tennis, and basketball were a few of the recreational activities that he would be introduced to. Most of these activities took place through the school's physical education department, but some were offered through community facilities, such as the YMCA and the community recreation center.

Poor social skills also present a challenge to engaging in recreational and leisure activities. As extreme examples, consider a student with autism who became very upset in the local gym and pushed over a piece of weight equipment, or a young man who became upset with the children at the local swimming pool and chased a young child. Both were banned from returning to the sites. Other students might participate cooperatively in recreational activities but demand to leave after a short period. In contrast, Craig refuses to leave when an activity is over. Transition plans for students like these should target social skills and challenging behaviors within the context of recreational and leisure activities.

Opportunities for Recreation and Leisure

With adequate supports, students with autism can participate in a wide range of leisure activities. Students can be helped to expand their areas of interest, make broader choices, and participate in a variety of activities. If students have limited interests and or are resistant to new experiences, the transition team should target expansion of students' choice-making skills and range of opportunities. A place to start would be to compile lists of recreational and leisure activities in the school and local community that students can be guided to participate in.

School Activities

High schools have dozens of clubs and sports teams, and they sponsor recreational activities such as trips, sports events, and dances, all of which students with autism might enjoy. Often students do not participate in these activities because they lack awareness, the skills to make choices, or the means to attend events. The school is the first place to look to help expand students' recreational and leisure opportunities. Transition teams should discuss possibilities that might suit students and determine ways to encourage them and provide support as they take part in the selected activities.

Publicly and Privately Sponsored Activities

Most communities have private and public recreational facilities, such as neighborhood swimming pools, public parks and recreational facilities, YMCAs, health and fitness clubs, and programs through local universities and community colleges. Students with autism may find fully inclusive activities or activities specifically designed for students with developmental disabilities.

Trips and Outings

Leisure activities may involve trips to places of interest, such as restaurants, movies, concerts, the theater, or sporting events; or to special events, such as the county fair. Supports can be arranged to facilitate the student's participation in such trips with the school, other organizations, family members, or friends.

Exercise and Sports

Students with autism can be fully included into local health clubs and fitness centers. They can also attend adaptive exercise classes designed for individuals with disabilities. For example, Maria found the aerobics class at the local fitness center too fast paced for her; she responded by retreating into the corner and reciting dialogues from *Finding Nemo*. When the local county recreation center offered adapted aerobics for individuals with developmental disabilities, Maria joined the class. This class was more to her liking, and she was able to fully participate.

Hobbies, Games, Crafts, and Art

Students without disabilities often have a variety of hobbies, games, and art projects that they enjoy. Students with autism often will not seek out these experiences to try, but with guidance and support they can come to enjoy and even excel in these pursuits.

Social Events

Although a popular image of autism is that individuals retreat into their "own little world," the truth is that many students with autism enjoy the company of other people. Dances, parties, barbecues, and other social events can be special and enjoyable occasions. Learning how to host these events by planning, issuing invitations, and holding the event can be an achievable goal for many students with autism.

Building on Interests

As mentioned, many students with autism have specific areas of intense interest. Their enjoyment often extends to the most trivial aspects of the object of their interests, such as the time a certain train arrives in a certain city on Saturdays (not their train or their city). Teams can build on students' interests by helping them enjoy these interests within certain boundaries and limits. For example Jeff was overly interested in routes and would spend hours each day studying maps. His transition team focused on developing a weekly schedule that allowed Jeff designated times to pursue his interest in routes without having it dominate his life to the point where it was hard for him to get anything else done.

Supports for Recreation and Leisure

Students' transition plans should include supports that will help them broaden their range of recreational and leisure opportunities. Without such supports, students may remain limited in their recreational and leisure pursuits and perhaps miss out on fun, fulfilling activities. Some examples of possible supports follow.

Physical Education and Adaptive Physical Education

Physical education in the transition years can serve as the gateway to an enriched recreational life in adulthood. Teaching students to swim, play basketball, bowl, play tennis, dance, and play other games and sports can provide them with critical recreational and fitness skills. Once they make the transition from school to the community, they will either be on their own or under someone's care. If they are on their own it may be difficult for them to learn new sports, but if they have foundational skills from their physical education classes they can continue to enjoy the activities they have participated in. If students are under the care of others after transition, their caregivers may not have the skills to teach them sports and games. If students have learned those skills in school, however, caregivers can very likely help them participate. For example, Craig learned to swim in middle school physical education and moved into a supported living arrangement after high school graduation. His staff cannot swim, but they can escort him to the community pool each week so that he can continue to enjoy swimming.

High school physical education classes can also help transition-age students develop fitness and fitness skills that will provide health benefits into adulthood. Building up fitness through jogging, cycling, or other aerobic activities will make students healthier and give them the knowledge and skills to remain fit.

Jeff's team decided to target recreational and fitness skills as a key transition goal. His family reported that he seemed to enjoy going to the pool but was not safe in the water. An adaptive physical education program was worked out so that Jeff would spend the next year learning to swim. The team also felt that Jeff would benefit from some additional fitness-related recreation and determined that the most reasonable exercise for him was walking. They decided to build fitness walking into his schedule four times per week, especially as he was gaining unhealthy amounts of weight and tended to be rather sedentary. They hoped that taking daily walks would become a habit that would continue into the years to come. Because of Jeff's occasional aggression, the team recognized that his behavior support plan might need to be extended to encourage cooperation on walks and at the swimming pool.

Supervision

Supervision is a common support for students with severe autism. These students may need close, ongoing supervision to enjoy the recreational activities their community has to offer. With sufficiently close supervision, even students with frequently challenging behaviors can enjoy the local gym or the swimming pool. Students with less severe autism may need initial supervision, which can be faded out or occur on an occasional basis.

Training in Logistics and Content

Students may need specific training in logistics and content of recreational activities. For example, a young woman may need to be taught how to gain entry to a dance and how long she needs to stay there. She might also need to be taught how to dance and the protocol for having and keeping a dance partner. It is not unusual for two individuals with autism to be dancing, and mid-dance one of them wanders away!

Social Skills Training

Poor social skills can be a major barrier to acceptance into recreational and leisure opportunities. Specific social skills may need to be targeted and taught if students are to have a successful recreational experience. A young man with autism might attend school dances but spend his time there reading *TV Guide*. Social skills training for this student might include greeting other students and asking a girl to dance. Training can be supplemented by checklists and reminders. This student, for instance, may benefit from a reminder list that prompts him to ask a girl to dance every four songs, maintain good posture (no rocking), and keep his *TV Guide* in his coat pocket.

Behavior Support Plan

Students with challenging or dangerous behaviors may need a behavior support plan, as outlined in Chapter 2. This plan can be extended to include recreational activities, often using the same strategies as in the classroom. Specific strategies may need to be added, such as those that encourage good sportsmanship.

Recreational Choice Making

Students with autism may benefit from a specific goal in making recreational choices. Students should be exposed to the variety of recreational activities in their community and taught how to make choices about those activities. Students who can read can make choices from written lists, newspaper announcements, and other postings of activities. Students who cannot read will need more assistance (Cobigo, Morin, & Lachappelle, 2007; Thomson, Czarnecki, Martin, Yu, & Martin, 2007). For instance, they might use a picture system to make choices. In both cases, the students are presented with a broader range of choices than they themselves would initiate and are taught how to select from those choices activities that seem interesting to them.

HEALTH AND SAFETY

One of the more obvious critical life skills is the ability to maintain one's health, yet many students with autism grow into adulthood dependent on their parents to keep them healthy. Some individuals will always need a caregiver to help them maintain a healthy life. Others can learn at least some components of healthy living and practice them independently. Several aspects of healthy living are presented here for consideration by transition teams to discuss with students and their family members.

Illness and Injury

Students should learn how to identify illness or injury in themselves and what to do about it. Many students with autism can learn first aid skills. Signs of illness, how to self-treat, and when to call a doctor can also be taught. If the student is able to use the telephone and make appointments, he or she should learn how to call the doctor and make an appointment. The student might also learn how to arrange to get to the doctor.

Nutrition

Some students with autism have healthy eating habits when living at home; however, if they move out on their own they may be at high risk for making poor food choices. As for many young adults beginning to live independently, food choices for young adults with autism may be based on flavor, enjoyment, and convenience rather than on health. However, if students have training in good nutrition during the transition years, it is possible that those skills will be carried forward into adulthood.

One student provides an example of poor nutrition training. When he lived at home, he received no formal training in nutrition. He ate the meals that his parents prepared. They kept an ample supply of pizza and other frozen meals that he could make himself on evenings when they would not be home. They also gave him a steady supply of money, which he spent at fast-food restaurants. After he graduated from high school, the student moved into his own apartment and did his own grocery shopping. His main purchases were the pizzas and frozen meals that he had enjoyed so much on his parents' nights out and also fast-food meals. As a result, he gained 30 pounds in his first year out on his own.

Another student was able to make wiser food choices. Her mother rarely bought frozen meals, and the family hardly ever ate out. During the student's transition years, she learned about nutrition and food preparation, and she practiced food preparation skills at her restaurant job. By the time she moved into her own apartment, she was eager to try the recipes she had learned in school and at home. She particularly enjoyed preparing salads at her job, and this skill translated well to her own living situation.

Emergencies

Although some students with autism will need round-the-clock supervision, many will be able to at least spend time alone, if not live alone, once they reach adulthood. These students need to learn how to prevent emergencies and respond appropriately if one occurs.

Students should receive safety instruction for using tools, equipment, and other items that can present a danger. Kitchen safety is an obvious example. Those who are cooking need to learn how to turn the stove, oven, and other appliances on and off. It is important to identify and address inadvertent hazardous behaviors as well, such as a ritual of lining up items. An obvious danger is presented by an individual intent on lining up the knobs on the stove in a certain way, specifically, in the *on* position.

When cleaning, students need to know how to safely use various products. Skills training on following product warning labels may be required (Collins & Griffen, 1996). For example, students should be taught not to mix certain products together because harmful fumes could be created and to open the window to help ventilate the room while cleaning.

Students who might be using tools and appliances, especially electric ones, need to be taught how to use them safely. The importance of keeping small appliances out of water is an example. Students with autism often have difficulty with abstract thinking and problem solving. Unless safety is specifically taught, students will be a hazard to themselves and perhaps others. The transition team needs to identify the kinds of safety challenges that students might face and target those challenges.

Students should also be taught how to handle emergencies and basic safety. Some examples of home emergencies may include responding to a fire in the home or an accident or illness requiring immediate medical attention. Students should be taught to dial 911 and report emergencies. The student must also know how to evacuate a home in case of a fire. If the student has an accident or extreme illness, he or she needs to know how to contact help. The student may also have to respond to an unplanned event, such as a plumbing problem requiring the water to be shut off to prevent flooding or a power outage due to a storm. Other basic safety rules, such as not allowing strangers into one's home and keeping windows and doors locked (Collins & Griffen, 1996), can be included in the curriculum.

Fitness

A variety of fitness activities were covered in the section on recreational activities. Students with autism should learn how to build these fitness activities into their weekly schedule, whether they walk for 45 minutes daily or join a club and learn to jog or body build. Individuals with autism are often people of routine and habit. If fitness habits are established during the transition years, it is likely they will be carried through into adulthood.

MONEY MANAGEMENT

Money management is another important life skill that can lead to greater independence. Skills taught may range from making a simple purchase, such as a snack from a vending machine, to following an established budget and paying monthly bills. Following are some challenges students may face in learning to manage money and strategies that can be used to support them.

Challenges in Money Management

Money management may present several challenges to students with autism. Two aspects of money management generally cause difficulties: 1) understanding the value of money and 2) handling money appropriately.

Understanding the Value of Money

Students with autism often have difficulty understanding the value of money. At the most basic level, students may be unable to count, make change, or even recognize different coins and bills. At the next level of understanding, students can recognize coins and bills but lack an understanding of the relationship between work and money and money's value in the marketplace. At the third level, students have some understanding of the relationship between work and money and understand, in general, what different kinds of items cost. Students at this level, however, may have difficulty with higher levels of money management—that is, saving, budgeting, and making ends meet.

The transition team needs to assess the level at which the student operates and plan goals for progress. During transition, instruction must focus on the understanding of the practical use and budgeting of money.

Handling Money

Students with autism might have difficulty with the proper use of money. Poor reasoning and social skills often result in poor money management. Transition teams need to be aware of common pitfalls in the use of money if they are to help students gain the skills they need to handle their money appropriately.

One problem with the use of money is the tendency to hoard. Rather than seeing money management as an end, students with autism might focus on the means—saving coins, bills, and any money that comes their way. A reluctance to part with money interferes with proper budgeting. A young person with autism who has 15 uncashed or undeposited paychecks sitting in his or her drawer is not managing money effectively.

Some students do the opposite—they immediately spend every dollar that comes their way. They do not link money with the future. Their use of money is concrete; if they have $50, they want to spend it that day. These students need instruction in how to save up for something they want.

Failing to understand the concept of money ownership, coupled with a tendency to be taken advantage of, create problems for some students with autism. Some students will readily part with their money if asked. Jeff was once convinced to regularly give his money to his co-workers.

Internet shopping and credit cards can pose a danger to students with autism, as they can to other young people. In general, it is a useful skill to be able to shop on the Internet or make a credit card purchase. Problems arise when the individual lacks budgeting skills or a proper sense of money ownership. One young man's family was saddled with thousands of dollars of debt as a result of his Internet shopping sprees. A young woman with Asperger's syndrome used the ATM to deplete her savings account of several thousand dollars and make meaningless purchases without her family's knowledge.

Students with autism may also lack banking skills, and they may overspend from their bank accounts. Some students become anxious in banks when confronted with the tasks of making out deposit slips, waiting in line, and dealing with the bank teller. Some students have the math skills to balance checking accounts but lack other necessary skills needed to effectively manage their money.

Supports for Money Management

There are a number of supports that can be used to promote money management skills. This includes instruction as well as supervision and oversight.

Goal Setting and Instruction

Transition teams need to help students set realistic money management goals as part of the transition process. Instructional protocols should be developed that are suited to the needs of the learner. Some money management training can be classroom based, such as teaching how to identify coins and bills, do calculations with money, make change, create budgets, and balance a bank account. Other training should be community based—in stores, in a bank, and in other places where money will change hands. Community-based money management training includes not only how to bank money but also how to spend money, such as making shopping lists, choosing items in stores, and making purchases.

Computer-based video instruction has been used to teach verbal responses to questions presented by cashiers and purchasing skills in fast-food restaurants (Mechling, Pridgen, & Cronin, 2005). Results have indicated that these responses and skills can be taught to students with moderate to severe disabilities. This tool may be useful for some students with autism.

Jeff needed training in understanding the value of money and in the ability to safeguard his funds. He had very poor budgeting skills and would often spend an entire paycheck on his way home, often coming home with haphazard purchases for which he had no receipts and that he did not need. He would demand pricey items from his parents, and he had no savings plan. Jeff was easily taken advantage of and had "loaned" his co-workers money without hope of repayment.

Jeff's team selected strategies to help Jeff with money management. His teacher instructed him in setting up a weekly budget and opening and managing a bank account. Using his weekly budget, Jeff learned to set aside some money for small expenditures and to save for larger ones. Jeff was also given social skills training on how to say no when peers asked him for money.

Supervision and Oversight

Many students will need supervision or oversight in the handling of their money. Realistic individual goals need to be developed for fading of supervision. For students with severe autism, ongoing supervision will always be necessary. Using their own money for items in a vending machine might be as independent as some students will get. Other students with autism can reasonably expect to handle their own funds and create and follow budgets.

PERSONAL APPEARANCE

Many students with autism are very careful and appropriate with their personal hygiene and grooming; for others this area is a challenge (Smith et al., 1995). Unlike their peers without autism, they are less likely to take grooming and hygiene cues from their environment. Some possible challenges and supports in personal hygiene are described in the following sections.

Challenges in Hygiene

Poor hygiene and grooming can create problems in school and larger problems at work. Students may face challenges because of rituals, refusal to participate in certain grooming activities on a consistent basis, and difficulty learning or remembering how to perform certain activities to maintain good hygiene.

Rituals

Some students with autism may have rituals that extend to grooming. They may be overly attached to certain articles of clothing and want to wear those items daily, without washing them. They may not dress appropriately for the weather, perhaps because of active resistance or lack of understanding. Maria, for instance, needs to be reminded to wear a coat in the winter. In contrast, Craig wants to wear his coat daily, even in the summer. Some students might wear too many layers of clothing; Craig, if allowed, would wear six pairs of underpants to school. A preference for certain types of clothing may clash with a workplace dress code. Jeff is required to wear slacks and a button-down shirt to work, but he continues to wear jeans even though his employer has expressed her disapproval.

Hygiene

Students might refuse to shave, shower, brush their teeth, or perform other hygiene tasks. Some students with autism and severe intellectual deficits require a great deal of assistance with hygiene. At times, family members have a difficult time providing that assistance.

At age 16, Maria remained dependent on her mother to complete hygiene and grooming tasks. Some of the tasks she could do by herself, but she needed reminders. She continued to demand assistance from her mother on other tasks even though it appeared that she was capable of doing them alone. Her team targeted some hygiene and grooming skills for instruction so that Maria could learn to do them alone. Other hygiene and grooming tasks were targeted to increase Maria's independence and willingness to do them without prompts and assistance from her mother. Team members used several strategies to help her acquire these skills, including instruction, checklists, and picture cues. To heighten Maria's interest in hygiene and grooming, trips to the manicurist and hair stylist were periodically scheduled. Scented lotions, deodorants, and shampoos; special bath soaps; and bath sponges were used to increase Maria's interest in hygiene activities. She was also given incentives, such as praise and attention, for making improvements in hygiene and grooming and doing so independently.

Supports for Hygiene

Transition teams should target critical hygiene and grooming goals, if necessary, and determine appropriate supports. Supports may involve instruction, supervision, or positive behavior support strategies.

In many cases, the student may only need to be taught how to perform the hygiene or grooming skill. Teams cannot be shy about targeting and teaching these skills. Once the student leaves school, there will be fewer opportunities for instruction. Jeff, for example, certainly has the awareness to learn the hygiene skills a young man should have. However, because his family was somewhat intimidated and embarrassed about teaching him these skills, he was never fully taught how to take care of himself. His transition team can target goals for him and determine proper instructional strategies.

Some students need more supervision to properly take care of themselves. If the amount of supervision is targeted by the transition team, the student's grooming and hygiene should improve. These supervision guidelines can set the stage for the supports that will be needed after graduation.

Sometimes self-management strategies can help students acquire hygiene skills. For example, the student may be provided with a grooming and hygiene checklist to follow and check off each morning. Other times, parents or other caregivers will need to use the checklist to guide the student through the necessary tasks. If necessary, a system of motivation or rewards can be used to support the student in achieving good hygiene and grooming.

SOCIAL SKILLS

Poor or limited social skills will affect students' ability to initiate and maintain relationships with others, particularly their peers, and their ability to function at home, in school, at work, and in the community. Individuals with autism can often learn the skills necessary to perform the duties of their job but may experience difficulty with the social aspects of the workplace. High school offers perhaps the best opportunity for teaching students the social skills they will need for maintaining a job and making friends. The sections that follow discuss particular challenges students face in the social arena and supports that can help them meet these challenges.

Challenges in Social Skills

Social skill challenges may surface from difficulties in communicating (verbally and nonverbally), accepting authority, respecting boundaries, and relating to others. Students with autism may lack a spontaneous sharing in the enjoyment, interests, or achievements with others and lack reciprocity, all of which negatively affect social relationships.

Poor Conversational Skills

Students with autism often lack good conversational skills. There are a variety of ways in which their conversations can create problems, especially at work. They may talk too much in general or too much about topics that are not of interest to others. For example, Jeff can lecture for hours about his interest in maps. This type of narrow conversation does not interest his co-workers and makes it difficult for them to converse with Jeff. Other students with autism might ask questions of friends or co-workers that are too personal (e.g., about their marital status, income, hair color). Students with autism might also reveal information about themselves that is too personal.

Lack or Absence of Nonverbal Communication

Individuals with autism may not understand how to properly use eye contact, facial expressions, physical proximity, and gestures in conversations with others. They might not look others in the eye when speaking or listening, or they might stare during conversations. For example, Maria was being instructed on how to set up her work station by a co-worker. Instead of looking at her co-worker directly, Maria looked at her for a second or two and then stared up at the ceiling.

Some individuals may not show appropriate facial expressions. For example, while a classmate described his feeling of loss due to the death of his dog, Jeff listened with a big grin on his face. In other circumstances, the person's facial expressions may not seem to match what he or she is saying. For example, Jeff talked about his birthday party and how happy he was to see his grandparents without breaking a smile.

Lack of social awareness of boundaries can lead to invading another individual's personal space. A young adult with autism might stand too close to others when talking to them. Sometimes, he or she may make uncomfortable physical contact with others, like giving hugs to acquaintances or strangers.

Other problems may result from an inability to understand common nonverbal cues. For example, Jeff was talking to his co-worker in the hall. The co-worker began to repeatedly glance at his watch to signal a need for Jeff to wrap up the conversation so they could get back to work. Finally the co-worker stated, "I really need to go," and walked away as Jeff continued to talk. Soon afterward, the supervisor came by and told Jeff to get back to work.

Difficulty Accepting Authority

Some workers with autism have difficulty accepting their supervisor's authority. Refusing to follow a supervisor's instructions, arguing, complaining, and making unreasonable demands can make it difficult to keep a job. Accepting corrections, suggestions, and criticism and adapting to change are necessary but often difficult skills for the worker with autism.

Individuals may also have problems accepting the authority of those in the community. A bus driver, bank teller, or grocery store clerk could request accurate fare, a completely filled-out deposit slip, or a smaller bill, and this could cause the person with autism to argue, complain, or even act violently toward him- or herself or the authority figure.

Difficulty Respecting Boundaries

People with autism often have difficulty respecting boundaries. Physical boundaries apply to space, equipment, or materials. Consider Jeff's job at the greenhouse. When he needed more supplies or certain types of equipment, he would barge into the supervisor's office and take them. If he wanted to make a telephone call, he would demand to use the supervisor's telephone. He did not understand what his position in relation to his boss meant in terms of boundaries. When on a social outing with friends, Jeff would often attempt to touch his female friends' feet, resulting in his friends feeling uncomfortable.

Inability to Relate to Others

Often the worker with autism learns how to get along with a boss or co-workers, and in many cases the boss or co-worker learns how to get along with the worker with autism. More severe problems can arise when workers with autism must interact with the public. For instance, they might be rude to customers. Often the trigger for this rudeness is the customer's interruption of the worker to ask for help or information. The problem can be compounded if the customer does not accept the help provided and demands more. When working at the video game store, Jeff explained that the problem when he answered customers' questions was that they did not pay attention. He asked, "If they are not going to pay attention, what is the point of them coming to the store?" Although the real problem likely was that the customers could not understand him when he answered their questions, he perceived this as a willful lack of attention and blamed them.

Maria had made friends with several other young women who attended her computer class at the community college. When report cards came out, one young lady shared her disappointing failing grade with Maria, and Maria responded by giggling and running away, which hurt her friend's feelings. Maria's giggling and running away is a typical response for her when she is unable to gauge how she should respond in a certain situation, but certainly this was perceived as a mean and hurtful reaction by her friend.

Inability to Take on Another Person's Perspective

Some individuals may have trouble taking on another person's perspective. They may have difficulty empathizing and feeling for others. For example, when Jeff's sister was hospitalized due to an automobile accident, he asked his parents if he could turn off her heart monitor (the beeping noise it made was too loud) and watch his favorite television program.

As mentioned previously, people with autism may fail to spontaneously share in the enjoyment, interests, or achievement of others. For example, Jeff's father announced a raise at work and his plans to take the family out to eat to celebrate. Jeff showed no expression. At dinner, he appeared sullen on an occasion that should have been a good time for all. Maria's little sister announced that she was on the honor roll at school. While Maria's mother congratulated her sister, Maria turned indifferently and walked out of the room.

Lack of Reciprocity

A lack of reciprocity can affect social relationships. For example, Jeff has difficulty taking turns with others in conversation. He talks continuously and does not give the listener a turn to speak. As a result, many of his peers purposefully avoid him. Furthermore, if someone offers to help him with something, he will not accept their assistance.

Initiating conversations or social interactions may present difficulties for some students. For example, Maria is reluctant to start conversations. She rarely asks questions or makes comments. In addition, she often does not respond to another person's conversation, questions, or comments.

Supports for Social Skills

Supports should be developed after assessing an individual's current social skills. Assessment should include an analysis of data from informal and formal sources, including observations of the person across settings and interviews with those that know him or her best. A variety of strategies can then be used to teach social skills, such as social skills training, Social Stories, and positive behavioral support. More discussion of these supports can be found throughout this book, most thoroughly in Chapter 2. Some students with autism may benefit from individual or group counseling that focuses on the development of acceptable social behaviors.

Students with autism may need specific training in social skills for the workplace (Hillier, Fish, Cloppert, & Beversdorf, 2007; Wehman, Targett, et al., 2007). Generally, it is not enough to merely explain to students why they need a particular skill or why they need to behave in a particular way. Explaining to Jeff why he needed to be helpful to customers did not change his behavior. He continued to be rude and insist that there was no point in customers' coming to the video game store if they were not going to pay attention to what he told them. Jeff needed specific instructions and specific training on how to deal with customers. In the school setting, this training can be done by teachers, job coaches, transition specialists, and counselors.

Jeff's team considered high school the best time to make assessments and provide training in using appropriate social skills at work. Some potential problems, including verbal abuse and staring at women's feet, had already been identified at his first job placement and were addressed in his behavior support plan. The team members decided that as Jeff went to work in different settings, they would pay close attention to the types of social supports he needed and implement either formal or informal plans for improvement. Jeff's team members hoped that this approach would result in a gradual development of good work habits and good social skills in the workplace over the course of Jeff's transition years.

Careful Assessment of Needs

Transition teams must make very careful assessments of students' social skills. Job trials and job placements are ideal settings for training. It is important that social skills be viewed as behaviors that can be learned rather than as inherent and unchangeable traits.

Target Behaviors

It is helpful to specifically target the social responses a student needs to learn. For instance, Jeff needs to learn to say to a customer who asks for assistance, "Follow me," and take the customer to a co-worker who can provide assistance. He also needs to learn what topics of conversation are interesting to his co-workers, and how long he can talk. When he is with friends, Jeff needs to learn to respect others' boundaries and not stare at feet. Jeff needs to learn where to get supplies and equipment and under what circumstances it is appropriate to approach his boss.

Sometimes problems related to social skills can be remedied by improving communication skills. If students have trouble taking direction, they could be taught to say, "I'll do it." If students have difficulty accepting correction or criticism, they might need to learn to say, "I'll fix it." Students who complain at work could be taught to write their complaints in a notebook and share them with their job coach once per week.

Checklists

Students may benefit from having checklists or written reminders that tell them how to handle certain social situations. One young man had a list of social rules for work that he used to respond when his boss gave him instructions or criticized his work. One young woman, who tended to ask personal questions and reveal too much personal information about herself, carried a list of acceptable conversation topics.

Social Skills Training

Direct instruction may be an effective method for teaching social skills, especially if care is taken to encourage generalization. Individuals with autism often have trouble generalizing a learned skill to new contexts and need to be taught specific skills within the context of where they are used. If skills are taught in school but also practiced at home, they will be generalized more quickly to the workplace or other community settings. Some examples of skills that can be taught using direct instruction are initial and continued attention, turn taking, following directions, choice making, and the basics of conversation.

Social skill support groups have also been described as a way to help people with autism learn and improve social skills (Hillier, Fish, et al., 2007), although few such groups have been developed for adolescents and young adults with autism. One type of social skill support group teaches individuals with autism to take turns in conversations, the topics of which are presented by the group facilitator. In another type of social skill support group, the leader gives specific instructions on an adaptive social response. Group members then take turns rehearsing with one another.

Social Stories

Social Stories are most useful for students who have basic language skills. The stories provide accurate information about situations a student may find difficult. Each story describes a social situation in writing or pictures or combination of the two. The content focuses on the important social cues of the situation, the events and reactions the individual might expect, the actions and reactions that might be expected of the student, and why these reactions are appropriate. The goal of the story is to help the individual comprehend certain situations and increase his or her comfort level. A review of research studies (Sansosti, Powell-Smith, & Kincaid, 2004) showed that Social Stories can help reduce problem behaviors, increase social awareness, and teach new skills. In some cases in these studies, the new behaviors were maintained and generalized to other situations even after the story was faded out. It should be noted that these studies were based on very small numbers of students.

Videotaping

Videotaping may be used to teach social skills, either by showing the adolescent footage of him- or herself or by showing demonstrations by other people (Ayres & Langone, 2005). First, a recording is made. During viewing, the student and a team member discuss what the student (or other individual) on the tape is doing and/or what the person could have done differently in that situation. Then a tape is made of the student (or other individual) attempting the new or alternative behavior, and this is viewed and discussed. Videotaping can also be used to rehearse social interactions. Positive effects of combined video- and computer-based instruction to teach social skills have also been described (Simpson, Langone, & Ayres, 2004).

Behavior Support Plans

Behavior support plans, described in Chapter 2, can be used to increase appropriate social behaviors. For a plan to be effective, everyone involved in carrying it out must follow key principles and adhere to the protocol. Refer to Chapter 2 for more details.

WORK HABITS

Students with autism often need direct instruction in good work habits. The transition years are an ideal time to provide this instruction. Instruction can be classroom based and can also be provided through job experiences that are part of the transition plan (Branham, Collins, Schuster, & Kleinert, 1999). Work habits that are critical to job success are described in the following sections.

Challenges to Good Work Habits

Individuals with autism are often at risk for losing their jobs due to poor work habits rather than to inability to perform the task. A good transition plan needs to identify any challenges to good work habits that the student may have. Strategies can then be developed to help the student overcome those challenges and develop better work habits.

Poor or Erratic Attendance

Employers expect good attendance. Spotty attendance among workers with autism can be due to logistical problems, such as transportation issues, or to more personal factors, such as a refusal to go to work. Sometimes behavioral issues result in poor work attendance. On days Maria got extremely upset and scratched herself, her mother would determine that she was too overwhelmed to go to work and would keep Maria home. Consequently, every month Maria missed several days of work.

Related to good attendance is respecting arrival, break, lunch, and dismissal times. As noted earlier, Jeff was often late to work because he walked instead of waiting for the bus, and this caused a problem for his boss.

Low Productivity

Some students with autism are hard, consistent workers. They enter transition with strengths in this area. These students can make a valuable contribution to the workplace. Other students with autism need to improve in this area. Some students may have a short attention span. After several minutes on a task or an activity, they are ready to move on to a new one. Other students are easily distracted, and those distractions can be an obstacle to productivity. When Jeff started his job at the video game store, he often forgot his work and instead read the backs of all the video game boxes. He did this because he loved video games, and having to unpack and stock them was actually very distracting for him.

Inaccuracy

Some people with autism are very precise and detail oriented. Their precision is a strength that will be useful in the workplace. Other individuals with autism do their work in a very hurried, careless manner, resulting in errors. Learning to work accurately is a critical skill that they will need in order to succeed at work.

Supports for Work Habits

Training and supports can be used to help develop and encourage good work habits. Some of these are described in the following sections.

Instruction in Work Habits

A primary support for good work habits is systematic instruction in those habits. This instruction is most productive when delivered in high school during the transition years. Once a student graduates, poor work habits are likely to result in job termination after several warnings go unheeded. While the student is in high school, he or she may be more willing to take instruction. Observing students' work habits and then teaching students how to improve them should be a primary activity of the transition years.

Supervision

Poor work habits can also be improved through increased supervision, either permanent or temporary, during work experiences. Job coaches and transition specialists can assess work habits, then provide sufficient supervision to allow the student to learn better habits while meeting their employers' needs.

Other Strategies

Reminders, checklists, written schedules, and strategies added to behavior support plans can also be used to teach and encourage good work habits. Jeff was given a written schedule, with designated break times. He was successfully taught to use that schedule to govern his break times. Maria's work attendance was improved by adding money rewards to her behavior plan. She earned daily wages based on attendance, with bonuses for having longer periods of good attendance. Whereas her paycheck was not particularly meaningful to her, earning daily money rewards was. Jeff was given increased supervision by his job coach to keep him in his assigned area of the video game store. Once his tasks were completed, he was allowed to spend 15 minutes on the floor reading the backs of the new video games.

MAINTAINING DIGNITY

Behaviors associated with autism may cause a lack of dignity for students. They may engage in embarrassing behaviors without realizing that they are embarrassing themselves. In addition, co-workers, supervisors, peers, and neighbors can easily mistake lapses in dignity for willful misconduct. The following sections discuss challenges relating to maintaining one's dignity and supports to help students meet these challenges.

Challenges in Maintaining Dignity

Behaviors associated with autism that may result in a lack of dignity include self-stimulatory behaviors, such as rocking, finger-flicking, spitting, and spinning. Some behaviors are especially embarrassing, such as public masturbation, staring at women's feet, or other openly sexual behaviors. Some students have compulsive rituals, such as touching the walls, touching floors, and walking in patterns. Sometimes rituals can be verbal, such as Maria's recitations of long sections of movie dialogue. Difficulty dealing with anger or frustration can lead to outbursts of crying, yelling, and cursing. In some cases, outbursts can escalate into violence.

Autism itself presents challenges to learning how to maintain dignity. Students without autism generally learn socially acceptable behaviors either by watching peers or by direct feedback from peers or others. Often, however, students with autism cannot learn how to be acceptable and dignified merely by watching peers, and direct instruction often fails to result in behavior change. The normal channels for teaching students to maintain their dignity around peers and, later, around neighbors, co-workers, and employers are often not effective for students with autism.

Generalization, or the ability to take what one has learned in one environment and display it in another environment, is often limited in students with autism (Smith, Belcher, & Wehman, 1997). For instance, through patient teaching by his transition teacher, Jeff was able to learn to enter the classroom and greet the other students appropriately. He also learned to take turns in conversation and talk about topics other than his special interests. These skills, however, which he learned in his transition class, did not generalize to his job setting. There, he was eager to go from co-worker to co-worker and talk about his interest in maps. His inability to generalize took a toll on his dignity at work. Co-workers would laugh at him behind his back.

Supports for Maintaining Dignity

Successful transition will often depend on the transition team's ability to assist with the resolution of these behaviors so that students can enter adulthood with some measure of dignity. Some behaviors can be taught by direct instruction. In other cases, the behaviors will need to be managed by support personnel and behavior support plans. Auxiliary support services may be helpful, including counseling and psychiatric intervention. An in-depth treatment of these strategies is provided in Chapter 2.

PULLING IT ALL TOGETHER

This chapter has explored the challenges with critical living skills that people with autism may face and possible strategies transition teams can use to help students gain these skills, preparing them for a more independent life once they graduate from high school. It is important to teach students these skills regardless of their post–high school plans, because a life lived as independently as possible is fulfilling.

10

Living in the Community

Pamela Sherron Targett and Marcia Datlow Smith

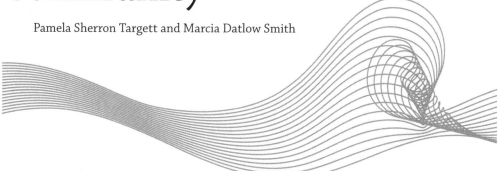

Housing can be one of the most difficult transition issues for individuals with autism. Historically, those with severe disabilities have lived at home with family members or in large institutions. Public opinion and policies about housing for all individuals with disabilities have changed. These improvements, largely energized by the Olmstead (1999) decision, give individuals with autism and their families greater choice in housing, which can enhance the quality of life. In the Olmstead decision, the Supreme Court ruled that individuals with disabilities must be offered services in the most integrated setting. The court encouraged states to establish an effective plan for placing people with disabilities in the least restrictive setting and a waiting list for community-based services to ensure that services will be provided and people will be moved off the list at a reasonable pace.

Even with a greater variety of residential options available, however, few individuals with autism move to more independent and integrated settings. A small percentage of adults with autism live alone (Billstedt, Gillberg, & Gillberg, 2005; Howlin et al., 2004; Wagner et al., 2005). Some reside in long-term hospitals or institutions, but most continue to live at home with their families (Howlin et al., 2004; Seltzer, Krauss, Orsmond, & Vestal, 2001). Wagner et al. (2005) surveyed out-of-school youth and found that 80% of those with autism were still living at home, and only 4% were living on their own. In a follow-up study by Howlin et al. (2004), less than 5% of adults with autism (mean age, 29.3 years) lived independently, and nearly 40% still lived at home.

Table 10.1.   Differences between traditional approaches to housing and supported independent living for people with autism

Traditional housing options	Supported living in an independent environment
The organization has decision-making authority.	Where to live is based on choice, not disability label. The person is supported to make choices and is assisted with fulfilling personal desires and wishes.
The person is expected to adapt to service.	Services are individualized. The person is assisted with learning new skills and developing interests in the residential setting of his or her choice.
The person is expected to choose only from available resources.	Resources are developed as needed to meet individual needs and desires and facilitate obtainment of personal goals. Services ensure participation in the community, including spending time with friends and family.
If needs change, the person's life may be disrupted rather than supported as he or she is transferred to another setting.	Services are flexible and change as indicated by the person's desires and needs.

Nonetheless, the shift has been away from individuals with disabilities living together in group situations or in some form of supervised living to supported living in an independent environment and home ownership (Racino, 2003; Taylor, 2006). Choice and self-determination are at the heart of this trend. Although traditional services still exist, adults with disabilities, family members, and service providers are increasingly looking for ways to create housing options and tailor support to meet an individual's needs within his or her preferred setting. Some of the differences between the traditional approach and the supported independent living approach are provided in Table 10.1.

This is good news for Jeff, Craig, Maria, and their families as they think about their futures. Parents will continue to age and eventually will not be able to provide support, and an earlier move toward independent living will likely lead to future levels of independence. This may not only benefit the person with autism but may also help decrease worry among parents who are deeply concerned about what the future will hold for their son or daughter upon their death.

Like other young adults, individuals with autism may want to reside on their own rather than remain at home with their parents. There is little doubt that they will face many challenges in this endeavor. Independent living requires a number of complex skills, from the general increased demands of independence to specific tasks linked with activities of daily living and monetary responsibilities (see Chapter 9). Regardless, like anyone else, young adults with autism should be able to live away from home if they wish to. Parents of individuals with autism should be able to see their children live on their own, just as other parents do. Mothers of children with autism who live away from home report great benefits for their children, whereas mothers whose grown children reside with them report negative consequences for them, including complacency, not being pushed to be independent, and social isolation (Krauss, Seltzer, & Jacobson, 2005).

Parents of adolescents with autism experience elevated caregiving demands (Holmes & Carr, 1991) and have higher levels of stress and depression than parents of children with other disabilities (Abbeduto et al., 2004). Respite services or relief staff can help alleviate some of this stress, yet just one in five families report using such services (Levine, Marder, & Wagner, 2004). It seems reasonable to assume that stress and strain on caregivers would be lessened as a child with autism becomes more independent.

The important question for successful supported living in an independent environment is "What support does the person need to live the most independently in the community setting of his or her choice?" Answering this question can be a first step toward developing creative living arrangements that are best suited to the individual's personal needs, wants, and dreams. Potential supports can be identified and eventually provided or facilitated in flexible ways to meet the unique needs of the individual. Note that this type of support sounds similar to the way individuals with autism are supported in the workplace, as described in Chapter 7.

Support for home living might include teaching the individual home safety skills, such as learning when and how to leave the area during a suspected fire. It may include instruction on daily living skills, such as cleaning the house, preparing food, or maintaining good hygiene. For many people with autism, supports for home living should address adjusting to the social demands of housemates, neighbors, and nonparental caregivers. Fortunately, more and more residential agencies are shifting to a support role rather than a provider role (i.e., planner, organizer, controller, and deliverer). Some of the guiding principles behind this approach are provided in Table 10.2.

In this chapter, we examine housing options, potential sources for funding, and what skills individuals with autism should be taught to increase their chances to live as independently as possible in the community setting of their choice. We also follow Craig, Maria, and Jeff as they make the transition from home to community living.

It is important to note the following words of caution. Residential success is often hampered by a lack of necessary supports. Failure to provide needed supports at the outset can result in a move back to the individual's family home. Another unfortunate outcome of lack of supports is that the family fills in the support gap, often for decades. This burden becomes less tenable as parents age. To avoid these problems, it is important to choose a residential option that provides enough support for the person to succeed under a worst-case adjustment scenario. Residential choices and nice apartments do not cure autism. It is imperative that support needs are adequately assessed and addressed at the outset. Once the transition is made from school to community living and certain funding arrangements are in place, it can be very difficult to address those needs later. It is best to start out

Table 10.2. Recommended practice guidelines

Everyone can live in the setting of his or her choice when given appropriate support.

Readiness to live in the place of one's choice (home) cannot be predicted.

People should be taught skills needed to live as independently as possible in the setting where they choose to live. They do not first have to live in a segregated or congregated living situation to learn such skills.

The person with a disability should make residential decisions to the greatest extent possible.

One size does not fit all. Supports should be tailored to personal needs.

Supports should be flexible.

When possible, a combination of natural and paid support should be provided.

with the most conservative scenario, and if all goes well, to fade supports and increase independence as the individual experiences success.

RESIDENTIAL OPTIONS

Smith and Philippen (2005) described a variety of living arrangements, including living with family, with a foster family, independently, in a partially-supported living situation, and in a fully supported situation. Some people may choose to remain living at home with family. Others may decide to pursue living in an existing community housing option with supervision or a residence specifically intended for individuals with autism. Still others may prefer having some support in an independent environment, such as their own house or apartment. Table 10.3 provides some examples of housing options. It is important to note that the options are not listed in order of desirability. The transition team plays an important role in helping the individual build the skills to live as independently as possible no matter which residential option is eventually chosen. Some of these skills are discussed in this chapter. The team also plays an important role in directing family members and other interested parties to resources related to home living, such as CILs and Social Security benefits planning and outreach specialists.

Living with Family Members

Some individuals with autism may continue living with their family as adults or perhaps move into a more independent setting on the homestead's premises, such as a garage apartment or an in-law suite. Support in this setting may continue to come primarily from family members and friends, or an independent living provider may be hired. Many individuals with autism live at home with their parents

Table 10.3.   Examples of community living arrangements

Type of arrangement	Description
Family living	Living with parents or family members, either in the same dwelling or perhaps in an apartment-like setting on the premises (e.g., in-law suite, garage apartment)
Group home	Living in a home in a residential setting for four or more individuals with disabilities
	Residents must meet entrance criteria
	House manager and/or around-the-clock support staff on duty
	May or may not be specifically for individuals with autism
Supervised apartment	Individuals with disabilities rent apartments in a particular complex
	Residential manager is on the premises in his or her own apartment and provides various supports to residents
	May or may not be specifically for individuals with autism
Shared living	Living with one or more roommates without disabilities in a single-family house, townhouse, or apartment
	Each person shares joint expenses; in some circumstances a person may receive free room and/or board in exchange for providing particular supports to the resident with autism
Independent living	Living on one's own or with spouse and children in a house, townhouse, or condominium purchased by the homeowner in a residential neighborhood with or without support

well into adulthood. If the adult child with autism is going to remain in the home setting, family members must receive up-to-date information about autism and recommended practices, including implementation of behavior support plans as described in Chapter 2. Equipped with this information, more families may become more willing to consider alternative ways to support their son or daughter to live in a community setting.

Structured and Supervised Settings

Other people with autism may opt for a more structured or supervised residential option, such as a group home or supervised apartment. The residence may or may not be specifically designed with individuals with autism in mind.

Group homes are purchased or rented and usually house four or more residents, who are supported by on-site house managers and/or staff. Supervised apartments are located in community complexes. Depending on the level of support residents need, the dwellings may be clustered together in close proximity or dispersed throughout an apartment complex.

There is often a waiting list for structured or supervised residential options. When a space does become available, several factors may be taken into consideration to match someone from the waiting list to the residence. For example, if rooms are shared, gender is considered. Staff-to-resident ratios based on the potential newcomer's support needs must be considered as well. Age of residents is another factor.

Typically, a person can visit the potential residence prior to making his or her final decision about moving in. If the individual decides not to move in, his or her place on the waiting list is usually not affected. Available housing options, rules, regulations, and funding, among other things, will vary by state, county, city, and community. Table 10.4 lists some consideration for people thinking about a group or supervised apartment housing option.

Table 10.4.   Factors to consider when selecting supervised apartment or group home setting

Is the residence in a desirable/acceptable community setting?

Are residents respected and treated like adults?

Do residents make decisions and choices rather than being told what to do (e.g., daily schedules, what to wear, what to eat, where to go)?

Is the management style supportive or supervisory?

Are all residents treated the same, or are different levels of support provided based on individual needs?

What are the support needs of the other residents, and how might this affect the individual considering moving there?

Are residents allowed to decorate and keep their private areas however they choose?

What other areas in the home can residents go to for privacy?

Are there any house policies that all residents must comply with? What happens if a resident chooses not to follow a set rule? How are disputes among residents settled?

Are residents assigned housekeeping duties, or are these rotated among residents? Can a resident purchase housekeeping services if he or she does not want to do housekeeping?

Are residents encouraged to do what they can for themselves and taught new skills to become more independent?

If transportation is available, is it accessible with or without support?

Are residents required to participate in group outings to shop, do other errands, participate in leisure activities, and so on, or are these activities planned to meet individual desires or requests?

Residential programs designed specifically for adults with autism may provide an appropriate living arrangement for those needing intensive support. Such programs began in the 1970s and incorporated the use of instructional and behavioral techniques to help individuals develop new skills (Holmes, 1990; Van Bourgondien & Reichle, 1997; Wall, 1990). The research suggests that these residential treatment models resulted in increased community participation (Luce & Dyer, 1995), increased independent functioning and interpersonal behavior (Persson, 2000), and a higher quality of life (Van Bourgondien, Reichle, & Schopler, 2003). Again, this type of option is typically reserved for those individuals who may be at risk of harm without ongoing supervision. Over time, some people with autism may be able to shift from this intensive support option to one that is less intensive.

Developing Individualized Housing Options

As noted previously, more and more people with disabilities are opting to develop their own housing options (Taylor, 2006). This may be done alone or, depending on the state, in coordination with an agency. The transition team should identify local resources and direct family members there for assistance. Using a person-centered approach, a person with autism and his or her family work together to locate housing and develop the needed support system. For example, the person may live in his or her own home or rent a house or an apartment. The person may live alone or with one or more roommates. Support may range from in-home skills training for meal preparation or clothes cleaning to services such as shopping for groceries or paying monthly bills.

In supported living arrangements, the person with autism receives a combination of supports (including direct service and/or skills training) based on his or her skills and abilities. For example, one person may live in an apartment and have paid supplemental staff come in and assist with certain activities throughout the week. Another individual may share his or her home with someone and also have a neighbor next door who is paid or volunteers to offer emergency support service if required. Still another person may have ongoing support provided by a few hired staff who are on the premises at different times of the day. Some individuals are readily able to live independently; others may need to learn certain skills to reach this level. Still others may always require ongoing support.

Supervision levels in independent living situations will range from no supervision to around-the-clock supervision. For example, if a person with autism demonstrates a behavior that could lead to self-injury or injury to others if the person is left unattended, supervision may be crucial. Likewise, if an individual is not able to recognize emergency situations or hazards, some form of supervision would be required—perhaps nighttime support could be provided by a roommate or an on-call support provider who lives nearby.

Supports also must be flexible and change as the person's needs change. For example, over time an individual may learn new skills that increase independence in the home, or the person may move to another place and no longer have access to a provider's support services. Factors such as these result in a change to existing supports.

Due to the nature of the challenges that some individuals with autism face, an array of residential options are needed. A variety of individual and interacting fac-

Table 10.5. Factors to consider for an independent living environment

What housing option does the young adult with autism and the family prefer? What are the first, second, and third choices?

Is the first-choice residential option available? If not, can it be developed? What about the second and third options?

What safety and support needs are anticipated for this person in an independent community living situation?

Can the supports be offered in the preferred setting? If not, what skills would the person need to learn and what supports are required to live in the preferred setting?

How much will it cost to live there? (Be sure to calculate living expenses, taxes, etc.)

What funding assistance, if any, is available?

Will the person have access to the community when desired?

If public or private transportation is needed, what is the cost?

What transportation is available (for work and community access) and at what times of day?

If the person is employed, will the setting affect employment? What is the commute time to and from work? If the person is unemployed, will the setting promote employment (e.g., business and industry in the area, transportation available)?

tors must be taken into account when considering independent living environments. Some of these factors are listed in Table 10.5.

FUNDING FOR HOUSING

Housing funding assistance may be available to people with autism. The transition team should be familiar with local, state, and federal resources so that they can connect individuals with autism and family members with financial resources. Referral to CILs and Social Security benefits planning and outreach specialist should be offered to families as well. This section will briefly examine federal housing assistance and Section 8 rental assistance. A quick review of trends in the banking industry for home loans will also be provided. Remember that resources will vary from place to place. The U.S. Department of Housing and Urban Development (HUD) web site is a good place to begin research on funding options.

Federal Housing Assistance

The federal government funds most housing assistance. HUD is the federal agency for administration and oversight of affordable housing programs. The main office is based in Washington, D.C., and there is at least one field office in each state to oversee regional administration and oversight. HUD contracts with public and private agencies and governments to administer housing assistance. Generally, the primary agencies that HUD contracts with include Public Housing Authorities (PHAs); city, county, and state governments; and housing developers.

Affordable community housing may also be available. This may include public housing projects developed and owned by the PHA, Section 8 vouchers administered by the PHA, and privately owned rental housing, which offers affordable rent because the owners receive some form of assistance.

Congress provides new funding each year to increase the number of households that will receive assistance. This might include block grant funding, a lim-

ited number of Section 8 vouchers for which PHAs may apply, mainstream Section 8 vouchers open to application by nonprofits and public housing authorities, and funding to refurbish deteriorating housing projects.

The Section 8 voucher provides the greatest flexibility to individuals with low incomes. Although there are a few restrictions, vouchers are generally portable, making them available to use on a rental unit anywhere. Once a rental unit is approved, the resident pays a percentage of his or her income as rent. The balance of the rent is paid to the landlord through the voucher program. This offers an effective way to obtain decent and affordable housing; however, many people become frustrated with the application process, rules, regulations, and long waiting lists.

Home Ownership

Many people with disabilities have low incomes, and their ability to accumulate savings is often limited. To overcome this barrier to home ownership, low down payment requirements are usually incorporated into home ownership programs for people with disabilities. In addition, banks are slowly adopting more flexible down payment requirements to allow individuals with disabilities greater access to mortgage financing. Some lenders may allow the down payment or assistance with closing costs to come from a gift from family, friends, a special needs trust, religious organizations, community groups, and so forth (Galbraith, 2001).

Grants may also be available to assist with down payment or closing costs. Sources include independent living centers, developmental disabilities councils, state human service agencies, state and local housing trusts, state housing finance agencies, rural community development programs, and local housing funds. In addition, nontraditional sources of income from food stamps, Medicaid, and community-based waiver services that help the person cover monthly living expenses may be taken into consideration (Galbraith, 2001).

Banks may also be willing to consider nontraditional credit options for those with no or poor credit histories. Service providers and state home ownership agencies can work with individuals with disabilities to assist in clearing up bad credit or establishing credit for the first time. Individual development accounts may be one way to build assets to buy a home. These are dedicated savings accounts similar in structure to an individual retirement account (IRA).

Collaborations or home ownership coalitions coordinated by a lead agency may be another resource to help a person reach the goal of home ownership. Lead agencies may be nonprofits that address housing or disability issues, or they may be local, county, or state housing and human services agencies. Ideally, all interested and necessary parties are included in program design and implementation. This includes lenders, real estate agents, developers, service providers, state housing and human service agencies, and home buying counseling agencies. Lead agencies play a key role in aggregating the government and private funding needed for down payment assistance and other costs (Galbraith, 2001).

BUILDING SKILLS FOR HOME LIVING

Learning to live on one's own requires being able to complete a number of complex activities. Therefore, home living skills training should begin early and continue throughout the years. This means the school should play a major role in assisting students with autism in developing home living skills. Despite this fact, Cameto and colleagues (2004) reported that less than one third of transition plans had goals related to independent living, and only one third had identified supported living services for students exiting school. These findings indicate a lack of planning and shed light on why so many adults with autism remain at home as adults. Waiting until the last few years of school or until graduation to focus on home living skills is simply too late.

Transition Planning

Educators should work with students with autism and their families to explore future residential options and work toward specific goals for home living skills. Instruction for home living skills should be based on the presumption that all students, regardless of the severity of their disability, can master many of the skills required. Students should receive skills training in community-based settings during school; later, as needed, supports can be put in place to further promote independence.

Several studies demonstrate that individuals with autism can learn home living skills. Smith and Belcher (1985) improved the life skills of five adults with autism living in a group home by breaking skills into small steps and gradually increasing the level of assistance. A training program was implemented and evaluated that consisted of analyzing life skills into component steps and providing increasing levels of assistance according to a predetermined schedule. Five adults with autism who lived in group homes in the community served as participants. All five adults showed progress in targeted life skills, and four of the five achieved independence on their targeted skills.

An intervention using Social Stories (Gray, 1998) was implemented to improve the lunchtime eating behaviors of an adolescent with Asperger's syndrome (Bledsoe, Smith, & Simpson, 2003). Brown (1991) increased participation in daily activities and reduced problem behavior for adults with autism by using an individualized daily schedule and providing choices. Lasater and Brady (1995) used a multicomponent package consisting of self-assessment, behavioral rehearsal, and video self-modeling to increase self-help skills of an adolescent with autism. Reese, Sherman, and Sheldon (1998) used a differential reinforcement schedule to reduce aggressive and disruptive behaviors in an adult with autism in a residential setting. Simpson et al. (2004) demonstrated how video- and computer-based instruction could be used to improve social skills for students with autism. Ferguson, Smith, and Hagiwara (2005) used a PDA to increase the independence of an adolescent with Asperger's syndrome.

Skills to Teach

Some home living activities, such as eating, self-care, bathing, and maintaining appropriate hygiene, are vital, but many others are helpful (see the list of selected activities in Table 10.6). Some living skills were discussed in Chapter 9, including mobility, participation in recreational and leisure activities, money management, maintenance of personal appearance, and socialization. The focus in this section is

Table 10.6.   Examples of home living skills

Shopping
Preparing meals
Cleaning the home
Doing laundry
Knowing what to do in an emergency
Caring for pets
Caring for self when ill
Seeking help and assistance
Managing finances and paying bills
Managing time

on additional skills needed for home living: preparing meals, cleaning and maintaining the home, and caring for clothing.

Preparing Meals

Preparing meals is something that some individuals do not pick up naturally; for them, learning to prepare meals takes practice. The basic meal-preparation tasks to teach transition-age students with autism are food preparation, cleanup, and food storage. Depending on the level of skill a student already has with food preparation, he or she might be taught how to make a noncooked meal (e.g., a sandwich), heat a frozen entrée in the microwave, or cook food on the stovetop or in the oven. Setting the table, pouring a drink, and serving the food may also be taught. This may be difficult initially for students who are used to repetition of certain activities, such as Jeff's needing to be in his seat before a fork is placed at his setting, followed by a spoon. This is why learning independent living skills prior to the actual transition is beneficial. Safe practices related to food preparation must also be addressed. This may include making a meal that meets special dietary requirements, cleaning knives after cutting raw meat, preventing burns by using potholders to remove hot items from the oven, or keeping some items properly refrigerated until preparation time.

Cleanup skills should also be taught. Students might learn to remove dishes from the dining room table; wash dishes by hand or load, run, and unload a dishwasher; wipe counters and sink using antibacterial soap; clean up spills; and sweep or mop the floor.

Instruction should also cover proper food storage. This includes putting away groceries, keeping the refrigerator and freezer on proper settings, storing foods appropriately, and determining when to throw foods away.

Cleaning and Maintaining the Home

A dirty home will breed germs and be uninviting to guests. Students should be taught basic skills to keep their home clean, particularly the kitchen and bathroom. Some students with autism may already be particular about cleanliness; others may show little regard for a messy or dirty area. Again, it is easier to learn to clean and maintain a living space before students make the transition to an independent or semi-independent living arrangement. Having time to practice these skills will benefit the person with autism once in a new environment.

Students can learn to clean the bathroom by mopping the floor; scrubbing the tub, toilet, and sink; and wiping faucets and mirrors. Daily straightening of the bathroom may also be taught. Cleaning the kitchen—not just after every meal, but at least weekly—is important, too. Cleaning common rooms like a living room or den should be addressed. For example, students can be taught how to vacuum the floor, dust the furniture, and straighten the area on a scheduled basis. Bedroom cleaning skills include making a stripped bed, making a partially made bed, vacuuming, dusting, and putting away clothes (hanging, folding, or putting in laundry room) daily. Collecting trash from the various rooms and taking it outside for garbage collection is another important skill to teach. Housecleaning requires the student to learn how to use various types of equipment, such as a vacuum cleaner, mop, and broom. Students will also need to learn how to use cleaning products that may be sprayed or dispensed in other ways.

Cleaning regularly may be natural for some students, whereas others may need visual or verbal reminders to clean on a regular basis. Having a chore list on the refrigerator or in a PDA may help the person with autism remember to complete these tasks on a regular basis.

Caring for Clothes

Keeping clothes neat and clean may not be intuitive to a person with autism. Therefore, it is important to teach transition-age students how to properly care for their clothing. Students should be taught how to sort laundry in loads to wash according to the instructions, identify and treat stains, and operate the washing machine. They should also learn how to remove clothes from the washer, determine how to dry a particular item (hang to dry or put in dryer), and operate the dryer. Students should also be taught how to fold or hang and put away their clean towels, sheets, and clothing.

When teaching these skills, it is important to explain to the student why they are important. Students like Maria are not embarrassed by untidy clothing and do not understand the importance of wearing neat, clean clothing to work. Students like Jeff and Craig do not recognize the importance of housekeeping tasks such as taking the trash out. It is important to help these students understand why certain things need to be done, not just that they need to be done.

Behavioral Concerns

Behavioral concerns associated with autism may jeopardize an individual's success in a residential situation. Often, behavioral issues present the greatest obstacle to community living (Schall et al., 2006). Whereas housekeeping skills can be learned rather easily, behavioral challenges are harder to overcome. These issues need to be recognized and a plan developed for training and support. Following are some of the behaviors that may present challenges to residential adjustment.

Destructive Behaviors

Some individuals with autism, even those with high intellectual functioning, may exhibit destructive behaviors, such as aggression towards others, self-injury, or property destruction. Individuals who act aggressively or self-injure can pose a threat to their own safety as well as to the safety of housemates and neighbors. Property destruction can take a toll on the residence itself as well as on its contents. Holes in the walls, holes in the floor, destruction of furnishings and appliances, and even fire setting are risks in some severe cases. Not only is the destruction of property itself a problem, but the noises involved can also disturb neighbors.

Craig sometimes stuffs the toilet at his parents' house with paper and clothing. If he does this while living in a supported apartment, this behavior will not only affect his roommates but also the tenants in the rest of the building, who will experience plumbing problems. Craig may need to have restricted access to toilet paper. He may also need a behavior support plan and full residential supervision to monitor his use of the bathroom. If Craig is in the bathroom too long, a residential supervisor can check on him to make sure he is not flushing items down the toilet.

Rituals and Hoarding

Rituals associated with autism, especially hoarding, can create health and safety concerns. Saving and hoarding items such as supplies, newspapers, magazines, scraps of paper, and even items scavenged from trash cans can present a housekeeping nightmare. Hoarding of food, especially perishables, presents an even greater challenge.

Maria tends to hoard hygiene and grooming products, including scented lotions, shampoos, and soaps. If she does this while living in an apartment with roommates, it will present three problems. First, her room will become overrun with large quantities of these items. Second, she will experience budget problems, as she likes to purchase excessive amounts of these items during shopping trips. Third, she may be tempted to steal her roommates' soaps, shampoos, and other hygiene products and hide them in her room. Jeff may also be at risk for hoarding items. He loves maps, newspapers, and junk mail, but if he lets these items pile up in his room, they will create safety and fire hazards. Both Maria and Jeff would benefit from behavioral interventions to limit their hoarding. For example, Maria's mother can limit Maria to two extra of each type of hygiene item and not allow her to buy more until one of her extras is gone. Because she was particularly fond of lotion, Maria can be given a shoebox to keep lotion in. She can have as much lotion as can fit in the box. Jeff may benefit from a large filing cabinet in which he can keep as many of his collectibles as can fit. Once the cabinet is full, he will have to make room for new items.

Noise

Noisemaking can be a challenging behavior in a residential setting. Some individuals with autism may yell, scream, sing, or talk loudly. Sometimes these outbursts are due to anger, but in other cases they simply reflect a failure to properly modulate voice volume. Some people talk aloud to themselves, which can be particularly disturbing to others if they do this after bedtime hours. A loud voice can disturb housemates as well as neighbors. Jeff sometimes screams if he gets frustrated while completing a task such as balancing his checkbook. Craig has a limited vocabulary but communicates with other vocalizations, and these vocalizations can disturb roommates or neighbors late at night. Sometimes it is not a person's loud voice that is disturbing but loud music or a loud television program. Behavior support plans and social skills training may be needed to address issues related to noise.

Elopement

Some individuals with autism may have a problem with *elopement*, or going off unauthorized and unsupervised from their living situation. While living in a supervised apartment, one woman with autism, who had very fond memories of a prior caregiver, made several unplanned, unsupervised, and uninvited visits to this individual's home. Another young adult with autism had a fondness for soda from the local convenience store. He made several nighttime trips to the convenience store in search of soda. The problem was that he exited his apartment by jumping from his second floor balcony at 2 A.M. On one occasion he was found nude and limping by a passing motorist as he made his way to the nearby convenience store. To ensure their safety, individuals with elopement issues need close supervision, behavior support plans, and perhaps alarms on doors and windows.

Poor Social Skills

Poor social skills are a hallmark of autism and of course present special challenges in all residential situations. Whereas families have had 20 years or more to adjust to and accommodate the young adult with autism, neighbors and housemates who are less familiar with the individual might not be so accommodating. Poor social skills can be disturbing to housemates as well as neighbors. Learning to both share and respect boundaries can be very difficult for the young adult with autism. Counseling, support groups (Hillier, Campbell, et al., 2007), social skills training, and perhaps supervision and behavior support plans may be needed to properly support an individual in his or her transition to life away from home. Video-based instruction for children with autism is also being used to successfully teach a variety of functional skills to young adults with autism (Ayres & Langone, 2005). Although this area of research is expanding, more detailed studies are needed to better describe various aspects of video-based instruction.

The Unexpected

As one parent whose grown son moved into his own apartment said, "Learning to do the laundry was not the problem. The problem was the unexpected." Given the difficulties associated with autism, such as poor judgment, poor problem-solving skills, difficulty with change, and difficulty with abstract thinking, it is not hard to imagine the many ways in which the unexpected can create problems in a residential setting. For example, although one woman with autism had been doing well with caring for her clothes and personal hygiene, she began to come to work unwashed and wearing dirty clothes. After further investigation, it was found that a water pipe had burst in the woman's house. Her housemate was able to turn off the water to avoid flooding, but no one called the landlord to have the problem resolved, which meant that no one in the house was able to cook with water, wash the dishes, bathe, or wash clothing.

When planning for residential options, it is imperative that the transition team consider how the student's behavioral challenges could affect the living situation. The need for behavioral supports, which might range from social skills training to intensive behavior support plans, must be assessed. Similarly, sufficient supervision must be planned to ensure the peace and safety of all concerned and the viability of the placement. Even students with the most challenging of behaviors can succeed in living situations outside the family home; however, that success depends on sufficient supports.

Other Skills

Depending on the situation and the student's desires and needs, other home living skills may be taught, such as taking medications, watering plants, caring for pets, and mowing the lawn. To successfully carry out the daily living activities that have been covered, individuals with autism must also learn self-management skills, including time management. Some might develop a natural rhythm for these activities, but others will need to rely on schedules and devices to help them. This might include using calendars, appointment books, or alarm watches. Independence has been increased among children with autism by teaching routines and using activity schedules (McDuff, Krantz, & McClannahan, 1993). This may also be a way to increase the level of independence and functioning in the home for adults with autism; however, it needs further exploration.

Determining What to Teach

Educators and support staff need to know which home living skills to teach. Taking a close look at the individual's current and future home living environments should provide the basis for the content of a *home living instructional program*. This approach, often referred to as an *ecological inventory*, involves the following steps:

1. Identifying and surveying current and future home living environments

2. Dividing the home living environments into subenvironments or places in the home where certain activities occur, such as the kitchen or living room

3. Inventorying the subenvironments by listing relevant activities performed there, such as meal preparation and food storage

4. Determining the skills required for performing those activities, such as making a sandwich and putting away groceries

This approach was used to design instruction that would prepare Jeff for living in the community. As discussed in Chapter 8, Jeff plans to move into an apartment after his first year of college. Since his junior year of high school, Jeff has been talking about how awesome it would be to live in the same apartment complex as his uncle. During Jeff's junior year, his teacher surveyed his current (home) and potential future environment (apartment) to determine what skills to teach him. It was too early to know whether a unit would be available in that specific apartment complex, so Jeff's teacher visited two settings Jeff liked and determined the skills that would be needed to live in either place. If Jeff's future residential environment had been unknown, his teacher could have visited several apartments and homes that are typical of future options (within a certain area and budget) and listed the skills most commonly required.

After the future home living environment has been identified, such as Jeff's expected apartment, the next step is to determine the physical areas within the setting. In Jeff's case, this included a living room, dining room, kitchen, bathroom, and bedroom. Next, each area (e.g., kitchen) can be broken down further into the activities that occur there (e.g., meal preparation) and the skills (e.g., make a sandwich) required to participate in the activity. An example of a partial ecological inventory that Jeff's team developed for apartment living is shown in Table 10.7.

An ecological inventory is important for identifying activities that may be unique to a particular environment. For example, locking the front door from the inside of a home will vary; some doors may have deadbolts or chains, whereas others may require a key. Due to variability in home living situations, teachers should always try to incorporate a variety of examples into their teaching. For example, students should be taught how to turn on and off different types of light switches. Other examples of home activities that may be done in different ways are using small and large appliances, setting the temperature of a room, disposing of garbage, using an alarm clock, and turning the water on in the shower.

Once activities are identified from ecological inventories, the next step is to plan an instructional program. First, each skill needs to be analyzed and a task analysis developed. Then natural cues are identified. Natural cues describe the way the materials or environment looks just before completion of the step. Table 10.8 shows a task analysis for drying clothes in a dryer.

Next, a specific assessment of a person's ability to complete important home living activities is conducted. An informal assessment of Jeff's skills would take

Table 10.7.   Partial ecological inventory for apartment living

Subenvironment	Activity	Skills
Living room	Vacuuming	Deciding when to vacuum
		Locating vacuum cleaner
		Operating vacuum cleaner
		Changing bag or filter
		Putting vacuum away
	Socializing with others	Inviting friends over
		Greeting others
		Talking about shared interests
		Asking for help from others
	Watching television	Deciding what to watch
		Turning television on
		Using remote to operate channel selection and volume
		Turning television off
Kitchen	Preparing food in the microwave	Selecting what to cook
		Operating microwave to cook item according to instructions
		Removing item from microwave
	Washing dishes	Determining if dishes in dishwasher are clean or dirty
		Loading glasses and cups
		Loading plates
		Loading silverware
		Loading pots
		Putting soap in washer
		Turning on dishwasher
		Interrupting cycle to add items
		Unloading items

Table 10.8. Task analysis for operating clothes dryer

Natural cue	Step in task analysis
Buzzer goes off on washer or clock	Open the washing machine door
Washer door open	Pull wet clothes out of washer
Wet clothes out of washer	Place in clothes basket
Wet clothes in basket	Open the dryer door
Dryer door open	Put wet clothes into the dryer
Wet clothes in dryer	Check and remove any material from lint compartment
Cleaned lint compartment	Close the dryer door
Dryer door closed	Set the dry cycle
Dry cycle set	Push "On" button to start the drying cycle

place in the environment where the activity is typically performed. One method for conducting informal assessment is to develop a task analysis for each activity, observe the student performing the activity (without instruction) and record which steps the student performs correctly or incorrectly or does not attempt. After the assessment, the data are analyzed to determine priority areas for instruction.

If Jeff performs a step correctly, this is recorded. If he does not perform a step correctly, the teacher will stop him and arrange the natural cues for the next step. This strategy highlights steps that need to be taught. It also illustrates the type of assistance needed for the learner to perform a step. Jeff will receive instruction on a variety of home living skills to help prepare him for life in the community. If he is not able to master particular skills over time, supports will need to be considered. For example, Jeff may need a neighbor to be accessible during nighttime hours or in the event of an emergency. If a spontaneous relationship does not develop, his parents might consider recruiting someone and possibly even paying them for these services.

Teaching Jeff home living skills can decrease his dependency on his family and others and increase his ability to live on his own. Even if Jeff is not able to master all the skills he needs, he may be able to live in the community if the proper supports and necessary funding can be found or created and the plan can be put into action.

Jeff Moves Out

After living at home his freshman year in college, Jeff moved into a supervised apartment. He lived with two roommates and had the services of support staff 10 hours per week. Staff assisted Jeff with meal planning, budgeting, paying bills, shopping for major purchases, and completing chores around his apartment. Because his high school teachers and parents had taken the time to teach him important home living skills, he made the transition smoothly and loves having his own space and increased responsibility.

Craig Moves Out

Craig was able to move out of his parents' home after high school. He opted to live in a three-bedroom apartment with two other roommates. Individuals with disabilities also occupy two other apartments located on the same floor. Staff trained in supporting residential living for persons with autism provide ongoing support in the apartment. Because Craig has a behavior support plan to address his challenging behavior, including self-injury, his residential staff were trained in that plan.

Residents of the apartments can receive support to conduct activities such as housekeeping, shopping, and banking; have someone do it for them; or make use of community services, such as home delivery of groceries. Residents can also receive support with cooking.

In this setting, support is also offered to assist residents with decision making. This includes assistance to ensure that each resident's needs are expressed and considered. For example, Craig received assistance to select roommates and decide which leisure activities he wanted to participate in. Opportunities are also created for a range of experiences and choices in daily living.

Maria Moves Out

Maria's school advised her and her mother to start thinking about future housing well in advance. During her last 2 years in high school, and her first year attending community college, Maria received instruction on home living skills in a community apartment setting a few times per week. Her mother was contacted about an impending opening in a small house shared by people with and without disabilities—a shared living environment. This is the place where Maria's best friend was living. Maria was invited to spend the weekend at the house. During this time, her mother interviewed her potential housemates, who provided support to the other housemates with disabilities in exchange for reduced rent, and observed Maria in the setting. Her first impressions were very positive. She also received favorable reviews about the shared living environment from Maria's friend and

Table 10.9. Maria's mother's checklist for potential shared living arrangement

Area	Notes
Philosophy of setting	Philosophy is person centered. Residential supports would be designed around Maria's needs and desires; steps would be taken to maximize her independence. She would be given choices and have input into how her life is structured.
Residents	The fellow residents seem friendly, happy, and healthy. Data indicate they are satisfied with supports.
Staffing	Resident statements reflect person-centered philosophy. The residents without disabilities who provide supports to those with disabilities do not frequently turn over.
Building	The house is clean, accessible, and located in a safe area.
Location	Transportation to and from the community is accessible; Maria could get to work and activities that she would enjoy.
Daily activities	Residents who choose to work are employed in the community. Maria and her fellow residents would be encouraged to go to work in the community as opposed to attending day support programs or sheltered workshops. Maria would choose her own schedule and would regularly participate in shopping, home maintenance activities, and so forth.
Leisure and recreation	Maria would have a variety of choices and can also have outings geared specifically to her interests or desires.
Emergency procedures and safety record	Adequate emergency procedures are in place and residents receive evacuation training. The home has a good safety record.

Table 10.10.   Maria's home living choices

Cleaning	Food preparation	Schedule
Maria likes to make her bed and clean up her room. Maria does not like to perform any cleaning that requires use of a sponge and water. Maria likes to vacuum, but it may aggravate her allergies. If she performs this task, be sure she takes an allergy pill. Maria likes to clean early in the morning; once her routine is started for the day, she does not like to be interrupted to perform a chore.	Maria likes cereal for breakfast. She does not like eggs but enjoys other breakfast foods, particularly pancakes. Maria can make a sandwich. She does not like mayonnaise and has an allergy to rye, so this type of bread should be avoided. Her favorite sandwich is turkey with Swiss cheese and mustard on wheat bread. Maria loves all types of Mexican food. She can make tacos. Maria likes chicken, turkey, and beef. She does not like pork. She can make a simple chicken casserole. Maria enjoys making salads and pizza. Maria likes to eat popcorn while watching television at night. She can make it in the microwave.	Maria likes to get up by 8 A.M. during the week to start her day. Maria varies her bedtime. On weekdays she usually goes to bed around 11 P.M. On weekends she will choose to stay up past 2 A.M. watching television. Maria uses an alarm watch to help her stay on schedule. If changes are made to her set schedule, she will need assistance setting the alarms.

the friend's parents. Some of the criteria she took into consideration are listed in Table 10.9.

At the end of the weekend, Maria reported that she wanted to live there, so plans were made for her to move into the house at the end of her first year in college. Her future housemates told Maria and her mother that they wanted to learn more about Maria's likes, dislikes, and preferences before she moved in. This contributed to a quality lifestyle for Maria when she moved to her new residence. A section of her choices profile is provided in Table 10.10. Maria has really enjoyed living independently in the house and one day plans to own her own home.

PULLING IT ALL TOGETHER

Individuals with autism and their families now have a greater choice in housing options than previously. The shift has been away from individuals with disabilities living together in group situations or in some form of supervised living to living in a supported independent environment or owning a home.

Some of the differences between the traditional and the supported independent living approach were described in this chapter. This chapter also examined various housing options, potential sources for funding, and what skills students with autism should be taught to increase their chances to live as independently as possible in the community setting of their choice.

Afterword

Paul Wehman, Marcia Datlow Smith, and Carol Schall

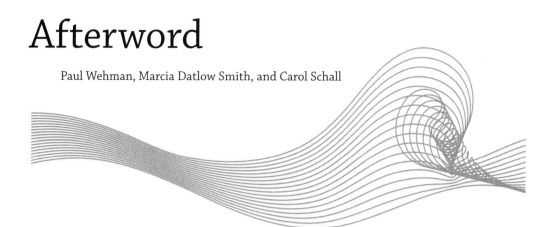

This book has been about the journey from adolescence into young adulthood for individuals with autism. For Jeff, Craig, Maria, and any teenager—with or without autism—there have been and are going to be obstacles along the way that have to be overcome. The transition years are a critical time for preparing young people for such challenges and paving the way to a successful future.

As this book has illustrated, with advances in education, teaching, applied behavior analysis, public attitudes, and employment opportunities, the future is brighter than ever for individuals with autism. It is clear that opportunities will abound and that society is more receptive to learning about autism, understanding individual differences among those who have autism, and taking advantage of the untapped human resource and potential that exists within these young people.

Although there is much wonderful news for young people with autism, it is vitally important that they and their families proceed with some caution. High-quality programs now exist for individuals with autism, but there are a great many that are mediocre. The most common issue is that the staff—the teachers, teaching assistants, psychologists, and administrators—have not had sufficient training in good program design. In discussing the design of school programs in this book, we have tried to underscore the importance of three key elements:

1. What skills and activities are taught and how functional they are in real life

2. How these skills are taught

3. Where the skills are taught

Lack of attention to any of these three points will render instruction ineffective. Young people with autism and the people who support them must determine how to gain access to programs that yield good community integration and employment outcomes.

There are four especially important take-home messages in this book. In closing, we would like to recapitulate each of these points. First, we have done our best in presenting what we know *now* about what youth like Jeff, Craig, and Maria can do. We have tried not to overpromise or be unrealistic. Some who read this book may feel we have, and we certainly respect those feelings, but we think the accomplishments and promise for each of these three individuals is positive—certainly when compared with what their situations would have been like just 10–15 years ago. With that said, it is highly likely, even probable, that there will be more promising outcomes, more uplifting possibilities, and more exciting aspirations in the future. We do not know what drug and pharmacology holds; we do not know how many workplaces will embrace and include workers with autism in their companies; we do not know whether universities will mandate teaching strategies that will more effectively reach a wider range of students; and, especially, we still do not know the full potential of young people with autism, especially at the higher end of the spectrum. In all likelihood, many have much more intellectual potential that is currently understood. As researchers delve deeper into the potential of people with autism, more opportunities may well arise.

Second, the nature and intensity of the supports made available to youth with autism will almost completely define the quality of a program and outcomes associated with the program. People who receive too much support will never achieve their full potential. People who receive too little support also will not achieve their full potential because they may not overcome antisocial behaviors—running away, screaming, hitting, destroying property—that will not be tolerated by society. Youth who receive too little support also will not be empowered to learn and generalize the skills they need to be successful in community college, shopping malls, apartments, and worksites. The level of needed support must be very carefully assessed, and we have tried to emphasize this point throughout the book.

Third, we recognize that early intervention is a crucial part of this entire process. The sooner students with autism have community-based learning experiences in recreational sites, community shopping malls, volunteer work, and then paid work activities, the sooner they will establish the competence necessary to be successful in these settings. Early intervention means real training in real work sites with enough regularity and structure that these skills become embedded in the student's portfolio of capabilities.

Fourth, we cannot emphasize enough how terribly important transition planning is. A careful review of the different options for services presented in Chapter 6, along with the work options in Chapter 7 and college options in Chapter 8, should make it apparent that these outcomes are not simply going to happen on their own. Living in the community, managing benefits, getting help for services, finding a job, and getting funding for support on the job will only happen with *planning.* This planning must start by the time the student is 14–16 years old at the latest, and the sooner the better. It takes too long for these activities to be put into place without a plan.

In conclusion, the future is brighter than ever but the challenges are also greater than ever. In the short term, families who know what they want and determine how to get it will succeed on behalf of their children. In the longer term, all of us must advocate for state and federal governments to adopt progressive policies that more fully embrace many of the ideas presented in this book. With the number of young people being diagnosed with autism, we cannot wait a second longer.

References

Abbeduto, L., Seltzer, M.M., Shattuck, P., Krauss, M.W., Orsmond, G., & Murphy, M.M. (2004). Psychological well-being and coping in mothers of youths with autism, Down syndrome, or Fragile X syndrome. *American Journal on Mental Retardation, 109*(3), 237–254.

American Psychiatric Association. (2000). *Diagnostic and statistical manual of mental disorders* (4th ed., text rev.). Washington, DC: Author.

Attwood, T. (2006). *The complete guide to Asperger's syndrome.* London: Jessica Kingsley.

Autism Society of America. (2001). *Position paper on the national crisis in adult services for individuals with autism: A call to action.* Available online at http://www.autismservicescenter.org/articles2.htm

Auxter, D., Halloran, W., Berry, H., & O'Mara, S. (1999). The precarious safety net: Supplemental Security Income and age 18 redetermination. *Journal of Vocational Rehabilitation, 14*(4), 196–202.

Axelrod, S. (1983). *Behavior modification for the classroom teacher* (2nd ed.). San Diego: Academic Press.

Ayres, K.M., & Langone, J. (2005). Intervention and instruction with video for students with autism: A review of the literature. *Education and Training in Developmental Disabilities, 40*(2), 183–196.

Bartlett, T. (2004, May 14). Back from the brink: More colleges try to help students who struggle with their courses. *Chronicle of Higher Education, 50*(36), A39.

Bellini, S. (2006). *Building social relationships: A systematic approach to teaching social interaction skills to children and adolescents with autism spectrum disorders and other social difficulties.*

Shawnee Mission, KS: Autism Asperger Publishing.

Berkman, K.A., & Meyer, L.H. (1988). Alternative strategies and multiple outcomes in the remediation of severe self-injury: Going "all out" nonaversively. *Journal of The Association for Persons with Severe Handicaps, 13*(2), 76–86.

Billingsley, F.F., & Romer, L.T. (1983). Response prompting and transfer of stimulus control: Methods, research, and a conceptual framework. *Journal of The Association for the Severely Handicapped, 8,* 3–12.

Billstedt, E., Gillberg, C., & Gillberg, C. (2005). Autism after adolescence: Population-based 13- to 22-year follow-up study of 120 individuals with autism diagnosed in childhood. *Journal of Autism and Developmental Disorders, 35*(3), 351–360.

Black, R.S., Mrasek, K.D., & Ballinger, R. (2003). Individualist and collectivist values in transition planning for culturally diverse students with special needs. *Journal for Vocational Special Needs Education, 25*(2, 3), 20–29.

Bledsoe, R., Smith, B., & Simpson, R.L. (2003). Use of a Social Story intervention to improve mealtime skills of an adolescent with Asperger syndrome. *Autism, 7*(3), 289–295.

Braddock, D., Hemp, R., Parish, S., & Rizzolo, M. (2002). *The state of the states in developmental disabilities: 2002 study summary.* Boulder: University of Colorado, Coleman Institute for Cognitive Disabilities and Department of Psychiatry.

Branham, R.S., Collins, B.C., Schuster, J.W., & Kleinert, H. (1999). Teaching community skills to students with moderate disabilities: Comparing combined techniques of classroom simulation, video-tape modeling, and community-based instruction. *Education and Training in Mental Retardation and Developmental Disabilities, 34,* 170–181.

Briel, L.W., & Getzel, E.E. (2001). Internships in higher education: Promoting success for students with disabilities [Electronic version]. *Disability Studies Quarterly, 21*(1).

Briel, L.W., & Getzel, E.E. (2005). Internships and field experiences. In E.E. Getzel & P. Wehman (Eds.), *Going to college: Expanding opportunities for people with disabilities* (pp. 271–290). Baltimore: Paul H. Brookes Publishing Co.

Brinckerhoff, L.C., McGuire, J.M., & Shaw, S.F. (2002). *Postsecondary education and transition for students with learning disabilities* (2nd ed.). Austin, TX: PRO-ED.

Brooke, V., Inge, K.J., Armstrong, A.J., & Wehman, P. (Eds.). (1997). *Supported employment handbook: A customer driven approach for persons with significant disabilities.* Richmond: Virginia Commonwealth University, Rehabilitation Research & Training Center on Supported Employment.

Brown, F. (1991). Creative daily scheduling: A nonintrusive approach to challenging behaviors in community residences. *Journal of The Association for Persons with Severe Handicaps, 16,* 75–84.

Brown, F., & Snell, M. (2000). Meaningful assessment. In M. Snell & F. Brown (Eds.), *Instruction of students with severe disabilities* (5th ed., pp. 70–115). Upper Saddle River, NJ: Merrill.

Brown, L., & York, R. (1974). Developing programs for severely handicapped students: Teacher training and classroom instruction. *Focus on Exceptional Children, 6*(2), 1–11.

Burgstahler, S. (2005). The role of technology in preparing for college and careers. In E.E. Getzel & P. Wehman (Eds.), *Going to college: Expanding opportunities for people with disabilities* (pp. 179–198). Baltimore: Paul H. Brookes Publishing Co.

Burt, D.B., Fuller, S.P., & Lewis, K.R. (1991). Brief report: Competitive employment of adults with autism. *Journal of Autism and Developmental Disorders, 21*(2), 237–242.

Callahan, M. (2004, June). What is customized employment? *The Advance, 15*(1)2.

Cameto, R., Levine, P., & Wagner, M. (2004). *Transition planning for students with disabilities. A special topic report from the National Longitudinal Transition Study-2 (NLTS-2).* Menlo Park, CA: SRI International.

Carr, E.G., Dunlap, G., Horner, R.H., Turnbull, A.P., Sailor, W., Anderson J.L., et al. (2002). Positive behavior support: Evolution of an

applied science. *Journal of Positive Behavior Interventions, 4,* 4–16.

Carr, E.G., Horner, R.H., Turnbull, A.P., Marquis, J.G., McLaughlin, D.M., McAtee, M.L., et al. (1999). *Positive behavior support for people with developmental disabilities: A research synthesis.* Washington, DC: AAMR.

Centers for Disease Control and Prevention. (2007). Surveillance summaries: Prevalence of autism spectrum disorders. *MMWR, 56* (SS1). Atlanta: Author.

Charlop-Christy, M.H., & Daneshvar, S. (2003). Using video modeling to teach perspective taking to children with autism. *Journal of Positive Behavior Interventions, 5*(1), 12.

Charlop-Christy, M.H., Le, L., & Freeman, K.A. (2000). A comparison of video modeling with in vivo modeling for teaching children with autism. *Journal of Autism and Developmental Disorders, 30*(6), 537–552.

Chin, H.Y., & Bernard-Opitz, V. (2000). Teaching conversational skills to children with autism: Effect on the development of theory of mind. *Journal of Autism and Developmental Disorders, 30*(6), 569–583.

Cobigo, V., Morin, D., & Lachappelle, Y. (2007). Assessing work task preferences among persons with intellectual disabilities: An integrative review of the literature. *Education and Training in Developmental Disabilities, 42*(3), 286–300.

Collins, B. (2007). *Moderate to severe disabilities: A foundational approach.* Upper Saddle River, NJ: Pearson.

Collins, B.C., & Griffen, A.K. (1996). Teaching students with moderate disabilities to make safe responses to product warning labels. *Education and Treatment of Children, 19,* 30–45.

Conroy, M.A., Asmus, J.M., Sellers, J.A., & Ladwig, C.N. (2005). Use of an antecedent-based intervention to decrease stereotypic behavior in a general education classroom: A case study. *Focus on Autism and Other Developmental Disabilities, 20,* 223–230.

Cooper, J.O., Heron, T.E., & Heward, W.L. (1987). *Applied behavior analysis.* New Jersey: Prentice-Hall.

deFur, S.H., Getzel, E.E., & Trossi, K. (1996). Making the postsecondary education match: A role for transition planning. *Journal of Vocational Rehabilitation, 6,* 231–241.

Deschamps, A. (2004). Traveling the road from high school to college: Tips for the journey. *Transition Times, 9*(1), 1–2.

Dew, D., & Alan, G. (2007). *Rehabilitation of individuals with autism spectrum disorders* (Institute on Rehabilitation Issues Monograph No 32.) Washington, DC: The George Washington University, Center for Rehabilitation Counseling Research and Education.

Duffy, J.T., & Gugerty, J. (2005). The role of disability support services. In E.E. Getzel & P. Wehman (Eds.), *Going to college: Expanding opportunities for people with disabilities* (pp. 89–115). Baltimore: Paul H. Brookes Publishing Co.

Dunlap, G., Kern, L., & Worcester, J. (2001). ABA and academic instruction. *Focus on Autism and Other Developmental Disabilities, 16*(2), 129–136.

Dymond, S. (2004). Community participation. In P. Wehman & J. Kregel (Eds.), *Functional curriculum for elementary, middle, and secondary age students with special needs* (2nd ed., pp. 259–291). Austin, TX: PRO-ED.

Eaton, H., & Coull, L. (1999). *Transitions to postsecondary learning: Self-advocacy handbook for students with learning disabilities and/or attention deficit disorder.* Vancouver, British Columbia, Canada: Eaton Coull Learning Group.

Education for All Handicapped Children Act of 1975, PL 94–142, 20 U.S.C. §§ 1400 *et seq.*

ENDependence Center of Northern Virginia. (2008). *Persons with disabilities ending dependence.* Retrieved January 23, 2008, from http://www.ecnv.org/

Fairweather, J.S., & Shaver, D.M. (1991). Making the transition to post-secondary education and training. *Exceptional Children, 57*(2), 264–268.

Fast, Y. (2004). *Employment for individuals with Asperger syndrome or non-verbal learning disability: Stories and strategies.* London and Philadelphia: Jessica Kingsley Publishers.

Federal Register, January 17, 2001, Vol. 66, No. 11, pp. 4379–4435.

Federal Register, June 26, 2002, Vol. 67, No. 123, pp. 43154–43149.

Ferguson, H., Myles, Smith, B., & Hagiwara, T. (2005). Using a personal digital assistant to enhance the independence of an adolescent with Asperger Syndrome. *Education and Training in Developmental Disabilities, 40*(1), 60–67.

Field S., & Hoffman, A. (1996). *Steps to self-determination: A curriculum to help adolescents learn to achieve their goals.* Austin, TX: PRO-ED.

Field, S., & Hoffman, A. (1999). The importance of family involvement for promoting self-determination in adolescents with autism and other developmental disabilities. *Focus on Autism and Other Developmental Disabilities, 14*, 36–41.

Field, S., & Hoffman, A. (2007). Self-determination in secondary transition assessment. *Assessment for Effective Intervention, 32*, 181–190.

Fisher, M., & Meyer, L.H. (2002). Development of social competence after two years for students enrolled in inclusive and self-contained educational programs. *Research and Practice for Persons with Severe Handicaps, 27*, 165–174.

Foley, B., & Staples, A.H. (2003). Developing augmentative and alternative communication (AAC) and literacy interventions in a supported employment setting. *Topics in Language Disorders, 23*(4), 305–325.

Forest, M., & Pearpoint, J.C. (1992). Putting all kids on the MAP. *Educational Leadership, 50*, 26–31.

Frith, U. (2003). *Autism: Explaining the enigma* (2nd ed.). Malden, MA: Blackwell Publishing.

Galbraith, S. (2001). A home of one's own: The role of housing and social service agencies. In A.J. Tymchuk, K.C. Lakin, & R. Luckasson (Eds.), *The forgotten generation: The status and challenges of adults with mild cognitive limitations* (pp. 141–168). Baltimore: Paul H. Brookes Publishing Co.

García-Villamisar, D., & Hughes, C. (2007). Supported employment improves cognitive performance in adults with ASD. *Journal of Intellectual Disability Research, 51*(2), 142–150.

García-Villamisar, D., Wehman, P., & Diaz Navarro, M. (2002). Changes in the quality of autistic people's life that work in supported and sheltered employment: A 5-year follow-up study. *Journal of Vocational Rehabilitation, 17*(4), 309–312.

Gervey, R., Gao, N., & Rizzo, D. (2004). Gloucester County One-Stop Project: Baseline level of access and satisfaction of One-Stop customers with disabilities. *Journal of Vocational Rehabilitation, 21*(2), 103–115.

Getzel, E.E. (in press). Addressing the persistence and retention of students with disabilities in higher education: Incorporating key strategies and supports on campus. *Exceptionality.*

Getzel, E.E., & Briel, L.W. (2006). Pursuing postsecondary education opportunities for individuals with disabilities. In P. Wehman, *Life beyond the classroom: Transition strategies for young people with disabilities* (pp. 355–368). Baltimore: Paul H. Brookes Publishing Co.

Getzel, E.E., Briel, L.W., & Kregel, J. (2000). Comprehensive career planning: The VCU Career Connections Program. *Work, 14*, 41–49.

Getzel, E.E., & Kregel, J. (1996). Transitioning from the academic to the employment setting: The employment connection program. *Journal of Vocational Rehabilitation, 6*, 273–287.

Getzel, E.E., & McManus, S. (2005). Expanding support services on campus. In E.E. Getzel &

P. Wehman (Eds.), *Going to college: Expanding opportunities for people with disabilities*. Baltimore: Paul H. Brookes Publishing Co.

Getzel, E.E., McManus, S., & Briel, L.W. (2004). An effective model for college students with learning disabilities and attention deficit hyperactivity disorders. *NCSET Research to Practice Brief, 3*(1). Retrieved January 20, 2004, from http://www.ncset.org/publications/re-searchtopractice/NCSET ResearchBrief_3.1.pdf

Getzel, E.E., & Thoma, C.A. (2006). Voice of experience: What college students with learning disabilities and attention deficit/hyperactivity disorders tell us are important self-determination skills for success. *Learning Disabilities: A Multidisciplinary Journal, 14*(1), 33–39.

Getzel, E.E., & Wehman, P. (Eds.). (2005). *Going to college: Expanding opportunities for people with disabilities*. Baltimore: Paul H. Brookes Publishing Co.

Grandin, T., & Duffy, K. (2004). *Developing talents careers for individuals with Asperger syndrome and high-functioning autism*. Shawnee Mission, KS: Autism Asperger Publishing Co.

Gray, C.A. (1998). Social Stories and comic strip conversations with students with Asperger syndrome and high-functioning autism. In E. Schopler, G.B. Mesibox, & L.J. Kunce (Eds.), *Asperger syndrome or high-functioning autism?* (pp. 167–198). New York: Plenum Press.

Gray, C.A., & Garand, J.D. (1993). Social Stories: Improving responses of students with autism with accurate social information. *Focus on Autistic Behavior, 8*(1), 1–10.

Greenbaum, B., Graham, S., & Scales, W. (1995). Adults with learning disabilities: Educational and social experiences during college. *Exceptional Children, 61*(5), 460–471.

Griffin, C., Brooks-Lane, N., Hammis, D.G., & Crandell, D. (2007). Self-employment: Owning the American dream. In P. Wehman, K.J. Inge, W.G. Revell, Jr., & V.A. Brooke (Eds.), *Real work for real pay: Inclusive employment for people with disabilities* (pp. 215–235). Baltimore: Paul H. Brookes Publishing Co.

Griffin, C., & Hammis, D. (2003). *Making self-employment work for people with disabilities*. Baltimore: Paul H. Brookes Publishing Co.

Griffin, C., Hammis, D., & Geary, T. (2007). *The job developer's handbook: Practical tactics for customized employment*. Baltimore: Paul H. Brookes Publishing Co.

Griffin, C., & Targett, P.S. (2006). Job carving and customized employment. In P. Wehman, *Life beyond the classroom*. Baltimore: Paul H. Brookes Publishing Co.

Grinker, R.R. (2007). *Unstrange minds: Remapping the world of autism*. New York: Basic Books.

Hagner, D., & Cooney, B.F. (2005). "I do that for everybody": Supervising employees with ASD. *Focus on ASD and Other Developmental Disabilities, 20*(2), 91–97.

Halpern, A.S., Herr, C.M., Doren, B., & Wolf, N.K. (2000). *Next S.T.E.P.: Student transition and educational planning, teacher manual* (2nd ed.). Austin, TX: PRO-ED.

Harding, T., Blaine, D., Whelley, A.T., & Chang, C. (2006). A comparison of the provision of educational supports to students with disabilities in AHEAD versus Non-AHEAD affiliated institutions. *Journal of Postsecondary Education and Disability, 18*(2), 125–134.

Haring, T.G., & Breen, C.G. (1992). A peer-mediated social network intervention to enhance the social integration of persons with moderate and severe disabilities. *Journal of Applied Behavior Analysis, 25*(2), 319–333.

Harris, R., & Robertson, J. (2001). Successful strategies for college-bound students with learning disabilities. *Preventing School Failure, 45*(3), 125–131.

Harrower, J.K., & Dunlap, G. (2001). Including children with autism in general education settings: A review of effective strategies. *Behavior Modification, 25*, 762–784.

Hart, D., Grigal, M., Sax, C., Martinez, D., & Will, M. (2006). Postsecondary education options for students with intellectual disabilities. *Research to Practice, 45*, 1–4. Retrieved January 10, 2008, from Institute for Community Inclusion web site: http://www.communityinclusion.org/article.php?article_id=178&staff_id=19

Hart, D., Zimbrich, K., & Parker, D.R. (2005). Dual enrollment as a postsecondary education option for students with intellectual disabilities. In E.E. Getzel & P. Wehman (Eds.), *Going to college: Expanding opportunities for people with disabilities* (pp. 253–267). Baltimore: Paul H. Brookes Publishing Co.

Held, M.F., Thoma, C.A., & Thomas, K. (2004). The John Jones show: How one teacher facilitated self-determined planning for a young man with autism. *Focus on Autism and Other Developmental Disabilities, 19*, 177–188.

Hieneman, M., Childs, K., & Sergay, J. (2006). *Parenting with positive behavior support: A practical guide to resolving your child's difficult behavior*. Baltimore: Paul H. Brookes Publishing Co.

Hillier, A., Campbell, H., Mastriani, K., Vreeburg Izzo, M., Kool-Tucker, A.K., Cherry, L., et al. (2007). Two-year evaluation of a vocational support program for adults with autism spectrum. *Career Development for Exceptional Individuals 30*(1), 35–47.

Hillier, A., Fish, T., Cloppert, P., & Beversdorf, D.Q. (2007, Summer). Outcomes of a social and vocational skills support group for adolescents and young adults on the autism spectrum. *Focus on Autism and Other Developmental Disabilities, 22*(2), 107–115.

Hitchings, W.E., & Retish, P. (2000). The career development needs of students with learning disabilities. In D.A. Luzzo (Ed.), *Career counseling of college students: An empirical guide to strategies that work* (pp. 217–231). Washington, DC: American Psychological Association.

Holmes, D.L. (1990). Community-based services for children and adults with autism: The Eden family programs. *Journal of Autism and Developmental Disorders, 20,* 339–351.

Holmes, N., & Carr, J. (1991). The pattern of care in families of adults with a mental handicap: A comparison between families of autistic adults and Down syndrome adults. *Journal of Autism and Other Developmental Disorders, 2,* 159–176.

Howlin, P. (2000). Outcome in adult life for more able individuals with ASD or Asperger syndrome. *ASD, 4*(1), 63–83.

Howlin, P., Alcock, J., & Burkin, C. (2005). An 8 year follow-up of a specialist supported employment service for high-ability adults with autism or Asperger syndrome. *Archives of Pediatrics & Adolescent Medicine, 159*(3), 266–269.

Howlin, P., Goode, S., Hutton, J., & Rutter, M. (2004). Adult outcomes for children with autism. *Journal of Child Psychology and Psychiatry, 45,* 212–229.

Hurlbutt, K., & Chalmers, L. (2002). Adults with ASD speak out: Perceptions of their life experiences. *Focus on ASD and Other Developmental Disabilities, 17*(2), 103–111.

Individuals with Disabilities Education Act (IDEA) of 1990, PL 101-476, 20 U.S.C. §§ 1400 *et seq.*

Individuals with Disabilities Education Improvement Act (IDEA) of 2004, PL 108-446, 20 U.S.C. §§ 1400 *et seq.*

Inge, K.J., & Targett, P. (2006). Identifying job opportunities for individuals with disabilities. *Journal of Vocational Rehabilitation, 25* (2), 137–139.

Inge, K.J., Wehman, P., & Dymond, S. (2005). Community-based vocational training. In P. Wehman, P.J. McLaughlin, & T. Wehman (Eds.), *Intellectual and developmental disabilities: Toward full community inclusion* (3rd ed., p. 368–369). Austin, TX: PRO-ED.

Iovannone, R., Dunlap, G., Huber, H., & Kincaid, D. (2003). Effective educational practices for students with autism spectrum disorder. *Focus on Autism and Other Developmental Disabilities, 18,* 150–165.

Janzen, J.E. (2003). *Understanding the nature of autism: A guide to the autism spectrum disorders* (2nd ed.). San Antonio, TX: PsychCorp.

Jennes-Coussens, M., Magill-Evans, J., & Koning, C. (2006). The quality of life of young men with Asperger syndrome. *Autism, 10,* 403–414.

Kakela, M., & Witte, R. (2000). Self-disclosure of college graduates with learning disabilities. *Learning Disabilities: A Multidisciplinary Journal, 10,* 25–31.

Kamps, D.M., Barbetta, P.M., Leonard, B.R., & Delquadri, J. (1994). Classwide peer tutoring: An integration strategy to improve reading skills and promote peer interactions among students with autism and general education peers. *Journal of Applied Behavior Analysis, 27,* 49–61.

Kanner, L. (1971). Follow-up study of eleven autistic children originally reported in 1943. *Journal of ASD & Childhood Schizophrenia, 1*(2), 119–145.

Kemp, D.C., & Carr, E.G. (1995). Reduction of severe problem behavior in community employment using an hypothesis-driven multicomponent intervention approach. *Journal of The Association for Persons with Severe Handicaps, 20*(4), 229–247.

Kim-Rupnow, W.S., & Burgstahler, S. (2004). Perceptions of students with disabilities regarding the value of technology-based support activities on postsecondary education and employment. *Journal of Special Education Technology, 19*(2), 43–56.

Kincaid, D. (1996). Person-centered planning. In L.K. Koegel, R.L. Koegel, & G. Dunlap (Eds.), *Positive behavioral support: Including people with difficult behavior in the community* (pp. 439–466). Baltimore: Paul H. Brookes Publishing Co.

Kincaid, D., Chapman, C., Shannon, P., Schall, C., & Harrower, J.K. (2002). Families and the Tri-State Consortium for Positive Behavior Support. In J.M. Lucyshyn, G. Dunlap, & R.W. Albin (Eds.), *Families and positive behavior support: Addressing problem behavior in family contexts* (pp. 309–328). Baltimore: Paul H. Brookes Publishing Co.

Kluth, P. (2003). *"You're going to love this kid!" Teaching students with autism in the inclusive classroom.* Baltimore: Paul H. Brookes Publishing Co.

Kluth, P., & Chandler-Olcott, K. (2008). *"A land we can share": Teaching literacy to students with autism.* Baltimore: Paul H. Brookes Publishing Co.

Koegel, L.K., Koegel, R.L., Harrower, J.K., & Carter, C.M. (1999). Pivotal response intervention I: Overview of approach. *Journal of*

The Association for Persons with Severe Handicaps, 24(3), 174–185.

Koegel, L.K., Talebi, J.L., Koegel, R.L., & Carter, C.M. (2006). Improving social-communication, empathy, and pragmatics in individuals with Asperger syndrome. In R.L. Koegel & L.K. Koegel (Eds.), *Pivotal response treatments for autism: Communication, social, and academic development.* Baltimore: Paul H. Brookes Publishing Co.

Koegel, R.L., Koegel, L.K., & Parks, D.R. (1995). "Teach the individual" model of generalization: Autonomy through self-management. In R.L. Koegel & L.K. Koegel (Eds.), *Teaching children with autism: Strategies for initiating positive interactions and improving learning opportunities* (pp. 67–77). Baltimore: Paul H. Brookes Publishing Co.

Kohl, F.L., McLaughlin, M.J., & Nagle, K. (2006). Alternate achievement standards and assessments: A descriptive investigation of 16 states. *Exceptional Children, 73,* 107–123.

Krantz, P.J., & McLannahan, L.E. (1993). Teaching children with autism to initiate to peers: Effects of a script-fading procedure. *Journal of Applied Behavior Analysis, 26*(1), 121–132.

Krauss, M.W., Seltzer, M.M., & Jacobson, H.T. (2005). Adults with autism living at home or in non-family settings: Positive and negative aspects of residential status. *Journal of Intellectual Disability Research, 49*(2), 111–124.

Kregel, J. (2001). Promoting employment opportunities for individuals with mild cognitive limitations: A time for reform. In A.J. Tymchuk, K.C. Lakin, & R. Luckasson (Eds.), *The forgotten generation: The status and challenges of adults with mild cognitive limitations* (pp. 87–98). Baltimore: Paul H. Brookes Publishing Co.

Lasater, M.W., & Brady, M.P. (1995). Effects of video self-modeling and feedback on task fluency: A home-based intervention. *Education & Treatment of Children, 18*(4), 389–407.

Lattimore, L.P., Parsons, M.B., & Reid, D.H. (2006). Enhancing job site training on supported workers with ASD: A reemphasis on simulation. *Journal of Applied Behavior Analysis, 39,* 91–102.

Leconte, P.J. (2006). The evolution of career, vocational, and transition assessment: Implications for the summary of performance. *Career Development for Exceptional Individuals, 29,* 114–124.

Lerman, D.C., & Rapp, J.T. (2006). Antecedent assessment & intervention of stereotypy. In J.K. Luiselli (Ed.), *Antecedent assessment and intervention: Supporting children and adults with developmental disabilities in community*

settings. Baltimore: Paul H. Brookes Publishing Co.

Levine, P., Marder, C., & Wagner, M. (2004). *Services and supports for secondary school students with disabilities: A special topic report from the National Longitudinal Transition Study-2 (NLTS-2).* Menlo Park, CA: SRI International.

Lipka, S. (2006). For the learning disabled, a team approach to college. *Chronicle of Higher Education.* Retrieved November 13, 2007, from http://chronicle.com/weekly/v53/i17/17a03601.htm

Luce, S.C., & Dyer, K. (1995). Providing effective transitional programming to individuals with autism. *Behavioral Disorders, 21*(1), 36–52.

Luecking, R., & Gramlich, M. (2003). Quality work-based learning and postschool employment success. Issue brief: Examining current challenges in secondary education and transition. *Education and Training in Developmental Disabilities, 2,* 1–5.

Machalicek, W., O'Reilly, M.F., Beretvas, N., Sigafoos, J., & Lancioni, G.E. (2007). A review of interventions to reduce challenging behavior in school settings for students with autism spectrum disorders. *Research in Autism Spectrum Disorders, 1,* 229–246.

Madaus, J.W. (2003). What high school students with learning disabilities need to know about college foreign language requirements. *Teaching Exceptional Children, 36*(2), 62–66.

Mancil, G.R., Conroy, M.A., Nakao, T., & Alter, P.J. (2006). Functional communication training in the natural environment: A pilot investigation with a young child with autism spectrum disorder. *Education and Treatment of Children, 29,* 615–633.

Martin, J.E., & Marshall, L.H. (1995). Choice-Maker: A comprehensive self-determination transition program. *Intervention in School and Clinic, 30,* 147–156.

Martin, J.E., Van Dycke, J., D'Ottavio, M., & Nickerson, K. (2007). Student-directed summary of performance: Increasing student and family involvement in the transition process. *Career Development for Exceptional Individuals, 30,* 13–26.

Matson, J.L., Matson, L.L., & Rivet, T.T. (2007). Social-skill treatments for children with autism: A review. *Behavior Modification, 31,* 682–707.

Matson, J.L., & Nebel-Schwalm, M. (2007). Assessing challenging behavior in children with autism spectrum disorders: A review. *Research in Developmental Disabilities, 28,* 567–579.

McDuff, G.S., Krantz, P.J., & McClannahan, L.E. (1993). Teaching children with autism to use photographic activity schedules: Maintenance and generalization of complex response chains. *Journal of Applied Behavior Analysis, 26,* 89–97.

Mechling, L.C., Pridgen, L.S., & Cronin, B.A. (2005). Computer-based video instruction to teach students with intellectual disabilities to verbally respond to questions and make purchases in fast food restaurants. *Education and Training in Developmental Disabilities, 40*(1), 47–59.

Miller, L. (2006, May). *Continuation of benefit payments to certain individuals who are participating in an approved program of vocational rehabilitation, employment services, or other support services: A summary of the revised Section 301 regulations.* Richmond: Virginia Commonwealth University, Rehabilitation Research & Training Center on Workplace Supports, Youth Transition Demonstration Technical Assistance Office.

Miller, L. (2007). *Understanding in-kind support and maintenance.* Richmond: Virginia Commonwealth University, Rehabilitation Research & Training Center on Workplace Supports.

Miller, L., & O'Mara, S. (2003, April). *Social Security disability benefit issues affecting transition-aged youth* (Briefing Paper Vol. 8). Richmond: Virginia Commonwealth University, Rehabilitation Research & Training Center on Workplace Supports, Benefits Assistance Resource Center.

Miller, L., & O'Mara, S. (2006). Social security disability benefit issues affecting transition-age youth. In P. Wehman, *Life beyond the classroom: Transition strategies for young people with disabilities* (4th ed., pp. 387–410). Baltimore: Paul H. Brookes Publishing Co.

Miltenberger, R.G. (2006). Antecedent interventions for changing behaviors maintained by escape from instructional activities. In J.K. Luiselli (Ed.), *Antecedent assessment and intervention: Supporting children and adults with developmental disabilities in community settings.* Baltimore: Paul H. Brookes Publishing Co.

Moon, M.S., Grigal, M., & Neubert, D. (2001). High school and beyond: Students with significant disabilities complete high school through alternative programs in postsecondary settings. *Exceptional Parent, 31*(7), 52–57.

Moore, A.S. (2006, November 5). A dream not denied: Students on the spectrum. *The New York Times Education Life,* Section 4A, p. 28.

Mount, B. (2000). *Person-centered planning: Finding directions for change using personal futures planning.* New York: Capacity Works.

Moxon, L., & Gates, D. (2001). Children with autism: Supporting the transition to adulthood. *Educational and Child Psychology, 18,* 28–40.

Mull, C., Sitlington, P.L., & Alper, S. (2001). Postsecondary education for students with learning disabilities: A synthesis of the literature. *Exceptional Children, 68*(1), 97–118.

Müller, E., Schuler, A., Burton, B.A., & Yates, G.B. (2003). Meeting the vocational support needs of individuals with Asperger syndrome and other ASD spectrum disabilities. *Journal of Vocational Rehabilitation, 18*(3), 163–175.

Myles, B.S., Grossman, B.G., Aspy, R., Henry, S., & Coffin, A.B. (2007). Planning a comprehensive program for students with autism spectrum disorders using evidence-based practices. *Education and Training in Developmental Disabilities, 42*(4), 398–409.

National Center for Special Education Research. (2007a). *Facts from NLTS-2: Secondary National Longitudinal Transition Study-2.* Washington, DC: U.S. Department of Education.

National Center for Special Education Research. (2007b). *Facts from NLTS-2: Secondary school experiences of students with autism.* Retrieved December 15, 2007, from http://ies.ed.gov/ncser/pubs/20073005/index.asp

National Organization on Disability. (2004). *N.O.D./Harris Survey of Americans with Disabilities: Landmark survey finds pervasive disadvantages.* Washington, DC: Author. Retrieved October 22, 2006, from http://www.nod.org/content.cfm?id=1537

National Postsecondary Education Cooperative. (2007). *Deciding on postsecondary education: Final report* (NPEC 2008-850). Retrieved December 20, 2007, from http://nces.ed.gov/pubs2008/2008850.pdf

National Research Council. (2001). *Educating children with autism.* Washington, DC: National Academies Press.

No Child Left Behind Act of 2001, PL 107-110, 115 Stat. 1425, 20 U.S.C. §§ 6301 *et seq.*

Nuehring, M.L., & Sitlington, P.L. (2003). Transition as a vehicle: Moving from high school to an adult vocational service provider. *Journal of Disability Policy Studies, 14*(1), 23–35.

Ochs, E., Kremer-Sadlik, T., Solomon, O., & Sirota, K.G. (2001). Inclusion as a social practice: Views of children with autism. *Social Development, 10,* 399–419.

Oggel, L., & Palko, S. (2004, April). Autism and assistive technology. *Autism E-News.* Retrieved January 18, 2008, from http://www.vcu.edu/ttac/autism/pdfs/e_news/enews_2004_apr.pdf

Olmstead, Commissioner, Georgia Department of Human Resources et al. v. L.C. & E.W. et al, 527 U.S. 581 (1999)

Palmer, A. (2006). *Realizing the college dream with autism or Asperger syndrome: A parent's guide to student success.* Philadelphia: Jessica Kingsley Publishers.

Paul, R. (2003). Promoting social communication in high functioning individuals with autistic spectrum disorders. *Child and Adolescent Psychiatric Clinics of North America, 12*(1), 87–106.

Pearpoint, J., O'Brien, J., & Forest, M. (1993). *PATH: Planning possible, positive futures.* Toronto: Inclusion Press.

Peck, B., & Kirkbride, L.T. (2001). Why businesses don't employ people with disabilities. *Journal of Vocational Rehabilitation, 16,* 71–75.

Persson, B. (2000). Brief report: A longitudinal study of quality of life and independence among adult men with autism. *Journal of Autism and Developmental Disorders, 30*(1), 61–66.

Prelock, P.A. (2006). *Autism spectrum disorders: Issues in assessment and intervention.* Austin, TX: PRO-ED.

Prince-Hughes, D. (2002). *Understanding college students with autism.* Retrieved September 7, 2007, from The George Washington University HEATH Center web site: http://www.heath.gwu.edu/node/191

Pumpian, I., Shepard, H., & West, E. (1988). Negotiating job-training stations with employers. In P. Wehman & M.S. Moon (Eds.), *Vocational rehabilitation and supported employment* (pp. 177–192). Baltimore: Paul H. Brookes Publishing Co.

Quill, K.A. (2000). *Do-watch-listen-say: Social and communication intervention for children with autism.* Baltimore: Paul H. Brookes Publishing Co.

Racino, J.A. (2003). There if you need and want them: Changing roles of support organizations. In J.A. Racino, P. Walker, S. O'Connor, & S.J. Taylor (Eds.), *Housing, support, and community choices and strategies for adults with disabilities* (pp. 107–136). Baltimore: Paul H. Brookes Publishing Co.

Reese, R.M., Sherman, J.A., & Sheldon, J.B. (1998). Reducing disruptive behavior of a group home resident with autism and mental retardation. *Journal of Autism and Developmental Disorders, 28,* 159–165.

Rehabilitation Act Amendments of 1998, PL 105–220, 29 U.S.C §§ 701 *et seq.*

Rehabilitation Act of 1973, PL 93-112, 29 U.S.C. §§ 701 *et seq.*

Rioux-Bailey, C. (2004). *Students with disabilities and access to community college: Continuing issues and new directions.* Retrieved March 20, 2008, from The George Washington University HEATH Center web site: http://www.heath.gwu.edu/node/181

Rubin, B. (2007, August 23). Help for when college years are not so carefree. *Chicago Tribune.* Retrieved August 24, 2007, from http://www.chicagotribune.com

Sansosti, F.J., Powell-Smith, K.A., & Kincaid, D.A. (2004). A research synthesis of Social Story interventions for children with autism spectrum disorders. *Focus on Autism and Other Disabilities, 19*(4), 194–204.

Savukinas, R. (2003). *Community colleges and students with disabilities.* Retrieved September 7, 2007, from The George Washington University HEATH Center web site: http://www.heath.gwu.edu/files/active/0/community_colleges_and_students.pdf

Sax, C.L. (2002). Person-centered planning: More than a strategy. In C.L. Sax & C.A. Thoma (Eds.), *Transition assessment: Wise practices for quality lives* (pp. 13–24). Baltimore: Paul H. Brookes Publishing Co.

Schall, C. (2002). A consumer's guide to monitoring psychotropic medication for individuals with autism spectrum disorders. *Focus on Autism and Other Developmental Disabilities, 17,* 229–235.

Schall, C., Doval, E.C., Targett, P.S., & Wehman, P. (2006). Applications for youth with ASD spectrum disorders. In P. Wehman (Ed.), *Life beyond the classroom: Transition strategies for young people with disabilities* (4th ed., pp. 535–575). Baltimore: Paul H. Brookes Publishing Co.

Schaller, J., & Yang, N.K. (2005). Competitive employment for people with autism: Correlates of successful closure of competitive and supported employment. *Rehabilitation Counseling Bulletin, 49,* 4–16.

Scott, J., Clark, C., & Brady, M. (2000). *Students with autism: Characteristics and instruction programming.* San Diego: Singular Publishing Group.

Seltzer, M.M., Krauss, M.W., Orsmond, G.I., & Vestal, C. (2001). Families of adolescents and adults with autism: Uncharted territory. In L.M. Glidden (Ed.), *International review of research on mental retardation* (Vol. 23, pp. 267–294). San Diego: Academic Press.

Seltzer, M.M., Shattuck, P., Abbeduto, L., & Greenberg, J.S. (2004). Trajectory of development in adolescents and adults with autism. *Mental Retardation and Developmental Disabilities Research Reviews, 10*(4), 234–247.

Sharp, M.N., & Hawes, M.E. (2003). Collaboration between general and special education: Making it work. *Issue Brief: Examining Current*

Challenges in Secondary Education and Transition, 2(1). Retrieved July 15, 2007, from http://www.ncset.org/publications/issue/NCSET IssueBrief_2.1.pdf

Sicile-Kira, C. (2004). *Autism spectrum disorders: The complete guide to understanding autism, Asperger's syndrome, pervasive developmental disorder, and other ASDs.* New York: Berkeley Publishing Group.

Siegel, B. (2003). *Helping children with autism learn: Treatment approaches for parents and professionals.* New York: Oxford.

Simpson, A., Langone, J., & Ayres, K.M. (2004). Embedded video and computer based instruction to improve social skills for students with autism. *Education and Training in Developmental Disabilities, 39*(3), 240–252.

Simpson, R.L. (2005). Evidence-based practices and students with autism spectrum disorders. *Focus on Autism and Other Developmental Disorders, 20*(3), 140–149.

Simpson, R.L., de Boer-Ott, S.R., & Smith-Myles, B. (2003). Inclusion of learners with autism spectrum disorders in general education settings. *Topics in Language Disorders, 23,* 116–123.

Sitlington, P.L., & Clark, G.M. (2007). The transition assessment process and IDEIA 2004. *Assessment for Effective Intervention, 32,* 133–142.

Sitlington, P.L., Neubert, D.A., Begun, W., Lombard, R., & Leconte, P. (2007). *Assess for success: A practitioner's handbook on transition assessment* (2nd ed.). Thousand Oaks, CA: Corwin Press.

Small Business and Self-Employment Services (SBSES). (2008*). Vocational rehabilitation state offices.* Retrieved January 28, 2008, from http://www.jan.wvu.edu/sbses/vocrehab.htm

Smith, G.J., McDougall, D., & Edelen-Smith, P. (2006). Behavioral cusps: A person-centered concept for establishing pivotal individual, family, and community behaviors and repertoires. *Focus on Autism and Other Developmental Disabilities, 21,* 223–229.

Smith, M. (1986). Managing the aggressive and self-injurious behaviors of adults disabled by ASD in the community. *Journal of The Association for Persons with Severe Handicaps, 10,* 228–232.

Smith, M. (1987). Treatment of pica in an adult disabled by ASD by differential reinforcement of incompatible behavior. *Journal of Behavior Therapy and Experimental Psychiatry, 18*(3), 285–288.

Smith, M. (1990). *ASD and life in the community: Successful interventions for behavioral challenges.* Baltimore: Paul H. Brookes Publishing Co.

Smith, M. (1994). Increasing work productivity of employees disabled by ASD. *Journal of Vocational Rehabilitation, 4*(1), 60–65.

Smith, M., & Belcher, R. (1985). Teaching life skills to adults disabled by ASD. *Journal of ASD and Developmental Disorders, 15,* 163–175.

Smith, M., & Belcher, R. (1992). Challenging behaviors and leisure. *Journal of Leisurability, 19*(1), 24–28.

Smith, M., Belcher, R.G., & Juhrs, P.D. (1995). *A guide to successful employment for individuals with autism.* Baltimore: Paul H. Brookes Publishing Co.

Smith, M., Belcher, R., & Wehman, P. (1997). Autism. In *Exceptional individuals in school, community and work* (pp. 419–447). Austin, TX: PRO-ED.

Smith, M., & Coleman, D. (1986). Managing the behavior of adults with ASD in the job setting. *Journal of ASD and Developmental Disorders, 16,* 145–154.

Smith, M.D., & Philippen, L.R. (2005). *Community integration and supported employment.* Mahwah, NJ: Lawrence Erlbaum Associates.

Smith, M.R., & Sowers, J. (2003). *A day in the life of health science students: Faculty in-service training guide.* Portland: Oregon Health & Science University, Center on Self-Determination.

Smith, T. (2001). Discrete trial training in the treatment of autism. *Focus on Autism and Other Developmental Disabilities, 16*(2), 86–92.

Smull, M. (2005). *Essential lifestyle planning for everyone.* Annapolis, MD: The Learning Company.

Snell, M.E., & Brown F. (2006). *Instruction of students with severe disabilities* (6th ed). Upper Saddle River, NJ/Columbus, OH: Pearson/Merrill Prentice Hall.

Snell, M.E., Vorhees, M.D., & Chen, L.Y. (2005). Team involvement in assessment-based interventions with problem behavior, 1997 to 2002. *Journal of Positive Behavior Intervention, 7,* 140–152.

Social Security Act of 1935, PL 74-271, 42 U.S.C. §§ 301 *et al.*

Social Security Administration. (2007a). *2008 Redbook: A summary guide to employment supports for individuals with disabilities under the Social Security Disability Insurance and Supplemental Security Income programs.* Retrieved December 6, 2007, from http://www.ssa.gov/redbook/eng/main.htm

Social Security Administration. (2007b). *2007 annual report of the SSI Program.* Retrieved March 14, 2008 from http://www.socialsecurity.gov/OACT/ssir/SSI07/Redet_CDRdata.html

Social Security Administration. (2008a). *The Ticket to Work sites—Service provider information.* Retrieved June 11, 2008, from https://

secure.ssa.gov/apps10/oesp/providers.nsf/bystate

Social Security Administration. (2008b). *Understanding Supplemental Security Income: Spotlight on student earned income exclusion 2008 edition.* Retrieved March 11, 2008, from http://www.ssa.gov/ssi/spotlights/spot-student-earned-income.htm

Social Security Disability Amendments of 1980, PL 96-265, 94 Stat. 441.

Sparrow, S.S., Balla, D.A., & Cicchetti, D. (1984). *Vineland Adaptive Behavior Scales.* Bloomington, MN: Pearson Assessments.

Stevenson, C.L., Krantz, J.P., & McClannahan, L.E. (2000). Social interaction skills for children with autism: A script-fading procedure for nonreaders. *Behavioral Interventions, 15,* 1–20.

Stodden, R.A., Galloway, L.M., & Stodden, N.J. (2003). Secondary school curricula issues: Impact on postsecondary students with disabilities. *Exceptional Children, 70*(1), 9–25.

Sullivan, R.C. (2001). *Position paper on the national crisis in adult services for individuals with autism: A call to action.* Available at the Autism Society of America web site: http://www.autismservicescenter.org/articles2.htm

Targett, P., Young, C., Revell, G., Williams, S., & Wehman, P. (2007). Customized employment in One-Stop career centers. *Exceptional Children, 40*(2), 6–11.

Taylor, S.J. (2006). Supporting adults to live in the community: Beyond the continuum of care. In S.M. Pueschel (Ed.), *Adults with Down syndrome* (pp.173–182). Baltimore: Paul H. Brookes Publishing Co.

Temporary assistance for needy families. (2008). Retrieved March 12, 2008, from http://www.disabilityinfo.gov/digovpublic/public/DisplayPage.do?parentFolderId=180

Thoma, C.A., & Wehmeyer, M.L. (2005). Self-determination and the transition to postsecondary education. In E.E. Getzel & P. Wehman (Eds.), *Going to college: Expanding opportunities for people with disabilities* (pp. 49–68). Baltimore: Paul H. Brookes Publishing Co.

Thomas, S.B. (2000). College students and disability law. *Journal of Special Education, 33*(4), 248–257.

Thomson, K.M., Czarnecki, D., Martin, C.T., Yu, C.T., & Martin, G.L. (2007). Predicting optimal preference assessment methods for individuals with developmental disabilities. *Education and Training in Developmental Disabilities, 42*(1), 107–114.

Touchette, P.E., MacDonald, R.F., & Langer, S.N. (1985). A scatter plot for identifying stimulus control of problem behavior. *Journal of Applied Behavior Analysis, 18,* 343–351.

Tsatsanis, K.D. (2003). Outcome research in Asperger syndrome and autism. *Child and Adolescent Psychiatric Clinics, 12,* 47–63.

U.S. Department of Education, Institute for Education Services, National Center for Special Education Research. (2005). *National Longitudinal Transition Study–2 (NLTS–2), Wave 3 parent interview and youth interview/survey.* Washington, DC: Author.

Van Bourgondien, M.E., & Reichle, N.C. (1997). Residential treatment for individuals with autism. In D.J. Cohen & F.R. Volkmar (Eds.), *Handbook of autism and pervasive developmental disorders* (pp. 691–706). New York: John Wiley & Sons.

Van Bourgondien, M.E., Reichle, N.C., & Schopler, E. (2003). Effects of a model treatment approach on adults with autism. *Journal of Autism and Developmental Disorders, 33*(2), 131–140.

Virginia Commonwealth University. (2002, July). *Understanding 1619(b)* (Briefing Paper Vol. 6). Richmond: Virginia Commonwealth University, Rehabilitation Research & Training Center on Workplace Supports, Benefits Assistance Resource Center.

Virginia Commonwealth University. (2003, February). *Supplemental Security Income and age-18 redetermination key facts* (Vol. 1, No. 2). Richmond: Virginia Commonwealth University, Rehabilitation Research & Training Center on Workplace Supports, Benefits Assistance Resource Center.

Virginia Commonwealth University. (2005, March). *Parent to child deeming* (Briefing Paper Vol. 2.3). Richmond: Virginia Commonwealth University, Rehabilitation Research & Training Center on Workplace Supports, Benefits Assistance Resource Center.

Virginia Commonwealth University. (2008a). *Age 18 check-up for youth transition demonstration project participants: A guide for students, parents, and professionals fact sheet.* Retrieved January 17, 2008, from the VCU Work Support web site: http://www.worksupport.com/research/viewContent.cfm/597

Virginia Commonwealth University. (2008b). *Employment negotiation fact sheet.* Retrieved January 17, 2008, from VCU Work Support web site: http://www.worksupport.com/research/viewContent.cfm/493

Virginia Department of Education, Division of Special Education and Student Services. (2003). *Virginia's college guide for students with disabilities: You know you can do it! Here's how!* (pp. 14–19). Richmond: Author.

Volkmar, F., Lord, C., Bailey, A., Schultz, R., & Kiln, A. (2004). Autism and pervasive developmental disorders. *Journal of Child Psychology and Psychiatry and Allied Disciplines, 45*(1), 135–170.

Volkmar, F., Paul, R., Klin, A., & Cohen, D. (2006). *Handbook of autism and pervasive developmental disorders: Vol. 1. Diagnosis, development, neurobiology, and behavior* (3rd ed.). Hoboken, NJ: John Wiley & Sons.

Wagner, M., Cameto, R., & Newman, L. (2003). *Youth with disabilities: A changing population. A report of findings from the National Longitudinal Transition Study (NLTS) and the National Longitudinal Transition Study-2 (NLTS-2).* Menlo Park, CA: SRI International.

Wagner, M., Newman, L., Cameto, R., Garza, N., & Levine, P. (2005). *After high school: A first look at the postschool experiences of youth with disabilities. A report from the National Longitudinal Transition Study-2 (NLTS-2).* Menlo Park, CA: SRI International.

Wagner, M., Newman, L., Cameto, R., Levine, P., & Garza, N. (2006). *An overview of findings from wave 2 of the National Longitudinal Transition Study-2 (NLTS-2).* Menlo Park, CA: SRI International. Available online at http://www.nlts2.org/reports/2006_08/nlts2_report_2006_08_complete.pdf

Wall, A.J. (1990). Group homes in North Carolina for children and adults with autism. *Journal of Autism and Developmental Disabilities, 20,* 353–366.

Walls, R.T., Haught, P., & Dowler, D.L. (1982). Moments of transfer of stimulus control in practical assembly tasks by mentally retarded adults. *American Journal of Mental Deficiency, 87*(3), 309–315.

Wehman, P. (2006). *Life beyond the classroom: Transition strategies for young people with disabilities* (4th ed.). Baltimore: Paul H. Brookes Publishing Co.

Wehman, P., Inge, K.J., Revell, W.G., Jr., & Brooke, V.A. (2007). *Real work for real pay: Inclusive employment for people with disabilities.* Baltimore: Paul H. Brookes Publishing Co.

Wehman, P., & Kregel, J. (2004). *Functional curriculum for elementary, middle, and secondary age students with special needs* (2nd Ed.). Austin, TX: PRO-ED.

Wehman, P., Revell, G., & Brooke, V. (2003). Competitive employment: Has it become the first choice yet? *Journal of Disability Policy Studies, 14*(3), 163–173.

Wehman, P., Revell, W.G., Brooke, V., & Parent, W. (2005). Supported employment for persons with intellectual and developmental disabilities. In P. Wehman, P. McLaughlin, & T. Wehman (Eds.), *Intellectual and developmental disabilities: Toward full community inclusion* (3rd ed., pp. 411–444), Austin, TX: PRO-ED.

Wehman, P., Targett, P., & Young, C. (2007). Off to work for individuals with autism: A supported employment approach. *Autism Advocate, 46*(1), 54–58.

Wehman, P., & Wittig, K. (in press). *Transition IEPs.* (3rd ed.). Austin, TX: PRO-ED.

Wehmeyer, M.L. (2002). Self-determined assessment: Critical components for transition planning. In C.L. Sax & C.A. Thoma (Eds.), *Transition assessment: Wise practices for quality lives* (pp. 25–38). Baltimore: Paul H. Brookes Publishing Co.

Wehmeyer, M.L., Gragoudas, S., & Shogren, K.A. (2006). Self-determination, student involvement, and leadership development. In P. Wehman, *Life beyond the classroom: Transition strategies for young people with disabilities* (4th ed., pp. 41–69). Baltimore: Paul H. Brookes Publishing Co.

Wehmeyer, M.L., & Kelchner, K. (1995). *The Arc's Self-Determination Scale.* Arlington, TX: The Arc National Headquarters.

Weiner, J.S., & Zivolich, S. (2003). A longitudinal report for three employees in a training consultant model of natural support. *Journal of Vocational Rehabilitation, 18,* 199–202.

West, M., Hill, J., Revell, G., Smith, G., Kregel, J., & Campbell, L. (2002). Medicaid HCB waivers and supported employment: Pre- and Post-Balanced Budget Act of 1997. *Mental Retardation,* 40(2).

Wilson, K., Getzel, E., & Brown, T. (2000). Enhancing the post-secondary campus climate for students with disabilities. *Journal of Vocational Rehabilitation, 14*(1), 37–50.

Witte, R.H., Philips, L., & Kakela, M. (1998). Job satisfaction of college graduates with learning disabilities. *Journal of Learning Disabilities, 31*(3), 259–265.

Wittenburg, D., Golden, T., & Fishman, M. (2002). Transition options for youth with disabilities: An overview of the programs and polices that affect the transition from school. *Journal of Vocational Rehabilitation, 17,* 195–206.

Wolman, J.M., Campeau, P.L., DuBois, P.A., Mithaug, D.E., & Stolarski, V.S. (1994). *AIR Self-Determination Scale and User Guide.* Stanford, CA: American Institute on Research.

Workforce Investment Act (WIA) of 1998, PL 105–220, 29 U.S.C. §§ 2801 *et seq.*

Yeargin-Allsopp, M., Rice, C., Karapurkar, T., Doernbert, N., Boyle, C., & Murphy, C. (2003). Prevalance of autism in a U.S. metropolitan area [Electronic version]. *Journal of American Medical Association, 289,* 49–55.

Zafft, C., Hart, D., & Zimbrich, K. (2004). College career connection: A study of youth with intellectual disabilities and the impact of postsecondary education. *Education and Training in Developmental Disabilities, 39*(1), 45–53.

Zwart, L.M., & Kallemeyn, L.M. (2001). Peer-based coaching for college students with ADHD and learning disabilities. *Journal of Postsecondary Education and Disability, 15*(1), 1–15.

Resource Guide

Carol Schall

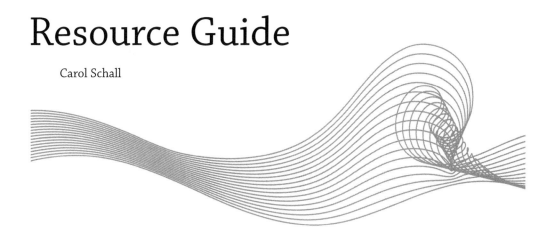

NATIONAL ORGANIZATIONS

Achieving Higher Education with
Autism/Developmental Disabilities
(AHEADD)
353 Spahr Street, Pittsburgh, PA 15232
412-848-9355
http://www.aheadd.org/

American Association on Intellectual and
Developmental Disabilities (AAIDD)
444 North Capitol Street, NW, Suite 846,
Washington, DC 20001
800-424-3688
http://www.aaidd.org

The Arc of the United States
1010 Wayne Avenue, Suite 650, Silver Spring,
MD 20910
301-565-3842; 800-433-5255
http://www.thearc.org/

Association for Persons in Supported
Employment (APSE)
1627 Monument Avenue, Richmond, VA 23220
804-278-9187
http://www.apse.org/

Association for Positive Behavior Support
(APBS)
Post Office Box 328, Bloomsburg, PA 17815
570-389-4081
http://www.apbs.org

Association of University Centers on Disabilities
(AUCD)
1010 Wayne Avenue, Suite 920, Silver Spring,
MD 20910
301-588-8252
http://www.aucd.org/

Autism Society of America (ASA)
7910 Woodmont Avenue, Suite 300, Bethesda,
MD 20814
301-657-0881; 800-328-8476
http://www.autism-society.org/

Beach Center on Disability
University of Kansas, Haworth Hall, Room
3136, 1200 Sunnyside Avenue, Lawrence, KS
66045
785-864-7600
http://www.beachcenter.org/

Center for the Study of Autism
c/o Autism Research Institute, 4182 Adams
Avenue, San Diego, CA 92116
http://www.autism.org/

Council for Children with Behavioral Disorders
http://www.ccbd.net/

Council for Exceptional Children (CEC)
1110 North Glebe Road, Suite 300, Arlington,
VA 22201
1-888-232-7733
http://www.cec.sped.org/

Division on Career Development and
Transition
http://www.dcdt.org/

Division on Developmental Disabilities
(focusing on individuals with cognitive
disabilities/mental retardation, autism,
and related disabilities)
http://www.dddcec.org/

Job Accommodation Network
Post Office Box 6080, Morgantown, WV 26506
800-526-7234
http://www.jan.wvu.edu/

MAAP Services for Autism and Asperger, Inc.
Post Office Box 524, Crown Point, IN 46307
219-662-1311
http://www.maapservices.org/

National Center on Secondary Education and
Transition (NCSET)
Institute on Community Integration,
University of Minnesota, 6 Pattee Hall, 150
Pillsbury Drive SE, Minneapolis, MN 55455
612-624-2097
http://www.ncset.org/

National Dissemination Center for Children
with Disabilities (NICHCY)
Post Office Box 1492, Washington, DC 20013
800-695-0285
http://www.nichcy.org/

National Professional Development Center on
Autism Spectrum Disorders
FPG Child Development Institute, The
University of North Carolina at Chapel Hill
CB# 8180, Chapel Hill, NC 27599
919-966-2622
http://www.fpg.unc.edu/~autismPDC/

Organization for Autism Research
2000 North 14th Sreet, Suite 710
Arlington, VA 22201
703-243-9710
http://www.researchautism.org

Research and Training Center on Community
Living
204 Pattee Hall, 150 Pillsbury Drive S.E.,
Minneapolis, MN 55455
612-624-6328
http://rtc.umn.edu/

TASH
1025 Vermont Avenue, Floor 7, Washington,
DC 20005
202-263-5600
http://www.tash.org

ThinkCollege.net
617-287-4310 (voice); 617-287-4350 (TTY)
http://www.thinkcollege.net/

Virginia Comonwealth University (VCU)
Rehabilitation Research and Training Center
on Workplace Supports and Job Retention
1314 West Main Street, Post Office Box 842011,
Richmond, VA 23284
804-828-1851
http://www.worksupport.com/

STATE RESOURCES

In an effort to further connect individuals with autism, their parents, teachers, and direct support providers with resources, I list a few specific agencies that are most relevant to transition-age youth with autism. Although I cannot provide an extensive list of every support available in every state, it is my hope that you can use these targeted resources to find additional local information.

E *State departments of education, offices of special education*—These state agencies are responsible for ensuring that the requirements of the Individuals with Disabilities Education Improvement Act of 2004 (PL 108-446) are implemented in every public school in the state.

V *State vocational rehabilitation agency*—These state agencies provide education, training, counseling, and other services to prepare individuals with autism for work. The state agency will be able to direct you to local offices in your area.

U *University Centers for Excellence in Developmental Disabilities Education (UCEDD)*—Although not every state has a UCEDD, these centers often have grant projects to improve outcomes for people with disabilities in their states. Many UCEDDs also provide direct clinic services as well. These centers are frequently active in statewide policy development and can offer resources to parents and professionals seeking more information about state systems.

Ⓐ *Autism training and technical assistance centers*—Many, but not all, states have special programs that provide training, technical assistance, and resources to citizens in their states with an interest in autism. Where possible, I have tried to include these resources so that you can contact them for more information.

Alabama

Ⓔ Alabama Department of Education, Special Education Services
334-242-8114; 800-392-8020 (in AL)
http://www.alsde.edu/

Ⓥ Department of Rehabilitation Services
334-281-8780
http://www.rehab.state.al.us/

Ⓤ Civitan International Research Center, University of Alabama at Birmingham
205-934-8900; 800-822-2472
http://www.circ.uab.edu

Alaska

Ⓔ Office of Special Education, Alaska Department of Education
907-465-2972
http://www.eed.state.ak.us/tls/sped/

Ⓥ Division of Vocational Rehabilitation
907-465-2814
http://labor.state.ak.us/dvr/home.htm

Ⓤ University of Alaska Anchorage, Center for Human Development
907-272-8270
http://www.alaskachd.org

Ⓐ Alaska Autism Resource Center, Special Education Service Agency
907-334-1300
http://www.alaskaarc.org

Arizona

Ⓔ Exceptional Student Services, Arizona Department of Education
602-542-4013
http://www.ade.az.gov

Ⓥ Rehabilitation Services Administration, Department of Economic Security
602-542-3332; 800-563-1221
http://www.de.state.az.us/rsa

Ⓤ Institute for Human Development, Northern Arizona University
928-523-4791
http://www.nau.edu/~ihd

Ⓐ Southwest Autism Research and Resource Center
602-340-8717
http://www.autismcenter.org/

Arkansas

Ⓔ Arkansas Department of Education
501-682-4221
http://arksped.k12.ar.us

Ⓥ Arkansas Rehabilitation Services, Department of Workforce Education
501-296-1616
http://www.arsinfo.org

Ⓤ Partners for Inclusive Communities
501-682-9900; 800-342-2923
http://www.uams.edu/partners/

California

Ⓔ Special Education Division, California Department of Education
916-445-4602
http://www.cde.ca.gov/sp/se/

Ⓥ Department of Rehabilitation
916-263-8987; 916-263-7477 (TTY)
http://www.dor.ca.gov

Ⓤ Tarjan Center at University of California, Los Angeles
310-825-0170
http://www.tarjancenter.ucla.edu

Ⓤ University of Southern California, Childrens Hospital Los Angeles (UCEDD)
323-669-2300
http://www.uscuap.org

Colorado

ⓔ Exceptional Student Services Unit, Colorado Department of Education
303-866-6694
http://www.cde.state.co.us

ⓥ Division of Vocational Rehabilitation, Department of Human Services
303-866-4150
http://www.cdhs.state.co.us/dvr/

ⓤ JFK Partners, University of Colorado Health Sciences Center
303-864-5261
http://www.jfkpartners.org

Connecticut

ⓔ Bureau of Special Education, Department of Education
860-713-6912
http://www.sde.ct.gov/sde/cwp/view.asp?
a=2678&Q=320730

ⓥ Bureau of Rehabilitation Services, Department of Social Services
860-424-4848
http://www.brs.state.ct.us

ⓤ University of Connecticut, A.J. Pappanikou Center for Excellence in Developmental Disabilities
860-679-1500; 860-679-1502 (TTY); 866-623-1315
http://www.uconnucedd.org

ⓐ Eden Connecticut
860-455-9231
http://www.edenservices.org/services_
connecticut.html

Delaware

ⓔ Exceptional Children and Early Childhood Group
302-739-5471
http://www.doe.state.de.us/Exceptional_
Child/ececehome.htm

ⓥ Delaware Division of Vocational Rehabilitation
302-761-8275; 302-761-8336 (TTY)
http://www.delawareworks.com/dvr/
welcome.shtml

ⓤ University of Delaware, Center for Disabilities Studies
302-831-6974; 302-831-4689 (TTY)
http://www.udel.edu/cds

ⓐ Brennen School, Delaware Autism Program
302-454-2202
http://www.christina.k12.de.us/schools/
Brennen/

District of Columbia

ⓔ Office of Special Education, DC Public Schools
202-442-5468
http://www.k12.dc.us/

ⓥ DC Rehabilitation Services Administration, Department of Human Services
202-442-8663
http://dhs.dc.gov/dhs/cwp/view.asp?a=3&
Q=492432&dhsNav=|30989

ⓤ Center for Child and Human Development, Georgetown University
202-687-5000
http://gucchd.georgetown.edu/

Florida

ⓔ Bureau of Exceptional Education and Student Services, Florida Department of Education
850-245-0475
http://www.fldoe.org

ⓥ Division of Vocational Rehabilitation, Department of Education
850-488-6210; 800-451-4327
http://www.rehabworks.org

ⓤ Mailman Center for Child Development, University of Miami School of Medicine
305-243-6801
http://pediatrics.med.miami.edu

ⓐ Center for Autism and Related Disabilities (CARD)/ Florida Atlantic University
888-632-6395; 561-297-2023
http://www.coe.fau.edu/card/

ⓐ CARD/Florida State University
800-769-7926; 850-644-4367
http://autism.fsu.edu/

(A) CARD/University of Central Florida
888-558-1908; 407-737-2566
http://www.ucf-card.org/

(A) CARD/University of Florida
352-846-2761; 800-754-5891
http://www.card.ufl.edu

(A) CARD/University of Florida, Jackson
904-633-0760
http://www.hscj.ufl.edu/peds/aut/

(A) CARD/University of South Florida
800-333-4530; 813-974-2532
http://card-usf.fmhi.usf.edu/

Georgia

(B) Division for Exceptional Students, Georgia
Department of Education
404-656-3963
http://www.gadoe.org

(V) Vocational Rehabilitation Program,
Georgia Department of Labor
404-235-0156
http://www.vocrehabga.org

(U) Institute on Human Development and
Disability, Center for Excellence in
Developmental Disabilities Education,
Research, and Service, The University of
Georgia
706-542-3457
http://www.ihdd.uga.edu

(A) Emory University School of Medicine,
Emory Autism Center
404-727-8350
http://www.psychiatry.emory.edu/
PROGRAMS/autism/

Hawaii

(B) Special Education Services Branch, Hawaii
Department of Education
808-733-4400
http://www.doe.k12.hi.us

(V) Division of Vocational Rehabilitation,
Department of Human Services
808-692-7719
http://hawaii.gov/dhs/self-sufficiency/vr/

(U) Center on Disability Studies, University of
Hawaii at Manoa
808-956-5011
http://www.cds.hawaii.edu/

Idaho

(B) Bureau of Special Population Services,
Idaho Department of Education
208-332-6800
http://www.sde.idaho.gov/specialed/

(V) Division of Vocational Rehabilitation
208-334-3390 (V/TTY)
http://www.vr.idaho.gov

(U) Center on Disabilities and Human
Development, University Center on
Excellence/University of Idaho
208-885-3559
http://www.idahocdhd.org

Illinois

(B) Illinois State Board of Education
217-782-4870
http://www.isbe.net/spec-ed/

(V) Division of Rehabilitation Services,
Department of Human Services
800-843-6154 (V/TTY)
http://www.dhs.state.il.us/ors/

(U) Institute on Disability and Human
Development, Department of Disability and
Human Development, University of Illinois at
Chicago
312-413-1647 (V); 312-413-0453 (TTY)
http://www.ahs.uic.edu/dhd

(A) Illinois Autism/PDD Training and
Technical Assistance Project
630-889-7398
http://www.illinoisautismproject.org

Indiana

(B) Division of Exceptional Learners, Indiana
Department of Education
317-232-0570
http://www.doe.state.in.us/exceptional

V Vocational Rehabilitation Services, Indiana Family and Social Services Administration, Division of Disability and Rehabilitative Services
317-232-1319; 800-545-7763, ext. 1319
http://www.IN.gov/fssa/

U Indiana Institute on Disability and Community at Indiana University, Bloomington
812-855-6508; 812-855-9396 (TTY)
http://www.iidc.indiana.edu

A Indiana Resource Center for Autism (IRCA), Indiana Institute on Disability and Community
812-855-6508; 812-855-9396 (TTY)
http://www.iidc.indiana.edu/irca

Iowa

B Student and Family Support Services, Department of Education
515-281-5735
http://www.state.ia.us/educate/

V Iowa Vocational Rehabilitation Services, Department of Education
515-281-6731; 800-532-1486
http://www.ivrs.iowa.gov

U Iowa's University Center for Excellence on Disabilities, Center for Disabilities and Development
319-356-1335
http://www.healthcare.uiowa.edu/cdd/index.asp

A Regional Autism Services Program, Child Health Specialty Clinic
319-356-4619
http://www.medicine.uiowa.edu/autism services/

Kansas

B Student Support Services, Kansas State Department of Education
785-291-3097
http://www.kansped.org

V Kansas Rehabilitation Services, Department of Social and Rehabilitation Services
785-368-7471
http://www.srskansas.org/rehab/

U Kansas University Center on Developmental Disabilities, University of Kansas
785-864-4295; 785-864-5051 (TTY)
http://www.healthcare.uiowa.edu/cdd/index.asp

A Autism Asperger Resource Center
913-588-5988
http://www.autismasperger.org

Kentucky

B Division of Exceptional Children's Services, Kentucky Department of Education
502-564-4970
http://www.education.ky.gov

V Office of Vocational Rehabilitation, Education Cabinet, Department of Workforce Investment
502-564-4440
http://ovr.ky.gov

U Human Development Institute, Center for Excellence in Developmental Disabilities
859-257-1714
http://www.ihdi.uky.edu

A Kentucky Autism Training Center
502-852-5555; 800-334-8635
http://louisville.edu/education/kyautism training/

Louisiana

B Division of Educational Improvement and Assistance, Louisiana Department of Education
225-342-3513
http://www.louisianaschools.net/lde/index.html

V Department of Social Services, Louisiana Rehabilitation Services
225-219-2225; 800-737-2958 (in LA)
http://www.dss.state.la.us

U LSUHSC-Human Development Center (UCEDD)
504-556-7573
Web: www.hdc.lsuhsc.edu

Maine

E Office of Special Services, Department of Education
207-624-6650; 207-624-6800 (TTY)
http://www.maine.gov/education/speced/specserv.htm

V Bureau of Rehabilitation Services, Department of Labor
207-623-7944
http://www.maine.gov/rehab/

U Center for Community Inclusion and Disability Studies, University of Maine (UCEDD)
207-581-1207; 800-203-6957
http://www.ccids.umaine.edu

Maryland

E Division of Special Education/Early Intervention Services, Maryland State Department of Education
410-767-0238
http://www.msde.state.md.us

V Maryland Division of Rehabilitation Service, Workforce and Technology Center, Maryland State Department of Education
410-554-9385
http://www.dors.state.md.us/

U The Kennedy Krieger Institute
443-923-9300
http://www.kennedykrieger.org

A Center for Autism and Related Disorders (CARD) at the Kennedy Krieger Institute
443-923-7630
http://www.kennedykrieger.org/kki_cp.jsp?pid=1394

A Community Services for Autistic Adults and Children (CSAAC)
240-912-2220
http://www.csaac.org/

Massachusetts

E Special Education Planning and Policy Development Office, Department of Education
781-338-3000; 781-338-3388
http://www.doe.mass.edu/sped

V Massachusetts Rehabilitation Commission
617-204-3600; 800-245-6543 (in MA only)
http://www.mass.gov/mrc/

U Institute for Community Inclusion/UCEDD, UMass Boston
617-287-4300; 617-287-4350 (TTY)
http://www.communityinclusion.org

A The May Institute
781-437-1205
http://www.mayinstitute.org/

Michigan

E Office of Special Education and Early Intervention Services, Michigan Department of Education
517-373-0923
http://www.michigan.gov/mde

V Michigan Rehabilitation Services, Michigan Department of Labor & Economic Growth
517-373-3390; 800-605-6722
http://www.michigan.gov/mrs

U Developmental Disabilities Institute, Wayne State University
313-577-2654
http://www.wayne.edu/DDI

A University of Michigan Autism and Communication Disorders Center
734-936-8600
http://www.umaccweb.com/

Minnesota

E Special Education Policy, Minnesota Department of Education
651-582-8590; 651-582-8201 (TTY)
http://education.state.mn.us

V Rehabilitation Services Branch, Department of Employment and Economic Development
651-296-7510; 800-328-9095
http://www.deed.state.mn.us

U Institute on Community Integration (UCE), University of Minnesota
612-624-6300
http://ici.umn.edu/

Ⓐ The Minnesota Autism Project hosted by the Metro ECSU
612-638-1519
http://www.ecsu.k12.mn.us/programs
Services/specialEducation/asdMNproject.html

Mississippi

Ⓔ Office of Special Education, Department of Education
601-359-3498
http://www.mde.k12.ms.us/special_education/

Ⓥ Mississippi Office of Vocational Rehabilitation, Department of Rehabilitation Services
601-853-5232
http://www.mdrs.state.ms.us

Ⓤ Institute for Disability Studies, University of Southern Mississippi
601-266-5163; 888-671-0051 (V/TTY)
http://www.ids.usm.edu

Missouri

Ⓔ Division of Special Education, Department of Elementary and Secondary Education
573-751-4444
http://www.dese.mo.gov/divspeced/

Ⓥ Division of Vocational Rehabilitation, Department of Education
573-751-3251
http://www.vr.dese.mo.gov

Ⓤ UMKC Institute for Human Development, Health Sciences Building
816-235-1770; 800-444-0821 (V)
http://www.ihd.umkc.edu

Ⓐ Judevine Center for Autism
314-432-6200
http://www.judevine.org/

Montana

Ⓔ Special Education Division, Montana Office of Public Instruction
406-444-4429
http://www.opi.state.mt.us

Ⓥ Vocational Rehabilitation Programs, Department of Public Health and Human Services
406-444-2590
http://www.dphhs.mt.gov/dsd/govt_programs/vrp/vrs/

Ⓤ University of Montana Rural Institute, Center for Excellence in Disability Education, Research, and Service
406-243-5467; 800-732-0322
http://ruralinstitute.umt.edu

Nebraska

Ⓔ Special Populations Office, Nebraska Department of Education
402-471-2471 (V/TTY)
http://www.nde.state.ne.us/SPED/sped.html

Ⓥ Vocational Rehabilitation, Nebraska Department of Education
402-471-3649
http://www.vocrehab.state.ne.us

Ⓤ Munroe-Meyer Institute (UCEDD)
402-559-5702
http://www.unmc.edu/mmi

Ⓐ Nebraska Autism Spectrum Disorders Network, University of Nebraska-Lincoln, Special Education Department
402-450-6298
http://www.nde.state.ne.us/autism/

Nevada

Ⓔ Office of Special Education, Elementary and Secondary Education, and School Improvement Programs, Nevada Department of Education
775-687-9142
http://www.doe.nv.gov

Ⓥ Rehabilitation Division, Department of Employment, Training, and Rehabilitation
775-684-4040
http://detr.state.nv.us/rehab/index.htm

Ⓤ UCEDD, Research and Education Planning Center, College of Education, University of Nevada-Reno
775-784-4921 (V/TTY); 800-216-7988
http://repc.unr.edu

New Hampshire

E Bureau of Special Education, New Hampshire Department of Education
603-271-6693
http://www.ed.state.nh.us

V Division of Adult Learning and Rehabilitation, New Hampshire Department of Education
603-271-3471
http://www.ed.state.nh.us/education/

U Institute on Disability/UCED, University of New Hampshire
603-862-4320 (V/TTY); 800-238-2048 (in NH)
http://www.iod.unh.edu

New Jersey

E Office of Special Education Programs, New Jersey Department of Education
609-633-6833
http://www.state.nj.us/education

V Division of Vocational Rehabilitation Services, New Jersey Department of Labor
609-292-5987; 609-292-2919 (TTY)
http://www.wnjpin.state.nj.us/

U The Elizabeth M. Boggs Center on Developmental Disabilities, University of Medicine and Dentistry of New Jersey, Robert Wood Johnson Medical School
732-235-9300
http://rwjms.umdnj.edu/boggscenter

A The Eden Family of Services
609-987-0099
http://www.edenservices.org/

A Douglass Developmental Disabilities Center
732-932-3902
http://dddc.rutgers.edu/

A New Jersey Center for Outreach and Services for the Autism Community (COSAC)
609-883-8100; 800-4-AUTISM
http://www.njcosac.org/cosac2/Home%20Page

A Youth Consultation Services
973-482-8411
http://www.ycs.org/

A Asperger Syndrome Education Network (ASPEN)
732-321-0880
http://www.aspennj.org

New Mexico

E Special Education Bureau, Public Education Department
505-827-1457
http://www.ped.state.nm.us

V Division of Vocational Rehabilitation
505-954-8500; 505-954-8511 (V/TTY); 800-224-7005
http://www.dvrgetsjobs.com/

U Center for Development and Disability (CDD), University of New Mexico
505-272-3000
http://cdd.unm.edu

A SouthWest Autism Network (SWAN)
800-270-1861
http://cdd.unm.edu/swan/

New York

E Office of Vocational and Educational Services for Individuals with Disabilities (VESID), State Education Department
518-474-2714
http://www.vesid.nysed.gov

U Developmental Disabilities Center, St. Lukes–Roosevelt Hospital Center
212-523-6230

U Westchester Insitute for Human Development
914-493-8204
http://www.wihd.org

U UCEDD Education, Research and Service, Rose F. Kennedy Center, Albert Einstein College of Medicine/Yeshiva University
718-430-8522
http://www.aecom.yu.edu/cerc/kennedy.htm

U Strong Center for Developmental Disabilities
585-275-0355
http://www.urmc.rochester.edu/strong/scdd

North Carolina

B Exceptional Children Division, Department of Public Instruction
919-807-3969/3971
http://www.ncpublicschools.org/ec

V Division of Vocational Rehabilitation Services, Department of Health and Human Services
919-855-3500; 919-855-3579 (TTY)
http://dvr.dhhs.state.nc.us

U Clinical Center for the Study of Development and Learning, University of North Carolina
919-966-5171
http://www.cdl.unc.edu

A Division TEACCH, University of North Carolina, Chapel Hill
919-966-5156
http://www.teacch.com/

North Dakota

B Office of Special Education, Department of Public Instruction
701-328-2277; 701-328-4920 (TTY)
http://www.dpi.state.nd.us/speced/index.shtm

V Vocational Rehabilitation Division, North Dakota Department of Human Services
701-328-8950; 701-328-8968 (TTY);
800-755-2745 (in ND)
http://www.nd.gov/humanservices

U North Dakota Center for Persons with Disabilities, Minot State University
701-858-3580; 800-233-1737
http://www.ndcpd.org

Ohio

B Office for Exceptional Children, Ohio Department of Education
614-466-2650
http://www.ode.state.oh.us

V Rehabilitation Services Commission
614-438-1210 (V/TTY)
http://www.state.oh.us/rsc

U Division of Developmental and Behavioral Pediatrics, Cincinnati Children's Hospital Medical Center
513-636-8383
http://www.cincinnatichildrens.org/svc/dept-div/disabilities/default.htm

U The Ohio State University UCEDD
614-292-2390
http://nisonger.osu.edu

A Ohio Center for Autism and Low Incidence (OCALI)
866-886-2254; 614-410-0321 (main business)
http://www.ocali.org/

Oklahoma

B Special Education Services, Department of Education
405-521-4873
http://www.sde.state.ok.us

V Department of Rehabilitation Services
405-951-3400; 800-845-8476
http://www.okrehab.org/

U Center for Learning and Leadership/UCEDD, University of Oklahoma Health Sciences Center College of Medicine
405-271-4500, ext 0; 800-627-6827
http://w3.ouhsc.edu/thecenter

Oregon

B Office of Student Learning and Partnerships, Department of Education
503-947-5600
http://www.ode.state.or.us

V Office of Vocational Rehabilitation Services; Department of Human Services; Children, Adults & Families Division
503-945-5880 (V); 503-945-5894 (TTY)
http://www.oregon.gov/dhs

U Center on Human Development, University of Oregon
541-346-3591
http://darkwing.uoregon.edu/~ivdb

Pennsylvania

B Bureau of Special Education, Department of Education
717-783-6913
Special Education Consultline:
800-879-2301(V/TTY)
http://www.pde.state.pa.us

V Office of Vocational Rehabilitation, Department of Labor and Industry
717-787-7312
http://www.dli.state.pa.us/landi/cwp/view
.asp?a=128&Q=168255&dsftns=4490

U Institute on Disabilities at Temple University UCEDD
215-204-1356 (V/TTY)
http://disabilities.temple.edu

A Advisory Board on Autism and Related Disorders (ABOARD)
412-781-4116; 800-827-9385
http://www.aboard.org

Rhode Island

B Office for Diverse Learners, Rhode Island Department of Elementary and Secondary Education
401-222-3505
http://www.ride.ri.gov

V Office of Rehabilitation Services, Department of Human Services
401-421-7005, ext. 301; 401-421-7016 (TTY)
http://www.ors.ri.gov

U The Paul V. Sherlock Center on Disabilities, Rhode Island College
401-456-8072; 401-456-8773 (TTY)
http://www.sherlockcenter.org

A The Groden Center
401-274-6310
http://www.thegrodencenter.org

South Carolina

B Office of Exceptional Children, South Carolina Department of Education
803-734-8224
http://www.ed.sc.gov

V South Carolina Vocational Rehabilitation Department
803-896-6500
http://www.scvrd.net

U University of South Carolina School of Medicine, Department of Pediatrics, Center for Disability Resources (UCEDD)
803-935-5248
http://uscm.med.sc.edu/cdrhome

A Autism Division
803-898-9609; 803-898-9600 (V/TTY);
888-376-4636
http://www.state.sc.us/ddsn/autism/
autism.htm

South Dakota

B Special Education Programs, Department of Education, Office of Educational Services and Supports
605-773-3678
http://doe.sd.gov/oess/specialed/index.asp

V Division of Rehabilitation Services, Department of Human Services
605-773-3195
http://dhs.sd.gov/drs/

U Center for Disabilities, Health Science Center
605-357-1439; 800-658-3080 (V/TTY)
http://www.usd.edu/cd

Tennessee

B Division of Special Education, Department of Education
615-741-2851; 888-212-3162
http://www.state.tn.us/education/speced/

V Division of Rehabilitation Services, Department of Human Services
615-313-4714
http://www.state.tn.us/humanserv

U Boling Center for Developmental Disabilities, The University of Tennessee Health Science Center
901-448-6512; 888-572-2249;
901-448-4677 (TTY)
http://www.utmem.edu/bcdd/

Ⓤ Vanderbilt Kennedy Center for Excellence in Developmental Disabilities
615-936-8852; 866-936-8852;
800-273-9595 (TTY)
http://kc.vanderbilt.edu/kennedy/ucedd/index.html

Texas

Ⓔ Special Programs, Monitoring, and Interventions, Texas Education Agency
512-463-9414; 800-252-9668
http://www.tea.state.tx.us/special.ed

Ⓥ Department of Assistive and Rehabilitative Services
800-628-5115
http://www.dars.state.tx.us

Ⓤ Center for Disability Studies, University of Texas at Austin, Pickle Research Campus
512-232-0740; 800-828-7839;
512-232-0762 (TTY)
http://tcds.edb.utexas.edu

Ⓤ Center on Disability and Development at Texas A&M University, Department of Educational Psychology
979-845-4612
http://cdd.tamu.edu

Utah

Ⓔ Special Education Services, State Office of Education
801-538-7757
http://www.schools.utah.gov/sars/

Ⓥ Utah State Office of Rehabilitation
801-538-7530 (V/TTY)
http://www.usor.utah.gov

Ⓤ Center for Persons with Disabilities, Utah State University
435-797-1981
http://www.cpd.usu.edu

Ⓐ Autism Information Resources at the Utah Parent Center
801-272-1051; 800-468-1160 (V/TTY)
http://www.utahparentcenter.org

Vermont

Ⓔ Student Support Services
802-828-2755
http://www.state.vt.us/educ/new/html/pgm_sped.html

Ⓥ Vocational Rehabilitation Division, Department of Aging and Independent Living, Agency of Human Services
802-241-2186
http://www.vocrehabvermont.org

Ⓤ Center on Disability and Community Inclusion, University of Vermont (UCEDD)
802-656-4031 (V); 802-656-8499 (TTY)
http://www.uvm.edu/~cdci

Virginia

Ⓔ Division of Special Education and Student Services, Department of Education
804-225-3252; 800-292-3820
http://www.doe.virginia.gov/VDOE/sess

Ⓥ Virginia Department of Rehabilitative Services
804-662-7000; 804-662-7081; 800-552-5019;
800-464-9950 (TTY)
http://www.vadrs.org

Ⓤ Partnership for People with Disabilities, Virginia Commonwealth University
804-828-3876 (V/TTY); 800-828-1120
http://www.vcu.edu/partnership

Ⓐ Commonwealth Autism Service
804-355-0300; 800-649-8481
http://www.autismva.org

Ⓐ The Virginia Autism Council, Partnership for People with Disabilities, VCU
800-426-1595; 800-828-1120 (TDD)
http://www.autismtrainingva.org

Ⓐ Virginia Autism Resource Center
804-674-8888, ext. 5161; 877-667-7771
http://www.varc.org

Washington

Ⓔ Special Education Operations, Office of Superintendent of Public Instruction
360-725-6075
http://www.k12.wa.us/specialed

(V) Division of Vocational Rehabilitation, Department of Social and Health Services
360-725-3610; 800-637-5627 (V/TTY)
http://www1.dshs.wa.gov/dvr

(U) Center on Human Development and Disability, University of Washington
206-543-7701
http://www.chdd.washington.edu

(A) Autism Outreach Project
360-299-4090; 888-704-9633
http://www.esd189.org/autism/

West Virginia

(E) Office of Special Programs, Extended and Early Learning, Department of Education
304-558-2696; 800-642-8541
http://wvde.state.wv.us/ose

(V) Division of Rehabilitation Services
304-766-4601
http://www.wvdrs.org

(U) West Virginia University Center for Excellence in Disabilities
304-293-4692
http://www.cedwvu.org/

(A) West Virginia Autism Training Center, Marshall University
304-696-2332; 800-344-5115 (in WV)
http://www.marshall.edu/coe/atc

Wisconsin

(E) Division for Learning Support: Equity and Advocacy
608-266-1781; 800-441-4563
http://www.dpi.state.wi.us/dpi/dlsea/een

(V) Division of Vocational Rehabilitation, Department of Workforce Development
608-261-0050; 800-442-3477;
608-266-0283 (TTY)
http://www.dwd.state.wi.us/dvr

(U) Waisman Center, University of Wisconsin-Madison
608-263-5254
http://www.waisman.wisc.edu/

Wyoming

(E) Wyoming Department of Education
307-777-2555
http://www.k12.wy.us

(V) Division of Vocational Rehabilitation, Department of Workforce Services
307-777-7389
http://www.wyomingworkforce.org/

(U) Wyoming Institute for Disabilities, University of Wyoming
307-766-2761
http://wind.uwyo.edu/

Index

Page numbers followed by *f* indicate figures; those following by *t* indicate tables.

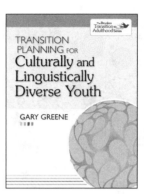